VETO PLAYERS

VETO PLAYERS

HOW POLITICAL INSTITUTIONS WORK

George Tsebelis

RUSSELL SAGE FOUNDATION NEW YORK

PRINCETON UNIVERSITY PRESS PRINCETON, NEW JERSEY

Library of Congress Cataloging-in-Publication Data

Tsebelis, George.
Veto players : how political institutions work / George Tsebelis.
p. cm.
Includes bibliographical references and index.
ISBN 0-691-09988-X (alk. paper)
ISBN 0-691-09989-8 (pbk. : alk. paper)
1. Comparative government. 2. Political planning. 3. Political science—
Decision making. 4. Legislation—European Union countries. I. Title.
JF51 .T745 2002
320.3—dc21   2002074909

This book has been composed in Times Roman

www.pupress.princeton.edu
www.russellsage.org

Printed in the United States of America

10 9 8 7 6 5 4 3

ISBN-13: 978-0-691-09989-7 (pbk.)

ISBN-10: 0-691-09989-8 (pbk.)

To Alexander and Emily

FOR THEIR INDISPENSABLE SUPPORT

Contents

List of Figures _____

List of Tables

Preface and Acknowledgments _____

THE BEGINNING OF THIS BOOK can be traced back, long before the beginning of my professional life in political science, to my undergraduate days at the Institut des Sciences Politiques in Paris, when I read Duverger and Sartori on parties and party systems, and Riker on political coalitions. Like the first two authors, I was interested in understanding how political systems work, and like the third, I was interested in understanding it in a simple way.

I remember trying to grasp the distinctions that the official classifications made: What is the difference between a parliamentary and a presidential system, besides the fact that, in the first, the legislative and the executive can dissolve each other while in the second they cannot? What is the difference between a two-party and a multiparty system, besides the fact that the first leads to a single-party government and the second does not? (In fact, being from Greece, a country with a multiparty system and single-party governments, I knew this stylized fact to be incorrect.) These matters quickly became more complicated and even incomprehensible when I considered multiparty democracies as did Sartori, because of "moderate" and "polarized" multipartyism: I could not understand why fewer than five parties were associated with a moderate system and more than six with a polarized one.

The years went by, and I went to Washington University in St. Louis for graduate school and learned the basic ideas about how at least one political system works (the U.S. Congress). Shepsle and Weingast taught me that politicians are rational and try to achieve their goals, that institutions are constraints to the deployment of human strategies, and therefore studying institutions populated by rational players leads us to understand different outcomes (institutional equilibria, according to Shepsle).

Though these insights were revealing and accurate in their description of U.S. institutions, they were not addressing my initial questions of different parties and different systems. I was looking for answers that did not exist at the time, because rational choice analysis was completely established in American politics but completely underdeveloped in comparative politics (as I discovered the year I entered the job market). In fact, my comparative classes were essentially replicating Duverger and Sartori instead of going beyond them.

In the beginning of my professional life, I addressed specific problems that I could solve rather than global comparative questions (tenure requirements being what they are, I would not be writing these lines if I hadn't). The questions remained with me for quite a while without any handle for answers until I saw Thomas Hammond present a preliminary version of a paper he was writing with Gary Miller that would later be published in the *American Political Science Review* as "The Core of the Constitution." Hammond and Miller were making an argument about the American Constitution: that adding players with the power to veto increases the set of points that cannot be defeated (the core); that providing the power to overrule such vetoes decreases the size of the core; and that the size of the core increases with the distance among chambers. As soon as I heard the argument I started wondering whether it could be generalized for other political systems, particularly parliamentary with strong parties. If so, we would have a general way of understanding legislating in all political systems.

My thinking was now focused on a series of questions generated by this paper. First, the analysis was presented in a two-dimensional space. What would happen if one increased the number of policy-relevant dimensions? Would the core continue to exist or would it disappear? Second, can the analysis apply to parliamentary systems that by definition do not have the separation of powers? Third, can the model apply to political parties instead of individual congressmen?

For my purposes, affirmative answers in all three questions were necessary. I tried to find the answers in 1992–93 while I was a National Fellow at the Hoover Institution. With respect to question 1, I read an affirmative answer in an article that claimed that as long as two chambers in a bicameral system do not have members with overlapping preferences, the core exists in any number of dimensions. I was disappointed, however, in what I considered the authors' very strong (that is, unrealistic) assumption of non-overlapping preferences. While looking at the proof, I discovered that it was mistaken and that the core did not exist except under extremely restrictive conditions. This discovery led me practically into despair. I felt that (non-overlapping preferences aside) I had come so close to answering questions that had puzzled me for many years, and now the answer was eluding me again.

The next step in the process was a series of models that have now been included in my previous book, *Bicameralism*, which demonstrate that even when the core does not exist, another concept from social choice theory, the "uncovered set" (see Chapter 1), provides very similar results.

I found a hint of the answers to questions 2 and 3 in Riker's 1992 article "The Justification of Bicameralism," where he argues that parties in coalition governments work essentially the same as chambers in a bicameral system: in both cases an agreement is necessary for a change in the status quo.

With these findings in mind, I wrote a paper attempting to compare across political systems by comparing the size of each system's uncovered set. The paper, alas, was too technical and well-nigh incomprehensible. Miriam Golden, who is usually a very tolerant reader of my work, made me understand these problems quite well: "Why are you doing these things? What do they tell me about the world?" Her clear words made me understand that I needed to take a different tack and make the findings relevant.

I decided to look at the winset of the status quo (see Chapter 1) instead of the uncovered set, and this provided a dramatic simplification that conveyed to readers the relevance of my analysis. Rewriting the paper on the basis of veto players and winset of the status quo did not change the substantive results, but made it much more comprehensible and usable. The paper was long, so after inquiring as to which journal would accept an article longer than usual I submitted it to the *British Journal of Political Science*. It was immediately accepted, published in 1995, and received the Luebbert Award for the best article in comparative politics in 1996.

At the same time I participated in a group organized by Herbert Doering that was studying West European legislatures. Doering promised me that if I were to write a veto players article for his edited volume, he would make sure that usable data on legislation from the project would become available to me for testing the veto players framework. His proposal led to a second article on veto players, as well as to a dataset that tested the main argument I was proposing: that many veto players make significant policy changes difficult or impossible. Doering had the brilliant idea to identify laws that produce "significant changes," using an encyclopedia of labor law written for international labor lawyers who practice law in different countries and need to know the significant pieces of legislation in those countries. The test corroborated the theory and was published in the *American Political Science Review* in 1999; it was the runner-up for the Luebbert Award for the best article in comparative politics in 2000.

While working on these issues I was constantly expanding the veto players theory, either on my own or along with other researchers. I wrote an article for a special issue of *Governance* dedicated to political institutions. In that article I calculated a missing link: what happens to policy outcomes when collective veto players decide by qualified majorities instead of simple majorities; in addition, I spelled out several of the consequences of policy stability. I demonstrated that policy stability affects government instability in parliamentary systems, and the role of judges and bureaucrats regardless of political regime. Later, reading the literature on bureaucracies and the judiciary, I discovered that there is a difference between indicators measuring institutional independence of judiciary and bureaucracies from the political system and behavioral independence of the same actors. My interpretation was that seemingly contradictory expectations of judicial and bureaucratic independence in the literature may be compatible after all. Working with Simon Hug, I analyzed the consequences of veto players on referendums. Working with Eric Chang, I discovered another indication of policy stability: the structure of budgets in OECD countries changes more slowly when the government is composed of many veto players.

My veto player findings were also being confirmed by my work on the European Union, where I was discovering the importance not only of actors who can veto, but also of actors who can shape the agenda. There was nothing new to the importance of the agenda-setting argument (McKelvey has said everything there is to know in his 1976 article), except that European institutions were quite complicated, and it was difficult to see how the many actors were interacting in a multiple dimensional setting. Having written an article on that subject, I proceeded to identify the differences introduced consistently by European treaties in three-year periods from 1987 until today. I have published some dozen and a half articles on the issue of E.U. institutions, some of them on my own, some with my students, and some with Geoff Garrett, trying to go beyond the statement that E.U. institutions are complicated. Much of this work led to controversies, and the findings are summarized in one chapter in this book. The relevance of the European Union to the veto players framework presented in this book is that E.U. institutions are too complicated and too variable to be analyzed any other way.

I would like to thank the editors of both the *British Journal of Political Science* and *American Political Science Review*, as well as Blackwell Publishing, publishers of *Governance*, for permitting me to reprint some of the ideas included in the original articles. While this book had an overwhelmingly long gestation period, I was very lucky to receive the helpful advice of extremely reliable people. I would like to thank Barry Ames, Kathy Bawn, Lisa Blaydes, Shaun Bowler, Eric Chang, William Clark, Herbert Doering, Jeffrey Frieden, Geoffrey Garrett, Barbara Geddes, Miriam Golden, Mark Hallerberg, Simon Hug, Macartan Humphreys, Anastassios Kalandrakis, William Keech, Thomas König, Amie Kreppel, Gianfranco Pasquino, Ronald Rogowski, Kaare Strom, Daniel Treisman, Jim Vreeland, and Paul Warwick for reading the manuscript, in whole or in part, and giving me extended comments that led sometimes to long discussions and longer revisions.

I would like to thank the Russell Sage Foundation for providing me with a fellowship that made intensive work on the project possible. Eric Wanner and his staff (in particular Liz McDaniel, who edited the whole manuscript) made my life there so pleasant. I only wish many happy returns were possible! (In fact, I tried very hard but in vain to persuade Eric to repeal the local twenty-second amendment and consider second applications.) I enjoyed every minute in New York, and the excitement of living in the "millennium capital of the world" improved my productivity (if not my production).

Chuck Myers of Princeton University Press read successive versions of the manuscript and provided me with many useful suggestions. He has been helpful and reliable throughout the publication process. Thanks go always to Wolfgang Amadeus Mozart for providing me with a stimulating environment while I was working. Finally (keeping the punchline last), I want to thank my children, Alexander and Emily, for providing me with the necessary emotional support to finish this extensive project.

VETO PLAYERS

Introduction

THIS BOOK IS ABOUT political institutions: how we think about them in a consistent way across countries; how they affect policies; and how they impact other important characteristics of a political system, like the stability of governments and the role of the judiciary and the bureaucracies. My goal is not to make a statement about which institutions are better, but to identify the dimensions along which decision making in different polities is different, and to study the effects of such differences.

Most of the literature on political institutions uses a single criterion to identify the main characteristics of a polity. For example, political regimes are divided into presidential and parliamentary, legislatures into unicameral and bicameral, electoral systems into plurality and proportional, parties into strong and weak, party systems into two-party and multiparty. The relationships among all these categories are underdeveloped. For example, how are we to compare the United States, a presidential bicameral regime with two weak parties, to Denmark, a parliamentary unicameral regime with many strong parties? What kinds of interactions do the combinations of different regimes, legislatures, parties, and party systems produce?

We see such interactions in the case of the European Union, which makes legislative decisions with the agreement of two or three actors (the Council of Ministers, the European Parliament, and, most of the time, the European Commission). Each of these actors decides with a different decisionmaking rule. Since the Nice Treaty of 2001, the Council of Ministers uses a triple majority to make decisions: a qualified majority of the weighted votes of its members; a majority of the E.U. members; and a qualified majority of the population (62 percent). The European Parliament decides by absolute majority (which, as we will see, is a de facto qualified majority). The European Commission decides by simple majority. The Council of Ministers is appointed by the member countries; the European Parliament is elected by the peoples of Europe; and the European Commission is appointed by the member countries and approved by the European Parliament. This political system is neither a presidential nor a parliamentary regime. It is sometimes unicameral, sometimes bicameral, and yet other times tricameral, and in addition one of its chambers decides with multiple qualified majority criteria. I will not even start a description of the party system, which is composed of several ideologies and even more nationalities. Thus the European Union is a blatant exception to all traditional classifications. In fact, it is described frequently in the relevant literature as "sui generis"; yet European institutions can be very well and very accurately analyzed on the basis of the theory presented in this book.

This book will enable the reader to study and analyze political systems regardless of the level of their institutional complexity. And it will do that in a *consequential* as well as a *consistent* way. "Consequential" means that we will start our analysis from consequences and work backward to the institutions that produce them. "Consistent" means that the same arguments will be applied to different countries at different levels of analysis throughout this book. The goal is to provide a theory of institutional analysis, subject it to multiple tests, and, as a result, have a higher level of confidence by corroborating it in several different settings.

Veto Players, Policy Stability, and Consequences

In a nutshell, the basic argument of the book is the following: In order to change policies—or, as we will say henceforth, to change the (legislative) status quo—a certain number of individual or collective actors have to agree to the proposed change. I call such actors *veto players*. Veto players are specified in a country by the constitution (the president, the House, and the Senate in the United States) or by the political system (the different parties that are members of a government coalition in Western Europe). I call these two different types of veto players *institutional* and *partisan* veto players, respectively. I provide the rules to identify veto players in each political system. On the basis of these rules, every political system has a configuration of veto players (a certain number of veto players, with specific ideological distances among them, and a certain cohesion each). All these characteristics affect the set of outcomes that can replace the status quo (the *winset* of the status quo, as we will call the set of these points). The size of the winset of the status quo has specific consequences on policymaking: significant departures from the status quo are impossible when the winset is small—that is, when veto players are many—when they have significant ideological distances among them, and when they are internally cohesive. I will call this impossibility for significant departures from the status quo *policy stability*.

In addition, political institutions sequence veto players in specific ways in order to make policy decisions. The specific veto players that present "take it or leave it" proposals to the other veto players have significant control over the policies that replace the status quo. I call such veto players *agenda setters*. Agenda setters have to make proposals acceptable to the other veto players (otherwise, the proposals will be rejected and the status quo will be preserved). In fact, they will select among the feasible outcomes the one they prefer the most. As a consequence, agenda-setting powers are inversely related to policy stability: The higher policy stability (meaning the smaller the set of outcomes that can replace the status quo), the smaller the role of agenda setting. In the limit case, where change from the status quo is impossible, it does not make any difference who controls the agenda.

If we know the preferences of veto players, the position of the status quo, and the identity of the agenda setter (the sequence of moves of the different actors), we can predict the outcome of the policymaking process quite well. This book will include such predictions and we will assess their accuracy.[1] However, most often the agenda setter will be a collective actor (in which case the preferences are not well defined)[2] or we will not know his exact location. For example, we will see (in Chapter 3) that in parliamentary systems the agenda setting is done by the government, but we do not know exactly how; similarly, in presidential systems the agenda setting is done by the legislature, but again we will not be able to identify the exact preferences of the conference committee that shapes the proposals. In all these cases, the only possible prediction can be based on policy stability, which does not require as much information to be defined.

Policy stability affects a series of structural characteristics of a political system. The difficulty a government encounters in its attempt to change the status quo may lead to its resignation and replacement in a parliamentary system. This means that policy stability will lead to government instability, as Figure I.1 indicates. Similarly, in a presidential system, the impossibility of the political system to resolve problems may lead to its replacement by a military regime ("regime instability" in Figure I.1). Finally, the impossibility of changing the legislative status quo may lead bureaucrats and judges to be more active and independent from the political system. I will provide theoretical arguments and empirical evidence for these claims in the chapters that follow. Figure I.1 provides a visual description of the causal links in the argument.

The implications of my argument as it differs from those most prevalent in the literature can be sketched in the following example. Consider four countries: the United Kingdom, the United States, Italy, and Greece. If one considers existing theories in comparative politics, these countries group themselves in different ways. For proponents of analysis on the basis of different regimes (Linz 1994; Horowitz 1996), the United States is the only presidential regime, while the other three countries are parliamentary. For proponents of more traditional analyses on the basis of party systems, the United States and the United Kingdom are lumped together as two-party systems, while Italy and Greece are multiparty ones (Duverger 1954; Sartori 1976). Cultural ap-

---

[1] See Chapter 11.

[2] In Chapter 2 I define the concept of "cyclical" preferences and demonstrate that collective actors deciding under majority rule have such preferences.

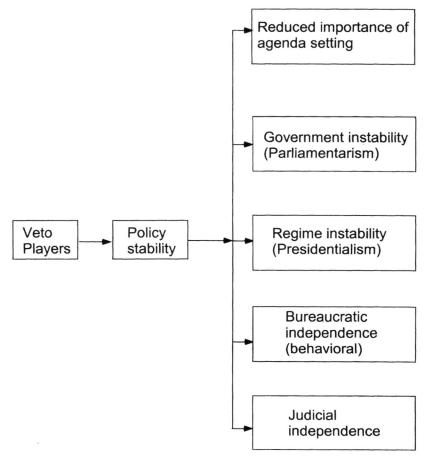

Figure I.1. Effects of many veto players.

proaches (Almond and Verba 1963) would also place the Anglo-Saxon systems together, in opposition to the continental European countries. Lijphart's (1999) consociationalism approach considers the United Kingdom a majoritarian country, Italy and Greece as consensus countries, and the United States as somewhere in the middle.[3]

In this book, Italy and the United States are countries with many veto players, and as such they will have high policy stability, while Greece and the United Kingdom have a single veto player, and consequently they may have

---

[3] On the one hand, the United States has two parties; on the other, it is a federal system.

high policy instability.[4] Note that Italy and the United States do not share any
characteristic according to traditional classifications (neither regime type, nor
party system, not to mention culture or consociationalism). Yet veto players
theory expects similar characteristics in these two countries. As a result of
policy stability or the lack of it, government instability will be high in Italy
and low in the United Kingdom and Greece; and the role of the judiciary and
bureaucrats much more important in the United States and Italy than in the
United Kingdom and Greece. Some of these expectations will be corroborated
by the data analyses in this book. Figure I.2 presents how existing classifications are cut across by the veto players theory. Neither regimes nor party
systems alone captures the characteristics that the veto players theory does.
In fact, the main argument in the book is that each configuration of traditional
variables is mapped on one specific constellation of veto players, so it is
possible that two countries are different in all traditional variables (regimes,
party systems, electoral systems, type of legislature, kinds of parties) and still
have the same or similar constellations of veto players. It is the constellation
of veto players that best captures policy stability, and it is policy stability that
affects a series of other policy and institutional characteristics.

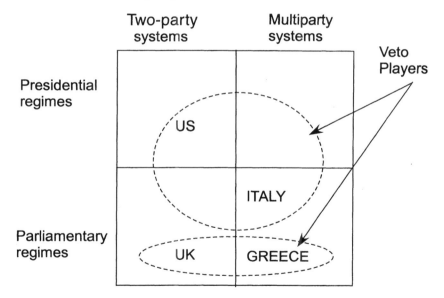

Figure I.2. Differences in classifications between regimes, party systems, and veto
players.

[4] Note the asymmetry in the expression: the countries with many veto players *will* have policy
stability, while the ones with one veto player *may* have instability. I explain the reasons for this
difference in Chapter 1.

In the pages that follow I examine both the causes and effects of policy stability. I will consider policy stability both as a dependent and an independent variable. I will identify the constellations of veto players that cause it, and consider its impact on other features such as government stability, bureaucracies, and the judiciary.

Substantive and Methodological Reasons
for Veto Players Analysis

Why do I start from policies and not from other possible points, such as institutions, political culture, behavioral characteristics, or norms? Even if one starts from policies, why focus on policy stability instead of the direction of policy outcomes? Finally, an important methodological question: why do I use the winset of the status quo instead of the standard concept of equilibrium? And how does this replacement of equilibria by winset of the status quo affect my analysis?

I start my analysis from policymaking (or, more accurately, from legislation and legislating) because policies are the principal outcome of a political system. People participate in a political system in order to promote the outcomes (policies) that they prefer. As a result, policymaking is important for political actors (parties or individual representatives), whether these actors have direct preferences over policies (like De Swaan 1973 assumes) or whether they care simply about reelection (this is Downs's [1957] simplifying assumption), or whether they are ideologically motivated (to follow Bawn's [1999a] approach).

Political actors propose different policies and are selected on the basis of the policies that they recommend. Politicians or parties are replaced in office when the policies they propose lead to undesirable outcomes or when they do not apply the policies they promised before an election. Obviously, the above statements are simplifications, but the bottom line is that the political system generates policy preferences and assures that these preferences are implemented. I do not imply that other characteristics like cultures, ideologies, norms, or institutions are not legitimate objects for study per se. What I do claim is that we are better in tune with a political system if we start our study from the policies that are implemented, and then work backward to discover how these policies defeated the alternatives. What were the preferences that led to these outcomes, and how were certain preferences selected over others by the political system?

But even if one focuses on policies as the basis of the intellectual enterprise, why focus on "policy stability," the impossibility of significantly changing the status quo instead of being more ambitious and studying the direction of change? There are three reasons for my choice.

First, policy stability affects a series of other characteristics of a political system, including institutional features, as Figure I.1 indicates. Second, it is an essential variable in the literature. Political scientists are often interested in the decisiveness of a political system—its capacity to solve problems when they arise. For example, in a thoughtful analysis of the effects of political institutions, Weaver and Rockman (1993:6) distinguish between

> ten different capabilities that all governments need to *set and maintain priorities* among the many conflicting demands made upon them so that they are not overwhelmed and bankrupted; to *target resources* where they are most effective; to *innovate* when old policies have failed; to *coordinate conflicting objectives* into a coherent whole; to be able to *impose* losses on powerful groups; to *represent diffuse, unorganized interests* in addition to concentrated, well organized ones; to *ensure effective implementation* of government policies once they have been decided upon; to *ensure policy stability* so that policies have time to work; to *make and maintain international commitments* in the realms of trade and national defense to ensure their long-term well-being; and, above all, to *manage political cleavages* to ensure that society does not degenerate into civil war.

While Weaver and Rockman are interested in the capabilities of governments, a great volume of economic literature starting with Kydland and Prescott (1977) is concerned with the credible commitment of the government *not* to interfere with the economy. Barry Weingast (1995) pushes the argument one step further and attempts to design institutions that would produce such a credible commitment. He proposes "market preserving federalism," a system that combines checks and balances that prevent government interference in the economy, with economic competition among units to assure growth. In a similar vein, Witold Henisz (2000a, 2000b) uses a long time-series of data to find that growth rates and investment are higher when the political system cannot change the rules of the economic game.

Bruce Ackerman (2000) adopts an intermediate position in a thoughtful and thought-provoking article. He suggests that the optimal institutional configuration is not one with many veto players, like the American system, or with few, as in the United Kingdom. Instead, he advocates the intermediate case of a parliamentary system with a senate that cannot veto all the time, and with the possibility of referendums that are called by one government and performed by another in order to diffuse the power of the government to set the agenda.

In all these diverse bodies of literature, the flexibility or the stability of policy is considered an important variable. Some scholars consider flexibility a desirable feature (in order to resolve problems faster); others point out that frequent interventions may worsen the situation.

I take a more agnostic position with respect to policy stability. It is reasonable to assume that those who dislike the status quo will prefer a political system with the capacity to make changes quickly, while advocates of the status quo will prefer a system that produces policy stability. It is not clear that a consensus exists (or is even possible) over whether a faster or slower pace of institutional response is desirable. Decisiveness in bringing about policy change is good when the status quo is undesirable (whether it is because a small minority controls the government, as with the French *ancien regime* or recent South Africa), or when an exogenous shock disturbs a desirable process (oil shock and growth in the 1970s). Commitment to noninterference may be preferable when the status quo is desirable (such as when civil rights are established), or if an exogenous shock is beneficial (such as an increase of the price of oil in an oil-producing economy). But regardless of whether policy stability is desirable or undesirable, the above literature indicates that it is important to study under what conditions it is obtained, which is a goal of this book.

The third reason to focus on policy stability instead of the direction of change is that my argument concentrates on institutions and their effects. While some researchers try to focus on the specific policy implications of certain institutions, I believe that specific outcomes are the result of both prevailing institutions *and* the preferences of the actors involved. In other words, institutions are like shells and the specific outcomes they produce depend upon the actors that occupy them.[5]

These are the three reasons I will use policy stability as my main variable. However, there will be times when information about the identity and preferences of the agenda setter is available, which will permit the formation of much more accurate expectations about policy outcomes. The reader will see in Chapter 11 that the institutional literature on the European Union has set and achieved such goals.

As for the main variable in this book, policy stability, we will see that it is defined by the size of the winset of the status quo.[6] Why do I use this concept

---

[5] As an example of my argument consider the following case, developed in Chapter 8: a significant component of the political economy literature argues that divided governments (which in my vocabulary means multiple veto players) cause budget deficits, or higher inflation. By contrast, my argument is that multiple veto players cause policy stability, that is, they produce high deficits if the country is accustomed to high deficits (Italy), but they produce low deficits if the country is familiar with low deficits (Switzerland or Germany).

[6] The more appropriate expression would be "winset of the default outcome." However, most of the time the default solution is the status quo. Rasch (2000) has identified countries where this provision is part of the formal rules. Even in cases where there is no such formal rule, votes comparing the status quo with the emerging alternative are taken on the floor of parliament. For example, in Herbert Doering's study of eighteen Western European countries in the 1981–91 period, of 541 bills, a final vote against the status quo had been taken 73 percent of the time (Doering *http://www.uni-potsdam.de/u/ls_vergleich/research*). In all these cases the final outcome is by definition within the winset of the status quo. In the cases where a final vote comparing the alternative with the status quo is not taken, the default alternative is specified either by rules or by a vote in parliament. If a majority in parliament can anticipate an outcome that they do not

instead of the widely accepted notion of (Nash) equilibrium? The absence of equilibrium analysis is due to the fact that in multidimensional policy spaces equilibria rarely exist. In fact, while in a single dimension equilibria of voting models are guaranteed to exist, Plot (1967) has demonstrated that in multiple dimensions the conditions for the existence of equilibrium are extremely restrictive. McKelvey (1976) and Schofield (1977) followed up the study by demonstrating that in the absence of equilibrium any outcome is possible.

On the other hand, the winset of the status quo has the self-imposing quality that it is the intersection of restrictions that each participant imposes on the set of outcomes. No rational player given the choice would accept any outcome that he does not prefer over the status quo.[7] In this sense my analysis is much more general than any other model (like bargaining, exclusive jurisdictions of ministers, or prime minister) that introduces a series of additional restrictions in order to produce a single equilibrium outcome.[8]

A Partial History of the Ideas in This Book

Some of the arguments in this book have already been made, even centuries ago. For example, terminology aside, the importance of veto players can be found in the work of Madison and Montesquieu. For Montesquieu (1977: 210–11), "The legislative body being composed of two parts, one checks the other, by the mutual privilege of refusing. . . . Sufficient it is for my purpose to observe that [liberty] is established by their laws." For Madison the distinction between the two chambers becomes more operative when the two chambers have more differences. In such cases, "the improbability of sinister combinations will be in proportion to the dissimilarity of the two bodies" (Federalist No. 62). The relation between government longevity and veto players can be found in the work of A. Lawrence Lowell (1896: 73–74). He identified one "axiom in politics" as the fact that "the larger the number of discordant groups that form the majority the harder the task of pleasing them all, and the more feeble and unstable the position of the cabinet."

---

prefer over the status quo, they can take steps to abort the whole voting procedure. Therefore, henceforth I use the expression "winset of the status quo" instead of "winset of the default alternative."

[7] Here I am excluding cases where a player receives specific payoffs to do so. For example, he may receive promises that in the future his preferences on another issue will be decisive. I do not argue that such cases are impossible, but I do argue that if they are included they make almost all possible outcomes acceptable on the basis of such a logroll, and make any systematic analysis impossible.

[8] Huber and McCarty (2001) have produced a model with significantly different outcomes depending on whether the prime minister can introduce the question of confidence directly, or has to get the approval of the government first.

More recently, literature on "divided government" has presented arguments about multiple veto players and policy stability (Fiorina 1992; Hammond and Miller 1987). Literature on bureaucracies has connected legislative output and bureaucratic independence (e.g., McCubbins, Noll, and Weingast 1987, 1989; Hammond and Knott 1996). Literature on judicial independence has connected judicial decisions with the capacity of the legislative body to overrule them (Gely and Spiller 1990; Ferejohn and Weingast 1992a, 1992b; Cooter and Ginsburg 1996). McKelvey (1976) was the first to introduce the role of the agenda setter in multidimensional voting games and demonstrate that an agenda setter can have quasi-dictatorial powers.

The furthest I have traced back ideas contained in this book was to a statement about the importance of agenda setting versus veto power contained in Livy's *History of Rome* (6.37), written over two thousand years ago: "The tribunes of the plebs were now objects of contempt since their power was shattering itself by their own veto. There could be no fair or just administration as long as the executive power was in the hands of the other party, while they had only the right of protesting by their veto; nor would the plebs ever have an equal share in the government till the executive authority was thrown open to them."

As for the importance of competition for setting the agenda (a subject discussed in Chapter 3), I was reminded of a quote in Thucydides that may qualify as the first expression of Downsian ideas in the political science literature:

> Pericles indeed, by his rank, ability, and known integrity, was enabled to exercise an independent control over the multitude—in short, to lead them instead of being led by them; for as he never sought power by improper means, he was never compelled to flatter them, but, on the contrary, enjoyed so high an estimation that he could afford to anger them by contradiction. Whenever he saw them unseasonably and insolently elated, he would with a word reduce them to alarm; on the other hand, if they fell victims to a panic, he could at once restore them to confidence. In short, *what was nominally a democracy became in his hands government by the first citizen.* With his successors it was different. *More on a level with one another, and each grasping at supremacy, they ended by committing even the conduct of state affairs to the whims of the multitude.*[9]

Finally, after I finished Chapter 5, where I argue that the possibility of referendums introduces an additional veto player (the "median voter") and as a result referendums make the status quo more difficult to change and bring

---

[9] Thucydides, *Histories*, Book II, 65.8–10; emphasis added. I thank Xenophon Yataganas for reminding me of the quote, as well as supplying the reference. Thucydides is here discussing the ability of a leader to persuade the people (like a president "setting the agenda"). In Chapter 3 I distinguish between this capacity and the more precise institutional feature of which veto player makes a proposal to whom.

results closer to the positions of the median, I discovered that this conclusion or a variation of it (depending on the meaning of the words) may be at least one century old. Albert Venn Dicey (1890: 507) said that the referendum "is at the same time democratic and conservative."[10]

It is probably the case that most of the ideas in this book are not original; some have been proposed centuries, even millennia ago. The value lies in the synthesis of the argument. This means that my task in this book is to explain why the propositions that I present fit together, and then try to corroborate the expectations with actual tests, or references to the empirical analyses produced by other researchers. Because the propositions presented in this book are part of the overall picture, the confidence in or incredibility of any one of them should strengthen or undermine the confidence to all the others.

Overview

The book is organized deductively. I start from simple principles, draw their implications (Part I), and then apply them to more concrete and complicated settings (Part II). I test for the policy implications of the theory first (Part III), and then for the structural ones (Part IV). This organization may surprise comparativists who like inductive arguments. Indeed, readers will have to go through some simple models first before we enter into the analysis of more realistic situations and before empirical results.

Is this sequence necessary? Why do I not enumerate the expectations generated by my approach and then go ahead and test for them? The answer is that I have to convince the reader that the conclusions of this book are different sides of the same mental construct. This construct involves veto players and agenda setters. Knowing their locations, the decisionmaking rule of each one of them, and their interactions generates similar expectations across a number of issues, ranging from regime types (presidential or parliamentary) to interactions between government and parliament to referendums to federalism to legislation to budgets to independence of bureaucrats and judges. And the same principles of analysis can be applied not only to countries that we have studied and analyzed many times before, but also to cases where existing models do not fit (like the European Union). The reader would not appreciate the forest if focused on the trees of each chapter. And I hope that it is the description of the forest that may help some of the readers identify and analyze trees that I did not cover in this book.

Part I presents the veto players theory for both individual (Chapter 1) and collective (Chapter 2) veto players. In the first chapter, I define veto players, agenda setters, and policy stability, focusing on individual veto players. I ex-

[10] Quoted in Mads Qvortrum (1999: 533).

plain why more veto players lead to higher levels of policy stability. In addition, I show that as distance among veto players becomes greater, policy stability increases and the role of agenda setting decreases. I also explain why all the propositions I present are sufficient but not necessary conditions for policy stability, that is, why many veto players with large ideological distances from each other will produce high policy stability, while few veto players may or may not produce policy instability. Finally, I demonstrate that the number of veto players is reduced if one of them is located "among" the others. I provide the conditions under which the addition of a veto player does not affect policy stability or policy outcomes. I call this condition the absorption rule and demonstrate its importance for the subsequent steps of the analysis. As a result of the absorption rule, a second chamber may have veto power but not affect policy outcomes, or an additional party in coalition government may have no policy consequences because its preferences are located among the preferences of the other coalition partners. One important implication of the absorption rule is that simply counting the number of veto players may be misleading, because a large proportion of them may be absorbed. I show that the best way of taking veto players into account is by considering not just their number, but their relative locations, and I demonstrate exactly how this can be done.

Chapter 2 generalizes the results when veto players are collective. Moving from individual to collective veto players focuses on the decisionmaking rule of a group: qualified majority or simple majority. Thus, Chapter 2 focuses on familiar decisionmaking rules. I explain that collective veto players in principle may generate serious problems for the analysis because they cannot necessarily decide on what they want. Their preferences are "intransitive," such that different majorities may prefer alternative A to B, B to C, and C to A at the same time, which makes the collective veto player prefer A to B directly, but B to A indirectly (if C is introduced in the comparison). I find a realistic way to eliminate the problem and to calculate the outcomes of collective choice when the decisions of veto players are made by simple or by qualified majority.

As a result of these two theoretical chapters, one can form expectations about policy stability and about the results of legislative decisionmaking in any political system regardless of whether it is presidential or parliamentary, whether it has a unicameral or bicameral legislature, whether there are two or more parties, or whether these parties are strong or weak. There is a veto player configuration of each combination of these traditional comparative variables, and more: veto players analysis takes into account the positions and preferences of each one of these actors, so the accuracy of analysis and expectations increases as more accurate policy preferences are introduced in the data.

Part II applies these theoretical concepts and expectations to the body of comparative politics literature, and compares the expectations generated by the traditional literature to the propositions generated in the first part. The main argument in the second part is that traditional analyses and variables have their impact on veto players, but this impact varies by specific institutional settings, and varies even more as a function of the preferences of the different veto players because of the absorption rule.

Chapter 3 compares different regime types and argues that the difference between democratic and nondemocratic regimes is the competitiveness of the agenda-setting process. As a result of political competition, politically successful elites approximate more the preferences of the median voter. Democratic regimes are classified into presidential and parliamentary; the veto players theory version of the difference is that the parliament controls the legislative agenda in presidential systems, while the government controls the agenda in parliamentary ones. This focus on agenda setting generates the opposite expectations from the traditional literature: it is the parliament that is powerful on legislative issues in presidential systems, and it is the government that controls power in parliamentary regimes.

Chapter 4 focuses further on the relationship between government and parliament in parliamentary regimes. It explains why most of the time the veto player configuration of a country is composed of the parties that participate in a government coalition, instead of the parties participating in parliament (the traditional party systems approach proposed by Duverger and Sartori). It also explains why "executive dominance," a fundamental variable in Lijphart's consociationalism analysis, can be understood as the institutional power attributed to the government to set the parliamentary agenda.

Chapter 5 focuses on referendums and explains why the inclusion of the possibility of a referendum increases the number of veto players in a country, and brings final outcomes closer to the median voter even if referendums do not occur. It also argues that the major differences among referendums revolve around the question of agenda control. This control is divided into two parts: who triggers the referendum, and who asks the question. An existing veto player may control both parts of the agenda-setting process and, in this case, his influence in legislation increases. Or, the referendum may be triggered not by a veto player, but the question may be asked by a veto player (popular veto) or not (popular initiative). Each one of these methods has different political consequences on the role of veto players and the median voter. For example, when the same player controls both dimensions of agenda setting (veto player referendum or popular initiative), the existing legislative veto players are eliminated.

Chapter 6 deals with federalism, bicameralism, and qualified majorities. Each one of these terms is translated into veto players theory in order to draw implications about the consequences of these institutions on policymaking. Federalism usually is accompanied by bicameralism (a second chamber representing the states and having veto power over important if not all pieces of legislation), or qualified majority decisionmaking. As a result, federalism increases the number of veto players, and therefore policy stability. I compare the properties of bicameral decisionmaking with qualified majorities, as well as with the combination of the two (existing in the United States as well as in the European Union).

Part III focuses on the policy implications of the above analysis. One expects higher policy stability as a function of veto players after taking into account the absorption rule. The identification of policy stability is not a trivial matter; two chapters are therefore dedicated to this issue.

Chapter 7 focuses on significant departures from the status quo. I consider legislation on working time and working conditions in parliamentary democracies and find that significant legislation is introduced in countries with one or few veto players more frequently than it is introduced in countries with many veto players, particularly if there are great ideological distances between these veto players. This finding is contrasted with the overall number of laws in different countries; this number is positively correlated to the number of veto players. As a result, countries with few veto players produce several significant laws and few nonsignificant ones, while countries with many veto players produce few significant laws and many nonsignificant ones. The chapter ends with the expectation that such systematic differences lead to a different concept of "law" in different countries.

Chapter 8 examines macroeconomic outcomes. A wide range of economic literature posits that the number of veto players is correlated with higher deficits, because different veto players require significant portions of the budget. In contrast, according to the veto players theory, more veto players lead to more inertia, and therefore countries with high levels of debt (Italy) will continue to have high deficits while countries with low levels of debt (Switzerland) will continue to have low levels of deficit. Similarly, the composition of the budget will change more in countries with few veto players, while countries with many veto players will rely more on an automatic pilot.

Part IV examines the institutional consequences of policy stability. According to the theory, policy stability will lead to government instability for parliamentary systems, regime instability for presidential systems, and independence of judges and bureaucrats. The chapters in this part examine these claims.

Chapter 9 analyzes the question of government stability. This chapter reexamines the claims in the literature that a country's party system (i.e., features of the parliament) affects government survival. By contrast, veto players theory claims that it is government characteristics that affect government survival. The two expectations are highly correlated because two-party systems produce single-party governments—single veto players—while multiparty systems produce coalition governments—multiple veto players. However, the correlation is not perfect. Multiparty systems may produce single-party majority governments as well as minority governments. As a result, the implications of the two theories can be separated empirically, and recent work (mainly by War-wick) has shown that it is government characteristics that matter.

Chapter 10 establishes the reasons why policy stability affects the role of bureaucrats and the judiciary and examines the empirical evidence. While the arguments for judicial and bureaucratic independence from the legislative system are similar, there is more empirical evidence available on judges than on bureaucrats.

Chapter 11 applies all the analysis developed in the book to a new political system, the European Union. The European Union is unusual because it is neither a country nor an international organization and has altered its constitution frequently (four times in the last fifteen years). In addition, the institutional structure of the European Union is quite complicated (Ross 1995) and does not fit existing classifications (it is neither presidential nor parliamentary, and it has one chamber that decides with three different qualified majorities). On top of that, the legislature is quite frequently tricameral, and the number of parties is extraordinary if one counts that they are defined by both nationality and ideology. As a result, the European Union provides an overwhelming challenge for most existing theories. Even for the veto players theory, the European Union is a significant challenge: I had to extend the theory presented in Part I (such as the discussion of "conditional agenda setting" and the calculation of a multicameral core) in order to study E.U. institutions. Hence, testing veto player predictions with E.U. data provides a powerful test of the theory.

In the Conclusion I return to the distinguishing features of the book. The deductive mode of presentation permits the same simple principles to be combined in the analyses of complicated phenomena. The introduction of the new variables (veto players) maps the legislative process in whatever level of detail is necessary and is significantly more accurate than any of the traditional theories. As a result, the expectations can be formulated in a sharper way and tested more easily.

The empirical evidence presented covers a wide range of policies, processes, and countries. The data quality is sometimes very reliable (Chapters 7 and 8), other times less so (Chapter 10); sometimes it originates in single-author (Chapter 7) or co-authored (Chapter 8) work, while other times it is based on other researchers' findings (Chapter 9). Finally, the position of the agenda setter is known quite accurately in some cases, enabling accurate predictions about the outcomes (Chapter 11), while at other times we will ignore the identity of the agenda setter in order to talk only about the policy stability of outcomes (Chapters 7 and 8). However, all this diversified evidence means that the theory under investigation is corroborated under a wide variety of conditions.

PART I

VETO PLAYERS THEORY

PART I EXPLORES the impact of different political institutions on policies. I base my analysis on policies because one can think of a political system as the means for collective decisionmaking. Consequently, all the actors in a political system, whether they are voters, representatives, or political parties, care about policy outcomes, either directly or indirectly—either because they have preferences over outcomes or because other things they like (such as reelection) depend on policy outcomes.

However, policy outcomes are the result of two factors: the preferences of the actors involved and the prevailing institutions. Given that the identity of players and their preferences are variable, while institutions are more stable, policy outcomes will vary depending on who controls political power as well as where the status quo is. For the time being we will consider the status quo as given and discuss its location more in detail when it becomes necessary.

In this book we will focus on the more stable part of the interaction and try to assess the outcomes focusing only on institutions, with *limited knowledge* of the identity of the actors that produce them. We will make predictions about the consequences of the number of actors involved or their relative positions, without knowing exact numbers or locations. Given that we know little about the identities and choices of the actors involved, we will be able to make statements only about the rate of change, or how much different institutional settings *permit* the change of the status quo. There is one immediate consequence from this method of study. I will be able to identify the conditions where change of the status quo is difficult or impossible (policy stability is high), but I will not be able to predict actual change. When policy change is possible, whether it occurs or not will be a matter of the specific choices of the actors themselves. Even if change is possible, it may not occur. In other words, all the propositions that follow provide necessary but not sufficient conditions to change the status quo. I will demonstrate in the first chapter that the implications of this statement are far from trivial.

In this part I provide the rules according to which all political institutions (regime types, parliaments, party systems, parties, and so on) are translated into a series of veto players—actors whose agreement is required for a change of the status quo. The number and the location of veto players affects policy stability, or how difficult it is to change the status quo. The sequence in which veto players make their decisions (who makes proposals to whom) affects the influence that these veto players have in the decisionmaking process. Whether these veto players are individual or collective affects the way they make decisions about policies. If they are individuals (a president or a monolithic political party), they can easily decide on the basis of their preferences. If they are collectives (a parliament or a weak political party), the location of the outcome depends on the internal decisionmaking rule (unanimity, qualified or simple majority) and who controls the agenda. Therefore, traditional political institutions like regime types, or number of chambers of parliament, or number, cohesion, and ideological positions of parties, or decisionmaking rules of all these actors, will be translated into some veto player constellation, which in turn will determine the policy stability of a political system.

This approach establishes the possibility of different institutional settings to provide policy change, but does not and cannot identify the direction of it. For the identification of the direction of change, the preferences of veto players are required, as well as the identity of the agenda setter and the location of the status quo. In other words, institutions in this book will resemble shells, and only when the occupants of these shells and the status quo are identified will specific predictions of outcomes be possible. However, as I demonstrate, there are important results that can be drawn even if one ignores the specific choices of the different actors involved. Such results cover, as I have argued, not only policy stability, but also a series of consequences of policy stability on other variables, like government or regime stability, the importance and independence of the judiciary, and the role of bureaucracies.

This part is divided into two chapters. The first chapter analyzes individual veto players, while the second focuses on collective veto players. The reason for the division is twofold. First, for didactic purposes, the division of the chapters facilitates a better understanding since the theory of individual veto players is simple, straightforward, and intuitive, while collective veto players introduce complications into the analysis (depending on the rules regulating their decisionmaking) and, as I show, approximations into the results. Second, the division is helpful because collective veto players, as I explain, have particularly serious problems as agenda setters, since different majorities may prefer to make different proposals, a problem that I address in detail in Chapter 2.

1

Individual Veto Players

IN THIS CHAPTER I define the fundamental concepts I use in this book, in particular *veto players* and *policy stability*. I demonstrate the connections between these concepts by using simple Euclidean spatial models. The chapter presents a series of propositions relating the number and the distance of veto players with policy stability. In essence, the argument presented in Sections 1.2 and 1.3 is that the greater the distance among and the number of veto players, the more difficult it is to change the status quo. The last section introduces sequence of moves into the picture, and makes the argument that the first mover (the agenda setter) has a significant advantage. However, this advantage diminishes as policy stability increases, that is, as the number of veto players and the distances among them increase.

1.1. Veto Players and Policy Stability

Veto players are individual or collective actors whose agreement is necessary for a change of the status quo. It follows that a change in the status quo requires a unanimous decision of all veto players.

The constitution of a country can assign the status of veto player to different individual or collective actors. If veto players are generated by the constitution, they are called *institutional* veto players. For example, the Constitution of the United States specifies that legislation, to be enacted, requires the approval of the president, the House of Representatives, and the Senate (ignoring override of presidential veto for the time being). This means that these three actors (one individual and two collective) are the institutional veto players in the United States.

Analyzing the political game inside institutional veto players may produce more accurate insights. If veto players are generated by the political game, they are called *partisan* veto players. For example, it may be that inside the House of Representatives, different majorities are possible, meaning that the House cannot be reduced any further as a veto player. Alternatively, it may be that the House is controlled by a single cohesive party, and the only successful pieces of legislation are those supported by this party. In this case, while the House is the institutional veto player, the majority party is the real (partisan) veto player. Similarly, in Italy, while legislation can be generated by the ap-

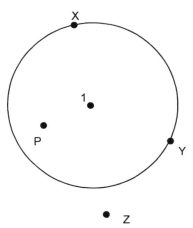

Figure 1.1. Circular indifference curves of a veto player.

proval of both chambers of the legislature (two institutional veto players), closer examination indicates that the partisan veto players are the parties composing the government coalition. We return to this point in Chapter 2.

Each individual veto player is represented here by his ideal point in an n-dimensional policy space. In addition, I assume that each veto player has *circular indifference curves*, that he is indifferent between alternatives that have the same distance from his ideal point. Figure 1.1 presents a two-dimensional space, where dimensions 1 and 2 might be the size of the budget for social security and defense, respectively. In these two dimensions a veto player (1) is represented in the center of the circle. The figure also represents four points, P, X, Y, and Z, in different locations. The veto player is indifferent between points X and Y, but he prefers P to either of them. He also prefers either of them to Z. As such, the circle with center 1 and radius 1X (henceforth (1, 1X)), or "the indifference curve that goes through X," also goes through Y, while point P is located inside the circle and point Z is located outside.

Both assumptions include several simplifications. For example, an individual actor may be interested in only one dimension instead of two or more. On a redistributive issue an actor may be interested in maximizing his share, and be completely indifferent to who else is getting how much. In addition, circular indifference curves indicate the same intensity of preferences in each issue. If these assumptions are invalid, the statements having to do with the ideological distances among veto players have to be reevaluated. However, the statements that depend simply on the number of veto players hold regardless of the shape of indifference curves. Hereafter, I will represent a veto player by a point (e.g.,

A), the status quo by another (SQ), and A will prefer anything inside the circle (A, ASQ) to the status quo.

I now define two more concepts. The first is the *winset of the status quo (W(SQ))*, the set of outcomes that can defeat the status quo. Think of the status quo as current policy. The winset of the status quo is the set of policies that can replace the existing one.[1] The second concept is the *core*, the set of points with empty winset—the points that cannot be defeated by any other point if we apply the decisionmaking rule. I usually refer to the core along with the decisionmaking rule that produces it. For example, the "unanimity core" refers to the set of points that cannot be defeated if the decision is unanimous. An alternative name for "unanimity core" that I also use is "Pareto set." In Figure 1.2, I present a system with three veto players, A, B and C, and two different positions of the status quo, SQ1 and SQ2. As noted, all decisions must be made by unanimity, since A, B, and C are veto players.

In order to identify the winset of SQ1 (W(SQ1)), one draws the indifference curves of A, B, and C that pass through SQ1 and identifies their intersection. I have hatched this intersection in Figure 1.2. A similar operation indicates that $W(SQ2) = \varnothing$, or that SQ2 belongs to the unanimity core of the three veto players system. It is easy to verify that $W(SQ2) = \varnothing$ as long as SQ2 is located inside the triangle ABC.[2] Thus the unanimity core is the entire triangle ABC as shaded in the figure.

I use both the smallness of the winset of SQ and the size of the unanimity core as *indicators of policy stability*. In Section 1.3, I demonstrate formally that these two indicators are almost equivalent (Proposition 1.3). Here, however, I provide arguments in favor of each one independently.

In each proposition, "the winset in case A is smaller than the winset in case B" means that the winset in case A is a subset of the winset in case B. Similarly, "the winset shrinks" means that under new conditions it becomes a subset of what it was before. The *policy stability* of a system, then, is the difficulty of effecting significant change in the status quo.

The definition of unanimity core logically leads to the conclusion that its size is a proxy for policy stability. Indeed, a bigger unanimity core produces a larger set of points that cannot be changed. For the time being, let us note that the argument for the smallness of the winset appears more complicated. I use the smallness of the winset of the status quo as a proxy for policy stability for the following reasons:

1. The bigger the winset of the status quo, the more likely that some subset of it will satisfy some additional external constraints;

---

[1] In Parts III and IV I discuss more interesting and productive ways to conceptualize the concept of status quo, but we do not need them here.

[2] If, however, SQ2 is located outside the triangle ABC, then it can be defeated by its projection on the closest side, so its winset is not empty.

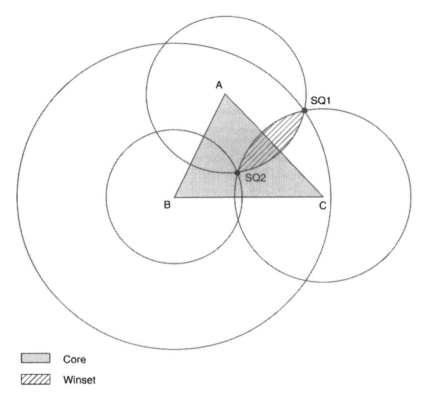

Core

Winset

Figure 1.2. Winset and core of a system with three veto players.

2. If there are transaction costs in changing the status quo, then players will not undertake a change that leads to a policy that is only slightly different, which means that the status quo will remain;

3. Even without transaction costs, if players undertake a change, a small winset of the status quo means that the change will be incremental. In other words, a small winset of the status quo precludes major policy changes.

Each of these reasons is sufficient to justify the use of the smallness of the winset of the status quo as a proxy for policy stability.

The two proxies for policy stability are complementary for different positions of the status quo. When the status quo is far away from all veto players, its winset is large (policy stability is low). As the status quo approaches one of the veto players, policy stability increases (since the winset of the status quo includes only the points that this veto player prefers over the status quo). Moving the status quo even further and locating it among the veto players may

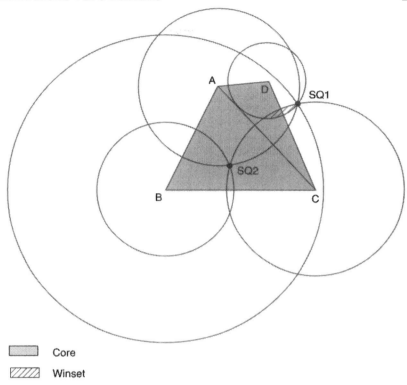

Core

Winset

Figure 1.3. Winset and core of a system with four veto players.

completely eliminate the winset of the status quo (as the case of SQ2 in Figure 1.3 indicates).

The above discussion indicates that policy stability crucially depends on the position of the status quo. However, of particular interest are propositions that are *independent* of the position of the status quo, for two reasons. First, in political science analyses it is not always easy to start by locating the status quo. For example, when a health-care bill is introduced, one does not know the status quo until *after* the bill is voted on. Indeed, a series of provisions having to do with mental health, for example, may or may not be included in the status quo depending on whether they were included in the bill itself.[3]

---

[3] An alternative approach would consider a policy space of extremely high dimensionality, and consider the status quo as the outcome generated by *all* existing legislation and the departures caused by any particular bill. Then we ignore the dimensions that have not been affected by the change. In my opinion this is a much more complicated procedure.

Second, political analysis that is dependent on the position of the status quo has necessarily an extremely contingent and volatile character (exactly as the status quo that it depends on). The analysis of the above legislation may become an extremely difficult enterprise (particularly if one considers this legislation over time). It is not my position that such an analysis is superfluous or irrelevant—quite the opposite. But one would like to see whether some comparative statements could be made independently of the position of the status quo, whether statements that are characteristic of a political system and not of the status quo are possible.[4]

In the remainder of this chapter I focus on the other factors that affect policy stability. In Section 1.2, I carry the analysis in two complementary parts: the case where the winset of SQ is non-empty, and the case where it is empty (when SQ is located inside the unanimity core). In Section 1.3, I demonstrate the high correlation of the two approaches.

1.2. Number of Veto Players and Policy Stability

1.2.1. Winset of Status Quo Is Non-empty

Figure 1.3 replicates Figure 1.2 and adds one more veto player: D. It is easy to see by comparison of the two figures that the winset of SQ1 shrinks with the addition of D as a veto player. Indeed, D vetoes some of the points that were acceptable by veto players A, B, and C. This is the generic case. Under special spatial conditions the addition of a veto player may not affect the outcome. For economy of space I do not present another figure here, but the reader can imagine the following: if D is located on the BSQ line between B and SQ so that the circle around D is included inside the circle around B, the addition of D as a veto player would not influence the size of the winset of SQ1.[5] I could continue the process of adding veto players and watch the winset of the status quo shrinking or remaining the same ("not expanding") with every new veto player. It is possible that as the process of adding veto players unfolds, at some point the winset of the status quo becomes empty such that there is no longer a point that can defeat the status quo. This would have been the case if D were located in an area so that SQ1 were surrounded by veto players. We will deal with this case in the next few paragraphs. Here let me summarize the result of the analysis so far. *If the winset of the status quo exists, its size decreases or remains the same with the addition of new veto players.*

---

[4] I discuss the very concept of "status quo" that is omnipresent in formal models and so elusive in empirical studies in Chapter 9 as the foundation of my analysis of government stability.

[5] I take up the point of when additional veto players "count," that is, affect the size of the winset of the status quo, in the next section.

1.2.2. Winset of Status Quo Is Empty

Let us now focus on SQ2 in Figure 1.3. It presents the case where the winset of the status quo with three veto players is empty. Given that $W(SQ2) = \varnothing$, the size of $W(SQ)$ is not going to change no matter how many veto players one adds. However, the addition of D as one more veto player has another interesting result: it expands the unanimity core. The reader can verify that the unanimity core now is the whole area ABCD. Again, it is not necessary that an additional veto player expands the unanimity core. It is possible that it leaves the size of the unanimity core the same, as would have been the case if D were located inside the triangle ABC. We will deal with this case in the next section. For the time being, the conclusion of this paragraph is as follows: *If there is a unanimity core, its size increases or remains the same with the addition of new veto players.*

Combining the conclusions of the previous paragraphs leads to the following proposition:

> **Proposition 1.1:** The addition of a new veto player increases policy stability or leaves it the same (either by decreasing the size of the winset of the status quo, or by increasing the size of the unanimity core, or by leaving both the same).

The comparative statics supported by Proposition 1.1 are very restrictive. Note that I am speaking for the *addition* of a new veto player. The phrasing implies that the other veto players will remain the same in the comparison. For example, it would be an inappropriate application of Proposition 1.1 to consider that if we eliminate one particular veto player and add two more the result would be an increase in policy stability. It would be equally inappropriate to compare two different systems, one with three veto players and one with four veto players, and conclude that the second produces more policy stability than the first. Thus, while Proposition 1.1 permits comparisons of the same political system over time, it does not usually permit us to compare across systems.

The following proposition, which I will call "numerical criterion," increases simplicity but reduces the accuracy of Proposition 1.1. The reason is that it ignores the cases where adding a veto player makes no difference on policy stability.

> *Numerical Criterion:* The addition of a new veto player increases policy stability (either by decreasing the size of the winset of the status quo, or by increasing the size of the unanimity core).

The "numerical criterion" has the same restrictions for comparative statics as Proposition 1.1. In addition, it may lead to wrong expectations because a new veto player does *not* always increase policy stability. This point should be underscored, because, as we will see in the empirical chapters, empirical research frequently uses the numerical criterion either to produce expectations or to test them. The propositions presented in the next section relax some of the above restrictions.

1.3. Quasi-equivalence and Absorption Rules, Distances among Veto Players, and Policy Stability

This section deals with the conditions under which adding a veto player affects (increases) policy stability. If it does not, I say that the new veto player is "absorbed" by the existing ones, which gives the title "absorption rule" to this section. As an interesting by-product of the analysis, we will see that the two different proxies for policy stability (the size of the unanimity core and the size of the winset) are almost equivalent, as well as under what conditions altering distances among veto players affect policy stability.

1.3.1. Quasi-equivalence and Absorption Rules

I present the argument in a single dimension first for reasons of simplicity. Consider the situation presented in Figure 1.4. Three individuals (they are not veto players yet) are located on the *same straight line*, and the status quo is anywhere in an n-dimensional space (a two-dimensional space is sufficient to depict the situation). In the remainder of this section I index the different winsets by the veto players, not by the position of the status quo, because my findings are valid for any possible position of the status quo.

Figure 1.4 presents the indifference curves of the three actors A, B, and C. Labels D, E, and F are the intersections of the indifference curves of A, B, and C with the line AC. Consider first that actors A and B (but not C) are veto players, and identify the winset of the status quo (W(AB)). Add C to the set of veto players; that is, endow C with the power to veto outcomes he does not like. It is easy to see that the winset of the status quo shrinks to W(ABC) (going through points D and F). In this case adding a veto player increases the policy stability of the system.

Now let us follow a different time path and assume that the initial veto players are A and C. The winset of the status quo is W(AC) (going through D and F). Adding B as a veto player does not affect its size. In other words, W(ABC) = W(AC).

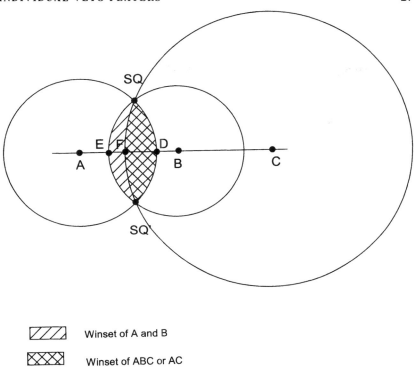

| Winset of A and B |
| Winset of ABC or AC |

Figure 1.4. Winset of VPs A and C is contained in winset of VPs and B (B is absorbed).

Why was policymaking restricted in the first case but not in the second? The reason is that if B is located between A and C, then F is located between E and D.[6] In other words, it is impossible for A and C to have joint preferences over the status quo that B will not share.

One can reach similar conclusions with respect to the unanimity core: adding B to veto players A and C does not affect the unanimity core of the system (which is the segment AC), while adding C to A and B expands the unanimity core from AB to AC.

In fact, the two conditions are equivalent: when a new veto player is added inside the segment connecting existing veto players (their unanimity core), it does not affect the winset of the status quo, and when it does not affect the winset of the status quo (for any position of SQ), it is located inside the segment defined by the existing veto players (their unanimity core). Indeed,

[6] It is easy to see from the triangle SQBC that the sum of two sides is longer than the third, so BC + BSQ > CSQ. It is also true that BSQ = BE and CSQ = CF. Replacing it we get BC + BE > CF, or CE > CF, or F is located between E and D.

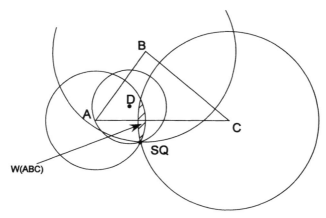

Figure 1.5. Winset of VPs A, B, and C is contained in winset of D (D is absorbed).

the only way that the three indifference curves will pass from the same two points (SQ and SQ′) is for the three points A, B, and C to be on the same straight line.

These arguments can be generalized in any number of dimensions. Figure 1.5 presents a two-dimensional example. To the three initial veto players A, B, and C, a fourth one, D. is added. If D's ideal point is located inside the unanimity core of A, B, and C (the triangle ABC), then D has no effect on the unanimity core or the winset of A, B, and C, regardless of the position of the status quo. If, on the other hand, D is outside the unanimity core of A, B, and C, it both expands the unanimity core and restricts the winset of the status quo (at least for some SQ positions).

Proposition 1.2 (absorption rule): If a new veto player D is added within the unanimity core of any set of previously existing veto players, D has no effect on policy stability.

Proof (by contradiction): Suppose that a new veto player D belongs to the unanimity core of a system of veto players S, and for some SQ it affects the size of the winset of the status quo. On the basis of Proposition 1.1, in this case the winset of the status quo shrinks. The previous propositions imply that there is a point X that all veto players in S prefer over the status quo, but D prefers SQ over X. Call X′ the middle of the segment of SQX and draw through X′ the hyperplane that is perpendicular to SQX. By construction all the veto players in S are located on one side of this hyperplane, while D is located on the other; consequently, D is not in the unanimity core of S.[7]

---

[7] I thank Macartan Humphreys for this elegant proof that is much shorter than mine.

Proposition 1.2 is essentially what distinguishes between the verbally awkward accuracy of Proposition 1.1 and the approximate simplicity of the *numerical criterion*. It explains under what conditions an additional veto player is going to make a difference or is going to be absorbed. This proposition makes a significant difference in empirical applications, because it identifies which veto players count. One important point has to be made here: the whole analysis is carried out under the assumption that there are no transaction costs in the interaction of different veto players. The reason that I make this assumption is that it is difficult to find any way to operationalize such costs across countries and time. However, this does not mean that such costs do not exist. If one relaxes the assumption of no transaction costs, even an absorbed veto player would add difficulty in changing the status quo.

Figure 1.5 can help us also to understand the relationship between the two criteria of policy stability we have adopted. We have already seen on the basis of the absorption rule that adding a veto player inside the unanimity core of others does not affect the winset of the status quo. Now we will see that the reverse is also true (that if we add a veto player and we do not reduce the size of the winset for any position of the status quo, the new veto player is located inside the unanimity core of the previous ones). As a result, the two criteria of policy stability are almost equivalent.

Proposition 1.3 (quasi-equivalence rule): For any set of existing veto players S, the necessary and sufficient condition for a new veto player D not to affect the winset of any SQ is that D is located in the unanimity core of S.

Proof: The proof of the absorption rule is also the proof of necessity. For sufficiency suppose that D does not belong in the unanimity core of S. I will show that there are some positions of SQ for which the winset of SQ is reduced if one adds D as a veto player. Consider a hyperplane H separating S and D, and select a point SQ on the side of D. Consider the projection SQ′ of SQ on H, and extend the line to a point X so that $SQX = 2SQSQ'$ (X is the symmetric of SQ with respect to H). By construction, all veto players in S prefer X to SQ, but D prefers SQ to X, so W(SQ) shrinks with the addition of D.

I call Proposition 1.3 the quasi-equivalence rule because it demonstrates that the two criteria of policy stability we used are almost equivalent: if adding a veto player does not increase the size of the core, it will not reduce the size of the winset of any status quo either. Similarly, if adding a veto player does not reduce the size of W(SQ) for any SQ, it will not increase the size of the core either. However, Proposition 1.3 does not imply that for *any position* of SQ increasing the core decreases W(SQ). The reason is that the two criteria of policy stability that we used have one important difference: the size of the core does not depend on the position of the status quo, while the winset of the status quo (by definition) does. As a consequence of Proposition 1.3, even if the size of the winset of the status quo did not seem as convincing a criterion of policy stability as the size of the unanimity core in the introduction to this part, now we know that the two are highly correlated.

1.3.2. Distances among Veto Players and Policy Stability

The goal of this section is to derive propositions involving the distances among veto players that are *independent of the position of the status quo*. In Figure 1.4 we demonstrated that *adding* B as a veto player has no effect, while adding C has consequences. Now we can shift the argument and consider a scenario where we *move* veto players instead of adding them. If we have only two veto players, A and B, and we move the ideal point of the second from B to C, then the winset of the status quo will shrink (no matter where the status quo is) and the unanimity core will expand, so policy stability will increase. In this case increasing the distance of two veto players (while staying on the same straight line) increases policy stability regardless of the position of the status quo.

Similarly, in Figure 1.5, adding D has no effect on stability. In other words, the system of the veto players ABC produces higher policy stability than the system ABD. Therefore, if we had only three veto players A, B, and a third and we moved that third veto player from point C to point D, the policy stability of the system decreases regardless of the location of the status quo. We can generalize these arguments as follows:

Proposition 1.4: If Ai and Bi are two sets of veto players, and all Bi are included inside the unanimity core of the set Ai, then the winset of Ai is included in the winset of Bi for every possible status quo and vice versa.

Proof: Consider two sets of veto players Ai and Bi, so that all of Bi are included inside the unanimity core of Ai. In that case, on the basis of Proposition 1.2, each one of the Bi would have been absorbed by the veto players in Ai. As a result, the intersection of winsets of all Ai is a subset of the winset of each Bi, which means that the intersection of winsets of all Ai is a subset of the intersection of winsets of all Bi.

Figure 1.6 provides a graphic representation of the proposition when Ai is a system of three veto players, and Bi is a system of five veto players included in the unanimity core of Ai. Note that despite the higher number of veto players in system B, the winset of any point SQ with respect to the veto player system A (indicated by W(A) in the figure) is contained inside the winset with respect to veto player system B (indicated by W(B)); thus policy stability in system A is higher. In fact, we can move B_1 further "out" until it coincides with A_1, then move B_2 to A_2, and then B_3 to A_3. The policy stability of the system Bi

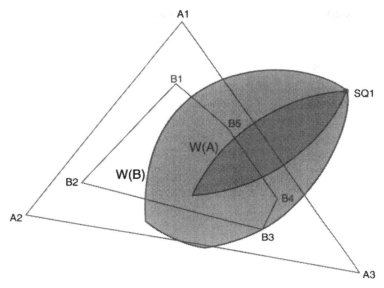

Figure 1.6. Veto players A1–A3 produce more policy stability than B1–B5 (no matter where the status quo is).

increases with each move (since the unanimity core expands). In the new system B_4 and B_5 are absorbed as veto players.

Proposition 1.4 is the most general statement about veto players in multidimensional spaces in this book. It permits comparisons across political systems, provided that we are discussing the same *range* of positions of the status quo. Let me explain this point more in detail. All the arguments I have made hold, regardless of the position of the status quo, but once the status quo is selected it is supposed to remain fixed. Until now, I have not compared policy stability of different systems for different positions of the status quo. For example, it is a reasonable inference from Proposition 1.4 to expect the policy stability of a system including communist, socialist, and liberal parties to be higher than the policy stability of a coalition of social democratic and liberal parties. However, this proposition would not involve different positions of the status quo. If the status quo in the first case happens to be very far away from the ideal points of all three parties, while the status quo in the second is located between the positions of the coalition partners, then the first system may produce a significant change in the status quo, and the second will produce no change. To be more concrete, policy stability does not imply that the first coalition will be unable to respond to an explosion in a nuclear energy plant by mobilizing the army if necessary. It is only with respect to similar positions of the status quo that the comparative statics statements make sense.

None of the four propositions I presented so far identifies the policy position that defeats the status quo. It is possible that the winset of the status quo is large, and yet the position that is selected to be compared with it (and defeat it) is located close to it. It is inappropriate to conclude from any of the four propositions that because the winset of the status quo is large in a particular case, the new policy will be far away from it. The correct conclusion is that when the winset of the status quo is small, the policy adopted will be close to it. In other words, each one of the propositions above should be read as presenting *a necessary but not sufficient* condition for proximity of the new policy with the status quo: if the new policy is away from the status quo it means that the winset is large, but if it is close it does not mean that the winset is small. Similarly, if we are inside the unanimity core there will be no policy change, but if there is no policy change we are not necessarily inside the unanimity core.

The points made in the previous paragraph are extremely important for empirical analyses. Let us call SQ and SQ′ the status quo and its replacement. Propositions 1.1–1.4 indicate the following: When the winset of the status quo is small, the distance between SQ and SQ′ (which is represented by |SQ-SQ′|) will be small. When the winset of SQ is large, |SQ-SQ′| can be either small or large. Aggregating across many cases will therefore present the following picture. *On average,* assuming that all possible distances are equally plausible,[8] large winsets will present bigger |SQ-SQ′| than small winsets. In addition, large winsets will present higher variance of |SQ-SQ′| than small winsets.

Figure 1.7 presents the relation between the size of the winset and the distance |SQ-SQ′| and leads to two predictions. First, on average, the distance |SQ-SQ′| will increase with the size of the winset of the status quo; and second, the variance of |SQ-SQ′| will also increase with the (same) size of the winset of the status quo.

Because of the high variance of |SQ-SQ′|, when the winset of the status quo is large the statistical significance of a simple correlation between size of winset and |SQ-SQ′| will be low because of heteroskedasticity. However, the appropriate way of testing the relationship between the size of the winset and |SQ-SQ′| is not a simple correlation or regression, but a double test that includes the bivariate regression and also the residuals of this regression.[9]

After discussing Propositions 1.1–1.4 and the way they should be tested empirically, we need to focus on one important issue completely omitted so far: the question of sequence.

---

[8] This is a questionable assumption, but one is needed here and I find nothing better to replace it.

[9] In fact, this is a much more general idea. Many relationships presented in comparative politics and in international relations are necessary but not sufficient conditions (think of B. Moore's "no bourgeois no democracy"). The appropriate test for such theories is not a simple regression, but a

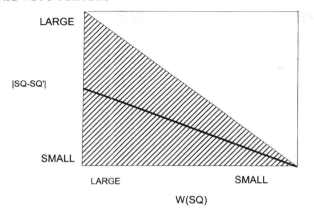

LARGE

|SQ-SQ'|

SMALL

LARGE   SMALL

W(SQ)

Figure 1.7. Distance of new policy from status quo as a function of size of W(SQ).

1.4. Sequence of Moves

So far we have been treating veto players in a symmetric way. All of them were equally important for us. As a result we only identified the set of feasible solutions: the winset of the status quo. However, in political systems certain political actors make proposals to others who can accept or reject them. If we consider such sequences of moves, we can narrow down significantly the predictions of our models. However, in order to be able to narrow down the outcomes we will need to know not only the precise identity but also the preferences of the agenda setter. As we will see, these requirements are quite restrictive.[10] This section aims to find out what difference it makes if one veto player proposes and another accepts or rejects.

Figure 1.8 presents the simplest possible case: two veto players. Given that both of them try to achieve their ideal point, or come as close as possible to it, if veto player A makes an offer to B, he will select out of the whole winset the point PA, which is closest to him. Similarly, if B makes an offer to A he will select point PB. It is easy to verify that there is a significant advantage to making proposals. In fact, the player who makes proposals will consider the winset of all the other veto players as his constraint, and select among all the

---

double test, that includes heteroskedasticity of residuals. In the empirical chapters I use multiplicative heteroskedastic regression to test necessary but not sufficient condition expectations.

[10] For example, we will see in Chapter 4 that in parliamentary systems governments control the agenda; however, we do not know who within a government is the agenda setter. In fact, different researchers have hypothesized different actors (prime minister, finance minister, relevant minister, bargaining among different actors, proportional weights, and so on).

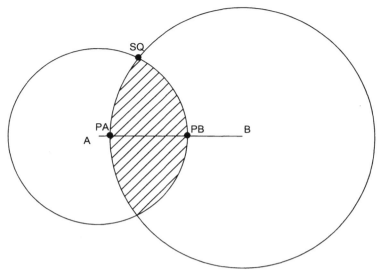

Figure 1.8. Significance of agenda setting.

points contained in this winset the one that he prefers. This is the advantage of the agenda setter, identified for the first time formally by McKelvey (1976).[11]

Proposition 1.5: The veto player who sets the agenda has a considerable advantage: he can consider the winset of the others as his constraint, and select from it the outcome he prefers.

Proposition 1.5 makes clear that the analysis of the previous three sections is valid even if one knows the sequence of moves and includes sequence in the analysis: one can subtract the agenda setter from the set of veto players, calculate the winset of the remainder, and then identify the point closest to the agenda setter.

As a consequence of Proposition 1.5, a single veto player has no constraints and can select any point within his indifference curve. As another consequence, as the size of the winset of the status quo shrinks (either because there are more veto players or because their distances increase), the importance of agenda setting is reduced. In the limit case where the status quo is inside the unanimity core (when there is no possibility of change), it does not matter at all who controls the agenda. As a third consequence, the importance of agenda setting increases the more centrally located the agenda setter is. I will single out these three corollaries because we will make use of the first in the discussion of

---

[11] But as we said already, the idea of agenda-setting advantage can be traced back to Livy.

single-party governments in Chapter 3 (both democratic and nondemocratic) and the other two in the discussion of the relationship between governments and parliaments in parliamentary systems in Chapter 4.

Corollary 1.5.1: A single veto player is also the agenda setter and has no constraints in the selection of outcomes.

Corollary 1.5.2: The significance of agenda setting declines as policy stability increases.

Figure 1.9 provides a graphic representation of Corollaries 1.5.2 and 1.5.3 that we will use frequently. Consider first the set of two veto players A and X, and the status quo SQ. The winset of the status quo is hatched, and if X is the agenda setter he will select the point X1 that is as close to his ideal point as possible. Now add B as another veto player in the system. The winset of the status quo shrinks (the crosshatched area), and if X continues to be the agenda setter, he has to select the point that he prefers inside this smaller winset. It is clear that the new outcome X2 will be *at least* as far away from X as point X1 was.[12]

The power of the agenda setter depends also on his location with respect to other veto players. In Figure 1.9, the agenda setter X was further away from both A and B than the status quo; that is why he had to make the proposal X2, which was far away from his ideal point. If the agenda setter is Y instead of X, he has to be concerned only with veto player A and make the proposal Y1 (since he is already close to B's ideal point). Finally, if the agenda setter is Z (inside the winset of the status quo) he can propose his own ideal point. Think now of the location of the status quo changing; in this case, an agenda setter will have more power the more centrally located among the veto players he is, because then he has a higher probability of being located more frequently inside the winset of the status quo.

Corollary 1.5.3: The significance of agenda setting increases as the agenda setter is located centrally among existing veto players.

This entire discussion makes two important assumptions. First, that all veto players have been taken into account. We will discuss how to count veto players in different countries in the second part. However, we will be considering only institutional or partisan veto players. If a case can be made that the army, the bureaucracy, or some interest group are veto players in a certain country,

---

[12] In an empirical study of German bicameralism Braeuninger and König (1999) find that the agenda-setting powers of the German government decline when legislation has to be approved by the upper chamber (Bundesrat).

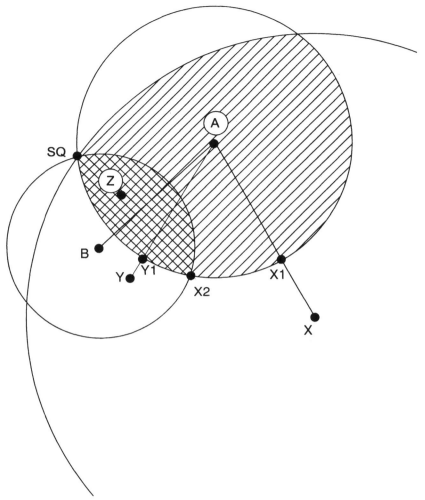

Figure 1.9. Importance of agenda setting decreases with more veto players and increases with the central location of agenda setter.

their preferences should be included in the analysis. Similarly, if in a certain policy area foreign actors can play an important role and exclude possible outcomes (the International Monetary Fund on financial policies of developing countries), these players should be also included in the set of veto players. Failure to include all veto players inaccurately specifies the size of W(SQ), although the outcome is still within the (mistakenly) hypothesized W(SQ).

Second, the ideal points of all veto players are well known by all of them (as well as by the observer). It excludes any uncertainty for one veto player about the ideal point of another, and consequently any strategic misrepresentation of preferences. If the assumptions of this chapter were met, one would observe all the time successful proposals by agenda setters being accepted by the other veto players. If this second assumption is not met, then proposals may fail and the policymaking process may start all over again. However, we will see in the second part that real institutions have provisions for the exchange of information among veto players.

1.5. Conclusions

This account completes in broad strokes all the theory in the book. Veto players are actors whose agreement is necessary for a change in the status quo. Policy stability is the term that expresses the difficulty for a significant change of the status quo. Policy stability increases in general with the number of veto players and with their distances (but see Propositions 1.1–1.4 for more accurate predictions). The empirical test of these predictions requires not a simple regression, but also tests of the variance of the distance between old and new policies. The veto player who controls the agenda-setting process has a significant redistributive advantage: he can select the point he prefers from the whole winset of the others (Proposition 1.5). However, this advantage declines as a function of the policy stability of the system (Corollary 1.5.2), that is, with the number of veto players and their distances from each other. Finally, the significance of agenda setting increases when the agenda setter is centrally located within existing veto players (Corollary 1.5.3).

Corollaries 1.5.2 and 1.5.3 provide the positional dimensions of agenda setting. Agenda setting becomes less important as the number of veto players increases, and more important as the agenda setter is located centrally within the veto players. In Chapter 4 we will study (some of) the institutional dimensions of agenda setting, that is, specific rules that enable some actors to make proposals and prevent others from changing them. The combination of institutional and positional dimensions of agenda setting is necessary for understanding its importance.

This chapter has dealt with all the issues that will be studied in this book. Conceptually we will just elaborate points made in this chapter, and empirically we will test the predictions formulated here. We start with the introduction of a significant dose of realism into these simple models. Does this analysis apply to collective veto players, since the constitutions of different countries do not speak of veto players but of collective actors such as parliaments, parties, and committees?

2

Collective Veto Players

ON THE BASIS of Chapter 1 we can analyze situations where the veto players are individuals (like the U.S. president), or have monolithic majorities (like a communist party), or decide by unanimity (like the Polish parliament in the early eighteenth century). However, such situations are rare. Most often decisionmaking involves participation of some collective veto player such as a committee, a party, or a parliament. Rare are the cases where such actors are monolithic, or even have a homogeneous majority inside them. And today cases that involve unanimous decisionmaking are exceptional. Therefore, we need to generalize and see whether the intuitions generated by Chapter 1 hold in more familiar configurations of preferences and modes of decisionmaking.

While this chapter is essential for moving away from simplifications and increasing the correspondence between theoretical concepts and political reality, it is significantly more technically demanding than the previous one. In addition, while the conclusions presented in Chapter 1 were intuitive to the point that they may have seemed obvious to readers, some of the ideas here are counterintuitive. This chapter reaches the conclusion that the analysis of Chapter 1 provides a very good approximation to political phenomena, but the argument is more challenging to follow.

The nontechnical reader may be tempted to skip a chapter that is significantly more difficult than the previous one, has counterintuitive results, yet reaches the same conclusions. To dissuade the reader from such a strategy, I precede my discussion with a long introduction, which explains the problems generated by collective veto players. I hope this will generate sufficient interest in the conceptual problems. However, should the reader remain unpersuaded, I summarize in the conclusion the most important ideas presented in this chapter. Thus a nontechnical reader may read the introduction and conclusion of this chapter and then proceed to the rest of the book. The reader who wants to apply veto players theory to cases not covered in this book (countries I do not discuss here, or decisionmaking at the state or local level) should complete the chapter in full.

2.1. Introduction

Transition from individual to collective veto players generates two problems. First, the configuration of the winset of the status quo may become complicated, that is, the *outcomes of decisionmaking become more complicated.* We will need to approximate these outcomes in some simple way. Second, collective veto players violate one important assumption we made about individuals: under majority rule, collective veto players cannot unambiguously choose the outcome they prefer. In other words, *the choices of collective veto players are ambiguous.* This is obviously more than a mere inconvenience, or a lack of descriptive accuracy; it may make collective veto players unable to make a proposal and thus undermine completely the analysis of the previous chapter. I will explain under what conditions this problem can be eliminated, and argue that these conditions occur frequently.

2.1.1. The Outcomes of Decisionmaking Are More Complicated

Consider the seven individual veto players (1, 2, . . . 7) and the status quo (SQ) presented in Figure 2.1. Which points can defeat the status quo by a unanimous decision of the seven veto players?

The points that can defeat the status quo can be located if we consider the points that each individual veto player prefers over the status quo. The reader is reminded that such points are located inside circles that go through the status quo, and have in the center the preferences of each veto player. The intersection of all these circles is the heavily shaded lens in Figure 2.1. Similarly, we can identify all the points that cannot be defeated by a unanimous decision of the seven veto players (the unanimity core). These points form the whole heptagon 1234567.[1] Indeed, any point inside the heptagon cannot be replaced without one of the veto players objecting. The hatched area in Figure 2.1 presents the unanimity core of this collective veto player.

What happens if this collective veto player uses less restrictive decision-making rules? What if decisions are made by qualified majority or simple majority instead of unanimity? The intuitions generated from Chapter 1 indicate that policy stability should decrease, that is, that more points could defeat the status quo (the winset of the status quo should expand), and fewer points should be invulnerable (the core should shrink). Let us consider one case of each rule, first, a qualified majority decision by six out of the seven actors, and second, a simple majority (four of the seven members).

The points that can defeat SQ by a qualified majority of six-sevenths (the six-sevenths qualified majority winset of SQ) can be identified if we consider the intersection of six of the seven circles around the points 1, 2, . . . , 7 of Figure 2.1. I present this area shaded lighter than the points that could defeat SQ under the unanimity rule (the unanimity winset of SQ), and, as the reader

---

[1] I have selected them in such a way that none of them is included in the unanimity core of the others, otherwise the unanimity core would have been a different polygon (with fewer sides).

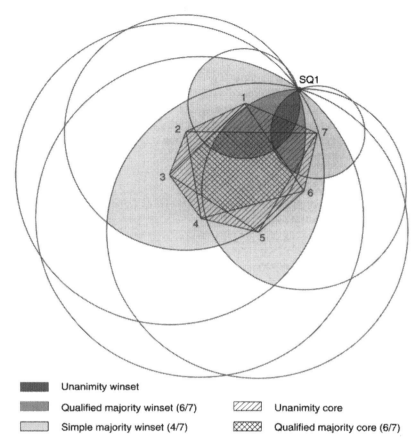

Figure 2.1. Winset and core of unanimity (7/7), qualified majority (6/7), and simple majority (4/7).

can verify, it includes this unanimity winset of SQ. In order to locate the points that cannot be defeated by a six-sevenths majority (the six-sevenths core), we consider all the possible combinations of six out of the seven players, and take the intersection of their unanimity cores.[2] In Figure 2.1 this intersection is represented by the cross-hatched area. The reader can verify that it is included in the unanimity core of the seven players.

What happens if the seven players decide by majority rule? In order to calculate the set of outcomes that defeat the status quo (the winset of SQ), we

---

[2] A more expedient way would be to connect the seven players by ignoring one of them each time (connect 1 and 3, 2 and 4, 3 and 5, and so on) and consider the polygon generated by the intersection of these lines.

have to consider the intersections of any four circles. The lightly shaded area in Figure 2.1 gives the area of the majority winset of SQ, and this area includes the qualified majority winset (which includes the unanimity winset). If we try to identify the core of majority decisionmaking we will see that this core is empty, that is, there is no point that cannot be defeated by majority rule. As we will see below, the conditions under which there is a point that cannot be defeated by any other point under majority rule are very exceptional indeed.

Figure 2.1 demonstrates two important points. First, policy stability generated by collective veto players follows the intuitions generated by Chapter 1: it decreases (that is, the winset of SQ expands and the core shrinks) as the decisionmaking rule moves from unanimity to qualified majority to simple majority. Second, the calculations become more complicated every time preferences of a collective veto player are not expressed by circles and the winset of collective veto players takes unusual shapes. This chapter aims at identifying a simple way of approximating the outcomes of the decisionmaking process (the points that can defeat the status quo) when a veto player is collective.

2.1.2. The Choices of Collective Veto Players Are Ambiguous

When an individual veto player compares three possible positions of SQ, we can assume that his preferences are *transitive*: if he prefers SQ1 over SQ2, and SQ2 over SQ3, then he will also prefer SQ1 over SQ3. This transitivity of preferences enables the individual veto player to select unambiguously among any set of alternatives, to identify the alternative that he prefers the most.[3] However, collective veto players deciding under majority rule do not have the same transitivity of preferences. Figures 2.2 and 2.3 provide in two steps the intuition behind the argument.

In Figure 2.2 there are three individual decision makers and the status quo located in the middle of the triangle 123. Let us first try to identify the points that defeat the status quo under simple majority rule. Following the rules set in Chapter 1, I draw the indifference curves (circles) of the three players and consider the intersections of any two of them. In the figure I have hatched W(SQ), which has a flower-like shape. The edges of the hatched area are the points of indifference of different majorities. In Figure 2.1 I represent the preferences of the coalition 1 and 3 with a different pattern, and I select a point SQ1 that defeats SQ because it is preferred by these two decisionmakers. Note that I have selected SQ1 at the edge of the petal. The only reason for this

---

[3] The individual may be indifferent between two alternatives. Indifference is different from ambiguity of preferences, as will become clear below. I ignore here cases of indifference for simplicity of exposition.

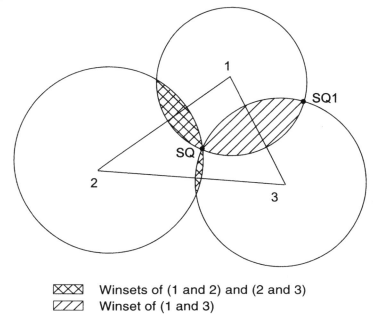

$\boxtimes\boxtimes\boxtimes$ Winsets of (1 and 2) and (2 and 3)
$\diagup\diagup\diagup$ Winset of (1 and 3)

Figure 2.2. SQ1 defeats SQ by majority (of 1 and 3).

choice is to minimize the subsequent drawing, but there is no loss of generality to the argument I present.

Let us now move to a second step: identify the set of points that defeat SQ1. In Figure 2.3 I have drawn the one additional circle required for this operation, the circle around point 2 (the other two circles already exist because of the selection of SQ1). The hatched area in Figure 2.3 are the points that defeat SQ1 by different majorities (winset of SQ1: (W(SQ1)).

I remind the reader that we started from SQ and identified the other two points as follows: SQ1 was a point that defeats SQ by majority rule (decisionmakers 1 and 3 prefer SQ1 over SQ). Similarly, SQ2 was a point that defeats SQ1 by majority rule (decisionmakers 1 and 2 preferred SQ2 over SQ1). If the collectivity of 1, 2, and 3 were a single individual that preferred SQ2 over SQ1 and SQ1 over SQ, then *by transitivity this individual would also prefer SQ2 over SQ*. However, this is not the case for our collectivity. It prefers SQ to SQ2. In other words, our collectivity has ambiguous preferences generated by majority rule:[4]

$$SQ2 \ \pi \ SQ1 \ \pi \ SQ \ \pi SQ2 \tag{2.1}$$

[4] In the above discussion I ignore indifference relations for reasons of simplicity of the exposition.

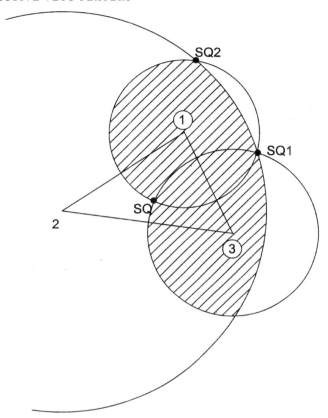

Figure 2.3. SQ2 defeats SQ1 by majority rule.

where π stands for "majority preferred." Note that the three preferences are not generated by the same majorities. Decisionmakers 1 and 2 are responsible for the first choice, 1 and 3 for the second, and 2 and 3 for the third. This ambiguity of preferences, this "intransitivity" of majority rule (to use the technical term) was known by Condorcet, but was explored and generalized extensively by Arrow (1951)[5] and in a spatial context by McKelvey (1976) and Schofield (1977, 1978).

For our purposes the best way to note the ambiguous pattern of preferences generated by majority rule and described by (2.1) is to highlight the fact that the collectivity cannot make up its mind between SQ and SQ2: SQ defeats SQ2 by direct comparison but it is defeated by SQ2 in a mediated or indirect

---

[5] Arrow has, of course, shown the impossibility of *any* decisionmaking rule to conform to five plausible and desirable requirements.

comparison (if SQ1 is compared with both of them, it eliminates SQ and is eliminated by SQ2).

Why should we care about the ambiguity of collective preferences, the fact that SQ directly beats SQ2, while it is indirectly defeated by SQ2? Because we do not know how SQ and SQ2 will be compared. We do not know which one is first on the agenda. More to the point, if the collectivity cannot make up its mind, strategic entrepreneurs will present a sequence of choices that lead to one or the other outcome. In fact, McKelvey (1976, 1978) and Schofield (1977, 1978) have shown that the problem is much more serious than my description presents it: these "intransitivities" can cover the whole space such that an astute agenda setter can present a society with a series of choices structured appropriately and lead it to *any* result he or she wishes.

This analysis may completely undermine the arguments I made in Chapter 1. Collective veto players cannot choose unambiguously by majority rule. This means that if a collective veto player controls the agenda and makes an offer to another veto player, a clear choice should *not* be expected because collective veto players come to contradictory results when they have to compare two points (let alone the infinity contained in the winset of the others).

In subsequent sections, I demonstrate that these objections, which could have been fatal for my arguments, are in fact mere inconveniences. The winset of a collective veto player may not be a circle, but a circle that contains it can be identified and the analysis can be carried out in an approximate way. Collective veto players may not be able to make choices in general, but under empirically plausible conditions they can select a small area among all the available alternatives. Thus the analysis of Chapter 1 holds approximately for collective veto players also.

However, there is a price to be paid. These approximations, while on the average accurate, are not always true. For example, as I demonstrated in the previous chapter, while the set of points that defeat the status quo shrinks with the distance of two individual veto players (along the same line, as Figure 1.4 demonstrates), with collective veto players it is possible to decrease the distance and decrease the size of the winset of the status quo. This can happen under specific distributions of the individual players and/or positions of the status quo. It is not a frequent phenomenon, but it is possible. As a result, I cannot present as theorems the claims made in this chapter, because positions of individual actors can be found to falsify such theorems. The claims will be presented as "conjectures" and the arguments for the validity of these conjectures will be presented.

The chapter is organized to mirror Chapter 1 (discussion of winsets first, of sequence afterward). I have interpolated one section: to discuss collective veto players deciding by qualified majority, which turns out to be quite different from simple majority. Thus the overall organization of the chapter is as follows. In Section 2.2 I identify the winset of a collective veto player by simple majority rule. In Section 2.3 I consider collective veto players who decide by qualified majorities, and explain the significant difference between simple and qualified majority decisionmaking. In Section 2.4, I deal with the question of sequence where collective veto players can generate more problems due to their inability to maximize. The overall finding of this chapter is that the analysis of Chapter 1 holds with very small adjustments.

2.2. Collective Veto Players and Simple Majorities

Let as assume that the agreement of a chamber of a legislature (like the U.S. House of Representatives) is required for a change in the status quo, and that this chamber decides by simple majority of its members. In our terminology the chamber is a collective veto player. However, no individual member inside the legislature has veto power over legislation. In order to find the winset of the status quo we have to identify the intersections of the indifference curves of all possible majorities.

Figure 2.4 presents the winset of the status quo for a five-member committee (I use the word committee because of the small number of members I present in order to simplify the graphics).[6] The political game inside this committee may support variable or stable coalitions. We will discuss the difference extensively in Part II. Here let us assume that any coalition is possible and try to locate W(SQ). Since W(SQ) is generated by the intersection of a series of circles, it has an unusual shape that makes the study of its spatial properties difficult. Ferejohn, McKelvey, and Packell (1984) located a circle where the winset of SQ by majority rule can be included. Here I report how one can identify this circle in three steps:

1. *Drawing of median lines.*[7] *Median* is a line connecting two points and having majorities on either side of it (including points on the line). For example, in Figure 2.4, AC, BE, BD, EC, and AD are median lines because they have on one side three points and on the other four (two of them are on the lines themselves).

2. *Identification of the "yolk."* Yolk is the smallest circle[8] intersecting all medians. In the figure this circle has center Y and radius r. It is tangent on median lines AD, AC, and EC. It intersects the other two median lines (BE and BD). Y is at a distance d from SQ.

3. *Drawing of circle (Y, d + 2r).* Figure 2.5 presents the yolk (Y,r), the status quo SQ in distance d from the center of the yolk Y, and two different median lines: L1 and L2. Given that there are majorities on both sides of these lines, the points SQ1

[6] As I show in Chapter 5, many members actually simplify the situation at least at the conceptual level, although graphics may become difficult to draw.

[7] Planes or hyperplanes in three or more dimensions.

[8] Sphere or hypersphere in three or more dimensions.

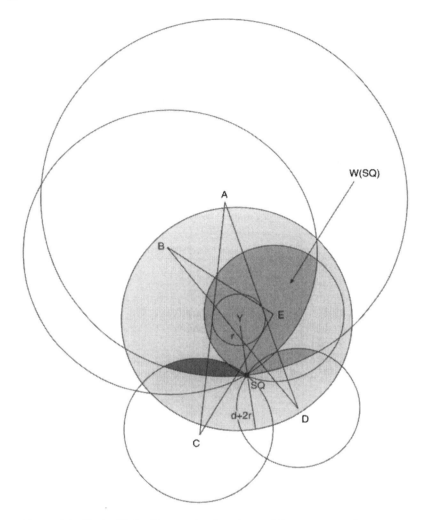

Figure 2.4. Circle (Y, d + 2r) contains the winset of the status quo of collective VP (ABCDE).

and SQ2 (symmetric of SQ with respect to these medians) belong also in the winset of the status quo (they are preferred over SQ by the majority of points that are on the opposite side of these lines than SQ). My goal is to draw a circle including all such points. For that purpose, I have to include the most distant location from SQ that a point symmetric to it with respect to a median line can obtain. Such a point is SQ3, which is symmetric with respect to a median line tangential to the yolk at the most distant point from SQ (point X in the figure). This point is in distance d + r

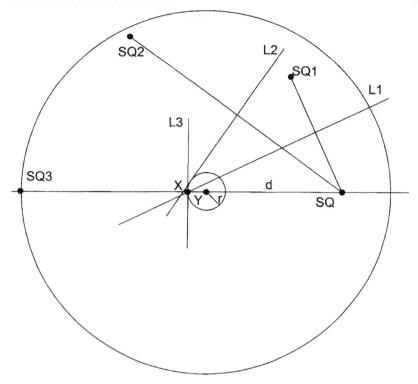

Figure 2.5. W(SQ) is contained inside the wincircle (Y, d + 2r).

from SQ, so the distance YSQ3 is d + 2r.[9] Consequently the circle (Y, d + 2r) includes SQ and all the symmetric points with respect to all possible median lines. I call this circle that includes the winset of the status quo of a collective veto player by majority rule the (majority) *wincircle* of the collective veto player. The basic property of the wincircle is that all the points outside it are defeated by SQ. The conclusion from this whole exercise is that we can replace the collective veto player ABCDE by a fictitious individual veto player located at Y (the center of the yolk of the collective one) with wincircle (Y, d + 2r).

How should we interpret these results? While individual veto players had circular indifference curves going through the status quo, collective veto players have indifference curves of unusual shape, generated by the different possible majorities that can support one point or another. The different possible majorities are the reason that the wincircle of the collective veto player has a radius larger than d by 2r.

[9] The distance SQSQ3 is 2(d + r), while YSQ is d. By subtraction we get the result.

There is an important difference between the analysis based on individual and collective veto players: For individual veto players the circular indifference curves are actual (i.e., generated from the assumptions of the model and the position of the veto player and SQ); for collective veto players the circular indifference curves are upper bounds or approximations. As noted, by the definition of wincircle there are no points of W(SQ) outside it.[10] In the remainder of this chapter I use these upper bounds of W(SQ) to approximate policy stability, because they can provide information about which points *cannot* defeat the status quo (where W(SQ) is *not* located). The reader is reminded that Propositions 1.1–1.4 provided sufficient but not necessary conditions for policy stability, so the use of the upper bound of W(SQ) is consistent with the arguments presented in Chapter 1 and preserves its conclusions.

As for the radius of the yolk of a collective veto player, it is an indication of its *m-cohesion*—of how well the majority is represented by the point Y located at the center of the collective veto player. So, as the radius of the yolk decreases, the m-cohesion of a collective veto player increases.

As the radius of the yolk increases (m-cohesion decreases), the wincircle of the collective veto player increases. While it is not always the case that an increased wincircle will entail an increase in the size of the winset of the status quo,[11] policy stability increases when the wincircle shrinks, since there are no points that can defeat SQ outside the wincircle.

> *Conjecture 2.1:* Policy stability increases as the m-cohesion of a collective veto player increases (as the radius of the yolk decreases).

It is interesting to note that on the average r *decreases* as the size of (number of individuals composing) the collective veto player *increases*. This is a counterintuitive result. The reason it happens is that additional points replace some of the previously existing median lines by others more centrally located. As far as I know, there is not a closed solution to the problem, but computer simulations have indicated that this is the case under a variety of conditions (Koehler 1990). This is why I will use again the term "conjecture."

> *Conjecture 2.2:* An increase in size of (number of individuals composing) a collective veto player (ceteris paribus) increases its m-cohesion (decreases the size of its yolk), and consequently increases policy stability.

---

[10] However, since the circles around collective veto players are the upper bounds of W(SQ), it is possible that two such upper bounds intersect while W(SQ) is empty.I thank Macartan Humphreys for presenting concrete examples of this point to me.

[11] In fact, one can construct counterexamples where the winset increases as the wincircle shrinks. Think for example of the following two situations: a triangle ABC and SQ is located on A. In this case W(SQ) is the intersection of the two circles (B, BA) and (C, CA). If one moves A inside the triangle BCSQ, then the radius of the yolk shrinks while the winset expands.

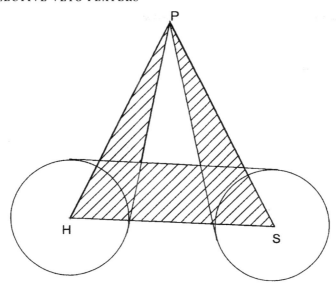

Figure 2.6. Possibility of incremental change when two VPs are collective (US).

I do not test the conjectures related to the cohesion of collective veto players in this book. As far as I know, there are no systematic data on internal cohesion of parties in parliamentary regimes. Even in the United States, where the positions of different members of Congress can be constructed on the basis of scores provided by different interest groups, the different methods raise methodological controversies.[12] Once such controversies are settled, if one can use voting records in legislatures to identify policy positions of individual MPs, such data would be used to identify party cohesion in the models I present. For the time being, I use the above analysis simply to make two qualitative points. The first has to do with the fact that most political players are collective. The second involves the dimensionality of the underlying policy space.

First, consider the implications from the fact that most veto players are collective and not individual. An example is provided by the U.S. Constitution: legislation requires approval by the House, the Senate, and the president (the first two by majority rule; I will not enter into filibuster, veto, and veto override until then next section).

Figure 2.6 compares two different cases: first, if all three veto players were individuals (or if the House and the Senate were each controlled by a single

---

[12] For a recent debate see McCarty, Poole, and Rosenthal (2001) and Snyder and Groseclose (2001).

monolithic party), and, second, the actual situation where the House and the Senate are collective veto players deciding by majority rule, in which case they are represented by the centers of their yolks, H and S.

When all three veto players are individuals, the image produced by Figure 2.6 is stalemate as long as the SQ is located inside the triangle PHS. In fact, we are located inside the unanimity core of the system of the three veto players, and no change is possible.

If, however, H and S are collective veto players, there is a *possibility* of incremental change. Humphreys (2001) has shown that this possibility exists *only* in the areas close to the sides of the triangle PHS as indicated by the hatched area in Figure 2.6.[13] I emphasize "possibility" because whether the winsets of the two collective players actually intersect depends on the preferences of individual members of Congress. Hence, instead of the absolute immobilism presented in the analysis with individual veto players, collective veto players *may* present the possibility of *incremental* change for certain locations of the status quo.

This analysis indicates that the possibility of change becomes more pronounced the less cohesive the two chambers are, as Conjecture 2.1 indicates. The political implication is that small deviations from SQ *may* be approved by the political system, and that such changes would be more important as the lack of cohesion of each one of the two chambers increases. Another way of thinking about this situation is that the more divided each one of the two chambers is, the more possibilities are presented to the president to achieve agreement on some particular alternative. In fact, if the two chambers are politically very close to each other, incremental change may always be possible.[14]

My second remark addresses the issue of multidimensionality of the policy space. In a seminal article on the U.S. Constitution, Hammond and Miller (1987) make the point that in two dimensions there will always be a core as long as the areas covered by members of each chamber do not overlap. Humphreys (2000) found that the probability that a bicameral core exists in two dimensions even if the preferences of members of the two chambers overlap is significant.[15] Tsebelis and Money (1997) showed that in a policy space with more than two dimensions, the core of a bicameral legislature rarely exists.

Political actors are usually composed of many individuals having preferences in multiple dimensions. Each one of these two factors increases the prob-

---

[13] This area is defined by the sides of the triangle and the tangent to the yolks of the two chambers as well as the lines through the president's ideal point tangent to each one of the two yolks.

[14] Technically, when the yolks of the two chambers intersect, the core of the political system *may* be empty.

[15] In a computer simulation he used two three-member chambers and the probability of a bicameral core was more than 50 percent.

ability that every possible status quo can be defeated in a political system.[16] Single dimensional analyses lead to median voter results: the median voter in a single dimension cannot be defeated (has an empty winset or constitutes the core); multidimensional models on the other hand have no median voter, every point can be defeated, and there is no equilibrium and no core. Riker (1982) raised this property of political systems into the essence of politics. According to his analysis, the difference between economics and politics was that economic analyses always reached an equilibrium, while multidimensional political analyses demonstrate that an equilibrium does not exist. The implication of this argument was that because such an equilibrium does not exist, losers are always looking for new issues to divide winning coalitions and take power.

My analysis shows that even if points defeating the status quo exist, they may be located very close to it, in which case the policy stability of the system will be high. Veto players replace the crude dichotomy of whether there is a core or not (or whether the winset of the status quo is empty) by a more continuous view of politics where the dependent variable is policy stability, which may exist even when there is no core, just because possible changes are incremental. The result of this approach is that we will be able to generalize in multiple dimensions instead of stopping because there are no equilibria.

2.3. Collective Veto Players and Qualified Majorities

In this section I examine the veto players decisionmaking process by qualified majority rule. The substantive interest of the section is obvious: quite frequently collective veto players decide by qualified majorities, like decisions to override presidential vetoes by the U.S. Congress (two-thirds), or verdicts by the Council of Ministers in the European Union (approximately five-sevenths), or conclusions on important institutional or constitutional matters in other countries (such as France or Belgium).

I argue that the actual importance of qualified majorities is even greater for two reasons. First, if a decisionmaking sequence includes a qualified majority at the end (as they usually do; see for example the veto override case in the United States, or resolutions in the Council of Ministers of the European Union, or some cases of overrule of the Bundesrat by the Bundestag), then the analysis of this sequence requires a backward analysis that *starts* from the results of this procedure.[17] Second, there are a series of cases where the official rules specify that decisions will be made either by simple or by absolute major-

---

[16] Technically, the core is empty.

[17] The process is called backwards induction. For such an analysis of the cooperation procedure in the European Union, see Tsebelis (1994) as well as the analysis in Chapter 11.

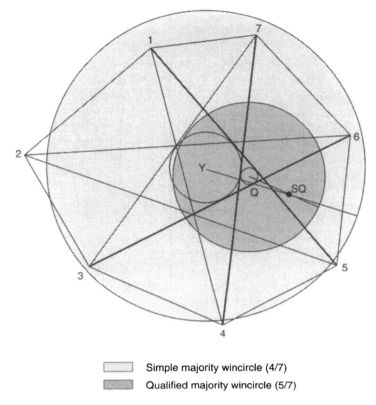

Simple majority wincircle (4/7)
Qualified majority wincircle (5/7)

Figure 2.7. Comparison of simple majority wincircle (4/7) with qualified majority wincircle (5/7).

ity, but the political conditions transform this requirement to an actual qualified majority threshold (I discuss these cases in detail in Chapter 6).

While conceptually a qualified majority occupies the intermediate category between the unanimity rule that I examined in Chapter 1 and the simple majority rule discussed in the previous section, the mechanics of locating a circle including the winset of the status quo by qualified majority are quite different. Because of the substantive importance of qualified majority decisionmaking and because of the technical differences between majority and qualified majority decisionmaking, I dedicate a whole section to this decisionmaking procedure.

Consider the center of the yolk (Y; defined in the previous section) of a collective veto player and the status quo as presented in Figure 2.7. I define as *q-dividers* the lines that leave on one side of them (including the line itself) a qualified majority q of individual points. Note the difference between q-dividers and median lines (or m-dividers): Median lines leave majorities of individual points *on each side* of them, while q-dividers leave a qualified majority *on one side only.* I define as *relevant q-dividers* the q-dividers that leave SQ and the q majority on opposite sides. The identification of a circle including the qualified majority winset of the status quo QW(SQ) is done again in three steps:

1. Draw all the relevant q-dividers. In Figure 2.7 I have selected a heptagon, and I am interested in five-sevenths qualified majorities. The selection of a heptagon presents the graphic simplification that the median lines (leaving at least 4 points on either side) and the q-dividers (leaving 5 points on one of their sides) are the same, so I do not need to complicate the picture. I also select the status quo SQ and identify the relevant q-dividers (the three heavy lines in the figure). Note that the relevant q-dividers pass between SQ and Y, and the q-dividers that leave Y and SQ on the same side are all nonrelevant.

2. Call q-yolk the circle (sphere or hypersphere) that intersects all q-dividers, and *q-circle* the circle (sphere or hypersphere) that intersects all the relevant ones. In Figure 2.6 the q-yolk is identical to the yolk, and the q-circle is the small circle between the yolk and the status quo. Note that while the centers of the yolk and of the q-yolk are close to each other (in our figure, by definition identical), the center of the q-circle moves toward the status quo because we consider only the relevant q-dividers.

3. Call Q and q the center and radius of the q-circle and draw the circle (Q, $d' + 2q$). This is the q-wincircle of the status quo—it contains the qualified majority winset of the status quo (QW(SQ)). The proof is identical to the one of majority wincircles (developed around Figure 2.5). The figure indicates that the q-wincircle is significantly smaller than the majority wincircle (as expected).

We can use the radius of the q-yolk of a collective veto player to define its *q-cohesion* in a similar way with the m-cohesion above. As the radius of the q-yolk increases, q-cohesion decreases. However, as Figure 2.7 indicates, an increase in the radius of the q-yolk indicates that the center of the q-circle will move further toward the status quo, and that, on average, will reduce the size of the q-wincircle. Again, this is conjecture because one can imagine counterexamples where the radius of the q-yolk increases and yet the size of the winset increases also. The above argument indicates that the comparative statics generated by q-cohesion are exactly the opposite from m-cohesion. Indeed, the more q-cohesive a collective veto player is (the smaller the radius of the q-yolk), the larger the size of the q-wincircle, while the more m-cohesive a collective veto player is (the smaller the radius of the yolk), the smaller its majority wincircle.

Another way of thinking about q-cohesion and policy stability is that a q-cohesive veto player will have a small core, which means that there will be few points in space that are invulnerable, and the further away from this point one goes, the larger the q-winset becomes. In the limit case where q members of a collective veto player are concentrated on the same point, this is the only point of the core, and the q-winset increases as a function of the distance between SQ and the location of the veto player.

> ***Conjecture 2.3:*** Policy stability decreases as the q-cohesion of a collective veto player increases.

There is one essential reason that conjectures 2.1 and 2.3 run in opposite directions: by definition median lines have a majority on both sides, while q-dividers have a qualified majority on one side only. A series of differences results. First, all median lines are relevant for the construction of the wincircle, while only the relevant q-dividers define the q-wincircle. Second, the yolk has to be intersecting all median lines, while the q-circle intersects only the *relevant* q-dividers who are located close to SQ (since by definition they are between SQ and different q majorities). Third, the wincircle has to include all the reflections of SQ with respect to medians, while the q-wincircle has to include only the reflections with respect to relevant q-dividers (see Figure 2.7).

The next comparative statics result is obtained by changing the qualified majority threshold. By increasing the threshold, one requires one or more individual decisionmakers to agree to a change of the status quo, which increases policy stability.

> ***Proposition 2.4:*** Policy stability increases or remains the same as the required qualified majority threshold q increases.

The above statement can be proven formally: it holds regardless of the distribution of the preferences of the members of a collective veto player. As we saw in Chapter 1, it is possible to increase the qualified majority threshold and maintain the size of the qualified majority winset (think for example of three players deciding by three-fifths or two-thirds majority rule).

Figure 2.7 gives us a visual representation of the circles containing the four-sevenths and five-sevenths qualified majority winsets of the status quo. The reader can verify that the winset as well as the wincircle shrinks as the required majority increases. This figure can help us gain insights of situations where a qualified majority threshold is modified, like the cloture rule in the U.S. Senate.[18] A cloture vote used to require a two-thirds majority, while now it requires only three-fifths. What difference does this change of rules make for policy stability? Given that four-sevenths (= .57) is close to three-fifths (= .60) and five-sevenths (= .71) is close to two-thirds (= .67), Figure 2.7 suggests that policy stability significantly decreases with this change of the cloture rule.

---

[18] Unlike the U.S. House of Representatives, there are no time limits on senators' floor speeches, so that senators can filibuster in order to prevent the adoption of any particular bill they dislike. The only way to interrupt a filibustering senator is by a vote of cloture.

These four conjectures and propositions indicate not only that the principles we identified in Chapter 1 also hold for collective veto players, but go one step further and analyze the importance of the m- and q-cohesion of collective players. What we said in Chapter 1 about the size of the winset of the status quo being a necessary but not sufficient condition for the distance between the status quo and the new policy also holds in the case of collective veto players, because we use the circle that includes the winset of the status quo. When this circle is small, the distance between SQ and SQ'will be small; when the circle is large, the distance |SQ-SQ'| may be large or small. These findings are summarized in the conclusion.

2.4. Sequence of Moves

The previous two sections resolved the problem of location of the simple and qualified majority winset of collective veto players. This section deals with a more serious problem. Given the cycles that characterize majority rule decisionmaking, can a collective veto player identify the point or points that are the most preferred among the set of feasible alternatives (the winset of the remaining individual or collective veto players)?

In order to resolve this problem I will *assume* that a collective veto player can make proposals inside a specific area called an *uncovered set*. Restricting the location of possible proposals is not an innocuous assumption. As we will see, it eliminates many outcomes from the feasible set. Thus a justification of this assumption will be necessary before we make use of it. This section is organized in four parts. First, I define the uncovered set of a collective veto player deciding by majority rule. Second, I explore the restrictive nature of this assumption. Third, I provide a justification for it. Fourth, I calculate the location of a proposal by a collective veto player when he uses the uncovered set of the feasible solutions.

2.4.1. Definition of the Uncovered Set

Figure 2.8 indicates how we resolve the problem of choice of collective actors. In this figure two points, X and Y, are presented along with their respective winsets, W(X) and W(Y). For reasons of simplicity, I omit the representation of the individual decisionmakers. Let us assume (again, without loss of generality) that Y defeats X (represented in both panels of the figure by the fact that Y is inside W(X)). Since Y∈ W(X), there are two possibilities about W(X) and

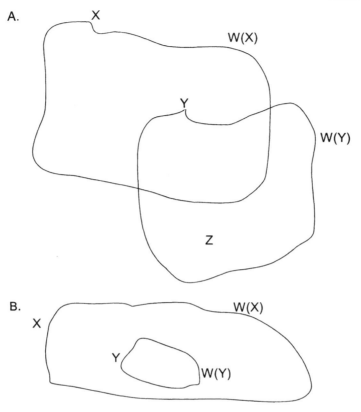

Figure 2.8. (A) Y does not cover X; (B) Y covers X.

W(Y). Either the two winsets intersect as in Figure 2.8A, or $W(Y) \subseteq W(X)$ (read "is a subset of") as in Figure 2.8B.[19]

Focusing on Figure 2.8A, since the two winsets intersect, I can always select a point Z such that $Z \in W(Y)$ and $Z \notin W(X)$. For that point Z we have:

$$Z \, \pi \, Y \, \pi \, X \, \pi \, Z \qquad (2.2)$$

In other words, in Figure 2.8A we can create a cycling pattern of preferences between X, Y, and Z. This pattern may be very useful for strategic actors, because the proponents of X, instead of admitting that their preferred solution is defeated, may introduce Z and ask for an indirect comparison, according to which Z defeats Y, and X defeats Z, so that X prevails.

[19] The cases that the two winsets have nothing in common or that $W(X) \subseteq W(Y)$ are excluded because of the assumption $Y \in W(X)$.

By contrast, in Figure 2.8B, where the winset of Y is a subset of the winset of X, it is impossible to find a point Z necessary to generate the cycling pattern. The relationship between X and Y in the second panel of 2.8 is such that not only does Y beat X, but anything that beats Y also beats X. We will call the relationship indicated in Figure 2.8B "a covering relationship."

Formally, a point Y *covers* a point X if and only if $Y \in W(X)$ and $W(Y) \subseteq W(X)$.

I use this definition of covering relationship when I speak about sequence. I argue that it makes no sense for an agenda setter to select covered points, that is, points that are defeated by others not only directly but also indirectly. Hence cases like point X in Figure 2.8B (but not in 2.8A) are excluded from consideration.

2.4.2. The Restriction of the Uncovered Set

Eliminating covered points from consideration may seem a reasonable assumption. But it is also a very restrictive assumption. If one eliminates the covered points (see Figure 2.8B), there are very few points that remain as valid choices. As demonstrated in Section 2.1 (Figure 2.5), the wincircle of the status quo of a collective veto player is a circle (Y, d + 2r), where d is the distance YSQ. As a result, any point located further away from the center of the yolk by *more than 2r cannot defeat SQ directly.* Applying the same reasoning twice leads us to the conclusion that any point further away than 4r *from the center of the yolk cannot defeat SQ indirectly.* As a result, all the points with distance from Y greater than d + 4r *are covered by SQ.*

McKelvey (1980) made use of this argument in order to locate the set of points that are not covered by any other, which is called the *uncovered set.* He started from the center of the yolk Y and argued that all points outside the circle (Y, 4r) are covered by Y. Consequently, this circle contains the uncovered set, or all points that are not covered by any point.

The uncovered set is a very powerful restrictive assumption. It moves the outcome from anywhere in space to a small circle centrally located inside the collective veto player. In fact, on the basis of the discussion surrounding Conjecture 2.2, as the size of a collective veto player increases, the uncovered set shrinks on average, so the larger the veto player, the more precise the prediction. How reasonable is the uncovered set assumption?

2.4.3. Can We Assume That the Outcome Will Be in the Uncovered Set?

The uncovered set is a concept of cooperative game theory. In what follows I first explain the fundamental assumptions of cooperative game theory and provide arguments supporting its use for the problem at hand. Second, I defend the use of the particular concept of uncovered set.

Cooperative game theory assumes that agreements made between different players are enforceable. The consequences of this assumption are dramatic. When agreements are enforceable, institutional features within the collective veto player such as agenda setting become irrelevant. Agendas merely determine the sequence in which different decisions are reached and strategic players act at every stage in a manner that promotes their (enforceable) agreement. Keeping the set of feasible alternatives constant, the only institution that matters in a cooperative game-theoretic analysis is the decisionmaking rule itself. In this sense, cooperative game theory is almost institution-free.

Is it reasonable to assume that agreements are enforceable within the agenda setter? There is one argument that can defend enforceability of agreements: reputation. If actors are interested in their reputations and suffer a sufficient reputational loss if they do not keep their word, agreements will be enforceable. Plausible conditions that may lead to enforceability of agreements are small groups, repeated interaction, or the existence of responsible political parties. The work of Robert Axelrod (1981) has mainly covered the first two reasons: with repeated interactions the shadow of future punishment is important. Similarly, small groups can sustain a strategy of punishing defectors. I will develop the case of parties a bit further: if individuals inside a collective veto player belong to parties and interact with each other as representatives of these parties, there is significantly more at stake than individual reputations. Defection from an agreement will be denounced to the other parties and to the population at large, and the consequences will be significant for the defector. As a consequence, the assumption of enforceable agreements is not far-fetched in the actual world of politics.

However, even if agreements were enforceable, why would they lead to the uncovered set? I provide three arguments. The first argument is that restricting the outcome to the uncovered set is equivalent to ignoring covered points, such as X in Figure 2.8B. Why would rational players agree to a covered point when a majority of them can make an agreement that will lead to Y and beats X not only directly but also indirectly? And if the choice between two contracts, one specifying X and the other Y, is obvious, then the enforceability assumption discussed before will actually lead to Y.

The second argument is that a series of other concepts like the Banks set (Banks 1985) or Schwartz's *Tournament Equilibrium Set* (TEQ; Schwartz 1990) produces outcomes in some subset of the uncovered set. For our purposes, the most significant is Schwartz's TEQ. Schwartz assumes that contracts between legislators are enforceable but legislators are free to recontract; that is, if they find a proposal that a majority coalition prefers, they can write an enforceable contract to support it. He also assumes that any two proposals can be directly compared. He calculates the smallest set within which this cooperative recontracting process is likely to produce outcomes. He calls this set TEQ and proves that it is a subset of the uncovered set.

The third argument is that even noncooperative games lead to centrally located equilibria. For example, Baron (1996) provides a model of infinitely repeated voting, and the equilibrium approximates the median voter. Results in multiple dimensions lead to expectations of convergence to the center of the policy space (where the uncovered set is located). For example, Baron and Herron (1999), using a two-dimensional model with three legislators, produce centrally located outcomes when the time horizon expands.

These arguments indicate (although do not prove) that the uncovered set is a reasonable assumption when one deals with decisionmaking inside committees (small groups with frequent interactions) or with interactions among parties. In their turn, decisions by larger actors like a chamber of a parliament are based on proposals by such small actors (either a formal committee or an informal gathering of party leaders, or the government), so assuming that covered outcomes will be excluded is not an arbitrary assumption under the circumstances. If the reader disagrees with this statement, he will be unable to restrict the prediction of the outcome any further than the winset of the status quo as calculated in Sections 2.2 and 2.3.

2.4.4. Calculation of the Induced Uncovered Set

For the readers who agree that restricting the outcomes to uncovered points of the agenda setter (within the winset of the status quo) is a reasonable restriction, the task is not over. We now have to identify these points.

One may think that the intersection of the uncovered set of the agenda setter with the winset of the other veto players would solve our problem. However, this is not a solution because the two sets may not intersect. In addition, some points in the winset of the other veto players may be covered by points that are themselves infeasible (do not belong in the winset).

The decisionmaking problem of the individual members of the collective agenda setter is the following: within the points of the feasible set (the winset of the other veto players), identifying the ones that are not covered by other feasible points. We will call the solution to this problem the identification of the *induced (on the winset of other veto players) uncovered set*.

Figure 2.9 helps us solve this problem on the basis of the analysis presented so far. Call W the area where a winning proposal has to be made (the winset of other existing veto players). Call Y the center of the yolk of the agenda setter. If Y were an individual veto player, he would make the proposal PI (the point of W closest to his preference Y). If we call the distance $YY' = d$ we know that any point outside the circle $(Y, d + 4r)$ is covered by PI (see Section 2.4.2).

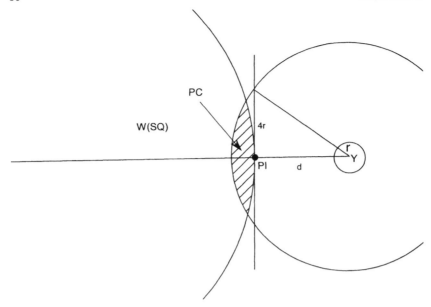

Figure 2.9. Area of proposal by collective VP.

Tsebelis and Money (1997) narrowed the area of the proposal even further by using more precise calculations. They demonstrated that the induced uncovered set is included in a circle (Y, sqrt(d^2 + ($4r^2$))). This is the hatched area in Figure 2.9, which is called PC (proposal by a collective). The reader can verify that the proposal of a collective veto player deciding by majority rule will be in the area that a fictitious individual located at the center of the yolk of the collective veto player would propose.

Proposition 2.5: If collective veto players make proposals within their induced uncovered set, they will make approximately the same proposals as individual ones (located in the center of their yolk).

The above proposition holds also for collective veto players that decide by qualified majorities, since a qualified majority proposal cannot be located outside the proposals made by a majority. So, collective veto players will behave approximately like individual ones not only in terms of the proposals that they will accept (as we saw in Sections 2.2 and 2.3) but also in terms of the proposals they make. The necessary assumption for the last statement is that collective veto players do not make covered proposals (i.e., proposals that are defeated both directly and indirectly by an alternative).

2.5. Conclusions

I started this chapter by presenting the difference between individual and collective veto players. Individual veto players decide by unanimity rule (since disagreement by any one of them can abort a change of the status quo), while collective veto players use qualified majority or simple majority for their decisions. We saw in Figure 2.1 that all the intuitions generated by Chapter 1 were valid, but that the set of points that defeats the status quo (W(SQ)) ceased to have the simple circular shape of individual veto players. The first goal of this chapter was to find a simple approximation of decisions under majority and qualified majority.

I calculated the *wincircle* of a collective veto player, a circle that contains the winset of the status quo by majority rule.[20] According to my calculations, policy stability *decreases* if the actors involved in a decision are collective veto players as opposed to individual ones. Collective veto players may reach outcomes when individual ones cannot agree. This may be the case with U.S. institutions, where disagreements among members of the House and among senators may provide the necessary room for compromises while individual decisionmakers (such as rigid parties controlling the majority of each chamber) would not be able to agree.

I replicated these calculations for qualified majority decisionmaking and calculated the *q-wincircle* of the status quo.[21] According to expectations, the q-wincircle shrinks as the required majority increases. In addition, the q-wincircle changes with the location of the status quo.

As a result of these calculations, I am able to replace collective veto players by fictitious individual ones and use the wincircles of the latter to discuss policy stability. However, these circles provide the necessary but not sufficient conditions for an outcome to defeat the status quo. Indeed, all points outside

[20] For simple majority decisionmaking I used previous analyses by Ferejohn, McKelvey, and Packell (1984), who identified the yolk of a collectivity deciding by majority rule as the smallest circle intersecting all the median lines, lines that have majorities on both sides of them. The center of the yolk Y is centrally located inside the collective veto player. One can think of it as the closest approximation to a multidimensional median. The radius of the yolk is a measure of dispersion of the members of the collectivity: a small radius means that the preferences are either concentrated or symmetrically distributed. In general the radius of the yolk decreases as the number of members of a collective veto player increases. I demonstrated that collective veto players will accept alternatives to SQ only if these alternatives are located inside a circle (Y, d + 2r) where Y is the center of the yolk, r is the radius of the yolk, and d is the distance YSQ.

[21] I identified the relevant q-dividers (the lines that leave a qualified majority q on one side of them and the status quo on the other). I considered the smallest circle that intersects all relevant q-dividers. I called this circle the q-circle with center Q and radius q. I demonstrated that the qualified majority winset of the status quo is located inside a circle (Q, d' + 2q) where Q and q are the center and radius of the q-circle, and d' is the distance QSQ. These statements become more concrete if one refers to Figure 2.7.

a wincircle or a q-wincircle are defeated by SQ, but not every point inside these circles defeats SQ. The approximation of the winset of the status quo by wincircles does not affect the empirical tests we will perform: a small wincircle is a necessary but not sufficient condition for a small distance |SQ-SQ'|. A test of the variance of |SQ-SQ'| is also necessary as in Chapter 1. Since wincircles are approximations, the accuracy of the corresponding tests will be reduced.

My analysis demonstrates that there is one significant difference between simple and qualified majority decisionmaking. In decisions by majority rule, policy stability increases with cohesion;[22] in decisions by qualified majority, policy stability decreases with cohesion.[23]

In order to proceed to issues of sequence of decisions, we needed additional assumptions. The required assumptions aim to address the generic problem of collective decisionmakers under majority rule: their collective preferences may be ambiguous. Indeed, it is possible that different majorities may have the following preference profile over three possible outcomes:

$$Z \pi Y \pi X \pi Z \text{ (where } \pi \text{ stands for majority preferred)}$$

This preference profile indicates that while Y is preferred over X directly, it is defeated by X indirectly (if one introduces Z in the comparison X is preferred over Z, which is preferred over Y). This ambiguity of choices (discrepancy between direct and indirect preferences) may induce strategic actors to introduce additional alternatives in order to upset outcomes they dislike. The assumption I introduce does not limit these strategic considerations of decisionmakers. It just states the following: If a collective veto player has to chose between X and Y, the preference of a majority is Y, and there is no alternative Z such that $Z \pi Y \pi X \pi Z$, then the choice will be Y. This may seem a simple and obvious assumption, but it has significant restrictive consequences: only proposals centrally located survive, and if the collective agenda setter makes a proposal inside the winset of existing veto players, this proposal will closely approximate the proposal that an individual agenda setter[24] would have made.

There are two points in this chapter that are counterintuitive, and that I need to single out. The first relates to the cohesion of collective veto players and policy stability: the more cohesive a collective veto player deciding by majority rule, the higher policy stability, while the more cohesive a collective veto player deciding by qualified majority, the lower policy stability. The second refers to the restrictions under which collective veto players will make similar

---

[22] Larger m-cohesion means smaller radius of the yolk, which leads to a smaller wincircle, so policy stability increases.

[23] Larger q-cohesion makes for a larger q-circle, which leads to a larger q-wincircle, so policy stability decreases.

[24] Located in the center of the yolk Y of the collective one.

proposals with individual ones: they should be making proposals that are not defeated both directly and indirectly by other available alternatives.

In conclusion, collective veto players approximate the behavior of individual ones. We can approximate their preferences by a wincircle (which includes the actual winset) whether they decide by simple or qualified majorities. We also have good reason to assume that they will make approximately the same proposals with individual veto players located in the center of their yolk.

The goal of this chapter was to move from individual to collective veto players. The introduction and conclusions provided the intuition behind my approach. The main part of the chapter provided the algorithm of identification of wincircles and q-wincircles, of proposals that may be accepted by collective veto players whether by simple or qualified majorities, as well as the algorithm to identify the proposals that collective veto players will make (assuming that covered points will not be chosen). I now move to the analysis of existing political systems on the basis of the theory presented.

PART II

VETO PLAYERS AND INSTITUTIONAL ANALYSIS

IN THE PREVIOUS part we identified differences of abstract veto player systems. We saw what happens if we add veto players, if new veto players are near or far from the existing ones, and if the unanimity core of a system of veto players includes the unanimity core of another one. We also saw what difference it makes if we take collective decisionmaking seriously and examine all different collective decisionmaking rules: majority, qualified majorities, and unanimity. In this part I apply the framework to specific institutional structures of interest to comparative political analysis: democratic and nondemocratic regimes, presidentialism and parliamentarism, unicameralism and bicameralism, two-party and multiparty systems, and strong and weak parties.

I have two distinct goals for this part. The first is to develop specific rules for the empirical analyses that follow: which institutions or parties count as veto players under what conditions, how we include the interactions of governments and parliaments in the analysis, and the effect of referendums or of qualified majority decisions for a political system. The second is to reexamine, on the basis of this analysis, prevailing ideas in comparative politics.

The findings in this part will be both positive and negative. Some parts of conventional wisdom are confirmed; others are spurious, while other aspects are questioned. For example, the distinction of regimes in presidential and parliamentary systems can be overcome, and within each of the categories the variance between specific systems is large. Actual political systems, therefore, instead of belonging to two distinct distributions, form a continuum where similarities can be greater across than within systems. As a result, veto players theory challenges some traditional distinctions like presidentialism versus parliamentarism used in comparative politics.

In addition, we will focus on different features of some of the conventional classifications and study additional properties of political systems. For example, instead of focusing on the party system of countries with parliamentary systems, the veto players theory focuses on the structure of government coalitions as well as some institutional characteristics (existence of a president or a second chamber able to veto legislation) with significantly different results.

This part is organized along the lines of traditional institutional analysis. Chapter 3 deals with regimes: democratic and nondemocratic, presidential and parliamentary. Chapter 4 deals with the relationship between governments and parliaments. Chapter 5 deals with direct legislation of citizens through referendums. Chapter 6 deals with federalism, bicameralism, and qualified majorities. The titles (with the possible exception of qualified majorities) are standard in any comparative politics book. I added qualified majorities as a subject to focus on because, as I argue, they are much more frequent (de facto) than one is led to believe by looking superficially at the letter of institutional arrangements.

While the titles are familiar, the logic of the analysis will usually contrast with traditional analyses while borrowing the concepts that are congruent with veto players. The main angles of analysis will be the properties of different constellations of veto players, and the identity of the agenda setter in each decisionmaking process. Chapters 3–4 make the argument that one can understand most of the differences among regimes, or in the interaction between governments and parliaments, by focusing on the issue of agenda setting. Chapter 3 argues that despite the expectations generated about the location of political power by the adjectives "presidential" and "parliamentary" associated with different regimes, agenda control belongs usually to the opposite player (the government in parliamentary systems and the parliament in presidential ones). Chapter 4, on the relations between government and parliament, analyzes the institutions of agenda control and argues that it is these institutions that regulate the interaction and not government duration as is argued in the literature (Lijphart 1999). Chapter 5, on referendums, argues that all referendums add one more veto player (the population) and their differences are based on the question of who controls each part of the agenda. Chapter 6 views the subject matters of federalism, bicameralism, and qualified majorities through the angle of the number of veto players. The chapter makes the argument that federalism has usually distinct institutions regulating decisionmaking at the national level, and that bicameralism and qualified majorities increase the number of veto players, but in ways that produce different policy outcomes.

3

Regimes: Nondemocratic, Presidential, and Parliamentary

IN THIS CHAPTER I introduce the reader to the debates in the traditional literature. Then, I explain the difference between regimes as a difference in essential features of the agenda-setting process: democratic and nondemocratic regimes differ in whether the agenda-setting process is competitive or not (a difference in the *process* of agenda setting); presidential and parliamentary regimes differ in the identity of the agenda setter (government in parliamentary systems, parliament in presidential ones; exactly the opposite from the expectations generated by the names). In addition, presidentialism versus parliamentarism is based on what is the permissible endogenous change (changes in government versus changes in legislative coalitions). As a result of this difference, parties in parliamentary systems are more homogeneous or at least more disciplined than in presidential systems. My overall argument is that most of the differences between regimes discussed in the traditional literature can be studied as differences in the number, ideological distances, and cohesion of the corresponding veto players as well as the identity, preferences, and institutional powers of agenda setters. The arguments developed in this chapter lead to the conclusion that the adjectives "presidential" and "parliamentary" associated with different regimes generate mistaken impressions about the distribution of power: agenda control most frequently belongs to governments in parliamentary systems and parliaments in presidential ones.

The chapter is organized in three parts. First, I discuss the main arguments in the literature on democratic versus nondemocratic and presidential versus parliamentary regimes. Then, I provide the perspective of the veto players theory on the issues raised by the traditional literature. Finally, I discuss some of the criticisms of veto players theory with regards to this analysis.

3.1. Authoritarian, Presidential, and Parliamentary Regimes in the Literature

It may be argued that an analysis that uses the number and properties of veto players as its independent variables is ignoring the most fundamental distinctions in the literature: the one between democratic and nondemocratic regimes, or between presidential and parliamentary regimes. Indeed, both a democratic and an authoritarian regime may have a single veto player, or a presidential and a parliamentary regime may have several veto players. Are there any differences? In order to answer this question I will first summarize some of the literature on democratic versus authoritarian regimes, and some on presidentialism versus parliamentarism. Of course, space does not permit more complete discussion of these subjects, each of which has an extensive bibliography.

3.1.1. Democratic versus Authoritarian Regimes

For many theorists democracy converges, or should converge, to the common good, as expressed by Jean-Jacques Rousseau in *Social Contract*. Rousseau believes we start with individual desires and sum them up, and "the sum of the difference is the general will." This very simple formulation of the general will has been criticized by Kenneth Arrow (1951) in his "impossibility" theorem and an extensive literature that followed.[1]

At about the same time, Joseph Schumpeter also criticized Rousseau and replaced his concept of democracy by elite competition for government. According to Schumpeter's definition: "The democratic method is that institutional arrangement for arriving at political decisions in which individuals acquire the power to decide by means of competitive struggle for the people's vote" (1950: 269).

According to subsequent models of democracy (Downs 1957), elite competition leads to moderation, at least when there are two political parties so that each one of them tries to attract the "median voter." Giovanni Sartori (1976), looking at existing party systems, extended the Downsian argument to the ones with fewer than five parties, and claimed that such systems represent "moderate" pluralism, while systems with more than six parties are likely to include "extremist" parties with centrifugal tendencies. In addition, elite competition leads to responsiveness of governments from fear of losing the next election.

Schumpeter's definition had a profound impact in political theory and the social sciences in general. It is considered a minimal definition of democracy and a necessary condition for it. In fact, subsequent analyses have, in general, enlarged the requirements. The first and probably most prominent extension of requirements of democracy (because of its use by international institutions in assessing which countries are democratic) is Robert Dahl's creation.

Dahl (1971: 2) reserves the term of democracy "for a political system one of the characteristics of which is the quality of being almost completely responsive to all its citizens." He poses five requirements for democracy. They include

[1] See Riker (1982b) for a review of this literature, and the conclusion that Rousseau's notion of general will cannot survive the criticism generated by this literature.

equality in voting, effective participation, enlightened understanding, final control over the agenda, and inclusion (Dahl 1982: 6). Given that these requirements are difficult to achieve under any circumstances, Dahl creates a new term, "polyarchy" (1971: 8) and proposes a series of seven restrictions necessary for it (1982: 10–11). These restrictions include rules about citizens' freedom of information, speech, and association, the right to vote and be a candidate, freedom of election, and policy decisions made by elected officials.

Other authors have criticized Dahl for being too formal. Some of these critics introduced additional criteria on inequalities (particularly of wealth and income). These conceptions expand democracy from the political to the social and economic spheres.[2]

On the other hand, Adam Przeworski (1999) has provided a minimalist defense of Schumpeterian democracy. Along with the literature stemming from Arrow, he accepts that democracy is not "rational, in the eighteenth-century sense of the term" (Przeworski 1999: 25). In other words, there is nothing that can be defined as the common good to be maximized (existence). If there were, the democratic process does not necessarily identify it (convergence), and if it did, democracy is not the only system that does (uniqueness). "It thus seems that choosing rulers by elections does not assure either rationality, or representation, or equality" (Przeworski 1999: 43). But according to this analysis there is something else that makes the Schumpeterian notion of democracy desirable, and here is where Przeworski's analysis departs from all other approaches that add requirements to Schumpeter's definition.

Przeworski takes away the elite competition part and replaces it by a lottery. This way he aborts any connection between elections and representation. "Note that when the authorization to rule is determined by a lottery, citizens have no electoral sanction, prospective or retrospective, and the incumbents have no electoral incentives to behave well while in office. Since electing governments by a lottery makes their chances of survival independent of their conduct, there are no reasons to expect that governments act in a representative fashion because they want to earn re-election" (Przeworski 1999: 45).[3]

Przeworski goes on to demonstrate that even this substandard system under certain conditions presents one significant advantage: that the losers in an election may prefer to wait until the next round rather than to revolt against the system. This peaceful preservation property a fortiori holds for Schumpeterian democracy, where citizens control electoral sanctions and representatives know that reelection depends on responsiveness.

This is a very short and partial account of the literature on democracy. I have completely ignored deliberative issues, that is, questions of transforming

---

[2] See Macpherson (1973) and Marshall (1965), and, more recently, Rueschemeyer, Huber Stephens, and Stephens (1992).

[3] For a more detailed analysis of democracy see Przeworski (1991).

the preferences of citizens.[4] My account demonstrates that most of the literature revolves around the Schumpeterian idea of elite competition for government that generates responsiveness of government to the people. On the other hand, nondemocratic regimes lack the transparency of leadership selection, and may lack representation, but (surprisingly?) on average do not produce inferior economic performance from democratic regimes (Przeworski and Limongi 1997, Przeworski et al. 2000).

3.1.2. Presidentialism versus Parliamentarism

The definitional distinction between presidential and parliamentary regimes is the political independence or interdependence of the legislative and the executive branches. According to Stepan and Skach (1993: 3–4): "A pure parliamentary regime in a democracy is a system of mutual dependence: 1. The chief executive power must be supported by a majority in the legislature and can fall if it receives a vote of no confidence. 2. The executive power (normally in conjunction with the head of state) has the capacity to dissolve the legislature and call for elections. A pure presidential regime in a democracy is a system of mutual independence: 1. The legislative power has a fixed electoral mandate that is its own source of legitimacy. 2. The chief executive power has a fixed electoral mandate that is its own source of legitimacy."

Stepan and Skach consider these definitions as providing "the necessary and sufficient characteristics" and being "more than classificatory." What is important here is that they articulate the consensus in the literature. Starting from Bageot (1867) (in Norton 1990) and going through Linz (1996), Lijphart (1992, 1999), and Shugart and Carey (1992), the political dependence between legislative and executive is the defining characteristic of parliamentarism. Elgie (1998) has criticized the distinction as being ambiguous and leading to different classifications of the same country, and Strom (2000) has tried to address the problems by providing a minimum definition of parliamentarism relying only on the possibility of the parliament to remove the government from office.

Most of the literature has focused on the implications of this distinction for different regimes. Are presidential systems better or worse than parliamentary ones? In particular, is presidentialism a stable basis for democracies? The most famous debate originated in an article written by Juan Linz (1996), who criticized the ability of presidentialism to sustain democratic regimes: "Perhaps the best way to summarize the basic differences between presidential and parliamentary systems is to say that while parliamentarism imparts flexibility to the political process, presidentialism makes it rather rigid" (Linz 1996: 128).

---

[4] For an up-to-date discussion of such problems see Shapiro (2001).

The reason for the flexibility of parliamentarism and the rigidity of presidentialism is the endogeneity of government formation in a parliamentary system. Once elections are held, either there is a majority party that forms the government, or the different parties enter into negotiations about government formation. The result of these negotiations is a government that is supported by parliament, and anytime this support is undermined or challenged, a confidence vote resolves the issue. In presidential systems, however, there is no mechanism for the resolution of conflicts between the executive and the legislative. As a result, the conflict may be resolved through extraconstitutional means: "Replacing a president who has lost the confidence of his party or the people is an extremely difficult proposition. Even when polarization has intensified to the point of violence and illegality, a stubborn incumbent may remain in office. By the time the cumbersome mechanisms provided to dislodge him in favor of a more able and conciliatory successor have done their work, it may be too late" (Linz 1996: 137–38).

However, Linz's analysis has been criticized as partial and extrapolating from the experiences of Latin American countries, Chile in particular. Donald Horowitz contested Linz's findings based on the cases of Sri Lanka and Nigeria (1996: 149):

> Linz's quarrel is not with the presidency, but with two features that epitomize the Westminster version of democracy: first, plurality elections that produce a majority of seats by shutting out third-party competitors; and second, adversary democracy, with its sharp divide between winners and losers, government and opposition. Because these are Linz's underlying objections, it is not difficult to turn his arguments around against parliamentary systems, at least where they produce coherent majorities and minorities. . . . Linz's thesis boils down to an argument not against the presidency but against plurality election, not in favor of parliamentary *systems* but in favor of parliamentary *coalitions*.

It is interesting to note two things in this debate. First, the arguments presented on both sides are subject to case selection bias. Indeed, each one of the two debaters extrapolates from a very limited number of cases, and although both present extremely interesting insights to the way political systems function, they are both vulnerable to inaccurate extrapolations from partial cases. Second, it is interesting to note how Horowitz's argument resembles the argument of this book, where what matters is not the regime type but the number of veto players. I return to this point in the next section.

More recent empirical analyses have corroborated Linz's expectations. For example, Stepan and Skach (1993) examine seventy-five countries and discover that democracy survived 61 percent of the time in parliamentary systems and only 20 percent in presidential ones. Similarly, Cheibub and Limongi (2001), examining "99 spells of democracies" between 1950 and 1990, come to the conclusion that the expected life of democracy under presidentialism is approximately twenty-one years, while under parliamentarism it is seventy-three years. The introduction of a series of economic level controls does not alter the results. Cheibub and Limongi (2001: 5) conclude: "Thus, it is clear that presidential democracies are less durable than parliamentary ones. This difference is not due to the wealth of countries in which these institutions were observed, or to their economic performance. Neither is it due to any of the political conditions under which they functioned. Presidential democracies are just more brittle under all the economic and political conditions considered above."

More interesting for the analysis presented in this book is the finding from Shugart and Carey (1992: 154–58) that strong presidential powers (both legislative and nonlegislative) are more likely to lead to breakdown. According to their data (which include presidential and semi-presidential regimes since the beginning of the century), regimes where the president had weak legislative powers broke down 23.5 percent of the time (4 out of 17), while the probability of a breakdown was almost double (40 percent of the time, or 6 out of 15) in regimes with legislatively strong presidents (Tsebelis 1995a). Shugart and Carey's finding is consistent with the theory of veto players presented here. As I argued in the Introduction, regimes with legislatively strong presidents have one additional veto player, so policy stability increases. As a result of increased policy stability the regime may be unable to provide policy changes when needed, which may lead to breakdown. A similar argument can be found in Przeworski et al. (2000: 134), who find out that when a president's party has between one-third and one half of the seats in parliament, the probability of collapse increases, and the presidential regime becomes "particularly vulnerable" because the president can veto legislation passed in parliament and the situation can lead to a political impasse.

However, survival is not the only property that divides presidential from parliamentary regimes according to the literature. Most of the scholars, at least in the eighties and early nineties, when the debates took place, believe that there is an important distinction generating a host of different characteristics. Linz (1994: 5) is just an example when he argues: "All presidential and all parliamentary systems have a common core that allows their differentiation." Perhaps Moe and Caldwell (1994: 172) have expressed the idea more forcefully: "When nations choose a presidential or a parliamentary form, they are choosing a whole system, whose various properties arise endogenously . . . out of the political dynamics that their adopted form sets in motion." I will mention the most important of them as they are presented in different parts of the literature.

Stepan and Skach (1993) present evidence that presidential systems cannot handle multipartyism. Indeed, their data indicate that there are no successful democracies with more than three parties that are presidential. They also observe that parliamentarism has a "greater tendency to provide long party-government careers, which add loyalty and experience to political society" (Stepan and Skach 1993: 22).

Strom (2000) provides theoretical foundations to this last observation about time horizons of personnel. In his analysis, "parliamentary democracy implies heavy reliance on ex ante control mechanisms, especially prior screening relative to ex post accountability" (Strom 2000: 273). In fact, in most parliamentary democracies ministers either have to be members of parliament or have to have parliamentary experience, so that the potential ministers have already been screened before their appointment.[5] In contrast, in the United States not only is there incompatibility between membership in the cabinet and Congress, but legislative experience is hardly a requirement for a cabinet member. According to Strom, the greater reliance of parliamentarism on screening rather than ex post accountability is due to the greater role of political parties. As a result, parliamentarism focuses on selecting the appropriate personnel, but may not pay as much attention as presidentialism in the specific actions of the selected representatives: "Parliamentary regimes may be better equipped to deal with problems of adverse selection . . . at the expense of another [problem], moral hazard" (Strom 2000: 278–79).

The role of political parties is another point of difference between presidentialism and parliamentarism emerging in the literature. As Strom in the above analysis indicates, it is generally considered that parties are more cohesive in parliamentary systems than in presidential ones. Diermeier and Feddersen (1998) argue that it is the confidence relationship, the threat of being voted out of office and losing agenda-setting powers, that makes parties more cohesive in parliamentary than in presidential systems; in fact interparty cohesion in parliamentary systems should be greater than intraparty cohesion in presidential systems (see also Persson, Roland, and Tabellini 2000).

However, more recent analyses raise questions about the strength of this stylized fact. With respect to parliamentary systems, Wornall (2001) has found that the parties of the German Bundestag suffer occasional collapses in cohesion, as evidenced in the roll call voting record. In her analysis of 615 votes taken between 1965 and 1995, Wornall finds that party cohesion dipped below the 90 percent level[6] on 28.5 percent of roll call votes. When the analysis is limited to the three parties constant throughout the period (the CDU/CSU, SPD, and FDP), cohesion was violated in 17.4 percent of cases. In addition, there are cases in which dissenting members determined the outcome of the vote. On thirteen votes (representing 2.1 percent of cases), the legislation

---

[5] The French Fifth Republic is an exception not discussed in Strom's analysis. According to his analysis, as well as in this book, France is a case of a parliamentary system.

[6] The cohesion measure is calculated as 1 - [(number of dissenters)/(total number of party participants)]. The number of dissenters is determined by identifying all members who did not vote with the majority (or plurality) of their party.

would have gone the way of the party plurality had dissenters cooperated and voted along party lines. This suggests that there is considerable dissent within the German legislative parties—even on roll call votes, when parties should be the most unified. Similarly, with respect to the presidential systems, Cheibub and Limongi (2001) find disciplined votes in support of the presidential program in Brazil.

Another difference discussed in the literature between the two types of regimes is the visibility of policy decisions. In parliamentary systems the influence of different actors is hidden (mainly in the secrecy of council of ministers' deliberations), while in presidential systems there is transparency in the decisionmaking process. For example, Peter Cowhey (1993) argues that U.S. foreign policy has more credibility than Japanese precisely because the U.S. presidential system leads to more systematic disclosure of information about policy making and increases the transparency of foreign policy choices both to voters at home and foreign allies.

In a similar vein of argument, Vreeland (2001) finds that government agreements with the IMF are more likely when more veto players participate in a government, and when the regime is presidential. The first argument is congruent with the argument made in this book, that the more veto players, the more difficult it is to change the status quo, so governments may try to use an additional incentive. The second argument is on the basis of the independence of the executive from the legislature: a president may want to impose the outcome on the legislature in take-it-or-leave-it fashion, while a parliamentary government cannot do the same thing, since all veto players participate in the government.

Finally, there has been some (nonsystematic) discussion about the provision of public goods in the different systems. American political scientists have examined pork barrel legislation,[7] finding that the diffused costs and concentrated benefits of geographically focused projects make it rational for individual congressmen to propose them despite their inefficiency. The only way that such projects will get adopted is by omnibus legislation, bills that include all such projects so that they get adopted all together instead of being rejected one by one. In fact, the argument can be extended even more: if a president vetoes such projects because of their inefficiency, Congress can make the situation worse by expanding the coalition and making it veto proof (by including the pet projects of two-thirds of the legislators of each chamber).

Linz (1994: 63) extends this argument to congressional parties in presidential systems in general because of the weakness of parties: "Not having responsibility for national policy, they would turn to the representation of spe-

---

[7] See Ferejohn (1974); see also Weingast, Shepsle, and Johnsen (1981), Shepsle and Weingast (1981), and Cohen and Noll (1991).

cial interests, localized interests, and clientelistic networks to their constituencies." Other scholars, such as Ames (1995), attribute pork barrel to electoral systems, not to regime type. However, the opposite argument has been made more recently by Persson and Tabellini (1999, 2000),[8] who argue that presidential regimes will have smaller government because the legislative game in these regimes is more competitive: different coalitions prevail from one piece of legislation to the other. As a result, voters have tighter control over their representatives and they reduce the level of rents. The argument is not convincing at the theoretical level because Persson and Tabellini (1999) ignore in their analysis (as well as in their models) the basic implication of a division of powers: most presidential systems provide legislative veto power to the president, which reduces political competition since one specific actor has to be part of *any* winning coalition (the president is a veto player according to the terminology of this book). In addition, a crucial assumption in their models is that agenda setting in presidential regimes is divided in two parts, over the size of the budget on the one hand, and over its distribution on the other, and the agenda is controlled by two different institutions or legislators, while agenda setting in financial bills belongs to the executive in both presidential and parliamentary systems. However, Persson and Tabellini (1999) provide empirical evidence to support their claim. Their empirical results are corroborated (qualitatively) by Charles Boix (2001), who finds a very strong negative coefficient of presidential regimes in the size of the public sector.

In conclusion, there is one result in the literature that is corroborated in all analyses: democracy survives better under parliamentarism than under presidentialism. However, it seems that all the other characteristics described in the literature, while based on insightful analyses, do not seem to be corroborated all the time. The ironclad distinction between presidentialism and parliamentarism that exists in Linz (1994) or in Moe and Caldwell (1994) is not the bottom line of the most recent analyses. For example, Eaton (2000: 371) concludes his review of the most recent literature on the subject of regime differences the following way: "in most cases fundamental distinctions between parliamentarism and presidentialism tend to wash out." Similarly, Cheibub and Limongi (2001: 25) argue, "The reality of both parliamentary and presidential regimes is more complex than what it would be if we were to derive these systems' entire behavior from their first principles. So, what explains the difference? We suspect that the main difference between the two regimes is due to the way the decisionmaking process is organized." To this set of questions I now turn.

[8] See also Persson, Roland, and Tabellini (2000).

3.2. The Veto Players Angle

The veto players take on these questions is quite different. In order to under-stand the differences not only between democratic and nondemocratic regimes, but also between presidentialism and parliamentarism, one has to focus on the process of law production:

—How are veto players selected?
—Who are the veto players? (Who needs to agree for a change of the status quo?)
—Who controls the legislative agenda? (Who makes proposals to whom and under what rules?)
—If these players are collective, under what rules does each one of them decide (simple majority, qualified majority, or unanimity)?

These three categories of regimes have significant differences in at least one of these dimensions. For example, the competitive process of veto player selection is the minimal definition of democracy as we saw in the first section. I will argue below that the issues of agenda control and cohesion of different veto players are in principle distinctions between presidential and parliamen-tary systems.

3.2.1. How Are Veto Players Selected?

The process required in the Schumpeterian definition of democracy makes the different elites competing for political power more representative of the opin-ions of the people they represent. Downs (1957) has presented a one-dimen-sional policy space model of this competitive process. His model is so well known I will not present it here again. In the chapter on referendums (Chapter 5) I present a multidimensional generalization of this model.[9]

There are several conclusions that have been drawn from Downsian models that have to be discussed and moderated. For example, one may conclude that because of competition, democratic regimes are more representative of the will of the public. In addition, one could claim that two-party competition leads to better representation of the public. Finally, one can think that while many democratic regimes have multiple veto players, authoritarian regimes have necessarily a single one. All these are reasonable inferences, but I will argue that they are by no means necessary conclusions of the Downsian model (or true for that matter).

---

[9] I apologize to the readers who are aware of the difference between a one-dimensional analysis (leading always to a median voter outcome) and a multidimensional analysis (where the median voter almost never exists) for having to wait until then for the answer.

First, while electoral competition is a built-in condition for the introduction of the preferences of the public in politics, it is neither a necessary nor sufficient condition for representation. The reader is reminded of Przeworski's (1999) arguments presented in the previous section. In addition, we saw in the Introduction to this book that more than two millennia ago, Thucydides was making similar arguments about Athenian democracy. His tastes were conflicting with the median voter and he was admiring the capacity of Pericles to deviate from the preferences of the public while blaming his successors for following "the whims of the multitude."[10] Hence democracies do not necessarily represent the preferences of the median voter.

On the other hand, authoritarian regimes do not necessarily deviate from the median voter preferences either. It is possible that the preferences of the public are very close or even identical to the preferences of the person in charge. For example, populist regimes like Peron in Argentina may present such similarities in preferences.

Second, another improper conclusion that people may take from Downsian models is that the competition of two teams of elites may lead to a more representative or moderate system than the competition of multiple teams. The reason is that with two parties in a single dimension, the outcome is necessarily the position of the median voter, while with more than two parties or with more than two dimensions most of the time, there is no equilibrium outcome. In fact, as Lijphart (1999) discusses, the argument that two-party systems lead to political moderation has been, for a long time, the prevailing wisdom in Anglo-Saxon political science. Again, this is not a necessary conclusion. In fact, more recent empirical analyses (e.g., Huber and Powell 1994, Powell 2000) have demonstrated that multiparty systems provide a closer mapping between the preferences of the median voter and the preferences of the government.

Finally, it is not true that nondemocratic systems have necessarily a single veto player. While the decisionmaking process in democratic systems is usually more transparent to outside observers (like journalists or political scientists) who have a good idea of how policy decisions are made, this is not the case in nondemocratic regimes. However, transparency does not necessarily mean multiple veto players, and lack of it does not imply a single one. Remmer (1989) has made a forceful argument that different authoritarian regimes in Latin America have very different structures and in some of them, one individual is responsible for political decisions, while in others many players are endowed with the power to veto decisions. I claim that the situation is not unlike decisionmaking inside political parties in democracies.

Political parties in democratic regimes are usually approximated by a single ideal point derived from their political manifesto. However, we do not know

---

[10] See the complete quote in the Introduction.

how this preference came about. Was it the preference of the leader of the party? Was it the compromise arrived at in an institution with few members (like a secretariat or a polit-bureau) or in a larger body (like a parliamentary group)? In the latter case, what was the decisionmaking rule? Were all members or some of them endowed with the power to veto the decision? The answers to all these questions are not answered with respect to both nondemocratic regimes and political parties, and instead we are assuming single decisionmakers. I am just pointing out our lack of information about how some decisions are made both in democratic and nondemocratic regimes and arguing that, as Chapter 2 demonstrates, replacing collective veto players by individual ones is a reasonable approximation in the absence of such information.

Therefore, what distinguishes democratic from nondemocratic regimes is whether the veto players are decided by competition between elites for votes or by some other process and there is no necessary distinction in terms of representation or in terms of the actual number of veto players. One has to study the specific regime in order to make decisions on these matters.

3.2.2. Veto Players in Different Regimes

Let us first identify what counts as a veto player. If the constitution identifies some individual or collective actors that need to agree for a change of the status quo, these obviously are veto players. For example, the U.S. Constitution specifies that an agreement of the House, the Senate, and the president (veto override excluded) is required for enactment of legislation. As a result, the Constitution specifies that there are three veto players. For reasons of simplicity in this section I will ignore that two of them are collective (Chapter 2 demonstrates that such a simplification is permissible). Consider now the special case that these three veto players have ideal points on a straight line. On the basis of the analysis of Chapter 1, one of them is absorbed, so in this case the United States would in fact have two veto players. Or, consider the situation where all three veto players are controlled by the same disciplined party (as was the case in the first one hundred days of the Roosevelt administration), then two of the three veto players are absorbed and, consequently, in this period there is only one veto player.

Consider now a unicameral parliamentary system. The constitution does not define who the veto players are or specify their number. Laws are voted by parliament, so, in a sense, the only veto player specified by the constitution is the parliament. However, let us assume that in this country a single party controls the government (as is generally the case in the United Kingdom or Greece). Then, this party is by definition the only veto player in the political system. It can implement any policy change it wishes, and no policy change that this party disagrees with will be implemented. Suppose that as a result of extraordinary political circumstances the single-party government is replaced by a two-party government like the coalition of the right and left in Greece in 1989, or a lib-lab pact in the United Kingdom. Now no law will be enacted unless both government partners agree on it. In other words, during this period Greece or the United Kingdom will be transformed into a two–veto players political system. More generally, the dynamics of a parliamentary system require the agreement of one (Westminster systems) or more (coalition governments) parties for the modification of the status quo. Each one of these parties will decide by a majority of their parliamentary group; consequently, each one of these parties is a (collective) veto player.

I will call *institutional veto players* individual or collective veto players specified by the constitution. The number of these veto players is expected to be constant but their properties may change. For example, they may be transformed from collective to individual (if one institution, deciding by simple majority, is controlled by a disciplined party) and vice versa. Also, their ideological distances may vary, and one or more of them may be absorbed.

I will call *partisan veto players* the veto players who are generated inside institutional veto players by the political game. For example, the replacement of a single-party majority by a two-party majority inside any institutional veto player transforms the situation from a single partisan veto player to two partisan veto players. Both the number and the properties of partisan veto players change over time. Parties may lose majorities, they may split, and they may merge and such transformations *may* have an effect on the number of partisan veto players. This is the point I will develop in the remainder of this section.

Consider a five-party parliament in a unicameral parliamentary system. According to the constitution, legislation is enacted when a majority of this parliament agrees to replace the status quo. Let us assume (to simplify matters) that the five parties are cohesive and that any three of them control a majority. The reader can consult Figure 2.4 in order to visualize such a system. The situation specified by the constitution is a single institutional collective veto player. According to Chapter 2, if we know the status quo SQ we can identify the (majority) wincircle. This is the lightly shaded circular area in the figure. We can also identify the exact set of points that defeat SQ (the darker shaded area W(SQ)).

Now consider that not all coalitions are possible but that three of the parties A, B, and C form a government. This alliance makes sure that none of them enters into coalitions with parties D or E. This additional information alters the number of partisan veto players as well as the expectations of the feasible solutions. The only points that can defeat SQ are located in the deeply shaded lens. Therefore, the new information transformed the analysis of the political system from one collective veto player to three individual ones and reduced the winset of the status quo.

In the previous scenario we moved from any possible coalition to one and only one and we omitted the intermediate case when several coalitions are possible as long as they do not include one particular party. One can think of such a political scenario when the Communists or some other specific party will be excluded from all possible majorities. In fact, such a case would be equivalent to a qualified majority requirement imposed on the legislature, a case that we studied theoretically in Chapter 2, and address again in Chapters 4 and 6 when we discuss qualified majorities.

These scenarios can help us analyze specific political situations. For example, what is the overall veto player configuration in a country with many institutional veto players if within each one of them there are many partisan veto players? The previous analyses indicate that we proceed in three steps: *First*, we locate institutional veto players in a multidimensional space. *Second*, we proceed to disaggregate them into the partisan players they are composed of in order to identify the individual or collective veto players inside each one of them. *Third*, we apply the absorption rules to this system: if some of the veto players are located in the unanimity core of the others, we can eliminate them because they do not restrict the winset of the status quo. For example, if we have a presidential bicameral system where one of the chambers decides by majority rule and the other by qualified majority rule (an example selected on purpose because the United States approximates it, given that important decisions require cloture of potential filibusters by a three-fifths majority in the Senate), then we will locate the area of intersection of the winsets of the two collective players and intersect it with the winset of the president. If a replacement of the status quo exists, it has to be located in the intersection.

Let us go to a less complicated situation: some laws in Germany (*zustimmungsgesetze*, or agreement laws) require the agreement of both the Bundestag and the Bundesrat; while for others (*einspruchsgesetz*) a majority in the Bundestag is sufficient for passage.[11] What is the difference between the two kinds of laws? In order to answer the question we have to differentiate between two possible situations depending on whether the majorities in the two houses are the same or different. If the parties that control the majority in both houses are the same, there is no difference between the two kinds of legislation (for simplicity, I assume that the positions of the parties in each house are identical). If the majorities are different, then the government coalition consisting of two parties will have to request the approval from one party of the opposition, which will raise the number of veto players in Germany to three. In this case, there will be a significant difference between *zustimmungsgesetze* and *einspruchsgesetz* and it will be much more difficult to adopt the first than the second.

---

[11] Sometimes a two-thirds majority in the Bundestag is required in order to overrule a two-thirds majority in the Bundesrat.

Similarly, in presidential systems there is a difference between laws and executive decrees. The former require involvement of many veto players (the ones existing in one or two legislative chambers and the president), while the latter require only presidential approval. We will return to this distinction in the next chapter.

There is also a difference between law and government decree in France, but it works in the exact opposite direction. Laws require a vote in parliament, while government decrees require an agreement in government. The president of France is part of the government but he has no veto power over legislation. As a result, the president can veto a government decree but cannot veto legislation. If the president is not supported by the parliamentary majority (a situation that in France is called cohabitation), laws are easier to pass than government decrees. This is exactly what Prime Minister Chirac did in the first cohabitation period (1986–88). When confronted with President Mitterrand's refusal to sign government decrees, he reverted the same documents into laws and made it impossible for the president to veto them.

I have deliberately focused on institutional and partisan actors that exist in every democratic system, and ignored other potential veto players, such as courts or specific individuals (influential ministers, possibly army officials) that may or may not exist in particular political systems. I address the issue of courts in Chapter 10. With respect to other actors, I will consider them as random noise at the level of this analysis, but I claim that they should be included in analyses of specific policy areas, or case studies. For example, in corporatist countries the veto players of the political system may be replaced by labor and management, the actual negotiators of specific labor contracts. Similarly, in analyses of the U.S. defense policy in the eighties and early nineties, one may have to include Senate Armed Services Chairman Sam Nunn as a veto player since he was able to defeat decisions of both President Bush (the appointment of secretary of defense) and President Clinton (legislation on gays in the military). Similarly, Senate Foreign Relations Chairman Jesse Helms was able to abort many of President Clinton's initiatives (particularly ambassadorial nominations). However, one should not jump from the consideration of one specific committee chair as a veto player to the inclusion of all committee chairs in Congress as veto players, and certainly not to all committee chairs in other systems as veto players.

In the case that arguments can be made that certain institutions or individuals have veto powers (whether formally like committees, or informally like in some cases representatives of the armed forces), analyses of decisionmaking should include these veto players and their preferences. Chapter 6 focuses on different decisionmaking modes (e.g., multiple collective veto players, qualified majorities) that can be used for the analysis of such cases.

3.2.3. Agenda Setting in Presidentialism and Parliamentarism

I discussed the power of agenda setting in Proposition 1.5. We can use this proposition in order to identify differences between presidential and parliamentary regimes. With respect to financial bills, the initiative belongs to the executive in both presidential and parliamentary systems. With respect to non-financial bills, however, as a general rule, in parliamentary systems the government makes a proposal to parliament to accept or reject, while in presidential systems, parliament makes a proposal to the executive to accept or veto. In this sense, the roles of agenda setting are reversed in the two systems. In addition, the names used for each one of these systems do not reflect the legislative reality: one expects presidents to be powerful in presidential systems, and parliaments in parliamentary. The analysis I present reverses the roles in the legislative arena. My argument is that if parliament is strong in parliamentary systems it is not because of legislation; it is because it can withdraw its support from the government and replace it. If the president is strong in presidential systems, it is not because of his power to legislate, but because of executive decrees and the power to make decisions on foreign policy and other matters.

This strange and surprising assessment has been identified by other authors, but to my knowledge the cause (agenda setting) has never been pointed out. For example, Seymour Martin Lipset (1996: 151) has argued: "The fact that presidencies make for weak parties and weak executives, while parliaments tend to have the reverse effect, certainly affects the nature and possibly the conditions for democracy. But much of the literature wrongly assumes the opposite: that a president is inherently stronger than a prime minister, and that power is more concentrated in the former." Similarly, Stepan and Skach (1993: 18) argue: "Here, then, is the paradox. Many new democracies select presidentialism because they believe it to be a strong form of executive government. Yet . . . presidential democracies enjoyed legislative majorities less than half of the time. . . . Executives and legislatures in these countries were 'stuck' with one another." In more picturesque fashion Lyndon Johnson gave the following one-liner: "Being president is like being a jackass in a hailstorm. There's nothing to do but stand there and take it" (quoted in Ames 2001: 158). Veto players theory argues that if parliaments are weak in parliamentary systems and strong in presidential ones, if presidents are weak and prime ministers strong, it is not for idiosyncratic or random reasons, but because agenda setting is controlled by governments in parliamentary systems and parliaments in presidential ones. This is a blanket statement that we will qualify in the next chapter.

One last and important point: the fact that the agenda setter has the powers identified in Proposition 1.5 does not mean that the other veto players become irrelevant, as demonstrated in the 2000 U.S. presidential race. If one accepts the argument that Congress controls the agenda, does it follow that the result

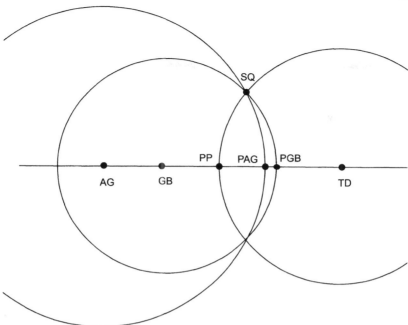

Figure 3.1. Difference between "Gore" and "Bush" presidency when the president controls or does not control the agenda.

of the election would not matter very much, or that it would matter more if the president controlled the agenda? Not necessarily, because the final outcome depends on the positions of the other veto players and the status quo.

Figure 3.1 presents a possible configuration of different players in order to make the point. Consider that the congressional agenda setter is House Majority Whip Tom DeLay and that the ideal point of candidate George Bush is located between the ideal point of candidate Al Gore and the Republican DeLay. For a status quo indicated in the figure, DeLay (TD) would make a different proposal to George Bush (PGB) than to Al Gore (PAG, had he been elected). In fact, the electoral result made a difference under the configuration of Figure 3.1 *because* the House controls the agenda. If the president controlled the agenda, both candidates would make the same proposal (PP) to the House.

This example is based on many questionable assumptions: I ignore the Senate to simplify the representation; I assume that DeLay would make the proposal, though he may have to negotiate with the more moderate Republicans (closer to Bush). However, it captures some important part of the political situation in the 1994–2000 period. Bill Clinton became better known for his ability to frustrate the Republican agenda (mainly the Republican "Contract with America") than promoting his own plans. One can, however, think of a few positive measures, such as the 1993 tax increase (passed in a Democratic-controlled House and Senate) and some trade measures (such as NAFTA and China, which occurred because Clinton led some Democrats into a coalition with Republicans) that were not merely designed to block Republican policies.

The reader may be surprised that, according to the above analysis, the result of the 2000 presidential election is more significant if the president has no agenda-setting powers than if he does. How does this analysis jibe with the powers of agenda setting discussed in Proposition 1.5? Here I compare two different players, assuming that they do not control the agenda, while Proposition 1.5 compares the power of veto players when they control the agenda or not. Proposition 1.5 in our example implies that both Bush and Gore would prefer to control the agenda than to leave it to DeLay, which is certainly true.

In a nutshell, this section has argued that agenda control for nonfinancial bills belongs to the parliament in presidential systems and to the government in parliamentary ones. In the next chapter, I flesh out this picture, and demonstrate that this prima facie difference of agenda setting has to be analyzed and documented on a country-by-country basis. The differences from one country to the next may be significant: some presidential systems may provide so many agenda-setting powers to the president that they look parliamentary, and some parliamentary systems may take away so many agenda-setting initiatives from the government that they look presidential.

3.2.4. Veto Player Cohesion in Presidentialism and Parliamentarism

The literature on presidentialism and parliamentarism has identified another significant difference (from the point of view of veto players) between the two types of regimes. Parties are more disciplined in parliamentary systems than in presidential ones, although, as discussed in Section 3.1, empirical evidence disputes the strength of this relationship.

The literature on electoral systems has provided a different source of variability of party discipline: the personal vote. Indeed, in electoral systems where candidates compete for a personal vote they are likely to pay attention to the demands of their constituency as well as to the demands of their party, while in situations where the candidate's chances depend only on the party leadership, loyalty to the party should be the rule.[12] Thus, party cohesion and discipline will be higher in systems without a personal vote.

As we have seen in Chapter 2, the internal cohesion of collective veto players affects the size of the area within which the winset is located. The lower the party cohesion, the lower is the policy stability. If we combine this argu-

---

[12] See Carey and Shugart (1995) for distinctions of different electoral systems along these lines.

ment with the findings of the literature on party cohesion in different regimes, we will conclude that *ceteris paribus* presidential systems have lower policy stability. This is a very strong *ceteris paribus* clause because it is probably impossible to keep everything else equal. The fact that parties lack discipline in presidential systems makes it difficult or even impossible to identify the origins of particular votes. As a result, it is difficult to identify partisan veto players in presidential systems. Whenever this is the case, we will be confined to the study of institutional veto players.

For example, in the United States under divided government, if parties were cohesive, only bipartisan bills would be passed, even ignoring the possibility of filibuster (which is discussed in Chapter 6). It is because parties are not cohesive that policymaking becomes possible. For example, Clinton passed his tax reform in 1993 with no Republican votes, while he passed his NAFTA agreement mainly with Republican votes. If such coalition shifts were not possible, there would have been fewer policy implementations in the Clinton presidency. But as a result of these shifts, we cannot replace institutional with partisan veto players in a presidential system.

On the other hand, not all presidential systems have the same party moderation as the United States, where almost every coalition is possible. In some presidential systems certain parties may not support government measures under any circumstances. If this is the case, we may not be able to replace institutional veto players with partisan ones, but we may be able to exclude some of the parties as possible veto players. This information would increase policy stability but would not provide the precision that we could have if we knew that a specific combination of parties would support some particular bill. We analyze this situation as a case of decisionmaking under qualified majority in Chapter 6.

3.3. Criticisms of Veto Players Theory

The difference in the analysis between regime types on the one hand and veto players on the other has been one of the strongest as well as the most criticized aspects of veto players theory. It has been the strongest because at the theoretical level one can analyze different kinds of regimes or other institutional settings within the same framework. It has been the most criticized, because different authors dispute that institutional and partisan veto players can be treated the same way. Therefore, here I will address some of the criticisms formulated in previous incarnations of the veto players theory and explain the way I have addressed them in this book.

The main critical argument was that while the conceptualization of different institutional settings in a unified framework in my original formulation of the veto players theory (Tsebelis 1995a) is a positive development, there is an important distinction between institutional and partisan veto players and the two should not be lumped together. Strom (2000) has made the most persuasive theoretical argument, and so I address his point first.

Strom discusses issues of delegation and accountability in parliamentary systems and makes the point that the chain of delegation is a single one in parliamentary systems (from voters to parliament, to prime minister, to ministers, to bureaucrats); while delegation in presidential systems occurs with competing principles and agents (voters to multiple representatives—president, House, Senate—and these representatives collectively oversee the bureaucrats). I address the issue of delegation to bureaucracies in Chapter 10 where I discuss bureaucracies. Here I want to focus on the criticism that Strom presents on the distinction between institutional and partisan veto players. Here is his criticism in its most general form:

> Although Tsebelis thus identifies intriguing similarities between presidential and multi-party parliamentarism, the distinction remains important for our purposes. . . . More generally, it is misleading to treat institutional and partisan veto players additively, since parties and the institutions in which they operate are not mutually independent, but rather highly interdependent. A credible veto player must have both opportunity and motive to exercise his or her veto. Partisan veto players may have motive (although this is not always obvious), but they do not generally have opportunity. Institutional veto players by definition have opportunity, though not necessarily motive. Interestingly, Tsebelis (1995: 310) discounts institutional veto players that have no discernible motive, i.e., when their preferences are identical to those of the other veto players, for example, in congruent bicameral legislatures. The same treatment should be accorded to partisan players that have no demonstrable opportunity to exercise veto. (Strom 2000: 280)

In order to support his argument, Strom brings the example of "oversized" coalitions, or extremist parties who may not want to veto a government policy and leave the government. Such players in his opinion can be bypassed, and cannot be counted the same way as institutional veto players.

Strom makes a series of correct points in the previous passage. It is true, for example, that in the article he refers to I had identified only identical veto players as cases for application of the absorption rule, and, as a consequence, I was applying this rule only to institutional veto players. In the current version of my argument I have presented the most general possible absorption rule, Proposition 1.2, where it does not matter if the players absorbed are institutional or partisan. For example, if in Figure 1.6 the system of veto players A is in one chamber of a legislature and the system of veto players B is in another chamber, the system B will be absorbed no matter whether this second chamber is the House or the Senate. Legislation that is approved by the system A of veto players will necessarily have the approval of the system B. Similarly, if a country had a bicameral legislature with one chamber composed only of the veto players in system A, and the other composed of the system of A's and one B, the overall situation would be equivalent with a unicameral legislature composed out of the three veto players of the system A. For example, in Japan the leading Liberal Democratic Party (LDP) lost the majority in the Senate in 1999. As a result, the LDP included representatives of the Liberals and the Komeito (Clean Government Party) in the government, although technically speaking their votes were not required for a House majority. Similarly in Germany if the Bundesrat is controlled by the opposition the situation is not politically different from a grand coalition: legislation that is not approved by both major parties will not be accepted. Or, in a presidential system, if the president's party has the same preferences as the president it will be part of any policymaking coalition, because if a bill does not get its support it will be vetoed by the president. The current version of the absorption rule is thus much more general than the one criticized by Strom and takes into account some of his objections.

It is also true that party members of oversized governments can be bypassed as veto players, while institutional veto players cannot, as Strom argues. I deal with this objection theoretically in Chapter 4 and present empirical evidence supporting my argument in Chapters 7 and 8.

Where Strom is not correct in my opinion is in the last part of his argument: "The same treatment [i.e., absorption] should be accorded to partisan players that have *no demonstrable opportunity* to exercise veto." Parties in government are there to agree on a government program. In fact, as we will see in the next chapter, such programs take a long time to be negotiated, and governments make serious efforts to have voted and implemented everything included in them, as de Winter (forthcoming) has carefully demonstrated. In addition, if new issues come on the political horizon, members of the different parties in government have to address them in common. If such a political plan is not feasible, the government coalition will dissolve, and a new government will be formed. Therefore the request that parties in government have "demonstrable opportunity to exercise veto" is either equivalent to participation in government or unreasonable. Indeed, participation in a government grants parties the right to veto legislation and to provoke a government crisis if they so wish. This is a sufficient condition for a party to qualify as a veto player. If "demonstrable opportunity" is on a case-by-case basis, it is impossible to be met empirically, because even cases where veto was actually exercised and legislation was aborted as a result may not be "demonstrable" given the secrecy of government deliberations.

Another type of criticism is empirically based. The argument is that on some specific issue different kinds of veto players have conflicting effects, so veto players should not be included in the same framework. Birchfield and Crepaz (1998: 181–82) present the argument as follows:

Not all veto points are created equal. We argue that . . . it is necessary to distinguish between "competitive" and "collective veto points" which are not only institutionally different but also lead to substantively different outcomes. Competitive veto points occur when different political actors operate through separate institutions with mutual veto powers, such as federalism, strong bicameralism, and presidential government. These institutions, based on their mutual veto powers, have a tremendous capacity to restrain government. . . . Collective veto points, on the other hand, emerge from institutions where the different political actors operate in the same body and whose members interact with each other on a face-to-face basis. Typical examples of collective veto points are proportional electoral systems, multi-party legislatures, multi-party governments, and parliamentary regimes. These are veto points that entail collective agency and shared responsibility.

These arguments seem similar to Strom's in the sense that they are intended to differentiate presidential from parliamentary systems, but they are significantly less precise. For example, the "face-to-face basis" does not distinguish the interaction between government and parliament on the one hand and conference committees in bicameral legislatures on the other. In both cases there is personal interaction but it is not very frequent, so it is not clear why parliamentarism is distinguished from bicameralism on this basis.

On the basis of outcomes, the authors argue that higher economic inequality is associated with competitive veto players, and lower associated with collective ones. In another article Crepaz (2002) finds similar results associated with Lijphart's (1999) first and second dimension of consociationalism, the "executive-parties dimension" and the "federal-unitary dimension." In the same article Crepaz equates the two distinctions: Lijphart's first dimension with the Birchfield and Crepaz "collective veto points" and Lijphart's second dimension with the Birchfield and Crepaz "competitive veto points."

I find some inconsistencies in these arguments and I consider the generalizability of their findings questionable. Lijphart's distinctions are not equivalent with those made by Birchfield and Crepaz. For example, the former includes the following five characteristics in his federal-unitary dimension: (1) unitary versus federal government; (2) unicameral versus bicameral legislatures; (3) flexible versus inflexible constitutions; (4) absence or presence of judicial review; (5) central bank dependence or independence. There is no reference to presidential government, which Birchfield and Crepaz consider a characteristic of "competitive veto players," and there is no reference of central banks, constitutions, or judicial review in the competitive veto players concept of Birchfield and Crepaz. Similarly, parliamentarism is a characteristic of collective veto players according to Birchfield and Crepaz, but not a characteristic of Lijphart's first dimension; corporatism is a characteristic for Lijphart, but not for Birchfield and Crepaz. As a result of these differences, I am not sure which characteristics are responsible for the inequality results.

If one eliminates the characteristics that are not common in the different indices (which would include presidentialism versus parliamentarism, which is not on Lijphart's list), the common denominator of the findings is that federalism increases inequalities but multipartyism reduces them. I can understand why federalism is likely to increase inequalities: some transfer payments are restricted within states. Consequently, if the federation includes rich and poor states, transfers from the former to the latter are reduced compared to a unitary state. I do not know why multiparty governments reduce inequality, and I do not know whether this finding would replicate in samples larger than OECD countries. If there is a connection, in my opinion, it should incorporate the preferences of different governments. It is not clear that all governments try to reduce inequalities, so that multiparty governments are "enabled" (as Crepaz claims) to do so more than single party ones. The usual argument in the literature is that the Left (as a single party government or as a coalition) aims at reducing inequalities, not some particular institutional structure.

Finally, even if there are answers to all these questions, the relationship between inequality and specific institutional characteristics is not a negation of the arguments presented in this book. Nowhere have I argued that veto players produce or reduce inequalities. In addition, this chapter argues that while there may be similarities among nondemocratic, presidential, and parliamentary regimes with respect to the number of veto players and the ideological distances among them, there are differences in terms of agenda setting and party cohesion. Nor have I ever argued that federalism has no independent effect besides the one operating through veto players. As I demonstrate in Chapter 6, federalism is correlated with veto players because it may add one or more veto players through the strong second chamber of a federal country, or through qualified majority decisions. As a result, federalism can be used as a proxy for veto players when information on veto players is not available.[13] However, this is not the only possible effect of federalism and it may also operate independently. For example, in Chapter 10 I argue that federal countries are more likely to have active judiciaries because these institutions will resolve problems of conflict between levels of government.

In conclusion, Strom has helped identify some weaknesses in earlier versions of my argument. The expansion of the absorption rule introduced in this book covers both institutional and partisan veto players. Strom has a valid argument with respect to nonminimum-winning coalitions, which I address in the next chapter. But he introduces too severe a restriction in parliamentary systems when he requires that "demonstrable opportunity to exercise veto" should be present for a party to count as a veto player. I argue that participation in government is a sufficient condition.

---

[13] In Chapter 10 I discuss an article by Treisman (2000c) using exactly this strategy.

3.4. Conclusions

I have presented a review of the differences between nondemocratic and democratic systems, as well as between presidential and parliamentary systems, and reexamined these literatures on the basis of veto players theory. This analysis led me to introduce the concepts of institutional and partisan veto players, and to identify such players in a series of situations. It turns out that the number of veto players may change over time in a country (if some of them are absorbed because they modify their positions), or that the same country may have different veto player constellations depending on the subject matter of legislation (like Germany).

With respect to veto players, while nondemocratic regimes are generally considered to be single veto player regimes, close analysis may reveal the existence of multiple veto players. The number of veto players is thus not a fundamental difference between democratic and nondemocratic regimes either.

My review of the literature on presidentialism and parliamentarism has pointed out that while there is a conclusive difference in terms of the probability of survival of democracy, all other differences are disputed in current political analysis. Analysis of presidentialism and parliamentarism points out that the most important difference between these regimes is the interaction between legislative and executive in parliamentary systems and their independence in presidential ones. The other differences seem fuzzy. In terms of veto players there are similarities between presidential and multiparty parliamentary systems, and they contrast with single party governments in parliamentary systems. There are differences between presidential and parliamentary systems in terms of who controls the agenda governments in parliamentary systems, parliaments in presidential ones (discussed further in the next chapter), and in terms of the cohesion of parties in each system (presidentialism is on the average associated with lower cohesion). We will focus on the question of who controls the agenda and how in the next chapter.

4

Governments and Parliaments

IN THIS CHAPTER I focus on agenda-setting mechanisms in more detail. I demonstrate that there are two important variables one has to examine in order to understand the power of the government as an agenda setter in parliamentary systems. The first is positional, the relationship between the ideological position of the government and the rest of the parties in parliament. The second is the institutional provisions enabling the government to introduce its legislative proposals and have them voted on the floor of the parliament—the rules of agenda setting. Both these questions are generated from the analysis in Part I. They focus on agenda setting and study the positional and institutional conditions for it. It turns out that my analysis has some significant differences from the existing literature.

The first difference is that we will be focusing on the characteristics of *governments* in parliamentary systems instead of the traditional *party system* focus (Duverger, Sartori). According to the traditional literature two-party systems generate single-party governments where the parliament is reduced to a rubber stamp of government's activities, while multiparty systems generate more influential parliaments. The party system analysis focuses on parliaments because they are the source from which governments originate—in technical terms, the "principals" who select their "agents." Veto players theory focuses on governments because they are the agenda setters of legislation, as noted in Chapter 3. Single-party governments will have all the discretion in changing the status quo, while multiparty governments will make only incremental changes.

A second difference between my analysis and existing influential literature is the question of who, within the government, controls the agenda. On the basis of my analysis, agenda setting belongs to the government as a whole. It is possible that in some areas it is the prime minister, in others the minister of finance, in yet others the corresponding minister. It can also be done through bargaining among the different government parties. All these possibilities are consistent with my approach, while other approaches assign agenda setting rights to specific government actors (Laver and Shepsle 1996, for example, to the corresponding minister).

A third difference regards the interactions between governments and parliaments. While most of the literature differentiates between presidential and parliamentary regimes, one researcher (Lijphart 1999), in his influential analysis of consociational versus majoritarian democracies, merges regime types (as this book does) and focuses on the concept of "executive dominance" as a significant difference between and across regimes. Executive dominance, in Lijphart's words, captures "the relative power of the executive and legislative branches of government" (Lijphart 1999: 129) and is approximated by cabinet durability in parliamentary systems. I argue that the interaction between executives and legislatures is regulated by an institutional variable: *the rules of agenda setting*. Let me explain what these differences involve.

The difference of an analysis on the basis of party systems (i.e., parties in parliament) or government coalitions (i.e., parties in government) may appear to be trivial. After all, multiparty systems lead usually to coalition governments, and two-party systems to single-party governments. However, the correlation is not perfect. For example, Greece (a multiparty country) has a government that completely controls the legislature. Besides the differences in empirical expectations (Greek governments are expected to be strong on the basis of veto players, while their single-party composition is a failure of understanding the relationship between governments and parliaments generated by party system analysis), the major difference is in the identification of causal mechanisms shaping the interaction between governments and parliaments.

I also argue that the veto players variable is not dependent on institutions or party systems alone, but derived from both of them. For example, veto players include not only partners in government, but also second chambers of the legislature or presidents of the republic (if they have veto power). In addition, a party may be significant in parliament and count in the party system of a country, but its approval of a legislative measure may not be required, in which case it will not be a veto player. Finally, one or more veto players, whether a government partner, a second chamber, or a president of the republic, may be absorbed and not count as veto players, as demonstrated in Chapter 1.

The question whether it is ministers that control the agenda or the whole government is a minor one; however, since my approach shares with that of Laver and Shepsle the importance attributed to agenda setting, I need to clarify that some empirical evidence conflicting with their expectations does not affect my analysis.

Equally trivial may seem the difference of whether the relationship between governments and parliaments is determined on the basis of government duration or agenda-setting rules. Yet government duration varies only in parliamentary systems, and consequently cannot be used as a proxy for executive dominance in presidential systems, or across systems; agenda-setting rules can be used across systems. In addition, I argue that there is no logical relationship between executive dominance and government duration, so a different variable is necessary for the study of the relationship between legislative and executive.

I demonstrate that this relationship can be captured by the rules regulating legislative agenda setting.

The chapter is organized into three sections. Section 4.1 studies the positional conditions of agenda setting. I focus on different kinds of parliamentary governments (minimum-winning coalitions, oversized governments, and minority governments) and study their ability to impose their preferences on the parliament. I demonstrate that when the agenda setter is located centrally among the other players, he is able to produce outcomes very close to his ideal point even if he does not control a parliamentary majority. Section 4.2 focuses on the institutional provisions of agenda setting. While all parliamentary governments have the ability to ask the question of confidence, in order to force parliament to comply with their preferences, they also have at their disposal a series of other weapons that enable them to shift outcomes in their favor. We study such institutional arrangements in some detail. Section 4.3 compares the results of Sections 4.1 and 4.2 with alternative influential approaches in the literature and shows the differences of veto players analysis with party systems accounts, ministerial discretion, or government duration as a measure of executive dominance. Most of this chapter studies parliamentary systems, because of restrictions in the literature. However, I do not miss opportunities to show how the arguments apply to presidential regimes as well.

4.1. Positional Advantages of Agenda Control

As I argued in Chapter 3, in parliamentary systems it is the government that controls the agenda for nonfinancial legislation. One of the major reasons is its capacity to associate a vote on a bill with the question of confidence (Huber 1996). Such a government initiative either forces the parliament to accept the government proposal or replaces the government. As a result, from our point of view every government *as long as it is in power* is able to impose its will on parliament (the italicized words are not trivial). My statement holds for any kind of parliamentary government, whether or not it controls a majority of legislative votes.

Some simple statistics suggest that the general assessment that governments control the agenda in parliamentary democracies is correct. In more than 50 percent of all countries, governments introduce more than 90 percent of the bills. Moreover, the probability of success of these bills is very high: over 60 percent of bills pass with probability greater than 0.9 and over 85 percent of bills pass with probability greater than 0.8 (Inter-Parliamentary Union 1986, Table 29).

However, even if governments control the agenda, it may be that parliaments introduce significant constraints to their choices. Or, it might be that parliaments amend government proposals so that the final outcome bears little resemblance to the original bill. I argue that most of the time, neither of these scenarios is the case. Problems between government and parliament[1] arise only when the government has a different political composition from a majority in parliament. By examining all possible cases of relationships between government and a parliamentary majority, I demonstrate that such differences are either nonexistent, or, if they do exist, the government is able to prevail because of positional or institutional weapons at its disposal.

There are three possible configurations underlying the relationship between government and parliament: minimum-winning coalitions (which are the textbook case), oversized governments (governments that include more parties than necessary to form a majority), and minority governments (governments not supported by a majority). These three categories are mutually exclusive and collectively exhaustive forms of government in parliamentary systems.

4.1.1. Minimum-Winning Coalitions

This is the most frequent (if we include single-party governments in two-party systems that are, by definition, minimum-winning coalitions) and least interesting case in our discussion. The government coincides with the majority in parliament, and, consequently, there is no disagreement between the two on important issues. As Figure 2.4 indicates, the minimum-winning coalition represented in government restricts the winset of the status quo from the whole shaded area of the figure to the area that makes the coalition partners better off than the status quo. There is one exception to consider: if the government parties are weak and include members with serious disagreements over a bill, the bill may be defeated in parliament. This, however, is only a marginal possibility because votes are public and party leaders possess serious coercive mechanisms that preempt public dissent (Italy was the only exception to the rule until the government introduced open votes in 1988 and did away with the problem of *franchi tiratori*—parliamentarians who voted to defeat and embarrass their own government). The most serious of these mechanisms is elimination from the list.

Even in cases where a secret ballot is required, party leadership may manage to structure the ballot in a way that enables them to monitor their MPs. A good example of such structuring comes from Germany. In 1972, Chancellor Willy Brandt was about to lose the majority supporting his coalition because of defections from his own party, the SPD, and his coalition partner, the FDP. On April 27 he faced a constructive vote of no confidence in the Bundestag.[1] According

---

[1] According to Article 67 of the German basic law, the chancellor cannot be voted out of office unless the successor has been voted into office.

to parliamentary rules, a vote of no confidence is a secret ballot, and the chancellor was afraid he might lose his majority. For that reason, he instructed the members of his coalition to stay in their places and not participate in the vote, thus effectively controlling possible defectors. The no-confidence measure failed by one vote: 247 of the 496 members of the Bundestag supported the leader of the opposition, Rainer Barzel (Tsebelis 1990).

In general, the coalition formation process gives an important advantage to governments. Either the leadership, or the leading party personalities, are included in the government, so when they come to an agreement it is difficult for other members of parliament to challenge or undo it. An example of the latter is the following statement from the Norwegian Prime-Minister Kare Willoch, regarding his coalition government: "I wanted their leading personalities in the government. It was my demand that their party leaders should be in government because I did not want to strengthen the other centers which would be in parliament. That was my absolute condition for having three parties in government" (Maor, 1992: 108).

4.1.2. Oversized Coalitions

Oversized majority governments are very common in Western Europe. Laver and Schofield (1990) calculate that 4 percent of the time (of the 218 governments they examine), a party that forms a majority alone will ask another party to join the government; 21 percent of the time, while there is no majority party, the coalition formed contains one or more parties more than necessary. In such cases, some of the coalition partners can be disregarded and policies will still be passed by a majority in parliament. Should these parties be counted as veto players, or should they be ignored?

Ignoring coalition partners, while possible from a numerical point of view, imposes political costs because if the disagreement is serious the small partner can resign and the government formation process must begin over again. Even if government formation costs can be avoided (by the formation of a government that includes all previous coalition partners without the disagreeing party) the argument is still valid, because the proposed reform will be introduced in parliament by a coalition that does not include the disagreeing party. Here is how Maor reports the position of a leader of the Liberal Party, a member of the government coalition in Denmark: "We could stop everything we did not like. That is a problem with a coalition government between two parties of very different principles. If you cannot reach a compromise, then such a government has to stay away from legislation in such areas" (Maor 1992: 107).[2]

---

[2] The government implied here is a minority government, but the logic applies equally to a minimum-winning or to oversized coalitions.

Simple arithmetic disregards the fact that there are political factors that necessitate oversized coalitions. Regardless of what these factors might be, for the coalition to remain intact the will of the different partners must be respected. Consequently, while the arithmetic of the legislative process may be different from the arithmetic of government, a departure from the status quo must usually be approved by the government before it is introduced to parliament, and, at that stage, the participants in a government coalition are veto players. This analysis indicates that, overall, oversized governments will have the same regularities as minimum-winning coalitions, but their relations will be weaker because they do not have to hold in every situation.

However, the above arguments have not persuaded Strom (2000), as we saw in Chapter 3. His argument is that some of the parties in oversized coalitions will not have the "opportunity to exercise veto." If this is the case, one should count only the parties that are required for a majority. It is not difficult to model the numerical requirements and locate the winset of an oversized coalition in the veto players framework: one can think that the parties composing the oversized government coalition do not decide by unanimity (as the political argument implies), but by qualified majority (as the number of votes permits). If, say, three of four oversized coalition parties are required for a majority decision, then we can identify the winset of the three-fourths of the government coalition. Chapter 2 shows that the (three-fourths) qualified majority winset is larger than the unanimity set of the government coalition and where the possible outcomes will be located.

To sum up, I provide a political argument for why the will of coalition partners should be respected as long as the government remains in place: because coalition partners in disagreement may depart from the government. Strom relies on a numerical argument that since in oversized governments the votes of some parties may not be necessary, these parties will not insist on their position, and bills will be approved without their votes. It is true that sometimes parties stay in coalitions and vote against specific policies (for example, in Israel the Labor Party remained inside the Likud coalition, yet made it known that it was against retaliation for the bombing of a Jerusalem Sbarro's in August 2001).[3] If this phenomenon does not happen frequently, then counting all government coalition partners as veto players will be a good approximation for empirical analyses. If, on the other hand, coalition partners vote frequently against their own government, then a qualified majority voting argument should be applied in empirical analyses. In Chapters 7 and 8 the reader can verify that counting all coalition partners as veto players provides a good approximation for policy stability.

---

[3] I thank Ron Rogowski for the example.

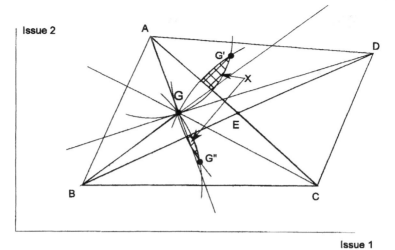

Figure 4.1. A minority government centrally located can avoid serious defeat (results in areas X).

4.1.3. Minority Governments

Minority governments are even more frequent than oversized coalitions. Strom (1990) has analyzed minority governments and found that they are common in multiparty systems (around one-third of the governments in his sample). Moreover, most of them (79 of 125) are single-party governments that resemble single-party majority governments. Laver and Schofield have argued that there is a difference between a governmental and a legislative majority. While their point is technically correct, I will argue that this difference has no major empirical significance. The reason is that governments (whether minority or not) possess agenda-setting powers. In particular, minority governments possess not only institutional advantages over their respective parliaments (which we will discuss in Section 3) but also have positional advantages of agenda setting, which we discussed in Chapter 1 (Corollaries 1.5.2 and 1.5.3). Let me focus further on these positional advantages. The party forming a minority government is usually located centrally in space. For this reason, it can select among many different partners to have its program approved by parliament (Downs 1957; Laver and Schofield 1990; Strom 1990). In order to develop this point further, consider a five-party parliament in a two-dimensional space like the one in Figure 4.1. What follows is an illustration of the argument, not a formal proof.

Figure 4.1 examines whether government preferences (G) can have parliamentary approval. The reader is reminded that any proposal presented on the parliament floor will either be preferred by a majority over G, or defeated by G.[4] Let us identify the set of points that defeat G. These points are located within the lenses GG' and GG". If the parliament is interested in any other outcome and the government proposes its own ideal point, a majority of MPs will side with the government.

To recapitulate, if a minority government is centrally located in space, it can be part of most possible parliamentary majorities and, consequently, move the status quo inside its own winset. In fact, most of the time it might not have to compromise at all, and it can locate the final outcome on its own ideal point. Consequently, assuming that the government controls the agenda, it can change the status quo in the way it prefers. This argument is very similar but not identical to Corollary 1.5.3. The difference is that there all actors were assumed to be veto players, while here they are not.

But if a point is selected from one of the two lenses GG' or GG", the government will lose the vote. The situation would be tolerable for the government if SQ were moved in the area of these lenses that is close to G, but the hatched areas called X are a serious defeat for the government. Right now we can claim that this is a low probability event, but this is a poor argument. Indeed, while it may be the case that *at random* it is not very likely that the outcome would be located in the two hatched areas X of the figure, legislative outcomes are not random. A coalition of parties A, C, and D would select a point in X in order to defeat and embarrass the government. Can the government avoid such a humiliation?

This brings us to the second category of advantages of a minority government over parliament, the institutional ones. This category of advantages is not limited to minority governments. Every parliamentary government has at its disposal some constitutional, as well as procedural or political means, to impose its will on important issues on parliament. Such institutional advantages are much more important for governments that do not enjoy the support of a stable majority in parliament, for obvious reasons. The government can force the majority of parliament to comply with its proposal. However, there is an additional reason generated from the theory presented in this book: minority governments most of the time have a single veto player. As a result, policy stability is low, and the significance of agenda setting is high (as Figure I.1 indicates). Thus on the basis of the theory presented in this book, if minority governments have institutional agenda-setting powers, they will make use of them more frequently than other forms of government (particularly oversized coalitions).

Let us focus on one particular mechanism that exists in several countries, as Heller (1999) demonstrates. Weingast (1992) described the mechanism as

---

[4] Indifference between the two is also a possibility. I will continue ignoring this case as in the past.

"fighting fire with fire," identifying it first in the U.S. Congress. The specifics are very simple: the government can make the last amendment on the bill under consideration. Consequently, when it sees that some hostile amendment is about to be adopted, it can modify this amendment in a way that protects its own bill. Let us use Figure 4.1 to see how the minority government can prevail. Suppose that the minority government presents a bill on its own ideal point G and an amendment in the undesirable area X is proposed on the parliament floor. This amendment would mean a significant political defeat for the government. The government, however, can "fight fire with fire" and propose an amendment in the nonhatched part of the two lenses (symmetric to the embarrassing proposal with respect to line AC; in fact, slightly closer to A and C). This amendment would command a majority in parliament (it would be voted by G, A, and C) and is located very close to the government preference (G). Let us now study such agenda-setting mechanisms.

4.2. Institutional Means of Government Agenda Control

Several constitutions provide governments with a series of agenda-setting powers, such as priority of government bills, possibility of closed or restricted rules, count of abstentions in favor of government bills, possibility of introducing amendments at any point of the debate (including before the final vote), and others. The most extreme in this regard is the constitution of the French Fifth Republic. In this constitution the following restrictions of parliamentary powers apply: According to Article 34, the parliament legislates by exception (only in the areas specified by this article, while in all other areas the government legislates without asking for parliamentary agreement); Article 38 permits legislation by ordinance (upon agreement of parliament); according to Article 40, there can be no increase in expenditures or reduction in taxation without the agreement of the government; Article 44.3 gives the government the right to submit votes under closed rule (no amendments accepted); Article 45 permits the government to declare that a bill is urgent, thus reducing the number of rounds in which the two chambers will shuttle the bill;[5] finally, the most powerful weapon of all, Article 49.3 permits the government to transform the vote on any bill into a question of confidence (Huber 1992; Tsebelis 1990: chap. 7). The picture of an impotent parliament is completed if one considers that the government controls the legislative agenda; that the parliament is in session less than half of the year (special sessions are limited to two weeks

---

[5] For a discussion of the navette system in France, see Tsebelis and Money (1997). Their argument is that reducing the number of rounds increases the power of the National Assembly (that has positions closer to the government).

and must have a specified agenda);[6] that the committee structure was designed to be ineffective (six large committees crosscutting the jurisdictions of ministries); and that discussions are based on government projects rather than on committee reports. Finally, even censure motions are difficult because they require the request by one-tenth of MPs (the right is not reusable during the same session), and an absolute majority of votes *against* the government (abstentions are counted in favor of the government).

The French government is an exception in terms of the breadth, depth, and variety of institutional weapons at its disposal. However, the German government possesses interesting institutional weapons as well, such as the possibility to ask for a question of confidence whenever it deems appropriate (Article 68), or the possibility to declare legislative necessity and legislate with the agreement of the second chamber (the Bundesrat) for six months (Article 81). Even the Italian government has the right to issue executive decrees (known as ordinances; Kreppel 1997). In addition, with respect to parliamentary legislation, it has the right to offer the last amendment on the floor (Heller 1999). The purpose of this section is to examine the literature on measures that empower the government with legislative agenda-setting powers.

As Chapter 3 has made clear, the most important of these measures is the attachment of the question of confidence on a bill, which is equivalent to the threat of government resignation, followed by dissolution of the parliament (Huber 1996). This measure exists in all parliamentary systems except Norway. However, this measure is like a threat of nuclear weapons in international disputes: it is extraordinary and cannot be used frequently. Here I will focus on weapons of lower range and higher frequency. The main reference to what follows are a series of three articles by Doering (all from 1995) on the institutions that assign legislative agenda-setting powers to the government. Doering (1995a) identifies and measures the seven variables I will present. Doering's analysis covers eighteen countries of Western Europe and combines data from previous analyses of parliamentary systems like *Parliaments of the World* (1986) with original research performed by an international group of scholars. What follows is the list of variables with explanations about their numerical values.

A. AUTHORITY TO DETERMINE THE PLENARY AGENDA OF PARLIAMENT

This variable has seven modalities; the two extremes are that the agenda can be determined by the government or by the parliament alone. Here is the entire list of possibilities:

---

[6] The Socialists, who had a heavy reform agenda, had to use seventeen such sessions in their first term (1981–86).

i. The government sets the agenda alone (United Kingdom and Ireland).

ii. In a president's conference, the government commands a majority larger than its share of seats in the chamber (France and Greece).

iii. Decision by majority rule at president's conference where party groups are proportionally represented (Luxembourg, Portugal, and Switzerland).

iv. Consensus agreement of party groups sought in president's conference, but the plenary majority can overturn the proposal (Austria, Belgium, Germany, Norway, and Spain).

v. The president's decision after consultation of party groups cannot be challenged by the chamber (Denmark, Finland, Iceland, and Sweden).

vi. Fragmentation of agenda-setting centers if unanimous vote of party leaders cannot be reached (Italy).

vii. The chamber itself determines the agenda (Netherlands).

This is the most important variable, although it guarantees only that the subjects proposed by the governments will be discussed, not the outcome of the parliamentary debates.

B. MONEY BILLS AS GOVERNMENT PREROGATIVE

While this prerogative belongs to the government in all countries, in some countries members of parliament are restricted from proposing money bills. For example, in the United Kingdom, "no member of the House of Commons can introduce a Bill the main purpose of which is to increase expenditure or taxation; nor can the relevant provisions of a Bill which proposes any such increase proceed much further unless a resolution authorising such increases has been moved by the Government and agreed to by the House of Commons" (Inter-Parliamentary Union 1986: 862).

France, the United Kingdom, Ireland, Portugal, and Spain belong in the category of countries that do not permit their MPs to propose money bills. Greece applies some restrictions, while the remainder of the countries apply very few or no restrictions at all to MPs on money bills.

C. IS THE COMMITTEE STAGE OF A BILL RESTRICTED BY A PRECEDING PLENARY DECISION?

Some of the first findings in the comparative literature on parliaments were that the importance of committees depends on whether they consider a bill before or after the floor sees it for the first time. "If a committee can consider a bill before it is taken up on the floor, the chances of the committee influencing or determining the outcome tend to be greater than when the lines of battle have been predetermined in plenary meetings. In general, where a strong commitment to utilize committees exists, the committees get the bills first" (Shaw 1979: 417). Most countries enable committees to play a serious role in the legislative process, while in three countries (Ireland, Spain, and the United Kingdom) the floor refers the bill to committees. In Denmark the floor decision is not strictly binding.

D. AUTHORITY OF COMMITTEES TO REWRITE GOVERNMENT BILLS

The question addressed by this section is on which text the floor decides. Does the government bill reach the floor with comments by the committee, or does the committee amend the government bill and submit its own proposal to the floor? There are four different possible answers:

    i. House considers original government bill with amendments added (Denmark, France, Ireland, Netherlands, and the United Kingdom).

    ii. If redrafted text is not accepted by the relevant minister, chamber considers the original bill (Greece).

    iii. Committees may present substitute texts, which are considered against the original text (Austria, Luxembourg, and Portugal).

    iv. Committees are free to rewrite government text (Belgium, Finland, Germany, Iceland, Italy, Norway, Spain, Sweden, and Switzerland).

E. CONTROL OF THE TIMETABLE IN LEGISLATIVE COMMITTEES

This issue combines the answers to two different questions: "Firstly, is the timetable set by the plenary parent body or by the committee itself? Secondly, may the plenary majority reallocate the bill to another committee or even take a final vote without a committee report, or does the committee enjoy the exclusive privilege of debating a bill as long as it thinks fit with no right of recall by the plenary?" (Doering 1995a: 237). The combination of the answers produces the following classification.

    i. Bills tabled before the committee automatically constitute the agenda. In Finland, Ireland, and the United Kingdom, where these rules are applied the government controls the committee agenda.

    ii. The directing authority of the plenary body with the right of recall. In Austria, France, Greece, Italy, Luxembourg, Norway, Portugal, and Spain, the plenary session can supervise the committee's agenda.

    iii. The committees themselves set their agenda but right of recall by plenary exists (Belgium, Germany, and Switzerland).

    iv. House may not reallocate bills to other committees. In Denmark, Iceland, Netherlands, and Sweden the committees themselves control their agenda.

F. CURTAILING DEBATE BEFORE THE FINAL VOTE OF A BILL IN THE PLENARY

Three questions are answered by the following classification. "1. May an exceedingly short time limit to curtail debate for the final vote be unilaterally imposed in advance by the government or its simple majority in the plenary over which the government normally commands? 2. May a limitation of debate only be imposed by mutual agreement between the parties? 3. Is there neither advance limitation nor possibility of closure of debate, thus theoretically opening up unlimited opportunities for filibustering?" (Doering 1995a: 240). The eighteen countries fall in the following categories.

    i. Limitation in advance by majority vote (France, Greece, Ireland, and the United Kingdom).

    ii. Advance organisation of debate by mutual agreement between the parties (Austria, Belgium, Denmark, Germany, Iceland, Italy, Luxembourg, Norway, Portugal, Spain, and Switzerland).

    iii. Neither advance limitation nor closure (Finland, Netherlands, and Sweden).

G. MAXIMUM LIFESPAN OF A BILL PENDING APPROVAL, AFTER WHICH IT LAPSES IF NOT ADOPTED

The shorter the lifespan of a bill if not adopted by parliament, the more imperative the agenda-setting power of the government. The lifespan of bills vary significantly by country from a six-month or one-year period to an infinite span.

    i. Bills die at the end of session (6 month–1 year) (Denmark, Iceland, and the United Kingdom).

    ii. Bills lapse at the end of legislative term of 4–5 years (Austria, Finland, Germany, Greece, Ireland, Italy, Norway, and Spain).

    iii. Bills usually lapse at the end of legislative term but carrying over is possible (Belgium, France, and Portugal).

    iv. Bills never die (except when rejected by a vote) (Luxembourg, Netherlands, Sweden, and Switzerland).

Table 4.1 provides the score each country receives in each of the seven agenda control variables. The next column provides an overall government agenda control variable that I use in this and other chapters.[7] While the variable "agenda control" is the most advanced currently in the literature, country scores on that variable should not be considered final. Doering has done an

---

[7] The numerical values attributed to each country have been calculated the following way: I used principal components and analyzed all seven of Doering's agenda control measurements. I used the first factor loadings to weigh each one of these variables (the first eigenvalue explains 47 percent of the variance) and normalized the weighted sum.

TABLE 4.1
Government Agenda Control, Duration, and Executive Dominance

Country	Plenary Agenda	Financial Initiative	Com- mittee	Re- write	Time Table	Financial Voting	Lapse Bill	Agenda Control	Gov't Duration (Lijphart)	Executive Dominance (Lijphart)
Austria	4	3	3	3	2	2	2	−0.044	5.47	5.47
Belgium	4	3	3	4	3	2	3	−0.170	1.98	1.98
Denmark	5	3	2	1	4	2	1	−0.106	2.28	2.28
Finland	5	3	3	4	1	3	2	−0.148	1.24	1.24
France	2	1	3	1	2	1	3	0.333	2.48*	5.52*
Germany	4	3	3	4	3	2	2	−0.126	2.82	2.82
Greece	2	2	3	2	2	1	2	0.280	2.88	2.88
Iceland	5	3	3	1	4	2	1	−0.170	2.48	2.48
Ireland	1	1	1	4	1	2	2	0.519	3.07	3.07
Italy	6	3	3	4	2	2	2	−0.219	1.14	1.14
Luxembourg	3	3	3	3	2	2	4	−0.053	4.39	4.39
Netherlands	7	3	3	1	4	3	4	−0.527	2.72	2.72
Norway	4	3	3	4	2	2	2	−0.063	3.17	3.17
Portugal	3	1	3	3	2	2	3	0.147	2.09	2.09
Spain	4	1	1	4	2	2	2	0.221	4.36	4.36
Sweden	5	3	3	4	4	3	4	−0.427	3.42	3.42
Switzerland	3	3	3	4	3	2	4	−0.135	1*	8.59*
United Kingdom	1	1	1	1	1	1	1	0.690	5.52	5.52

Source: Columns 1–7 from Doering (1995b).
   Agenda control as calculated in this study from Doering's (1995b) measures: "Government Duration" and "Executive Dominance" from Lijphart Table 7.1 (1999:132).
   * France and Switzerland are the only countries with different numbers for government duration and executive dominance.

excellent job compiling objective indicators about who can place items on the agenda and whether they can reduce discussion time on the floor or in the relevant committees, but further work is required. For example, the Heller (1999) and Weingast (1992) argument of "fighting fire with fire," that is, introducing a last-minute amendment I discussed with regard to Figure 4.1, has not been included in Doering's list. In fact, the identification of further such mechanisms or practices that governments can use to control the agenda is the most important avenue of study of government agenda control, and will improve the measurements that we currently have in Table 4.1. Finally, the table includes two columns from Lijphart's (1999) analysis, which I discuss in detail later.

4.3. Veto Players versus Other Approaches in Comparative Politics

I will compare the analysis I have presented so far with three influential approaches in comparative politics. The first (Duverger 1954, Sartori 1976) compares different countries on the basis of the characteristics prevailing in their party system. The second (Laver and Shepsle 1996) shares the focus on agenda setting, but attributes it to the corresponding ministers instead of to the government as a whole. The third (Lijphart 1999) studies the interaction between legislative and executive on the basis of government duration in parliamentary systems.

4.3.1. The Number of Parties in Parliament

In comparative politics, the party system of a country plays a crucial role in understanding the politics of the country. Beginning with Duverger (1951), the party system of a country has traditionally been connected with other significant features of the country, either as a cause or an effect. According to Duverger, the party system was both the result of a country's electoral system, and the cause of a certain type of interaction between its government and parliament.[8]

With respect to the effects of the party system on coalition formation, Duverger's argument was straightforward: two-party systems give the majority to a single party, and consequently produce stable governments that dominate parliament; multiparty systems generate coalition governments that can lose votes in parliament (including confidence votes), and are consequently weak and unstable. It should be clear from the previous discussion that when Duverger discusses the number of parties in the party system, he is referring to the number of significant parties in a country's *parliament*. For example, the United Kingdom is the archetypal two-party system because the Liberals, despite their votes, do not control a significant number of seats in parliament. This is a common feature of all the analyses I discuss: the number of parties in the party system is essentially defined as the number of parties in parliament.

Sartori (1976) elaborated on Duverger's model by, among other things, refining the typology. In particular, with respect to multiparty systems, he distin-

---

[8] I will not discuss the effects of electoral system on party system. The interested reader can find this information in Duverger (1954), Rae (1967), Lijphart (1994), Sartori (1996), and Cox (1997).

guished between moderate and polarized pluralism. The dynamics of party competition in moderate pluralism are similar to two-partyism: two coalitions compete for office, one of them wins, and both coalitions are close to the ideological center. In contrast, polarized pluralism includes a party that occupies the center and is opposed by bilateral oppositions on its left and its right. These oppositions are ideologically extreme and/or include antisystem parties. According to Sartori, the dividing line between moderate and extreme pluralism is "around" five parties. From his discussion, it becomes clear that the cutoff point is an empirical regularity, not a theoretical argument. Be that as it may, Sartori, following the foundations set by Duverger, expects the number of parties in a country's party system to affect the politics of that country.

One can find a common theoretical framework in all these analyses. On the basis of principal agent theories, Mathew McCubbins and his collaborators (McCubbins 1985, Kiewiet and McCubbins 1991, Lupia and McCubbins 2000) have studied the logic of delegation according to which an agent acts on behalf of another actor (the principal). In the government-parliament interaction, the principal is the parliament since it selects the government and it can replace it with a censure vote (Strom 2000). As a result, a government, like any other parliamentary committee, faces the dilemma of either obeying the parliamentary majority or being removed from power.

These theories are consistent and each adds to the others. They are also congruent with other bodies of work. For example, Almond and Verba's (1963) cultural analysis separates Anglo-Saxon democracies from continental ones, a distinction that is empirically almost identical with two-versus-multiparty systems. Powell (1982) found a correlation between two-party systems and executive stability but a very weak relationship between party systems and levels of violence.

All these arguments fail to acknowledge the role of government in promoting legislation. As we argued, governments shape legislative outcomes because of this agenda-setting power. Whether they can do it regularly and extensively depends not on the number of parties in parliament but on the institutional provisions of agenda setting, and the position of the government vis-à-vis the other parliamentary forces. For example, the Greek government is formed by a single party, and it has extensive agenda control (Table 4.1). It follows that the government will impose its will on parliament regularly and extensively. The fact that there are many parties in parliament is not relevant in this analysis.

4.3.2. Ministerial Discretion

In the previous discussion, the difference between veto players and conventional wisdom was the lack of recognition by traditional analyses of the power of agenda setting. This is not the case with more contemporary analyses in comparative politics. Huber (1996) analyzes the power of parliamentary governments to ask the question of confidence; Diermeier and Feddersen (1998) explain government cohesion on the basis of agenda-setting powers of the government; Persson and Tabellini (2000) use agenda-setting powers to explain the differences between presidential and parliamentary systems; Hallerberg and von Hagen (1999, 2001) focus on the role of ministers of finance on government control. Here I focus on one influential approach which argues that it is the corresponding minister that controls the government agenda (Laver and Shepsle's [1996] model of ministerial discretion). The Laver and Shepsle argument is not that ministers have exclusive decisionmaking rights in their area (although their models can be interpreted that way), but that they are making the proposals to the government in areas that no other person has the expertise and consequently are able to shape the government proposals. In their words: "Ministerial discretion results from the minister's ability to shape the agenda of collective cabinet decisions rather than to determine cabinet decisions once the agenda had been set" (Laver and Shepsle 1996: 33). In its turn, the government makes these proposals to the parliament and they get accepted with few modifications. "Perhaps the most distinctive feature of our approach is the assumption that most important policy decisions are taken by the executive" (Laver and Shepsle 1996: 13).

Veto players and ministerial discretion thus share the focus on agenda setting, but disagree on the identity of agenda setter. I think that while every parliamentary government ultimately controls the agenda by linking important legislation to a vote of confidence, it is not clear that inside the government the agenda is controlled by the corresponding minister. First of all, the prime minister also plays an important role in agenda formation. Second, the government coalition has negotiated a government program and a minister cannot submit legislation that disagrees with this program. Third, government meetings discuss substantive policy issues, and if ministers from other parties have political disagreements with a bill they will not accept it just because it was the proposal of the corresponding minister. Fourth, and most important so far, the ministerial discretion theory implies that changes in ministers (while the same coalition remains in power) would entail serious policy changes in the corresponding ministries. This is not the experience in the most extreme multiparty governments like the French IV Republic and post-war Italy. For example, Andre Siegfried, one of the fathers of French political science, makes the opposite point when he explains the "paradox of stable policy with unstable cabinets": "Actually the disadvantages are not as serious as they appear. . . . When there is a cabinet crisis, certain ministers change or the same ministers are merely shifted around; but no civil servant is displaced, and the day-to-day administration continues without interruption" (Siegfried 1956: 399).

The above arguments dispute whether agenda setting belongs exclusively to the corresponding minister. One can make an argument with a different tack: even if we (incorrectly) assume this to be the case, it makes little difference. Indeed, as we demonstrated in Chapter 1, more veto players restrict the winset of the status quo and, as a result, decrease the importance of agenda setting (Corollary 1.5.2). So, the more parties participate in government, the less important the role of ministers, even if we assume they have exclusive jurisdiction over the agenda. This is exactly what Huber and Shipan (forthcoming) find in their analysis of restrictions imposed by multiple principals (divided governments in both parliamentary or presidential systems) on bureaucrats and the executive.

Empirical tests corroborate the arguments above. The best empirical test of the ministerial influence thesis would be a test of policies along the lines indicated by the Siegfried quote: compare government policies under the same coalition but with different ministers and see whether differences are more significant than similarities. However, such a test has not been performed. Instead, Paul Warwick systematically tested one of Laver and Shepsle's implications about the duration of government coalitions. Laver and Shepsle identify equilibrium arguments according to their theory and expect the nonequilibrium governments to be more unstable.[9] Instead, Warwick discovers that it is majority status and the ideological range of governments and not the equilibrium status that significantly affect government duration. He concludes that parties in the government try to accommodate each other in forming policy and not permit ministers to make independent decisions concerning their portfolios.[10]

Similarly, Michael Thies (2001) analyzes the pattern of appointment of junior ministers in Italy, Germany, and Japan (both under single-party and coalition governments) and ascertains that in Italy and Japan junior ministers are overwhelmingly appointed out of different parties (and in Japan's single-party governments, out of different factions) from the corresponding ministers. The only exception to the identified pattern is Germany, but in this case Thies points out the importance of the chancellor and a series of other measures instituting collective decisionmaking (and responsibility) of government. He concludes that the exclusive jurisdiction model does not work for policymaking.

Finally, Lieven de Winter (2001) explores the way governments push the pieces of legislation included in their program (usually negotiated *before* the

---

[9] "Other things being equal, therefore (and in real life they may well not be), a party system that has no strong party and no empty-winset DDM [dimension by dimension median] cabinet seems likely to be more unstable than one that does" (Laver and Shepsle 1996: 78).

[10] In Warwick's words, his results "clearly bring into question the fundamental premise of ministerial autonomy. Considerable skepticism was expressed when Laver and Shepsle put the issue to a group of country experts . . . and this skepticism is supported here. . . . Coalition pacts cannot concern just the division of portfolios, nor can exercising power consist of letting each

distribution of ministries). Testing some five hundred pieces of legislation in eighteen European countries, he has found that governments "invest more resources in guaranteeing a smooth and swift legislative process, nursing the bill well from cradle (introduction to the legislature) to maturity (promulgation)" (2001: 3). More precisely, de Winter has found that bills covering the government program have a series of characteristics: they are more complex, less subjected to a plenary reading before the committee phase, more frequently treated by committees that are chaired by a majority MP, have majority MPs as rapporteurs, are more often submitted to a committee vote, have lower approval rate in committee and plenary and face different forms of committee dissent or plenary obstruction, have stronger voting discipline among both majority and opposition, are more frequently challenged in front of constitutional courts, and have a higher overall success rate. De Winter reports these findings as consistent with collective government responsibility, and inconsistent with the ministerial influence thesis.

4.3.3. Does Government Duration or Agenda Setting Define Executive Dominance?

According to the argument proposed in this book, the reasons that governments control the agenda (regardless of whether they are minimum-winning coalitions, minority governments, or oversized majorities) are either positional (governments in multiparty systems either have a majority supporting them or they are located in the center of the policy space) or institutional (a series of devices by which governments control the agenda that was presented in the previous section and summarized by the indicator "agenda control"). There is an alternative approach that I will now summarize and discuss in more detail for two reasons: first, because of its prominent position in the literature, and second, because it transcends the divisions by regime type that are so frequent in the literature. This discussion enables us to span *across* different regime types.

In *Patterns of Democracy*, Arend Lijphart (1999: 129) proposes an indicator of executive dominance: "How can the relative power of the executive and legislative branches of government be measured? *For parliamentary systems, the best indicator is cabinet durability*" (emphasis added). Lijphart differentiates his approach from what he calls the "prevalent" point of view according to which "cabinet durability is an indicator not just of the cabinet's strength compared with that of the legislature but also of regime stability" (1999: 129).

---

party do what it likes in the portfolios it receives" (Warwick 1999: 391). Laver and Shepsle (1999) dispute Warwick's conclusions. The interested reader should read the whole four-part exchange.

Lijphart cites Warwick's theory as an example of this point of view[11] and contrasts this approach with Siegfried's (1956) and Dogan's (1989) analyses, according to which the shift in ministerial personnel does not affect policies.

According to Lijphart, all the literature he cites agrees that cabinet durability is an indicator of executive dominance. The disagreement is whether government stability has an effect on the regime, and Lijphart and Siegfried and Dogan argue that it has no effect, while Warwick and most of the coalitions literature argue the opposite.

My argument is that government duration and executive dominance do not have the self-evident connection that Lijphart implies. If there is such a connection, the logical argument that leads to it should be made explicitly. In fact, I would argue even further: that government duration is logically independent of government power. Government duration is a function of when the government in power resigns or is voted down by parliament. Government resignation is an indication of a political disagreement between government and parliament, and whenever such a disagreement occurs the government will have to resign whether or not it is strong, or parties participating in a government for their own reasons will create disagreements in order to lead to the formation of a new government. None of these calculations has a systematic correlation with the power of the current government. Yet Lijphart uses executive dominance extensively in the theoretical part of his book: it is one of his indicators of consociationalism, and is connected with other features of democracies like the party system, the electoral system, or the concentration or sharing of power. In addition (and what may not be well known), executive dominance enters *all* the empirical assessments of Lijphart's analysis of democratic regimes because he uses factor analytic techniques, so the variable "executive dominance" is one of the indicators that generate the principal components of his analysis and all country scores on every issue are derivatives of this variable. Given the lack of theoretical justification, can we improve upon Lijphart's measurement of "executive dominance"? In order to answer this question we have to follow the steps of Lijphart's argument closely.

Lijphart constructs executive dominance based on government duration the following way. He first measures the average cabinet life of governments where the only feature that counts is party composition (governments with identical party compositions are counted as one even if the prime minister resigns, or if there is an election). He then uses the average cabinet life using several additional events as marking the end of a government: elections, change in prime ministership, change in the minimal winning, oversized coalitions, or minority status of a cabinet. The average of these two measures is

---

[11] "A parliamentary system that does not produce durable governments is unlikely to provide effective policymaking to attract widespread popular allegiance, or perhaps even to survive over the long run" (Warwick 1994: 139).

produced in Lijphart's (1999) Table 7.1, but there are some additional steps necessary for the creation of the "index of executive dominance." Here is the description of the rest of the process:

> Two important adjustments are required to translate the averages in the third column of Table 7.1 into a satisfactory index of executive dominance. First, some of the averages assume extreme values. Botswana, which has one-party cabinets made up of the Botswana Democratic Party from 1965 to 1996, is the most glaring example. Its four-year election cycle reduces the average duration in the third column to 17.63 years, but this is still more than three times as long as the average of 5.52 years for Britain—and there is no good reason to believe that the Botswana cabinet is three times as dominant as the British cabinet. Accordingly, any values higher than 5.52 years in the third column are truncated at this level in the fourth column. A much greater adjustment is necessary for the presidential systems and for the Swiss separation-of-powers system. In four of the six cases, cabinet duration gives a completely wrong impression of the degree of executive dominance. . . . Switzerland is a prime example of executive-legislative balance. Hence, I impressionistically assign it a value of 1.00 year. The same is appropriate for the United States and Costa Rica. On the other end France must be assigned the highest value for executive dominance— the same as Britain's. (Lijphart 1999: 133–34)

Eleven out of the thirty-six countries in Lijphart's study are assigned impressionistic values of the executive dominance index because the duration of their governments expressed as the average of the two measures had nothing to do with a balance of power between legislative and executive.

I argue that executive dominance is a matter of agenda control, that it reflects the ability of the government to have its proposals accepted the way they are as opposed to having them massively amended by parliament. If this is correct, the agenda control index I calculated in the previous section should have high correlation with Lijphart's "executive dominance" variable. This is actually the case: the correlation between Lijphart's index of "executive dominance" (replicated in Table 4.1) and the "agenda control" indicator that I developed in the previous section is statistically significant ($r = .496$ significant at the .05 level). It is interesting to note this correlation is much higher than the correlation between "executive dominance" and "duration" in Lijphart's own dataset. Indeed, for the restricted sample of eighteen countries derived from Doering's dataset, although Lijphart's two columns have identical numbers for all countries with the exception of Switzerland (duration is 8.59 and executive dominance is 1) and France (duration is 2.48 and executive dominance is 5.52), the correlation of "executive dominance" and "duration" is .29 (which is statistically nonsignificant since the F test provides the number .24). Of course, the eighteen countries that Table 4.1 covers are the easier half of Lijphart's countries. All of them are West European countries; all of them (with the exception of Switzerland) are parliamentary democracies.[12]

Lijphart's classification has the major advantage that it covers both presidential and parliamentary regimes. This is a point that should not be lost in the discussion. It is true that the duration variable cannot be used to generate indicators of executive dominance in presidential systems, and Lijphart uses "impressionistic" values. However, if one looks at the legislative abilities of presidents in presidential systems, one will come with results quite similar to Lijphart's classification of presidential regimes. Shugart and Carey (1992: 155) provide this information, and on the basis of their classification the Costa Rican president receives 1 (Lijphart score 1), the U.S. president receives 2 (Lijphart's score 1), Venezuela receives 0 (Lijphart's score 2), and Colombia 5 or 8 depending on the period (Lijphart's score 3). These two sets of numbers generate a .64 correlation coefficient, which means that legislative abilities of presidents in Latin American countries correlate quite well with Lijphart's executive dominance variable.

In the previous chapter, I separated presidential and parliamentary systems on the basis of legislative agenda control, and I claimed that basically, despite their name, parliamentary systems give most legislative power to the government, and most presidential systems give agenda control to the parliament. In this chapter, we started investigating this summary statement, and found significant differences in parliamentary systems. Do presidential systems have high variance in terms of agenda setting too? Unfortunately there is no comprehensive study like Doering's covering agenda setting in presidential systems, so we have to provide only a preliminary answer.

Based on Shugart and Carey (1992: 155) we can corroborate that agenda setting in presidential systems lies mainly with Congress. They ask whether presidents have the right to "exclusively introduce" legislation. Their answer is negative for all countries with popularly elected presidents, with the exception of Brazil, Chile (scored as 1, providing the assembly with unlimited amendment powers), and Uruguay (scored as 2, providing the assembly with restricted amendment powers). However, more detailed studies place such a uniform picture into doubt. For example, Londregan (2000: 88) argues that the Chilean president has significant agenda-setting powers: "Articles 65, 67, and 68 of the constitution permit the president to pass legislation despite opposition by a majority in one chamber provided he meets with the support of a superma-

---

[12] There may be a classification problem because the French Fifth Republic as well as Finland, Portugal, Iceland, Ireland, and Austria are usually classified as semi-presidential regimes. This is not a problem for veto players theory because for all these countries the number of veto players is calculated on the basis of legislative powers, so the French Fifth Republic is exactly like a parliamentary country. Lijphart uses the semi-presidentialism argument to give France a different score from the average of government duration, but does not alter the government duration scores of the other semi-presidential countries.

jority in the other, while article 70 of the constitution and articles 32 through 36 of the organic law of Congress contain powerful veto provisions that allow the president to have the last word in the legislative debate by introducing amendments along with his veto, amendments which must be voted up or down without further change by the Congress. As if these presidential powers were insufficient, articles 62 and 64 of the Constitution permit the president to propose and amend legislation, while the same articles plus article 24 of the organic law of Congress limit the ability of members of Congress to do so."

Similarly, Cheibub and Limongi (2001) argue that several Latin American presidents have the exclusive right to initiate legislation related to the budget. In addition, they make the argument that the president of Brazil actually controls the agenda and has most of his legislation approved by Congress. This is a position disputed by Ames (2001) in his recent book. Ames provides evidence that significant parts of presidential agendas have been withdrawn, not ratified, or rejected.[13] However, neither Cheibub and Limongi (2001) nor Ames (2001) provide the institutional details, and a significant part of their argument lies on the divisions within Congress itself. These specific examples indicate that a detailed study of agenda-setting powers in presidential systems is necessary.

There are two more general points that can be drawn from these more detailed country studies. The first is the importance of executive decrees for agenda-setting powers of presidents (Carey and Shugart 1998). For example, in Brazil presidents can use decrees to introduce legislation for thirty days. Such decrees become laws only when they are approved by the legislature, but the president can reissue such decrees indefinitely. This is a power that reverses the multiple veto player setting characterizing presidential systems, and uses it in favor of the president. If the president issues an executive decree, then it is difficult for Congress to alter his decision, particularly if he holds legislative veto powers (Eaton 2000: 362).

It is possible that the president is delegated decree powers for specific issues. In Russia legislators voted to delegate important decree powers to President Yeltsin in 1991 related to "banking, the stock market, . . . investment, customs activity, the budget, price formation, taxation, property, land reform and employment" (Parrish 1998: 72). One can hardly imagine any subject excluded from this list.

Even in the United States, the president has such strategies at his disposal. For example, Bill Clinton introduced his controversial "don't ask, don't tell" policy on gays in the military by executive decree, threatening at the same time to veto legislation that would overrule his decision. Similarly, George W. Bush altered many of Clinton's policies by executive decrees.

---

[13] See Ames (2001), Chapter 7 and, in particular, Tables 15 and 16, which provide pages of failed legislative agendas of Brazilian presidents.

Any agenda-setting study should therefore investigate the scope and frequency of executive decrees.[14]

Another "hidden" presidential agenda-setting power is the advantage presidents have vis-à-vis members of Congress is staff positions to research, draft, and support their proposals. Londregan (2001) argues that administrative support increases the "valence" of presidential positions and make them difficult for members of Congress to reject. This bureaucratic advantage may actually reduce the de facto agenda-setting powers of Congress. On the other hand, Congresses may easily be able to alter or even reverse this advantage if they realize how much it matters.

4.4. Conclusions

Legislative power is correlated with agenda-setting capacities. These capacities are attributed in general to governments in parliamentary systems and to parliaments in presidential ones, as Chapter 3 argued. However, when one looks more in detail the agenda-setting power in parliamentary systems varies.

In minimum-winning coalitions each one of the parties in government is a veto player and the outcome of votes in parliament (if parties can control their MPs) is identical to government proposals. In minority and oversized governments, the parties in government are politically but not arithmetically veto players. Minority governments require support from other parties and over-sized governments can ignore the positions of parties not necessary for a parliamentary majority. Consequently, in minority or oversized governments the expectations presented in the first part of this book will hold but with higher levels of error than in minimum-winning coalitions.

Looking at the agenda setters in more detail indicates that the degree of institutional agenda setting varies. For example, the government in the United Kingdom enjoys significantly higher agenda-setting privileges than the government of the Netherlands (see Table 4.1). I used all the available information and constructed an index of agenda-setting power covering eighteen countries of Western Europe. This index is based on actual procedures of legislating, as opposed to government duration and impressionistic assessments.

Unfortunately, similar analyses do not exist for presidential systems. In the previous chapter I separated different regimes on the basis of agenda setting. Here I focused on the variance in each category, and we saw that if we want to understand the relationship between the legislature and executive, we have to focus on specific questions of agenda control. If this becomes the focus of future research, we will be able to identify similarities in decisionmaking in countries like Italy, the Netherlands, and the United States as well as similari-

---

[14] See Cheibub and Limongi (2001) about the use of these powers in Brazil.

ties between Chile and Britain or France, despite their official classification in different categories. Similarly, minority governments in parliamentary systems may appear to be quite similar to particular presidential systems where the president has strong institutional powers and weak support inside the Congress. Indeed, in both minority governments and presidential regimes, the party in government and the party of the president have the privileged position that they will be included in any possible coalition (in fact, that they will select the composition of the coalition).

Studying agenda-setting powers in both presidential and parliamentary regimes will significantly increase our capacity to understand political institutions and compare the two. Lijphart's intuition that different political systems (presidential as well as parliamentary) should be ranked with respect to "executive dominance" is a big improvement upon the traditional distinctions of regime types. However, it is not duration but agenda-setting powers that are the foundation of whose preferences will prevail. Government duration is not a good substitute for agenda-setting powers not only because it does not apply to presidential systems, but also because it is not causally related to executive dominance in parliamentary systems either.

5

Referendums

THE MERE POSSIBILITY of a referendum introduces the preferences of the population in the policymaking process. I argue that this is equivalent to the introduction of a new veto player, and the outcomes that prevail (whether the referendum is actually used or not) approximate better the preferences of the public. In addition, policy stability in principle increases with the introduction of a new veto player.

However, the most interesting part of referendums is agenda control. I revisit themes developed in the introduction of this part, that is, whether the agenda-setting process is competitive or exclusive. The agenda setting of the referendum process is divided in two parts: first, who asks the question, and second, who triggers the referendum. If both parts of the agenda are controlled by the same player (whether an existing veto player, or a different actor in popular initiatives), the referendum process eliminates all other veto players. Thus the overall effect of referendums on policy stability depends on issues of agenda control.

Finally, how much the preferences of the public are approximated by different types of referendums also depends on the specific provisions of agenda control: if an existing veto player controls both parts of the agenda (both asking the question and triggering the referendum), he will simply use referendums to eliminate the input of other veto players; if agenda control is delegated through a competitive process, then the preferences of the public will be better approximated.

The chapter is organized into six sections. Section 5.1 deals with the question of what difference it makes if there is a possibility of referendums. In other words, what happens if the people can participate directly in the legislative process? Section 5.2 deals with the institutional differences among referendum processes. Some of them are controlled by existing veto players, others are delegated to popular initiative, and others split the agenda-setting process into two parts (triggering and asking the question) and delegate each one of them to a different actor. The final sections study each one of these processes in more detail.

5.1. Direct and Representative Democracy

What difference does it make if outcomes are selected directly by the people or indirectly by the people's representatives in parliament? For the proponents of referendums, decisions are by definition better if they are made by the people. The most famous argument to that effect comes from Rousseau (1947: 85): "Sovereignty cannot be represented for the same reason that it cannot be alienated; its essence is the general will, and that will must speak for itself, or it does not exist; it is either itself or not itself; there is no intermediate possibility. The deputies of the people, therefore, are not and cannot be their representatives; they can only be their commissioners, and as such they are not qualified to conclude anything definitively. No act of theirs can be law, unless it has been ratified by the people in person; and without that ratification nothing is a law."

We will revisit this quote at the end of the chapter. For the time being let us be less normative and more abstract and claim that outcomes selected by parliament will be preferred over the status quo by a majority in parliament, while outcomes selected by a referendum will be preferred by a majority of the population. The referendum result in a single dimension would be the preference of the median voter, but in multiple dimensions such a median voter very rarely exists. As we will see, the number of policy dimensions involved in a referendum is an open question. Sometimes multiple issues are lumped together; other times, efforts are made to separate issues and decide them one at a time. For example, referendums are sometimes used to approve (or disapprove) whole constitutions; on the other hand, the Italian Constitutional Court has decided that it will exclude popular proposals containing "such a plurality of heterogeneous demands that there was a lack of a rational, unitary matrix that would bring it under the logic of Article 75 of the Constitution" (Butler and Ranney 1994: 63–64).

This section will first make the argument that the number of underlying dimensions makes very little difference for the argument: referendum selected results are extremely well approximated by a median voter argument.[1] The second issue that we will address is that the preferences of this median voter may be significantly different from the policy selected by existing veto players.

5.1.1. "Median Voter" Preferences in Referendums

In Chapter 2 we demonstrated that the winset of the status quo when all people are voting is included in a circle (Y, d + 2r), where Y is the center of the yolk

[1] Throughout this chapter, I do not discuss referendums that require qualified majorities. There are few cases in which the law requires a certain percentage of electors or voters (e.g., in Denmark until 1953, 45 percent of electors; in the Weimar Republic, 50 percent of electors; in New Zealand from 1908 to 1914, 60 percent of voters) or a congruence between a majority of voters and a majority of states (e.g., Switzerland, Australia). In 1911 in New Zealand, 54 percent favoring prohibition had no effect, because the requirement was 60 percent of votes (Butler and Ranney 1978: 17). All the arguments in the text hold for qualified majorities also, as demonstrated in Chapter 2.

of the whole population of voters, d is the distance between Y and SQ, and r the radius of the yolk of the whole population. An argument that I did not present in Chapter 2, but can be found in Ferejohn et al. (1984), is that the winset of the status quo contains a second circle (Y, d − 2r). As a result, the boundaries of the winset of the status quo are located between two circles; both of them with center Y and one of them with radius (d + 2r), and the other with radius (d − 2r).[2]

We have also said that when the number of voters increases, the radius of the yolk (r) decreases on the average (Chapter 2). Consequently, for the millions of people who are the potential participants in a referendum in most countries or states r is (most of the time) exceptionally small. As a result, the winset of the status quo is contained between two circles that differ little from each other: 4r, when r becomes smaller and smaller.

What the previous two paragraphs indicate is that for a large population, the median voter may not exist but all median lines pass through a very small area (of radius r), so an "as if" median can be very well approximated by the center Y of the yolk of the population. In addition, the winset of the status quo for such a large population is also very well approximated by a circle of radius d. In other words, the multiplicity of voters simplifies rather than complicates the problem of identification of the median voter and the winset of the status quo. Note that through this analysis the number of underlying policy dimensions becomes irrelevant. While in a single dimension there is a median voter, in multiple dimensions an "as if" median voter (the center of the yolk of the population) is a very good approximation.

Figure 5.1 provides a visual representation of the argument. The yolk of the population is very small and has center Y. The winset of a point that has distance d from Y is the shaded area in the figure, and is located between the two circles with radii (d + 2r) and (d − 2r), so it can be approximated by the circle (Y, d).

5.1.2. Direct and Mediated Democracy

Denmark provides a couple of interesting examples of the differences between direct and mediated democracy. As Vernon Bogdanor (1994: 72) puts it: "It may seem a paradox that the Single European Act, which could not have gained a majority in the Folketing, received a majority in the country, while Maastricht, which enjoyed the support of parties with 80 percent of the seats in the Folketing, was rejected by the voters in 1992." Figure 5.2 helps us think the

---

[2] Obviously, the small circle exists only if d > 2r, that is, if the status quo has a distance greater than the diameter of the yolk from the center of the yolk.

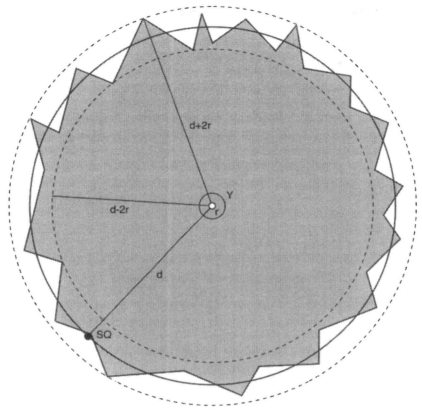

Figure 5.1. Winset of a large group of voters.

potential paradox through. Where would a parliamentary decision be located? If we know nothing about the parliament's decisionmaking except that it requires a simple majority, then according to what we have said in this book it would be a collective veto player, and the winset of the status quo would be located inside the circle (Y, d + 2r), where Y and r are the center and radius of the parliament's yolk, and d is the distance between the status quo and Y. If we need more accuracy, we would look at the intersection of any three of the circles representing the different parties that would lead to the shaded area in the figure. If we know some additional information about parliament's decisionmaking, we can incorporate it in the calculations and identify the winset of the status quo more accurately. For example, if we know that there is one parliamentary party that is certainly not included in the parliamentary decisionmaking, we can study the parliament as a collective veto player deciding by qualified majority. Or, alternatively, if we know the parties that form the

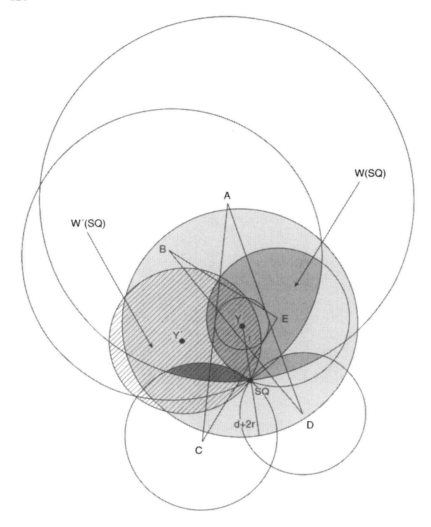

Figure 5.2. Difference between direct and mediated democracy.

government, we will identify the winset of the status quo by considering each one of them as a veto player and finding the intersection of their winsets. If the parties forming the government are A, B, and C, the outcome will be in the heavily shaded lens in the figure.

There is no reason to believe that the two processes (direct and representative democracy) will lead to the same outcome. Bowler and Donovan (1998) have made this point amply clear. In addition, Lupia (1992, 1993) has studied the information shortcuts that can inform voters about their interests in referendums. If we call Y′ the center of the yolk of the population, there is no guarantee that Y′ and Y will be identical. It depends on the electoral system whether every minority is represented in parliament. Even the purest proportional representation systems, like Israel or the Netherlands, cannot guarantee representation for minorities of one half of one percent, for example. Systems with higher thresholds, like Sweden's 4 percent or Germany's 5 percent, exclude many more. Finally, plurality electoral systems can severely underrepresent third parties or even eliminate them altogether.

Let me use an example known as the referendum paradox (Nurmi 1998: 336–37) to show one mechanism generating such a discrepancy. Suppose that there are ninety-nine voters, and nine MPs (each MP represents eleven voters). In addition, there are two parties: party A with two-thirds of the votes gets six MPs, and party B with one-third of the votes gets three MPs. This society has to vote on the question of whether X should replace the status quo. Let us assume that supporters of party A are split six to five in favor of the status quo, and that this pattern appears in every constituency, while proponents of party B are unanimous in favor of change. The parliament of the country would decide, six votes to three, to preserve the status quo, while a referendum would have produced change with sixty-three votes in favor and thirty-six against. The example indicates that a policy that is supported by almost two-thirds of the voters is rejected by two-thirds of their representatives in a country with a proportional representation electoral system!

In the figure I have selected a different point as the median of the population. One can see that the possible solutions under the two procedures have several points in common, but because of the difference between Y and Y′ these solutions do not coincide. This is only part of the story because there is no guarantee that the coalition prevailing inside the voters would be politically the same as the coalition prevailing inside parliament. For example, if there is a government of parties A, B, and C, the outcome would have to be located inside the heavily shaded area, while the outcome of a referendum could be anywhere inside the hatched area in the figure.

Hence the outcomes of direct and representative democracy may be different indeed. But can we locate these outcomes? Or can we have an algorithm that will help us understand in which areas the results will be? What we know from Chapter 1 is that the more veto players, the smaller the winset of the status quo, and the more the position of the corresponding median will be respected. But this statement compares outcomes within procedures, not across direct and representative democracy. For example, if a single party had a parliamentary majority in our Figure 5.2, the outcome would be located in its own ideal point. If parties A, B, and C are veto players and share control of the parliamentary agenda, the winset of the status quo shrinks and the heavily shaded area is closer to the parliament's median.[3]

There are lots of debates in the literature about the presumed or potential advantages and disadvantages of the two procedures. For proponents of direct democracy there are two main advantages: the first relates to outcomes that more closely fit the people's preferences (see Rousseau, above). The second is relevant to the education of citizens to democratic values. De Tocqueville has expressed this idea best: "Town meetings are to liberty what primary schools are to science: they bring it within the people's reach, they teach men how to use and how to enjoy it." For critics, from Plato to Stuart Mill to Schumpeter to Sartori, the major question is whether the average citizen has information and expertise to judge what best advances collective interests. Riker (1982) has added one additional issue: who controls the agenda is of major importance when questions are asked. Finally, legislation by referendums has raised objections on the basis that minority rights may be taken away. Gamble (1997) makes such a claim empirically, while Bowler and Donovan (1998) and Frey and Goette (1998) disagree on the magnitude of his results.

My goal in this section (or in the whole book, for that matter) is not to make a statement about which procedure is better, but to claim that there are differences in their outcomes and to study the effects of such differences for decisionmaking in political systems. If a parliamentary decision has to be ratified by the population (as is frequently the case in constitutional matters), then the outcome has to be located in the intersection of the parliamentary and the popular winsets. In other words, referendums create one additional veto player in the decisionmaking process: the people. There are two results from this introduction of a new veto player. First, in principle, it becomes more difficult to change the status quo, as I argued in Chapters 1 and 2. The qualifier "in principle" is because, as we shall see below, sometimes existing veto players are eliminated by the referendum process. Second, the final outcomes will approximate the preferences of the median voter better when the possibility of a referendum exists (whether the actual decision is made by a referendum or not).

Most of the traditional literature on referendums does not accept these points. In fact, it sees stability as contradictory to the will of the median voter; preferences on referendums thus reflect either one or the other. Butler and Ranney (1994: 21) summarize the conventional wisdom:

> As Magleby concluded in *Direct Legislation*, people who believe in undiluted representative democracy place the highest value on the virtues of *stability*, compromise,

---

[3] This argument is identical to Kalandrakis's (2000) formal result that in equilibrium, coalition governments will be less extreme than governments from two party systems. It is also consistent with the empirical results presented by Huber and Powell (1994) that multiparty governments are more representative of the median voter than single party majoritarian governments. However, both these studies do not differentiate between the parliament's median and the voters' median.

moderation, and access for all segments of the community, regardless of how small, and seek institutional arrangements that insulate fundamental principles from short-term fluctuations in public opinion. People who believe in coming as close as possible to direct democracy place the highest value on the virtues of change, participation, competition, conflict, and *majority rule* and seek institutional arrangements that maximize rapid and full responses to what popular majorities want.

There is empirical evidence in the literature in favor of both my expectations. With respect to the protection of the status quo, both Immergut (1992) and Neidhart (1970) argue that popular referendums empower its defenders. Immergut argues that after a policy proposal failed due to a referendum in 1911 in Switzerland, politicians became prudent and only minor reforms were possible. The federal government and the legislature remained hostage to powerful interest groups that could threaten a referendum challenge. For Neidhart, referendums have transformed Swiss democracy into a bargaining democracy where the government introduces legislation to interest groups first in order to avoid the referendum process.

The first scholar who provided empirical evidence of the respect of the will of the median voter was Pommerehne (1978). He discovered important differences in direct legislation and mediated legislation communities in Switzerland. Pommerehne built an econometric model based on a demand function of the median voter to study expenditure patterns in Swiss municipalities. He found that the model performs better for communities with direct legislation than for those without. In a similar study Feld and Savioz (1997) argued that direct legislation provides a check against politicians' wasteful spending habits. Matsusaka (1995) has produced similar results with Feld and Savioz with data from the American states. For the period 1960–90, his analysis suggests that states with popular initiatives had lower expenditures, taxes, and deficits. His model controls for economic and demographic factors, and includes a dummy variable for initiative states. The coefficient on the direct legislation dummy turns out to be negative, indicating that spending levels in initiative states are significantly lower. There is a significant political difference in the interpretation of these studies. The first shows evidence in favor of proximity to the interests of the median voter; the other two demonstrate a specific political outcome (regardless of the median voter's preferences). However, Matsusaka (2000) extended his analysis backward in time (covering the first half of this century) and found that spending was actually *higher* in initiative states. He concluded: "This seems to imply that the initiative is not inherently a device that reduces the size of government" (Matsusaka 2000). However, both of Matsusaka's findings could indicate proximity of outcomes to median voter preferences. Similarly, Elizabeth Gerber provides evidence that legislation on teenage abortion (Gerber 1996) or the death penalty (Gerber 1999) approximates better the preferences of the median voter in states with referendums than in states without, regardless of whether the legislation was actually introduced by a referendum or not. Finally, Hug (2001) developed new statistical techniques to estimate models of direct legislation and confirmed the theoretical expectation of proximity of outcomes to median voter preferences even in cases where the evidence used to be inconclusive. This analysis exhausts the similarities among all types of referendums. Now I will focus on the differences that relate to who controls the agenda of the referendum process.

5.2. Institutions Regulating Referendums

Most of the literature on referendums agrees that "the referendum label includes a variety of situations and usages that bear only a superficial similarity to one another" (Smith 1975: 294), and that different forms of referendums may imply very different consequences (Finer 1980: 214). However, the similarity of conclusions ends there. Disagreements arise when different authors try to classify different kinds of referendums or delineate the consequences that each kind implies.

For example, Smith (1975) uses two criteria to elaborate a "matrix of functional variance of referendums": on the one hand, "control," and on the other, "hegemonic effect." Butler and Ranney (1978) use four different categories: (1) government controlled referendums, (2) constitutionally required referendums, (3) referendums by popular petition, and (4) popular initiatives. Pier Vincenzo Uleri (1996) emphasizes legal aspects of referendums and multiplies the classification by using terms like Mandatory Referendum, Optional Vote, Initiative Referendum, Decision-Promoting, or Controlling, Rejective Vote, Abrogative Vote, and so forth.

More recently, researchers have focused on the strategic aspects of referendums, the degree that some player controls the agenda. My analysis is very similar to such approaches, and I use a classification similar to the one introduced by Hug (2001), following Mueller (1996), following the dichotomous criteria proposed by Suksi (1993).

Hug distinguishes referendums on the basis of three dichotomous criteria. First, he notes whether or not they are required. Second, he subdivides the nonrequired into two categories on the basis of whether they require an initiative to be undertaken by the people or not (active and passive). Third, he subdivides the active referendums on the basis of who controls the agenda, that is, whether the proposition on the ballot originates from the government or the opposition.

I agree with the logic behind Hug's classification, but his criteria do not generalize very well to different countries. For example, who is in government and who is in opposition is not clearly defined in a presidential regime, while who the existing veto players are is clear. Referendum agendas include two

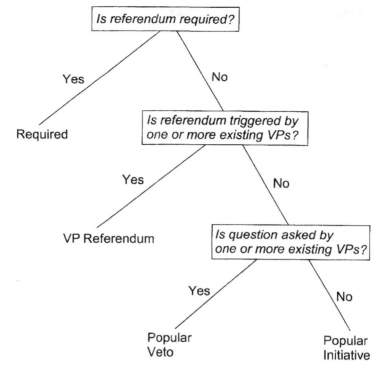

Figure 5.3. Questions defining different categories of referendums.

distinct issues to be decided: first, the decision whether or not there will be a referendum, which I call "triggering"; and second, the exact wording of the question. Figure 5.3 provides the underlying algorithm for my classification.

1. Required referendums. "Required" means that the government is obliged to submit a policy to the voters. No referendum initiative is undertaken. A particular document has to be ratified by the people in order to be enacted. In many countries, required referendums apply to constitutional changes. Such referendums exist at the state level in the United States and at the national level in Switzerland.

2. Veto player referendum. If a referendum is not required, an actor has to decide to hold a referendum. A first possibility is that the decision to hold a referendum belongs to one of the existing veto players. It could be the parliament (a collective veto player) or the government (one or more than one veto player) of a country, or some other particular veto player, like the president of the French Fifth Republic.[4] This referendum has often been labeled "plebiscite."

---

[4] As noted in Chapter 4, the French president is not a veto player in terms of legislation because he has no legislative veto. However, if the parliamentary majority is on his side, he is actually the

3. Popular veto. It is possible that an existing veto player formulates the question, but the triggering of the referendum is a prerogative of a different agent. Such referendums are essentially vetoes on the policies decided by existing veto players. The triggering actor may be the population at large through a signature process, as in Italy on certain laws (Bogdanor 1994), or as in Switzerland for most federal legislation, or as in the United States with "popular referendums" at the state level, or as in Denmark with some minority in parliament.

4. Popular initiative. It is possible that the proposal placed on the ballot does not originate in existing veto player legislation, but is a proposal written by some political group that collected the required signatures to be placed on the ballot. This type of referendum exists at the state level in the United States and also in Switzerland. Hug and Tsebelis (2002) present the exact actors that trigger referendums and ask the question in all countries of the world. In the following sections I will point out the strategic consequences of different types of nonmandatory referendums.

I will first focus on the case where both issues of the agenda are in the hands of one of the existing institutional or partisan veto players, and then I will investigate the case of a competitive agenda-setting process corresponding to referendums by popular initiative. Finally, I will examine more complicated institutions where the two issues of agenda setting are controlled by different players (one triggers the referendum and the other proposes the question).

5.3. Veto Player Referendums

Assume that a single veto player controls both parts of the referendum agenda: he can ask the question and trigger the referendum. Let us focus on Figure 5.2 and see under what conditions different possible agenda setters would actually call for a referendum. The referendum agenda setter has to calculate whether he prefers to select his most preferred point from $W'(SQ)$ or take his chances with $W(SQ)$. In order to simplify our calculations here, assume that a referendum has no political costs for the agenda setter. Obviously, this is an incorrect assumption, but one can address it easily by adding such costs in the calculations.

I consider two different cases of parliamentary decisionmaking: first, that there is a stable coalition of parties A, B, and C (I call this situation "parliamen-

---

leader (or one of the leaders) of this majority. For example, no political actor disputed that de Gaulle or Pompidou were the leaders of the majority when they were in power. No political actor disputed that d'Estaing was the leader of one of the two coalition partners in the government. Similarly, Mitterrand was the leader of the majority as long as there was a left-wing majority. Thus when the president's legislative party is part of the majority, he is a veto player (although not an additional one). The constitution of the Fifth Republic does not allow a president to proclaim a referendum against the will of his government.

tary" government); second, that any possible winning coalition among A, B, C, D, and E is possible (I call this situation a "presidential" system). In each one of these cases I consider two possible agenda setters: party A and party E (the first is part of the parliamentary system government; the second is not).[5]

Under complete information the referendum agenda setter is guaranteed to get his most preferred point from the popular winset of the status quo (W''(SQ) in Figure 5.2). Given that both A and E are located outside W''(SQ), they can achieve the points A' and E', respectively, when they control the referendum agenda. The question is, can indirect democracy offer to the referendum agenda setters a more attractive alternative? In order to answer this question we have to calculate the winset of the status quo of these two points W(A') (see Figure 5.4) and W(E') (see Figure 5.5).

Figure 5.4 presents exactly the same configuration of players as Figure 5.2, and identifies the point A', which is the best outcome the referendum agenda setter can achieve (A' is the intersection of the line AY with the circle (Y, YSQ)). Figure 5.4 also identifies the winset of A' (instead of W(SQ)), since player A can introduce a referendum and obtain A' as the outcome. Out of this, winset A will consider only the points included in the circle (A, AA'), and trigger a referendum for any point further away than A'. There is only one possible coalition that can approve points inside the (A, AA') circle: A, D, and E. Consequently, A has to select this coalition in order to get an outcome which he prefers over A' (preferably A''). In our idealized "presidential" system this is what will happen. In the case of a "parliamentary" system with A, B, and C in government, the situation is more complicated. Note that there is no point that all three A, B, and C prefer to A' because A' is in the unanimity core of A, B, and C. A has to choose between keeping the government in place or leading to a government resignation. Similarly, parties B and C may offer to approve outcome A' and avoid a referendum, or they might prefer to delegate their disagreement to a referendum. These calculations lead to three possible outcomes: Government ABC remains in power and adopts A' without a referendum. Government ABC remains in power and A' is adopted by referendum. The government resigns, and is replaced by another coalition that selects a feasible point from W(A').

Figure 5.5 presents exactly the same configuration of players as before, but identifies the winset of point E' instead of SQ, since player E can introduce a referendum and obtain it. Out of this winset only the points included in the circle (E, EE') can be considered, because E would prefer to trigger a referendum than to accept a point further away than E'. There are three possible coalitions that can approve points inside the (E, EE') circle: (ABE), (ADE), (CDE). Consequently, E has to select one of the available coalitions. In the

---

[5] In this case E is not a veto player. I include this counterfactual case for reasons of completeness.

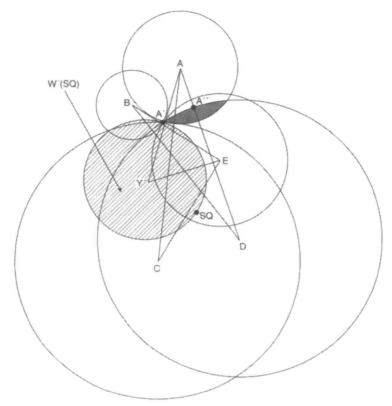

Figure 5.4. Possible outcomes when A controls the referendum agenda.

case that any coalition is possible (the "presidential" system above), E will select his own ideal point supported by (ADE). In the counterfactual case of a "parliamentary" system with (ABC) in government, the situation would be more complicated. E could use his advantage of referendum agenda setting to try to negotiate a different government: indeed, players A, D, and E may prefer a new coalition government. If the parties in government want to stick together, E will trigger a referendum and the government will lose.

In all these calculations, a presidential system where parties can shift coalitions on the basis of the subject matter under consideration was a more flexible system than a parliamentary one, where the existing government coalition was unable to adapt to the new policy environment generated by the referendum, even when agenda setting belonged to an existing veto player (A).[6] A parlia-

---

[6] And, of course, the same holds in the counterfactual case where a nonveto player (E) controlled the agenda.

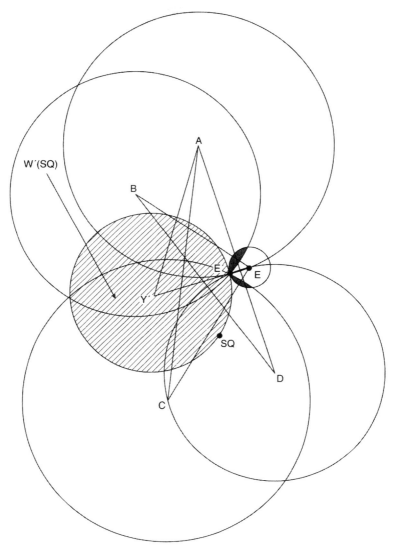

Figure 5.5. Possible outcomes when E controls the referendum agenda.

mentary system can produce similar outcomes by delegating a political issue
to a referendum, and leaving it outside the political conflict of the main parties.
For example, in the United Kingdom the referendum on participation in the
European Union had this special treatment because both parties were divided
and could not handle the issue without serious damage to their unity.

Given these calculations, strategically thinking parties in the legislature (particularly if, for some reason, they want to avoid a referendum) can assure the referendum agenda setter that they will do anything in their power to make the legislative process end up in an area that is at least as good for him as the result of a referendum. These mental experiments lead to the following conclusions. First, the position of referendum agenda setter translates into significant policy advantages. We made this point in the first two chapters, but here we go a step further: if a veto player controls the referendum agenda, he cancels other veto players as such. The reason is that the veto player with agenda control of a referendum can select whether to use the procedures of direct or representative democracy, and all other players have to provide him with the most advantageous solution. This is a very different analysis than the one presented by referendum advocates who consider referendums the expression of the will of the people (see Rousseau above). Second (and this is a consequence of the first), the legislative outcomes of representative democracy are altered if direct democracy is possible.

Let me use some examples from real referendums to show that the first conclusion is consistent with real political processes, not just mental exercises. I will deal with the second conclusion (the modification of outcomes of parliamentary process) in Section 5.4.

In France, the president of the republic can proclaim referendums under two different articles of the constitution. According to Article 11, "On the proposal of the government during parliamentary sessions, or on the joint proposal of the two Assemblies, published in the *Journal Officiel* the president of the republic may submit to a referendum any government bill dealing with the organization of the public authorities . . . which . . . although not in conflict with the constitution, would affect the working of institutions." The right to propose constitutional amendments according to Article 89 "belongs concurrently to the president of the republic, on the proposal of the Prime Minister, and the members of parliament. The amending project or proposal must be passed by the two assemblies in identical terms."

During his tenure (1958–69), de Gaulle proclaimed five referendums. He never waited for the government or the prime minister to propose any referendum to him. The proposals always came *after* de Gaulle's announcement. In addition, de Gaulle used Article 11 instead of the appropriate Article 89 for constitutional amendments, such as the referendum of 1962 when he changed the mode of election of the president from indirect to direct elections. There was no support for this action by almost any constitutional expert, but after the proposal was accepted, the question of constitutionality became moot. De Gaulle thus ignored the constitutional restrictions, and used the referendum initiative as his proper power.

What is more interesting is how he bundled the proposed questions so that he would not have to accept no for an answer—he lost only the last of five referendums he proposed. That referendum, in April 1969, asked the question: "Do you approve of the bill dealing with the creation of regions and the reform of the Senate?" "The bill was over fourteen tightly printed pages, comprised sixty-nine articles, and involved the modification or replacement of nineteen articles of the constitution" (Wright 1978: 156). In addition, de Gaulle framed the vote as a referendum on himself, telling the French people on April 10, "There cannot be the slightest doubt. . . . The continuation of my mandate or my departure obviously depends on the country's answer to what I ask. . . . What kind of man would I be . . . if I sought ridiculously to stay in office?" (Wright 1978: 158). Perhaps the packaging of the question was unusual for de Gaulle in 1969, but certainly not the association of the referendum result with whether he would remain in office. In 1961 he stated that "a negative or uncertain result would prevent me from pursuing my task." In 1962 he declared, "Your replies will tell me whether I may and whether I must continue my task." Of the two statements, the first was much more effective, since the president of the republic is also the commander-in-chief of the armed forces and it was made in the middle of a colonial war.

The threat of resignation when there was no clear alternative to de Gaulle was apparently the most critical element to the success of his referendum packages. When, in 1969, ex-Prime Minister Georges Pompidou stated that he would be available to serve his country as president if need be, de Gaulle's referendum failed and, true to his word, he resigned.

What has not been underlined in the literature covering these events is that all these maneuvers are instances of agenda control, which is the power of the actor who asks the question in referendums. This power had de Gaulle's opponents so frustrated that one of them (former prime minister Pierre Mendes-France) said: "Plebiscites? You do not discuss them: you fight against them." Another was more calm and philosophical but equally negative in his evaluation. De Gaulle (1971: 325) cited the thoughts of Vincent Auriol, president of the Fourth Republic: "The referendum is an act of absolute power. . . . While ostensibly making obeisance to the sovereignty of the people, it is, in fact, an attempt to deprive the people of its sovereignty, for the benefit of one man."

5.4. Popular Initiatives

I have heretofore dealt with referendums where the agenda setter enjoys monopoly power. Now I focus on referendums that delegate agenda-setting powers to the winner of a competitive process. The argument I advance here echoes the argument presented in Chapter 3 about the difference between democratic and nondemocratic regimes.

If different groups can become agenda setters in a referendum by winning the right to present their question to the electorate (signature collection), the legislative outcome will depend on how competitive the selection process is. If all potential agenda setters are included in the selection process, and if voters are informed, then the only way one can select proposals that can prevail (defeat not only the status quo but also possible alternatives) is to converge toward the preferences of the median voter. This result is a multidimensional generalization of the argument presented in Chapter 3, and it is possible because the winset of the status quo can be approximated by a circle, as demonstrated in Figure 5.1.

If some of the potential agenda setters are excluded from the process, then the remaining ones may be more extreme and the legislative outcome may be further away from the preferences of the median voter, if no group with preferences similar to the median voter is allowed to enter the agenda-setting process. As noted in Chapter 1, there is significant power in agenda setting.

As a consequence of this analysis, we have to focus on the process of selection of the agenda setter and assess how competitive it is. If, for example, what is required is signature selection by *volunteers*, then demands that are supported by a majority of the population are likely to get the volunteers necessary for their placement on the ballot, and initiatives that do not have enough volunteers are not likely to be supported by a majority. Consequently, such a process is a competitive one, and one can expect that the outcome will be located close to the preferences of the median voter.

If, however, what is requested for an issue to be placed on the ballot is signature selection by remunerated *professionals*, organized groups (even with ideal points far away from the median voter) are the only ones able to participate. In this case, the selection process for agenda setting will translate into outcomes that may be inconsistent with the preferences of the median voter. In all cases, the selected outcome has to be closer to the preferences of the median voter than the status quo.[7] So, again, despite the fact that the median voter makes the final decision, the result depends crucially on the preferences of the agenda setter.

Veto player referendums eliminate the existing veto players in legislatures, and so do popular initiatives. In fact, through popular initiatives, the whole legislative process is replaced by referendums. It is possible that existing veto players will try to avoid referendum challenges. However, the only points that cannot be successfully challenged are the ones close to the "as if" median voter (the center of the yolk of the population). Again, this point might not even be part of the winset of the status quo of mediated democracy, which means that

---

[7] I should repeat here that the radius of the yolk is assumed to be 0; otherwise, the selection of a point that is further from the center of the yolk than the status quo by up to 2r could not be excluded.

the existing veto players are canceled *because* the same player controls the whole referendum agenda.

5.5. Popular Vetoes

Nonmandatory referendums will be triggered by the actors with jurisdiction as a function of their own preferences. Existing veto players will select a referendum if they want to cancel other veto players, as I argued in Section 5.2. Nonveto players will select a referendum if the government-proposed result is not inside the winset of the median voter. Actually, this is true merely if they believe so, as the following story of the Italian divorce referendum indicates.

In December 1970, legal divorce was enacted in Italy for the first time. The most important provision of this law was that if the partners had been "legally separated" for five years, they could obtain a divorce. The response of the Catholic Church was immediate. The pope revealed that he had sent diplomatic notes to the government before the law's enactment, and clerics raised the issue of a referendum to abrogate the new law. In practice, although such referendums were specified by Article 75 of the Italian constitution, they had never taken place, and there was no legislation on its procedures. The government, bowing to Vatican pressure, passed such a law *before* the passage of the divorce law itself, so that Catholics, if they desired, could force a referendum to abrogate such a law when it passed. As it happened, in February 1971 the Italian bishops issued a declaration that marriage was indissoluble, and 1.4 million signatures were collected by June to force the referendum, nearly three times the required number.

What was interesting was the reaction of the political establishment to this referendum threat, which was not welcomed by the leadership of either the Communists or the Christian Democrats. First, in July 1971 there was an attempt to put forward a bill to make inadmissible any referendums that would protect ethnic and religious minorities *or marriage*. Then, the Communists introduced a new, improved divorce bill in the hope that it would replace the existing divorce law so that the process would have to start over again. When this maneuver failed (mainly because of the parliamentary timetable), the parliament was dissolved a year early in order to avoid the referendum being held in 1972. The new parliament had a slight right-wing majority, but the Christian Democrats did not try to repeal the law because they did not want to replace their alliance with the socialists with an alliance with the fascists, who were also against the divorce law. Finally, the referendum took place in 1974, three years after the signatures were collected (Butler and Ranney 1994). The result had not been foreseen by the proponents of the referendum, or by the Italian political establishment. It was a 60–40 defeat of the abrogation procedure, a humiliating outcome for the clerical coalition.

This account indicates that while the triggering player can force a referendum, the existing veto players can postpone it so that the balance of forces will improve in their favor, or modify the status quo so that the referendum will be either canceled or postponed further. These reactions of existing veto players aim at capturing the preferences of the median voter.

The accounts I have presented so far mainly assume well-informed voters. The situation is altered significantly under the more realistic assumption of incomplete information. As Wolf Linder (1994: 144) wrote in *Swiss Democracy*, "Money is . . . the single most important factor determining direct legislation outcomes." According to his account, campaign spending inequalities rise to ratios of 1:20 or 1:50, and "in Switzerland as in the American states, the high spending side wins 80–90 percent of the campaigns. It is exceptional for underdogs to win against 'big money.'" Lowenstein (1982) refines this claim for American States, arguing that when the side supporting the status quo significantly overspends the proponents of change, the odds are strongly in favor of the status quo. These arguments can be captured by an incomplete information model, according to which money is spent to persuade an uninformed median voter that one proposal is closer to his ideal point than another (regardless of the actual location of the three points).

5.6. Conclusions

Referendums—the possibility of direct legislation—significantly alter the rules and the outcomes of the legislative process. The mere possibility of introducing a legislative choice to the approval of the people introduces one additional veto player into the decisionmaking process: the median voter of the population. Although in multiple dimensions such a voter does not exist, as I argued in Section 5.1, an "as if" median voter can be identified, and the predictions will be very accurate approximations of the results. If the same player is able to trigger the referendum and also controls the wording of the question, then traditional legislative veto players are eliminated from the decisionmaking process, as we saw in Sections 5.3 and 5.4. Indeed, the analysis indicated that instead of the winset of the status quo, the relevant calculations involved the winset of the point that the referendum agenda setter can achieve.

The differences among referendums depend on who controls the agenda (triggering and question). If it is an existing veto player, it strengthens him at the expense of the others. If it is popular initiative, it favors the groups that can affect the agenda. If the agenda-setting process is competitive, it favors the median voter. As a result, existing veto players have to consider not only the winset of the status quo, but the preferences of the "as if" median voter as well.

Proponents of direct democracy argue that it expresses the will of the people, while opponents discuss the voters' lack of information that prevents them from making the right decisions. We saw that the preferences of the median voters in parliament and in the population may not coincide, and that the coalitions formed inside each one of these bodies may be different so that the outcomes of direct and representative democracy may be different.

The argument that the will of the people is expressed through referendums, as made by Rousseau, is wildly optimistic.[8] It does not take into account the role of agenda setting, triggering and asking the question. These two aspects of agenda setting may belong to the jurisdiction of a single player (veto player referendums, popular initiative) or be shared by two different players (mandatory referendums, popular vetoes).

As we saw, if the agenda setting is delegated to one veto player, it strengthens this actor vis-à-vis the other veto players. If the process of agenda setting becomes competitive, then the preferences of the median voter become more respected. As a result of this analysis, the median voter's preferences will be approximated better in countries or states with popular initiative; legislation in countries with popular veto will be more distant from the median voter's preferences, but not as much as in countries or states with mandatory referendums, or with veto player referendums.

[8] Or, more to the point, incorrect. It would have been optimistic had Rousseau been referring to popular referendums. However, I was very surprised to learn that he was in fact speaking so highly of referendums organized by the government, as Manin (2001) documents. In this case, perhaps Auriol's assessment cited earlier is more accurate.

6

Federalism, Bicameralism, and Qualified Majorities

THE TERM "FEDERAL" is used for countries where "(1) two levels of government rule the same land and people; (2) each level has at least one area of jurisdiction in which it is autonomous; and (3) there is some guarantee (even though merely a statement in the constitution) of the autonomy of each government in its own sphere" (Riker 1964: 11).

Researchers have focused on the effects of federalism on different policy outcomes, both at the theoretical and the empirical level. However, little agreement has emerged. For example, with regard to one of the most intensely studied matters in political economy, fiscal federalism, there is no agreement whether decentralization has beneficial consequences or not. Riker (1975: 144) has made the argument that there should be no policy differences between federal and unitary countries, while Rose-Ackerman (1981) and Dixit and Londregan (1998) provide arguments for why legislation will be different in these two types of states. In terms of the direction of potential differences, scholars such as Tiebout (1956), Buchanan (1950), Oates (1972), and Weingast (1995) have described economic benefits of decentralization. On the other hand, Davoodi and Zou (1998), Prud'homme (1995), Tanzi (1995) and Treisman (2000a, 2000b) point out problems associated with decentralization. Most of this literature examines the (beneficial) results of economic competition among states.

This book takes a different tack on federalism. I focus on the institutional structure of the federal government. There I observe frequently at least one of two different features: either the use of bicameralism with a second chamber having effective veto power over legislation, or the use of qualified majorities in policymaking. I argue that each one of these two institutional structures generates more veto players, so that federal countries have *ceteris paribus* more veto players than unitary ones. As a result, federal countries will exhibit higher levels of policy stability, as well as the other structural characteristics (independence of judiciary, of bureaucracies, and government instability if they are parliamentary) that follow the existence of multiple veto players.

While bicameralism (with effective veto of the second chamber) and qualified majorities are more frequent in federal countries, they are not exclusively used by them. For example, Japan has an upper chamber with the right to veto legislation proposed by the lower one, although it is not a federal country. Similarly in France (a unitary country), the government has the power to decide whether a bill will be decided by agreement of both chambers, or whether the lower chamber will overrule the upper one. Similarly with qualified majorities, while they may not be constitutionally required in many countries, they frequently become the result of the political game, as we will see in the third section of this chapter. Since neither of these two features is necessarily linked with federalism, I study them independently of each other and of federalism.

The chapter is divided in four parts. The first discusses why federalism has been such an elusive independent variable, and focuses on its implications on veto players. The second discusses bicameral institutions. The third analyzes qualified majority decisionmaking. The fourth addresses the combination of bicameralism and qualified majorities.

6.1. Federalism

Several analyses have pointed out important characteristics that unite or separate federal countries. For example, all federal countries involve constituent units that compete with each other for the attraction of citizens (Tiebout 1956). On the other hand, some federal countries have agencies for implementation of national policies at the federal level (e.g., the United States), while others do so at the state level (European Union, Germany).[1] In this part I concentrate on two issues, fiscal federalism and veto players. Fiscal federalism dominates the economics literature. Here I argue that while the theoretical arguments in favor of decentralization may seem compelling, the empirical evidence does not seem to support these theories. Then I focus on the institutions that most frequently prevail in different federal countries.

6.1.1. Fiscal Federalism

On the basis of Riker's definition cited above, federalism is a balance between constituent units willing to participate in the federation (and not depart from it) and the central government not taking away their autonomy. If either of these conditions does not hold, the federation will collapse (either transform itself to a group of independent states, or become a unitary state). However, Riker (1975: 144) did not believe that there would be policy differences between federal and nonfederal countries because of this balance between center and periphery. In fact, he proposed a thought experiment where eight pairs of countries (one of these pairs was Australia and New Zealand) were divided by the "federalism" variable but had very similar policies in most dimensions.

---

[1] See an excellent article by Scharpf (1988) on the issue.

But economists studying federalism pointed out two important differences between federal and unitary countries. First, Hayek (1939) suggested that because local governments and consumers have better information about local conditions and preferences, they will make better decisions than national governments. Second, Tiebout (1956) focused on the effects of competition among jurisdictions since people can "vote with their feet" and argued that federalism provides people with the choice among different menus of public goods.

However, these early approaches ignored the question of incentives of politicians to provide public goods and preserve markets. Weingast (1995: 24) focused on the following fundamental problem: "Markets require protection and thus a government strong enough to resist responding to the inevitable political forces advocating encroachments on markets for private gain. The fundamental political dilemma of an economic system is that a state strong enough to protect private markets is strong enough to confiscate the wealth of its citizens."

This problem of production of institutions strong enough to produce certain desirable outcomes, yet not able to abuse their strength, has appeared several times in the literature. For Przeworski (1991: 37), stable *democracy* "requires that governments be strong enough to govern effectively but weak enough not to be able to govern against important interests." For Weingast (1997), the *rule of law* is another mechanism that provides for strong but limited governments. For the founding fathers of the American Constitution, *checks and balances* was such a mechanism. For Ackerman (2000), it is a *limited separation of powers* (which, as I argued in the Introduction, is a limited number of veto players). Weingast applied the same analytic approach to the issue of federalism, and created the concept of "market preserving federalism."

Market-preserving federalism adds three characteristics to Riker's definition of political federalism: "(1) Subnational governments have primary regulatory *responsibility over the economy*; (2) *a common market* is ensured, preventing lower governments from using their regulatory authority to erect trade barriers against the goods and services from other political units; and (3) the lower governments face a *hard budget constraint*, that is, they have neither the ability to print money nor access to unlimited credit" (Weingast 1995: 5; emphasis in the original).

The originality of Weingast's analysis is that the conditions of market-preserving federalism are explicitly introduced as opposed to being *derived* as characteristics of federalism. Hence in Weingast's analysis not all federal countries present or tend toward these characteristics, while in other, more theoretical analyses fiscal competition increases the cost of a financial bailout and consequently serves as a commitment device for the federal government, and the combination of monetary centralization and fiscal decentralization hardens the budget constraint (see Qian and Roland 1998). For Weingast, in contrast, countries like Argentina, Brazil, and India, while federal, are not market-preserving federal countries and have low economic performance.

Unfortunately, Weingast has not yet produced a list of countries that meet his "market-preserving federalism" criteria. The classification of countries in this category is not straightforward because the United States, according to Weingast's analysis, qualifies as "market preserving" only up to the 1930s, while contemporary China, qualified by Weingast as market-preserving federalism, is not federal, strictly speaking. As a consequence, Weingast's intuitions cannot be tested directly. However, empirical analyses of economic performance of federal systems seriously questions the conclusions of economic analyses (at least of the first generation: Hayek [1939], Tiebout [1956] and Oates [1972]). In the most recent of these empirical analyses, Treisman (2000b) creates a data set including 154 countries and defines five different types of decentralization depending on the political institutions prevailing in a country, the number of tiers that different units can be classified, the size of the lower level units, and so on. His conclusions are that countries with higher levels of decentralization have higher levels of corruption, and lower levels of provisions of public goods indicating "quality of government," like childhood inoculation and reduction of adult illiteracy. He concludes: "The Tieboutian idea that decreasing the size of government units will strengthen competition between governments for capital, thus stimulating greater efficiency and honesty, is not supported. Countries with smaller first-tier jurisdictions tended to be perceived as more corrupt" (Treisman 2000b: 1). The same result holds with other measurements of decentralization as well: decentralization and corruption are positively correlated in Treisman's data.

6.1.2. The Institutions of Federalism

Riker's definition of federalism has been the starting point for the study of the institutions of federalism. Hicks (1978: 175) uses essentially Riker's definition and takes his points one step further in terms of their institutional implications: "If we agree that a federal system has the dual purpose of creating a nation and preserving the identity of its units, it is clearly essential that Constitution and institutions must be appropriately devised for both purposes. . . . The Constitution will provide for: (1) a probably large Assembly representative of all citizens and chosen from the units (or States), most likely in proportion to their relative populations; (2) a House of States or Senate, considerably smaller but normally providing strictly equal representation of all States."

Similarly, Bednar, Eskridge, and Ferejohn (2001: 9) discuss the institutional design of federalism: "Opportunism by the national government is best constrained by fragmenting power at the national level. By making it harder for a national will to form and be sustained over time, these mechanisms will tend to disable national authorities from invading state authority, especially as to controversial political issues (the most tempting target for national cheating on the federal arrangement). The foregoing fragmentation may be accomplished through a formal system of separation of powers and extra requirements (such as bicameral approval and presentment to the chief executive for veto) for legislation." They also point out the significance of two additional mechanisms: one informal, the fragmentation of the party system,[2] and one formal, an independent judiciary to control federal opportunism. Let us discuss these three mechanisms one at a time.

Most analysts associate federalism with "strong bicameralism" (to use Lijphart's terminology), that is, a system where the second chamber has formal veto and does not have the same composition as the first. Indeed, most federal countries have such a strong second chamber. What is not well known is that the bicameral constitutional form, which after the adoption of the United States Constitution became very frequent in federal countries, was not the first institutional arrangement characteristic of federalism. European federations like the United Netherlands, the Swiss Cantons, and the German Confederation were deciding by bargaining among the representatives of the different states (Tsebelis and Money (1997: 31). On the basis of these experiences, Montesquieu's ideal confederal republic was an association of small homogeneous states making decisions by unanimity (Inman and Rubinfeld 1997: 76), while Condorcet's way of avoiding the problems of majority cycling that he had discovered was decisionmaking by qualified majorities (Tsebelis and Money 1997: 38).

In philosophical terms, Montesquieu's conception of federalism was based on the small units that represented similar preferences, and the unanimity or qualified majority rule that reduced the probability of imposition of one state's preference on another. For Condorcet, bicameralism did not have any advantage that could not be achieved in an easier and more secure way by qualified majorities in one chamber.[3]

Madison developed his model of the federal republic set forth in *The Federalist* (especially nos. 10 and 51) by criticizing the vices of the Articles of Confederation, with respect to two main weaknesses: "First, the external and internal weaknesses of a government based on a compact among number of

---

[2] According to Bednar, Eskridge, and Ferejohn (2001), this fragmentation is produced by the appropriate electoral system. As we saw in Chapter 3, other mechanisms (e.g., the lack of vote of confidence in presidential systems) can also produce fragmentation.

[3] In "Lettres d'un bourgeois de New—Haven a un citoyen de Virginie" (written in 1787), he claimed: "But it is easy to see (and this matter can be rigorously demonstrated) that there is no advantage, with respect to the truth of decisions, in multiplying the legislative bodies, that one would not get in a simpler and more secure way by asking for a qualified majority in one chamber" (Condorcet 1968, vol. 9: 76; my translation from the original). In other parts of his work he gave examples of what one can call type I and type II problems of bicameralism: If a decision needs to be made by simple majority, it might be frustrated by the lack of congruent majorities in two chambers, and if a decision requires a qualified majority, it may be obtained with a lower number of votes in a bicameral system ("Est-il Utile de diviser une Assemblee nationale en plusieurs chambers?" in Condorcet [1968], vol. 9: 333–63).

small sovereign republics; and second, the heart of his case, the danger of majority tyranny within such small states. These two lines of argument controvert the two elements of Montesquieu's model of confederate republic: the compact solution and the small republic theory. The remedy for both failings Madison finds in the sovereignty of the people in the large compound republic" (Beer 1993: 245). Madison's argument also contradicts Condorcet's analysis, which provides equal weight to all possible majorities or qualified majorities, a point that we will return to in the conclusions of this chapter.

Consequently, both qualified majorities and bicameralism have been used as bases of federalism, but over time, it is the second that replaced the first. In contemporary federations, the European Union has employed qualified majority (or unanimity) decisionmaking to guarantee the preferences of its members. In fact, in the period before the European Parliament was elected (1979), and before it received formal powers (1987), qualified majority or unanimity decisionmaking in the Council of Ministers was the only mechanism protecting the interests of country members. Since 1987, the European Union has applied a combination of bicameralism and qualified majorities (see Chapter 11). As we will see in Section 6.4, the United States uses a similar combination of qualified majorities and bicameralism for political decisionmaking. In fact, it would probably be more appropriate to discuss "multicameralism" instead of bicameralism in the case of the United States and the European Union, because besides the two parliamentary institutions (the two houses in the U.S. case, and the council and parliament in the E.U. case), there is a third actor with veto powers: the president in the United States, and the Commission[4] in the European Union.

Why do qualified majorities and bi- or multicameralism increase the number of veto players? Because if we consider the legislature of a country as a single collective veto player deciding by majority rule, then both bicameralism and qualified majorities introduce additional constraints, by specifying that some or all of the simple majorities are not sufficient to make a decision. As a result, some parts of what used to be the winset of the status quo are not valid anymore, and the winset of the status quo shrinks.

Figure 6.1 provides the answer for the case of bicameralism. Suppose that there were six actors in a parliament, and consequently, four of them were necessary for a majority decision. Any combination of four of the six players would be sufficient to replace the status quo. Now suppose that we divide the six initial players into two groups, the group L1, L2, and L3 (representing the lower house), and the group U1, U2, and U3 (representing the upper house). If the requirement for a replacement of the status quo becomes congruent majorities in the two houses, some of the previous majorities (like (L3, U1, U2, U3) in the figure) are now invalidated, because they do not represent majori-

---

[4] For exceptions and more detailed discussion see Chapter 11.

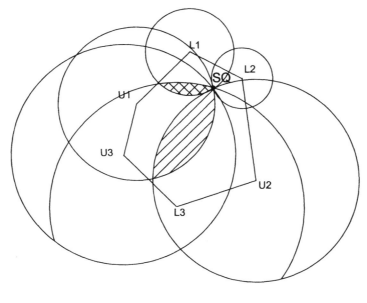

XXXX   Bicameral winset

ZZZZ   Additional winset of unicameral legislature

Figure 6.1. Winset of bicameral (by concurrent majorities) and unicameral (by quali-fied majority) legislatures.

ties in both houses. Figure 6.1 shows the winset of a bicameral system with crosshatch, and the winset of a unicameral but not bicameral legislature with single-hatch.

A similar argument can be made if instead of bicameralism one would intro-duce qualified majorities. If we consider the case of a five-sixths qualified majority, Figure 6.1 demonstrates that the winset of the point selected as status quo is empty. There is no coalition including five of the six players that agrees to a replacement of the status quo. In the sections that follow I focus on each one of these methods of increasing the number of veto players: bicameralism and qualified majorities.

A different mechanism that "makes it harder for a national will to form and be sustained over time" according to Bednar, Eskridge, and Ferejohn is the fragmentation of the party system. The idea that a fragmented party system will not be able to decide or to sustain its decisions may seem plausible, but it is not necessarily correct. As we have seen in Chapter 2, the winset of collective veto players may include points that are not included in the winset of an individual veto player. As a consequence, fragmented party systems *may* produce outcomes that nonfragmented ones could not (by taking some dissidents from one party and forming a majority). Fragmentation per se may make bargaining among different factions more difficult, but does not preclude outcomes.

Finally, another mechanism that weakens the central government according to Bednar, Eskridge, and Ferejohn is the existence of a strong and independent judiciary. As we will see in Chapter 10, there is indeed an association between federalism and an independent judiciary; however, it is not clear which is the direction of causation. Is it that federal countries create constitutions with a strong judiciary, or is it that the judiciary in federal countries becomes more independent and important since it has to adjudicate among different branches of government?

In conclusion, federalism is an elusive independent variable. It does not seem to cause the beneficial effects that the fiscal federalism literature predicted. It does not have any unique or necessary institutional feature (whether bicameralism, or qualified majorities, or fragmentation of parties, or independent judiciary), yet it is associated with most of these characteristics. My contention is that whether it is through bicameralism, or through qualified majorities (the most frequent associations over time), the number of veto players increases, and the characteristics associated with veto players (policy stability, government instability, independence of bureaucracies, the judiciary, and so on) become more pronounced.

6.2. Bicameralism

About one-third of parliaments in the world are bicameral (Tsebelis and Money 1997). In these bicameral legislatures, the composition as well as the power of the second chamber varies, as do the rules of how agreement is achieved (if necessary). I will deal with all these preliminary issues first, and then focus on decisionmaking under one set of rules that requires special analysis on the basis of veto players theory: the case where both chambers have veto power and are composed of weak parties.

6.2.1. Bicameral and Multicameral Diversity

The power of the second chamber varies from country to country. Sometimes the agreement of the upper chamber is necessary for the adoption of legislation (the United States, Switzerland, Italy), sometimes not (the United Kingdom,

Austria). It is quite common that federal countries have upper chambers with the right to veto legislation.

Another feature of bicameral countries is that the second chamber may have a similar or dissimilar political makeup to the first. Reasons for the differences in policy positions may be that the two chambers are elected from different constituencies (frequently in federal countries one represents the population and the other the states), or with different electoral systems, or they may simply have different decisionmaking rules. An example of different rules is provided by the U.S. Congress with the Senate's filibuster rule (which does not exist in the House): as a result of this rule, a qualified majority of three-fifths is essentially needed for legislation to clear the Senate, while a simple majority is needed for the House. I will analyze this case in detail below.

Even if both chambers have the same partisan composition, it does not follow that differences between them are eliminated. Even when its two chambers were nearly identical in political alignment, it took the Italian legislature seventeen years to adopt legislation on rape (*violenza sessuale*). The major issues were whether rape is possible in marriage, and whether the victim should always be the one who decides whether and when to go to court. Feminist organizations and women in parliament took different positions. As a result, party leaders did not want to interfere in the dispute, and legislation that was first introduced in 1977 was only adopted in 1995–96.[5]

Bicameral legislatures may therefore introduce a second institutional veto player (if the second chamber has the possibility to veto legislation). I will focus on cases fulfilling this veto requirement. However, it would be incorrect to assume that second chambers without veto power do not affect legislation. Tsebelis and Money (1997) have demonstrated that such chambers can influence outcomes, and sometimes can even abort legislation (like the House of Lords when it suspends legislation just before an election, which leads to the termination of bills).

Finally, while we are speaking about bicameralism, from the point of view of this book, it is easy to generalize to any number of chambers. For example, the U.S. political system, because of separation of powers between the president and the legislature on the one hand and federalism on the other, is de facto a tri-cameral system: it requires the agreement of three institutional veto players instead of two). In Chapter 2 I presented Figure 2.5 identifying an area containing the winset of the status quo of the U.S. tricameral system when one veto player (the president) is an individual, while the other two (the House and Senate) are collective. Similarly, one way of passing legislation in the European Union is by agreement of the European Commission, the European Parliament, and a qualified majority in the Council of Ministers, which means

---

[5] Gianfranco Pasquino, personal communication.

also that this system may be understood as tri-cameral.[6] I analyze the E.U. system under all sets of rules in Chapter 11.

If parties are cohesive, the different number of chambers may increase the number of veto players, but this does not complicate the analysis. For example, if the same majority controls both the upper and lower chambers and if the parties have the same ideal points, then cases like the disagreement between the Italian chambers will be rare, and one can perform the analysis in one chamber alone (technically, the veto players of the second chamber are absorbed). If a certain coalition controls the majority in one chamber but not in the second, then the parties required to form a majority in the second chamber have to be considered additional veto players. For example, as we saw in Chapter 3, if in Japan and Germany the ruling coalition does not control the Senate, one has to add as veto player the party required to control the upper chamber, whether the new veto player is included in the government coalition (as in Japan in 1999) or not (as in Germany).[7]

The one case that we have not covered in this preliminary discussion is the case where both chambers have veto power over legislation, and the parties in each one of them are not cohesive, as usually happens in bicameral presidential regimes.

6.2.2. Strong Bicameralism with Weak Parties

When parties are weak, the majorities that prevail in each chamber are not stable and the majorities of the two chambers do not necessarily coincide. As a result, a veto players analysis cannot move beyond the institutional level. Figure 6.2 provides a visual representation of the argument in a very simple case.

The two chambers (lower represented by L, upper represented by U) are drawn in two dimensions, and located away from each other. Any coalition in each one of them is possible, and they decide by congruent majorities. Under the above conditions, first there are some points that cannot be defeated by the decisionmaking rule in place. They are called the *bicameral core*. These points are along the segment LU. Indeed, any point over or under this segment can be defeated by its projection on the LU line. In addition, any point to the left

---

[6] Braeuninger (2001) studies theoretically multicameral systems, although his example addresses decisionmaking in international organizations.

[7] A prior question for the case of Germany is whether parties are cohesive to be considered as having the same preferences in both chambers. The most recent empirical research on the issue (König 2001) indicates that they are.

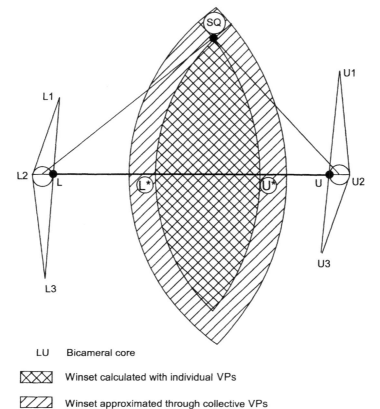

LU   Bicameral core

Winset calculated with individual VPs

Winset approximated through collective VPs

Figure 6.2. Bicameral core, and bicameral winset of SQ.

of L can be defeated by L1, L3, and a unanimity of U's. Similarly, any point
to the right of U can be defeated by U1, U3, and a unanimity of L's.[8]

Figure 6.2 also presents the winset of one particular position of the status
quo. The calculation has been performed in two different ways, exactly and
by approximation. For the exact calculation I consider the individual members of the two chambers and identify all the points that command congruent
majorities in the two chambers (crosshatched area). For the approximate calculation I use the concept of collective veto players introduced in Chapter 2,
draw the wincircles of each chamber, and consider their intersection. This
intersection is single-hatched in the figure, and as expected contains the winset
of the status quo.

[8] See Hammond and Miller (1987) and Tsebelis and Money (1997). The latter mistakenly draw
the core further than points L and U.

The location of the bicameral core in this analysis is important, because as we see in Figure 6.2 the bicameral winset is divided in half by the bicameral core. As a consequence, the closer the status quo to the bicameral core, the smaller the winset of the status quo (policy stability increases). In addition, the bicameral core is the major dimension of bicameral conflict. Given that points outside the core can be defeated (by congruent majorities) by their projection on the core, the real dispute between the two chambers is reduced to the adoption of a point in the L*U* interval.

However, the bicameral core is not guaranteed to exist particularly in high dimensional spaces (see Chapter 2). Tsebelis and Money (1997) have demonstrated that even in the absence of a bicameral core, the strategic situation is not modified significantly. They calculated the *uncovered set* of a bicameral legislature and showed that it includes the line that connects the centers of the yolks of the two chambers. Therefore, if the decision is made within the uncovered set (see Chapter 2), one has to locate the outcome using very similar calculations (the line that connects the centers of the two yolks, and the wincircles of the collective veto players).

For these reasons Tsebelis and Money (1997) have come to the conclusion that bicameralism shapes the conflict between the two chambers into a conflict along one privileged dimension (the one that connects the center of the yolks of the two chambers). This analysis is not significantly different than the analysis proposed in this book. As a result of either analysis, the larger the distance between the centers of the yolks of the two chambers, the smaller the possibility of change. Another conclusion that the two analyses share is that the outcome of bicameral negotiations depends on which chamber controls the agenda. In the analysis of this book, I identify the outcome when one of the two chambers controls the agenda-setting process. However, as Tsebelis and Money demonstrate, the actual agenda setting is a significantly more complicated process. Figure 6.3 addresses this issue.

As we discussed in Chapters 1 and 2, when one chamber makes a proposal to the other, they select the point closest to them from the winset of the status quo, so that the outcome will be L1 (or around L1) in the case when the lower chamber is the agenda setter, and U1 (or around U1) if the upper chamber controls the agenda. However, most countries have adopted more complicated rules, which are called the "navette"[9] system. The bill shuttles from one chamber to the other, either until agreement is reached[10] or until some other stopping rule is applied. In some countries, prolonged disagreement leads to the formation of a conference committee (France, Japan, Switzerland); in others the lower house makes the final decision (the United Kingdom, Austria); in others there is a joint session of the two chambers (Australia).

[9] "*Navette*" is the French word for shuttle.

[10] This means that the number of rounds is potentially infinite (Italy).

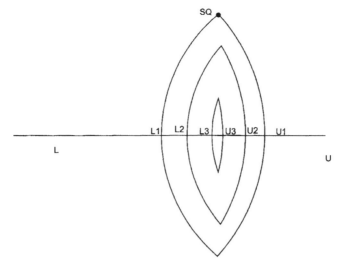

Figure 6.3. Bicameral outcomes under the navette system (alternating offers).

Tsebelis and Money have identified the differences in policy outcomes produced by these institutional arrangements. In their analysis they use the "impatience" of each chamber as an additional variable. Their argument is that each chamber prefers an immediate agreement over a postponement, and in order to reach this immediate agreement it is willing to make some concessions. The qualitative implications of this argument are presented in Figure 6.3. If the lower chamber makes an offer and there is the possibility of a new round of negotiations after a rejection, it will move to point L2 in order to avoid this rejection. If there are two rounds of negotiation, it will move even further to point L3, and so on. Similarly, if the upper chamber controls the agenda, and there is one round of negotiations in case of disagreement, it will propose U2 in order to avoid these negotiations; if there are two rounds of negotiations, it will propose U3 in order to avoid them, and so on. Note that all these institutional intricacies are covered by the veto players theory presented in this book, because here I have adopted the more general argument that the outcome is located within the winset of the status quo, and I do not attempt to finetune the prediction any further.

I can make the same argument with respect to conference committees. They control the legislative agenda, and they decide which particular outcome from the intersection of the winsets of the status quo of the two chambers will be selected. Hence the final outcome will be located inside the winset of the status quo of the two chambers, but the exact location depends on the composition and the decisionmaking rule inside the conference committee. The reader can refer to Figure 2.9 to visualize how a conference committee identifies the area within which it will make its proposal.

The analysis in this section leads to similar conclusions with the "divided government" literature in American politics. Some researchers (Fiorina 1992, Sundquist 1988) have argued that divided government will cause a reduction in significant legislation. Indeed, "divided government" in the terminology of this book is equivalent with "the two institutional veto players have significantly different preferences." However, empirical evidence collected by Mayhew (1991) on significant laws does not corroborate the divided government expectation.[11] Mayhew finds that there is no significant difference in legislation between periods of unified and divided government. There has been one important empirical response to Mayhew's finding. Sarah Binder (1999) has made the argument that Mayhew's data set requires "a denominator," that is, the set of potential laws (some of which were not passed because of divided government or other reasons). She identifies the set of such laws, and when she takes the ratio of actual legislation over this set of laws, she finds that the distance between the two parties as well as the distance between the two chambers have significant negative impact on the percentage of bills that become laws. Consequently, the most recent findings in the American literature are in agreement with the argument of this book. There is, however, a more theoretical response to Mayhew's argument that focuses on the question of qualified majority requirements in U.S. decisionmaking. I address this argument in the last section, after having a detailed discussion on qualified majorities.

6.3. Qualified Majorities

As we saw in the first part of this chapter, Condorcet, who did not believe in the virtues of bicameralism, was arguing that qualified majorities can produce the same outcomes of policy stability in a simpler and more certain way. In this section, I show two points: first, how qualified majorities can increase policy stability; second, how pervasive they are even if not explicitly specified by formal institutions.

6.3.1. Core and Winset of Qualified Majorities

Let us consider a collective veto player composed of seven members $(1 \ldots 7)$ who decides by a five-sevenths qualified majority. We can divide this collective veto player several times the following way: we can select any five points (say, $1 \ldots 5$), and then consider the pentagon composed of these five points (the

---

[11] For a debate on the Mayhew data set, see Kelly 1993 and Mayhew 1993.

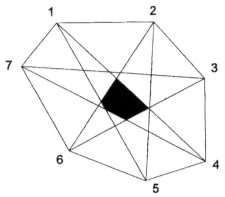

Figure 6.4. 5/7 majority core in two dimensions.

unanimity core of these five players). Any point included in this pentagon cannot be defeated by a unanimous agreement of the five selected players. If now we select all possible such combinations of five players, and there is an intersection of their unanimity cores, it means that any point in this area cannot be defeated by any five-sevenths qualified majority.

Figure 6.4 presents the intersection of the unanimity cores of all possible five-member combinations. This area is the five-sevenths core of the collective veto player. Such a core does not always exist, however, it is more frequent than a bicameral core. Indeed, Greenberg (1979) has shown that such a core always exists if $q > \frac{n}{(n+1)}$ where q is the required majority and n is the dimensionality of the policy space.

The reader can verify that the unanimity core always exists (regardless of the number of policy dimensions),[12] and that for points outside the core the winset of the status quo is not empty. In addition, if the qualified majority core exists and the status quo approaches this core, the winset of the status quo shrinks (policy stability increases).

A comparison of the bicameral core and the qualified majority core in an n-dimensional space (assuming that they both exist) indicates that the first is a single dimensional object, while the second is in general in n dimensions. And the shape of the core affects the size of the winset of the status quo (i.e., policy stability). For the winset of the status quo to be small in a bicameral system, the status quo has to be located close to one particular line, while under qualified majority rule, if the status quo is located centrally within the collective veto player, its winset will be small or empty (policy stability will be high).

What is the implication of this difference? A qualified majority decisionmaking is likely to leave centrally located policies either unchanged, or

---

[12] This is because n points define at the most an (n-1)-dimensional space.

produce incremental changes to them. Qualified majority decisionmaking is also likely to produce outcomes centrally located in space. The outcomes of bicameralism are more random. If the two collective veto players in a bicameral system are located on opposite sides of a policy question, bicameralism will focus the discussion on the issue. If, however, the two veto players are in agreement on the policy question, the issue is not likely to be discussed in a satisfactory way between the two chambers.[13] Let me produce some examples: if one chamber of a bicameral legislature is more rural and the other more urban, questions of agricultural subsidies are likely to be discussed, and a compromise on the issue identified. If, however, both chambers represent younger or older voters, a discussion of the social security issue or a compromise taking both sides of the issue into account may not occur.

6.3.2. Pervasiveness of Qualified Majorities

As we saw in Chapter 2, qualified majority requirements impose additional restrictions on the winset of the status quo. First, as the required qualified majority threshold increases, the winset of the status quo shrinks. Second, unlike the majority winset of the status quo, which is almost never empty, the qualified majority winset of the status quo may be empty. Third, and extremely important for the size of the qualified majority winset of the status quo (if it exists), is the q-cohesion of the collective player. As Conjecture 2.3 states, policy stability decreases when q-cohesion increases.

When collective veto players are deciding by qualified majorities, all these calculations are necessary in order to identify the location of the winset of the status quo. For example, this is the case for the Council of Ministers of the European Union, for the override of a presidential veto in the United States, for legislatures with respect to constitutional issues in Belgium, or for the lower chamber to overrule the upper in countries such as Chile and Argentina (see Tsebelis and Money 1997 for examples). However, what is not obvious is that the qualified majority calculations are necessary for some additional cases, which I call "qualified majority equivalents." Let me discuss such cases.

1. *Nonconstitutional requirements.* While the U.S. Senate formally makes decisions by a simple majority of its members, the possibility of filibuster modifies the situation significantly. If a senator decides to filibuster a bill, the only possibility to end his efforts is a three-fifths vote of the Senate to end debate and bring the bill up for a vote. Consequently, forty senators can prevent legislation from being adopted. For any significant legislation to pass the U.S. Senate, an agreement of the minority party is required (unless this party does

---

[13] It may or may not be discussed inside each one of the chambers, depending on the attitude of the majority.

not control forty seats). In other words, the U.S. Senate is a qualified majority (or supermajoritarian) institution. We will see the difference this "detail" makes in Section 6.4.

2. *Absolute majorities and abstentions.* Sometimes, constitutional requirements specify an absolute majority of the members of a parliament. For example, the European parliament has to propose amendments by the absolute majority of its members in certain legislative procedures. Similarly, the French National Assembly can pass a vote of no-confidence only by the absolute majority of its members. The German chancellor is invested (and replaced) by an absolute majority of the members of the Bundestag. If all the members of a legislative body are present and nobody abstains, then an absolute majority and a simple majority coincide. If, however, there are absentee members, or if certain members abstain from the vote, then the absolute majority requirement is equivalent to a qualified majority of the members who participate in the vote.

Consider that the percentage of abstentions and/or absentee votes is A. Of the remainder, the percentage of "yes" votes is Y (and the remainder $(1 - y)$ is "no" votes). An absolute majority requirement translates to $Y > \frac{(1/2)}{(1 - A)}$. This relationship gives the following "qualified majority threshold equivalents." If 50 percent of the members of the European Parliament (MEPs) are absent or abstain, a unanimity of votes is required for an amendment to pass. If 33.3 percent do not vote or abstain, the required threshold is three-quarters; if the percentage of nonparticipants is 25 percent, a decision requires two-thirds of the present MEPs, and so on. Since the absolute majority requirement translates to a qualified majority equivalent threshold in the European Parliament, this institution is sometimes unable to introduce amendments desirable to an (absolute) majority of its members.

3. *Unwilling or undesirable allies and simple majorities.* In the French Fourth Republic (1946–58), at the height of the Cold War, governments often made the statement that if the Communist Party voted in their favor they would not count the Communist votes. A statement of that form is equivalent to taking a percentage of votes away from the "yes" column and moving it to abstentions. Again, we are talking about qualified majority equivalence. Alternatively, some parties may refuse to support any possible government. They are known in the literature as "anti-system parties." The mere existence of such parties transforms simple majority requirements to qualified majorities. Consider, for example, that a new party is added to the five parties of a parliament (like the ones presented in Figure 2.4), and that all parties have the same number of votes (16.67 percent). If the new party is an anti-system party, that is, a party that votes "no" on every issue, then in order to obtain a majority, four of the six parties are needed to vote "yes." Since party six is always voting no, then the required majority is in fact four-fifths (four of the remaining five parties have to agree). Applying the reasoning I presented in Section 2.3, this

qualified majority equivalence substantially decreases the winset of the status quo. In fact, it may make any change of the status quo impossible.

Modeling some Latin American legislatures may require this technique of qualified majority equivalence. The reason is that Latin American parties are more disciplined than U.S. parties, but less so than European parties; consequently, winning coalitions may exclude some parties (that never support prevailing policies) but use different parties each time. In this case the analyst has to exclude the parties that never participate in majorities and see how the remaining parties form qualified majorities in order to produce the required votes.

Finally, as I wrote in Chapter 4, oversized governments in parliamentary systems may be modeled as qualified majority equivalents, because all coalition members are not needed for a particular policy to be adopted. Strom's (2000) arguments discussed in Chapter 4 would lead to such an approach. However, as the reader will verify from the empirical results of Chapters 7 and 8, I did not need such an approach to model the effects of oversized coalitions on the issues of workers' time, working conditions, and budget structures that these chapters cover.

To conclude, while qualified majorities per se are not a very frequent requirement, knowledge of the political reality prevailing inside different institutions or political systems may lead the researcher to use qualified majority equivalents, and to the analysis introduced in Section 2.3 to model particular institutions or political systems. Whenever qualified majorities become the decisionmaking rule (whether de facto or de jure), policy stability should increase, and outcomes should be expected to converge toward the center of the location of veto players.

6.4. Bicameralism and Qualified Majorities Combined

What happens if bicameralism is combined with qualified majorities, such that one of the chambers decides by simple majority but the other decides by qualified majority? This is the case of the U.S. Congress if we consider that the Senate has to make important decisions by filibuster-proof majorities (enabling a three-fifths majority to invoke cloture and end filibusters). This is also the case of E.U. institutions, because the Council of Ministers decides by qualified majority or unanimity.

Figure 6.5 replicates Figure 6.2, with the only difference that decisions in the upper chamber are made by unanimity. There are two major consequences of these more stringent requirements of decisionmaking in one of the two chambers, as shown in Figure 6.5. First, policy stability increases (since the winset of the status quo shrinks). Second, outcomes shift in favor of the less flexible chamber (whether one considers the whole winset of the status quo or

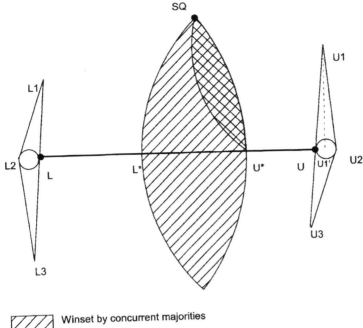

Winset by concurrent majorities

Winset by majority in lower and unanimity in upper chamber

Figure 6.5. Winset by concurrent majorities, and by unanimity in the upper chamber.

simply the intersection with the core or the line connecting the centers of the two yolks [in the figure, of all the points L*U*, only one survives]). I will use these results to analyze decisionmaking in the European Union in Chapter 11.

If we restrict the above analysis in one dimension, then the core of the bicameral system expands, and it is more difficult to upset the status quo. In particular, points between U1′ (the projection of U1 on the bicameral core) and U2 that could be modified under congruent majorities are now invulnerable under the new decisionmaking rule.

This is the essence of the argument that Keith Krehbiel (1998) presents in his influential book *Pivotal Politics*.[14] At the theoretical level Krehbiel introduces a one-dimensional model and identifies the "pivots" of decisionmaking (the 40th and 60th senators for filibuster and the 34th and 66th senators for veto override)

[14] See also Jones (2001a, 2001b).

and the size of the area included between the two pivots (the "gridlock area").[15] Empirically, Krehbiel identifies changes in the "size of the gridlock area" by using the size of the majorities in each chamber and calculating whether the support for the president increases (in which case the gridlock area shrinks) or decreases (in which case gridlock increases).

Krehbiel uses his model to reevaluate Mayhew's findings. Mayhew identified two major variables accounting for legislative productivity: the first was the first half of a presidential term (Mayhew 1991: 176–77), and the second was the "activist mood," which, in Mayhew's words, is an "elusive" way of capturing the idea that "in lawmaking, nothing emerges more clearly from a postwar analysis than that something special was going on from the early or mid-1960s through the mid-1970s" (Mayhew 1991: 177). By introducing the size of the gridlock area in a series of regressions, Krehbiel (1998: 70–71) is able to demonstrate that the statistical significance of Mayhew's variables disappears even if one considers alternative measures for these variables. The contribution is significant, because as Krehbiel modestly claims, it moves the analysis "a step beyond anecdotal support which is characteristic of much of the presidency theory" (Krehbiel 1998: 75).

Krehbiel's results are completely consistent with the theory presented in this book, but I want to introduce one important point of comparison. It is the dimensionality of the underlying space. For *Pivotal Politics*, the policy space is one-dimensional. In fact, the very title of the book and the definition of pivots implies a single policy dimension. In Krehbiel's analysis, "among the n legislators . . . two players may have unique pivotal status due to supermajoritarian procedures" (Krehbiel 1998: 23).

However, if one adds even a single policy dimension into the underlying model, the pivots multiply. In Figure 6.6A I present the single-dimensional argument, according to which the pivots are always the same no matter where the status quo is and no matter where the alternative proposal is (see also Krehbiel 1998: 23). In Figure 6.6B I add a second dimension, and consider only three voters, A, B, and C. Depending on where the alternative proposal is, the pivotal player may change (proposal PA makes voter A pivotal, proposal PB makes B pivotal, while proposal PC makes C pivotal). One can increase the dimensions and the alternatives to the status quo, and almost any one of a particular group of players will become "pivotal." This fundamental change from one to more than one dimensions is not an unusual feature of voting models or of Krehbiel's model. In fact, speaking about all spatial models Krehbiel (1988) has argued: "Simply expanding the dimensionality of choice space from one to two has profoundly destabilizing consequences." It is a distinctive feature of

[15] For a similar one-dimensional model taking into account committee positions, see Smith (1988). For multidimensional models see Shepsle (1979) and Shepsle and Weingast (1981, 1984, 1987).

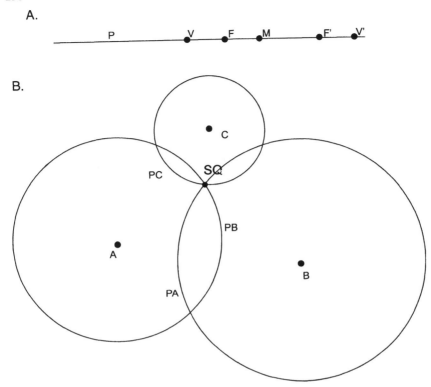

Figure 6.6. (A) Pivotal voters in one dimension (two filibuster (F,F) and two veto (V,V) pivots); (B) almost any voter can be pivotal in multiple dimensions.

veto players theory that its conclusions hold in any number of dimensions and regardless of whether veto players are individual or collective. The price I pay for this ability to generalize is that sometimes I have to restrict proposals in the uncovered set, and my conclusions hold only approximately (Chapter 2).

Is it reasonable to expand the dimensionality of space? Theoretically, the answer is a clear "yes" because we cannot rely on one-dimensional models if their results do not generalize. But even if theoretically this is the case, why not stick with a parsimonious model that works in one dimension? After all, Congress is a bicameral legislature, and, as I have claimed in Section 6.2, the bicameral core, or, in its absence, the line connecting the centers of the yolks of the two chambers, is the dominant dimension of conflict. Why not then report everything to this dimension? Because besides the positions of the different members of the legislature, it is important to know the positions of the president that are simply *assumed* in Krehbiel's model. Indeed, as Krehbiel argues, he assumes that the position of the president "is exterior to the legislative pivots" (Krehbiel 1998: 73), or, more generally, "to shift probabilistically between designated intervals of the policy space" (Krehbiel 1998: n. 27). If the president is not assumed, but his preferences are included, a one-dimensional model is not sufficient, because there is no reason to assume that his position is on this dimension. Braeuninger (2001) demonstrates that when n groups negotiate, the underlying space is of n-1 dimensions, which would mean, in the American case (with three veto players), a two-dimensional analysis. Given that the models in veto players theory hold in any number of dimensions, in the empirical chapters that follow I will undertake both single and multiple dimension estimations (Chapters 7 and 8). What Krehbiel calls "the gridlock area" is nothing but the core of the decisionmaking rule in multiple dimensions. In addition, in Chapter 11 I will examine another case of three institutional veto players (the European Union) and produce multidimensional models of the core of quite complicated procedures.

To summarize my argument, it is true that government in the United States is not just united or divided as several researchers have claimed, but it is also supermajoritarian because significant legislation cannot pass without clearing filibuster obstacles in the Senate, and most of the time the minority party controls the required forty seats. This means that divided government is built into U.S. institutions, not because of the requirement that all three veto players agree on a particular change of the status quo, but because of the filibuster rule that essentially prevents partisan legislation from passing the Senate. Krehbiel's (1998) contribution was to point out the significance of supermajoritarian procedures in order to understand American politics. I use the term "supermajoritarian" instead of "pivotal" because the latter presupposes a single dimension that cannot be taken for granted. His empirical results are an important first step, but they have to be replicated on the basis of multidimensional models.

6.5. Conclusions

Federalism has been studied both in the political science and the economics literature. The expectation was that decentralization would lead to decisions more appropriate for the people that they concerned. The empirical evidence does not corroborate this expectation.

I studied the institutions of federalism, and found out that two particular rules as well as their combination are used most frequently in federal countries: bicameralism and qualified majorities. Each one of these procedures as well as their combination increases the number of veto players, and consequently increases policy stability. The expectation is that federalism will not only increase policy stability but have the structural consequences associated with multiple veto players: independence of bureaucracies and the judiciary, government instability, and so on. It is of course possible that federalism has independent consequences as well. For example, federalism may increase the independence of the judiciary not only because the number of veto players increases but also because judges are asked to adjudicate among different levels of government. I discuss such effects in the corresponding empirical chapters.

While both bicameral and qualified majority institutions increase the number of veto players, there is a significant difference between the two: bicameral institutions work well only if the underlying dimension of conflict is captured by the centers of the yolks of the two chambers; qualified majorities are likely to preserve outcomes located centrally in the collective veto player.

All four chapters in Part II cover phenomena central in comparative political analysis: regime types, interactions between legislative and executive, referendums, federalism, bicameralism, and qualified majorities. I have reexamined the existing knowledge and sometimes ended up in agreement with the literature (democracy and competition), sometimes in conflict (government power is a derivative of agenda-setting power that is not equivalent to government duration), sometimes explaining existing disagreements (role of agenda setting in different types of referendums) and other times introducing a different angle of analysis (institutions of federalism instead of fiscal federalism, government composition instead of party system analysis). Rather than review the findings here, I focus on different mechanisms to increase or decrease the number or the distances of veto players examined in this second part.

In Part I, I considered the number and distances of veto players as given and looked at the implications on policy stability. In Part II, I studied different institutional configurations and their effects on the constellation of veto players of a polity. While it is clear that the policy positions of veto players affect policy stability either because of absorption (some veto players do not affect policy outcomes) or because of the ideological distances of veto players (if they converge policy stability decreases), there is one additional source of variation that I have discussed in each chapter but want to highlight as part of the conclusions. Specific institutional provisions may not always have the same result on veto players. The same institution may add or subtract veto players, or it may keep their number the same but alter their distances, thereby affecting policy stability.

I have made some of these points explicit in Part II. For example, referendums always add a veto player (the "as if" median voter), but depending on their agenda-setting rules they may eliminate existing ones. Indeed, when the same player controls both the question and triggering of a referendum, the existing veto players are eliminated. I have shown that in veto player referendums the position of the status quo ceases to be relevant, and the agenda setter can obtain an outcome in the winset of the "as if" median voter. We also saw that in popular initiative referendums, the different potential agenda-setting groups will concentrate on attracting a majority of the public and ignore the existing veto players.

Similar arguments can be made about bicameralism: the second chamber may or may not have veto powers. For example, the German Bundesrat has veto powers over legislation that has consequences on federalism, but not on other pieces. With respect to qualified majorities, different issues may require different thresholds.

In presidential systems, the president usually has the power to veto legislation, but typically there are provisions for a veto override of the legislature. To the extent that such provisions can be achieved, the veto override conditions reduce policy stability, since they provide a mechanism that the status quo can be changed despite the objections of the president.

But the most complicated (from a veto player perspective) institutional provision is the one of executive decrees. This institution usually subtracts veto players, but it can also add veto players, or leave the number of veto players the same but alter their ideological distances. The archetypal case of executive decrees would be a presidential decree in a presidential system (Carey and Shugart 1998): the president bypasses the other veto players, and makes the final decision in an area of his jurisdiction.

However, there are cases where government decrees add a veto player to the existing ones: in France, for example, the president of the republic is part of the government (in fact, presides over it), so he has to agree to a government decree. With respect to ordinary legislation he has no veto; thus he can be bypassed by the parties in government (assuming different presidential and parliamentary majorities). I discuss this point further in the empirical analysis of Chapter 7.

Finally, government decrees may preserve the number of veto players but alter their distances. For example, the Italian government has often used executive decrees as a way of bypassing parliament (Kreppel 1997). However, as I argued in Chapter 4, the parties' members of government are veto players in a multiparty system. Why is it easier to pass government decrees than parliamentary legislation if the veto players are the same? Kreppel's answer is that the members of the government are ideologically closer to each other than the leadership of the corresponding parties, so policy stability decreases. Proposition 1.4 and Figure 1.6 make the same point in the most general case: if the decisionmakers are closer to each other, the winset of the status quo expands, and policy stability is reduced.

In conclusion, while veto players theory sometimes comes to similar conclusions with existing literature, there are also many disagreements. But most important, there is no direct way of translating existing institutions into the number and distances of veto players. Some institutions have similar effects (federalism increases the number of veto players), while others alter their impact on veto players on the basis of specific institutional provisions (who controls the agenda on referendums, executive decrees). Most important, however, is the fact that the results of veto players analysis depend on the ideological positions of veto players: some of them may be absorbed; even if they are not absorbed, they may converge or diverge, and this will have serious implications for policy stability. Even the importance of agenda setting depends on the positions of veto players and the location of the agenda setter.

I wish to conclude by underlying the consistency of the veto players approach. I have discussed different influential approaches in each chapter: regime types, party systems, ministerial influence, executive dominance, fiscal federalism, pivotal politics, to mention but a few. Each one is based on different assumptions and leads to conclusions relevant to the subject matter for which it was developed. By contrast, veto players is based on the same set of principles developed in Part I, and it is these principles that have led us to all the agreements or disagreements with the literature, as well as all the conditional or qualified statements on institutions.

PART III

POLICY EFFECTS OF VETO PLAYERS

THE BASIC SET OF PROPOSITIONS introduced in Part I use policy stability as the dependent variable and the number and distances among veto players as the independent variables. I have explained why increasing the number of veto players (Proposition 1.1) and the unanimity core of them (Proposition 1.4) leads to higher policy stability. Part III will test these propositions.

There are several problems with empirical tests of these expectations. They stem from the relationship between legislative policies and legislative outcomes. The crux of the problem is that legislators have to design policies, while they have preferences over outcomes. For example, when the legislators of a country pass legislation on a specific issue, they take a series of steps: they define the problem they want to resolve; they define the conditions under which it occurs, or the specific set of conditions that they will address; they define the means by which they will interfere, and the extent to which they will use these means. As a result, a series of policy-related outcomes occurs. In terms of unemployment legislation, for example, some people, but not others, receive unemployment compensation; select individuals receive health care even if they are not employed; a certain number of administrators and medical personnel are used to address these problems; and they cost a certain amount of money out of the budget. All these outcomes are the issues legislators care about and which they had in mind when they were designing the unemployment policy.

However, it is possible that some of these results were not anticipated when the legislation was introduced: the definition of unemployment may have been so inclusive as to permit a series of private citizens to ask for unemployment compensation while they had some kind of employment, or may have provided exactly the same amount of health care coverage so that the number of required doctors increases, or unemployment may have increased for reasons not considered by the legislature. As a result of any of these conditions, the number of administrative or of medical personnel, or the amount of money required, may be different than the preferences of the legislators. In this case the legislators may decide to introduce new legislation amending the policies specified in the past, so that they will approximate the preferred outcomes better.

This may be a more or less accurate description of how policymaking works, but how are we going to introduce in this picture the variable of policy stability we are interested in? Are we going to focus on the act of legislating and see whether new laws differ from the previous ones even if the outcomes do not, or are we going to focus on outcomes regardless of whether they were produced by legislation or by exogenous shocks? Suppose that the legislature changes the definition of unemployment, but because unemployment is so low it makes little difference on the budget. Is this a significant policy change or an insignificant one? Alternatively, suppose that unemployment increases while legislation has remained exactly the same. Is this an indication of policy stability or of policy change?[1]

In the two chapters that follow I use both interpretations and try to focus on each while controlling for the other. In addition, the two chapters present models with a different number of dimensions of the underlying policy space. In Chapter 7 the dependent variable maps well on the Left-Right policy axis, so I estimate a single dimensional model. In Chapter 8 the dependent variable is clearly multidimensional, so the model I discuss uses multiple dimensions.

Chapter 7 deals with working time and working conditions legislation and focuses on significant legislative changes. I will define how I assess such significant pieces of legislation and use an intersubjectively testable measure for this definition. I have taken every possible step to define significant policy changes in a way that will be persuasive, and will certainly not depend on my own measurements. However, no matter how accurate this measure is, it is completely possible that two countries start from and arrive at the same policy outcomes, one by using significant policy changes and the other not. For example, if one country introduces a comprehensive piece of legislation on unemployment compensation, it is likely that any observer would consider this a significant piece of legislation. On the other hand, if the second country introduces several dozen legislative pieces for different social groups (e.g., agricultural workers, public sector, industry) on specific aspects of unemployment benefits (e.g., duration, conditions, amounts, health care), chances are that none of these pieces of legislation will be considered important. Chapter 7 is open to the "outcomes" criticism of policy stability. While I demonstrate that one country produces significant legislation and the other does not, it is possible that there is no difference in the outcomes over a long period of time.

Chapter 8 addresses macroeconomic policies and focuses on outcomes, without addressing the issue of policies directly. The outcomes considered are budget deficits, inflation, and the composition of budget of different countries. There is no way to see directly whether these outcomes were due to direct

---

[1] The distinction I am making here between legislation and outcomes is very similar to the one made in the political economy literature between instruments and outcomes (Alt and Crystal 1985).

government design, or to other government policies (like deterioration of trade because of foreign policy reasons), or to random events (changes in unemployment because of international conditions), or to a high or low sensitivity of the budget to outside factors. I will try to control for some of these possibilities by introducing dummy variables for each country, so that, whatever the policy reason affecting the budget structure, it is controlled for. However, this analysis is not immune to a "policies" objection to policy stability argument. It is possible that these changes in budget outcomes do not reflect changes in budget policies.

The independent variables for both chapters describing the over-time constellation of veto players in different countries can be found at: *http:// www.polisci.ucla.edu/tsebelis/.* The findings that these two chapters produce are congruent. Policy stability increases with the number of veto players, or, more precisely, as the range of a government coalition (the size of the unanimity core in a single dimension, and some different but equivalent measure in multiple dimensions) increases. In addition, when one tests for ideological distance alone, not only is the coefficient negative, but the error terms are heteroskedastic (exactly as Figure 1.7 indicates). In fact, I used a special estimation procedure (multiplicative heteroskedastic regression) to estimate both effects simultaneously. When multiple independent variables are introduced, the additional results are that policy stability decreases as the alternation (ideological distance) of each coalition to its predecessor increases. Finally, I test whether different types of governments (minimum-winning coalitions, minority, and oversized) affect policy stability, and I find that while minority governments and oversized coalitions have higher and lower policy stability, respectively, than minimum-winning coalitions, these results are small and statistically insignificant. Thus the argument made in this section is that policy stability, whether measured in outcomes or in policies, depends on veto players, as Part I specified.

7

Legislation

THE THEORY I PRESENT in this book predicts that policy stability (defined as the impossibility of significant change of the status quo) will be the result of many veto players, particularly if they have significant ideological differences among them. This chapter aims at making a direct and crossnational test of production of significant laws as a function of the number and ideological distances of veto players. I test these predictions using a new dataset of "significant laws" on issues of "working time and working conditions."[1]

Working time and working conditions is a legislative dimension highly correlated with the Left-Right dimension that predominates party systems across Europe. Consequently, we can find the ideological positions of different parties on the Left-Right dimension and use them as proxies of the ideological positions of parties with respect to working time and working conditions. According to this approach, given that all parties are located along the same dimension, one can identify the two most extreme parties of a coalition, and all the others will be "absorbed" since they are located inside the core of the most extreme ones (Proposition 1.2). The result of this analysis is that the ideological distance of the two most extreme parties in a government coalition, the *range* of this coalition, will be our independent variable. The number of significant laws will be a declining function of range. In addition, the number of significant laws will be an increasing function of the distance between the current government and the previous one, henceforth *alternation*. The reason is because each government will try to modify the policies that it disagrees with, and the larger the distance between the two governments, the larger the distance between the current veto players and the status quo is likely to be. Also, the longer a government stays in power, the more likely it is to produce significant legislation in the area under consideration (Tsebelis 1995a: 105). Finally, as I explained in Figure 1.7, the variance of the number of significant laws will be higher when the range of a coalition is small and lower when the range is large.

The chapter is organized into three sections. The first presents the dataset that combines information about significant laws in different West European countries with data about government coalitions (composition of governments and ideological positions of parties on a left-right scale). In this part, I explain

---

[1] I thank Herbert Doering for providing me with this dataset.

how the different variables used in this study are generated. The second part presents the results with governments being the unit of analysis and shows that the expectations of the model are corroborated. The third part uses countries as the unit of analysis and points out the inverse relationship between significant legislation and overall pieces of legislation that are produced in a country.

7.1. The Data

In order to test whether the number and ideological distance of veto players affects the production of significant laws, I created a dataset by merging data on significant legislation (laws and decrees) on "working time and working conditions" in sixteen countries of Western Europe for the period 1981–91, with data on coalition governments for the same countries and the same period.[2] In this section, I explain what was included in the original datasets as well as the additional manipulations for the construction of specific variables.

7.1.1. Significant Legislation

Doering and his team identified the number of significant laws for all Western European countries in the area of labor legislation (legislation on "working time and working conditions") for the period 1981–91. For that purpose they used the computerized database NATLEX that has been compiled by the International Labor Organization (ILO), located in Geneva. While this database was created in the early 1970s, the dataset only became complete since the beginning of the 1980s. Consequently, the beginning of the dataset that I analyze is January 1, 1981. This dataset has been indexed by subject matter, so that one can identify all laws put to a vote and all decrees issued on any specific topic in all European countries. While this database is of excellent use in identifying any subject in labor legislation and has been used by Doering and his team to generate reliable numbers of pieces of legislation in different areas, it provides no indication of "significant" legislation, the dependent variable for a test of the veto players theory.

The next step would have been to identify some proxy for importance. Such a proxy should not be size or length of legislation because a law can be written to enumerate areas of applicability (in which case length is correlated with significance) or areas of exception (in which case length is negatively correlated with significance). The alternative proxies that come to mind are the size

---

[2] I received the data on significant legislation from Herbert Doering, and the data on government coalitions from Paul Warwick.

of the budget needed for implementation, or the number of people affected by its enactment. Both criteria would indicate that a bill on euthanasia or on same-sex marriage would not be significant. This short discussion indicates that criteria for selection of "significant" laws have an important ingredient of subjectivity that can undermine the results of any analysis for a reader who does not share the same criteria for selection.

In the face of this problem, Doering had the brilliant idea of using the *Encyclopedia of Labor Law* to generate the variable "significant laws." The encyclopedia, edited by Roger Blanpain, was written for labor lawyers from one European country who wanted to practice law in another. According to the introduction, "*National Legislation* intends to make available to the subscribers and users of the Encyclopedia pertinent provisions of the *most important acts* of Parliament, governmental *decrees*, national, and interindustry wide major *collective agreements*, or other legal sources, where they cover a country as a whole." (Blanpain, Suppl. 194, July 1997: subsection 5; emphasis in the original). Each country is covered by a 150- to 250-page monograph authored by a law professor or a judge explaining to readers the significant legislation in the area. The monographs have a common pattern that facilitates subject matter identification. Norway and Iceland are not covered by the encyclopedia. Laws that were in the intersection of both sources (NATLEX and the *Encyclopedia*) are considered "significant," while laws existing only in the NATLEX database are considered nonsignificant.

Blanpain's *Encyclopedia* provided a validation test for the NATLEX database, since for the 1981–91 period, all the laws mentioned in Blanpain were included in NATLEX. This was not true for the period before 1981, which, in turn, validates the cutoff point for the study.[3] The dates of promulgation of the significant laws of each country were compared with the dates that governments were in power, so that laws were attributed to the governments that sponsored them.

7.1.2. Governments

The dataset on governments included the dates of beginning and end of governments in the sixteen countries of the study (Austria, Belgium, Denmark, Finland, France, Germany, Greece, Ireland, Italy, Luxembourg, Netherlands, Portugal, Spain, Sweden, Switzerland,[4] and the United Kingdom). The dates of

[3] These choices are described in more detail, along with legal questions that arise when a law is inadequately or insufficiently described, in Blanpain's encyclopedia, in an essay co-authored by Georgios Trantas. Trantas, a lawyer, followed Doering's idea and actually identified the intersection of Blanpain and NATLEX (Scholtz and Trantas 1995).

[4] This chapter follows closely Tsebelis (1999). One of the important differences is that I have now included Switzerland. The addition is important because Switzerland is the only one of these

the beginning and end of the study (January 1, 1981, to December 31, 1991) were considered the dates of the beginning or end of the government in office at that date.[5] On the basis of these dates of beginning and end of different governments, I calculated the duration in years of each one of them.

The dataset on governments used conventional methods to account for beginning and end of governments. Warwick (1994: 27) is explicit about what constitutes beginning: "A government typically begins when it is appointed by a head of state." As for ending, he adopts the criteria proposed by Browne, Gleiber, and Mashoba (1984:7).[6] However, the variable that matters for the veto players theory is the partisan composition of government. Therefore, two successive governments with identical composition should be counted as a single government, even if they are separated by an election, which changes the size of the different parties in parliament.[7] The reason is that the variable that enters into a veto players analysis is not the relative strength of different parties in government or parliament, but the fact that each of them needs to agree in order for legislation to pass.

In order to operationalize the above argument, I created a dataset of "merged" governments, in which successive governments with the same composition were considered a single government regardless of whether they were separated by a resignation and/or an election. Obviously, merging affects the values of duration and the number of laws produced by a government. To account for this change, I added the number of laws produced by different governments to be merged and credited the resulting government with this total number of laws. Duration was recalculated as the sum of the duration of consecutive governments (this excludes possible caretaker governments and periods when a resigned government waits to be replaced that would have been included if I recalculated on the basis of the new beginning and ending dates). As a result of merging, the number of cases in the dataset decreased to fifty-nine.[8]

---

countries that is not a parliamentary system, and consequently its inclusion with no substantive difference in results makes the veto players argument more credible.

[5] As a result, the governments of each country at the beginning and end of the period have been truncated (they lasted longer than indicated, and may have produced legislation outside the period of this study).

[6] According to Browne, Gleiber, and Mashoba (1984): "A government is considered terminated whenever: (1) parliamentary elections are held, (2) the head of government changes, (3) the party composition of the government changes, or (4) the government tenders its resignation, which is accepted by the head of state" (Warwick 1994: 28). On this fourth point Warwick presents a variation and counts as termination even resignations that are not subsequently accepted by the head of state.

[7] For a similar argument concerning Italian governments that succeed each other while the party (and sometimes the person) composition is the same, see Di Palma (1977: 31).

[8] It would have been fifty-eight, but I count the French government twice during the cohabitation period of 1986–88: I consider only the two participating parties as veto players with respect to legislation, but I add the president when I consider a government decree that they issued. This

The difference between the merged government dataset used in this study and the traditional method of counting governments becomes clear in the following two cases. First, in Greece, the Socialist government (PASOK) came into power in 1981 and, according to the dataset, produced four significant laws in the area of "working time and working conditions." In 1985, the Socialists were reelected and the new government produced two additional significant laws. According to the merged government dataset, the two PASOK governments are counted as one that did not complete its legislative program in the first period and continued changing the legislative framework of the rightwing governments of 1974–81 during its second term.

The second example is drawn from France. After François Mitterrand was elected president of the republic in 1981, he appointed Pierre Mauroy as the prime minister of a coalition government that included the Socialists and the Communists. That government produced four significant laws in the area under study. In 1983, a second Mauroy government with the same party composition replaced the existing Mauroy government. This second government stayed in power for one year, until the Communists dropped out of the coalition because of the austerity policies that Mitterrand was about to impose in order to remain in the European monetary system. The second Mauroy government did not produce any new laws on "working time and working conditions." In my dataset, the two governments count as one: in a three-year period the Socialist-Communist coalition produced four significant laws. Implicit in my account is that the second Mauroy government did not produce any laws because the first had completed its work in this area.[9]

7.1.3. Ideology

The government dataset included also the composition of different governments (the parties participating in government coalitions to which I added the positions of the president of Portugal and France and the Bundesrat in Germany and their "ideological scores" on the basis of three indices. The first was from Warwick's (1994) *Government Survival in Western European Parliamentary Democracies* (Warwick expanded the dataset collected by Browne, Gleiber, and Mashoba [1984], who had expanded the dataset collected by Dodd 1976). This index was generated from forty different measures that were developed from experts, party manifestos, and survey sources. Of the governments

---

produces a conservative estimate because I omit all the times that a cohabitation government produced no decrees as a result of its ideological divisions.

[9] All the calculations in this article were replicated with the traditional way of counting governments and led to the same qualitative results.

included in this dataset, the index ranged from a low of −6 (left) to a high of 5 (right).

The second index was provided by Castles and Mair (1984) in "Left-Right Political Scales: Some 'Expert' Judgments." These ideological scores were generated from a questionnaire survey of more than 115 political scientists from Western Europe and the United States (Castles and Mair 1984: 75). The questionnaire asked each respondent to place all the parties holding seats in his/her national legislature on the left-right political spectrum ranging from zero (ultra-left) to 10 (ultra-right), with 2.5 representing the moderate left, 5 the center, and 7.5 the moderate right. Castles and Mair present the results from those countries that had at least three respondents. The ideological score reported for each party was the average of available responses. Given the ten-point scale, the potential range of responses was (0, 10). Of the parties analyzed here, however, the low score was 1.4, received by the Communist Party of France, and the high was 8.2, received by the Gaullist Party.

The third index was drawn from Laver and Hunt's (1992) first dimension variable, "increase services vs. cut taxes." Respondents were professional political scientists (Laver and Hunt 1992: 38–41, 122). Each respondent was asked to locate the policy positions of both the party leaders and voters for each party in his/her country on the left-right spectrum. In addition to the parties that won seats in the most recent election, respondents were asked to evaluate every party that won at least 1 percent of the national vote, as well as any significant regional parties. The scale adopted by Laver and Hunt was a twenty-point scale (to accommodate for the fact that the countries included in their study contained up to fourteen parties to be placed on the scale). For the first dimension—taxes versus public services—respondents assigned each party a score ranging from 1 ("promote raising taxes to increase public services") to 20 ("promote cutting public services to cut taxes"). Among the cases included in the dataset, the Laver-Hunt (first dimension) variable ranged from a low of 2.1 to a high of 17.4.

Switzerland was not included in any of the datasets. It has had a government including the four major parties (Socialist, Liberal, Christian Democrat, and Farmers Party) throughout the period under study. I used the data generated for a similar government in Finland (four veto players including the Social Democratic Party, the Rural and Agrarian parties, and the People's Party) for the missing data on Switzerland. On the basis of Sani and Sartori's (1983) data reported in Laver and Schofield (1990: 255, 265), the Swiss government had a range of 3.4 (= 7.1 − 4.7) in their scale), while the Finnish range was greater[10] than 2.4 (= 6.3 − 3.9).

---

[10] Sani and Sartori do not report the position of all parties included in the Finnish government, so I could not make the exact calculation.

Laver and Hunt included the remaining fifteen countries in their study. Warwick did not code the parties of the French Fifth Republic, and Greece. In addition, some government parties in Ireland, Italy, Spain, and Sweden were not scored. Castles and Mair did not include Luxembourg, Portugal, and Greece.

On the basis of each of these measures of ideology, I was able to construct new variables representing the "range" of each government according to the index, as well as the "alternation" from one government to the next. The range variable was created by taking the absolute value of the distance between the most extreme parties of a coalition. These two parties were usually (but not always) the same for different indices. However, the correlations among the range variables calculated on the basis of the cases covered by all three indices were quite high.[11]

The alternation variable was calculated by finding the mid-range position of each government, and taking the difference between two successive governments.[12] Because this measure was calculated using the previous government, I needed information on the government preceding the one that was in power in 1981. Again, the three different indices produced highly correlated values of alternation for the cases covered by all three indices.[13]

7.1.4. The New "Range" and "Alternation" Variables

These three range and alternation variables covered different countries, and were calculated on the basis of different questions that were relevant to the left-right division. In order to preserve the size of my dataset, as well as use all the available information, I constructed new measures of range and alternation, based on the values of *all* available indices. To accomplish this, I standardized each one of the indices and then took the average of the standardized scores that were available for each case government. For standardization, I used only the values of the variables for the countries covered by all three indices. This procedure was run separately on all three range and alternation variables, resulting in three standardized range and three standardized alternation variables. The average range and alternation variables used all the available information in the following way: in the case that all three indices existed, the average was calculated on the basis of all three; for countries with two indices, only the

---

[11] The correlations between any two of these indices were above .8.

[12] The formula I used was the following: (maxgovt1 + mingovt1) − (maxgovt2 + mingovt2), where max- and min-govt1 are the ideological scores of the preceding government, and max- and min-govt2 are the ideological scores of the "current" government.

[13] The correlations between any two of these indices were also above .8.

average was calculated on the basis of the two standardized indices; in the cases covered by one single analyst (Greece), I used that one standardized score. In the regressions I used the absolute value of alternation as calculated above, because it makes no difference whether a left-wing government is replaced by a right-wing government, or vice versa.

7.2. Veto Players and Significant Legislation

In this section, I test all the predictions made in the introduction of this chapter. I test whether range negatively affects the number of significant laws while at the same time producing a heteroskedastic relation. I construct the variable *RANGE* (average normalized ideological distance of extreme partners of a government coalition, corrected for institutional rules like the president of Portugal, or the Bundesrat in Germany). I test whether this relationship is both negative and heteroskedastic (see Figure 1.7). I test whether alternation and government duration positively affect the number of significant laws by introducing a series of additional variables: *ALTERNATION* (absolute value of the average normalized difference between two successive governments), *DURATION* (years of a government in office), as well as others that turn out not to be significant (as predicted).

7.2.1. Testing for the Negative Effect of Range and for Heteroskedasticity

The expected relationship between *RANGE* and *LAWS* is that the first is a necessary but not sufficient condition for the second: a large range will prevent significant legislation, but a small range will not guarantee the existence of significant legislation. As noted in Chapter 1, the implication of this analysis is that *RANGE* and *LAWS* will be negatively correlated, *and* the squared (or the absolute value of) residuals of the estimated relationship will also be negatively correlated with *RANGE*. Heteroskedasticity has a negative impact on the significance of statistical coefficients (since it generates high standard errors). However, the existence of predicted heteroskedasticity should be in favor of my theory, not against it. In other words, the appropriate test for a theory predicting a sufficient but not necessary condition is a combination of a test of means (regression) with low statistical significance *and* a test of the variance (residuals) for heteroskedasticity. If both predictions turn out to be corroborated (as they are), then the confidence in the theory that predicted both relationships ought to be significantly higher than the p-value of any one coefficient.

TABLE 7.1
Multiplicative Heteroskedastic Regression Model of Significant Legislation

	Model 1 (includes RANGE)	Model 2 (excludes RANGE)
Dependent Variable: Number of Significant Laws		
Constant	1.1935****	1.2711****
	(.2017)	(.2246)
RANGE	−.4837****	
	(.0133)	
Dependent Variable: The Squared Error Term of Number of Significant Laws		
Constant	0.7110****	1.0910****
	(.1852)	(.1841)
RANGE	−0.7471****	
	(.1919)	
N	59	59
Prob > χ^2	0.000	0.000
Likelihood-ratio test:	$\chi_1^2 = 17.85$	Prob > $\chi_1^2 = 0.0001$

Standard errors in parentheses.
* $p < 0.1$ level
** $p < 0.05$ level
*** $p < 0.01$
**** $p < 0.001$
All tests are one-tailed.

Table 7.1 tests for these two expectations with a multiplicative heteroskedastic regression model.[14] The following two equations are tested simultaneously by maximum likelihood estimation:

Equation 1: $LAWS = a - b\ RANGE + \varepsilon$

Equation 2: $\varepsilon^2 \exp(p - q\ RANGE)$

As Table 7.1 indicates, both the coefficients of RANGE for equations 1 and 2 are highly significant. However, the null hypothesis is that both coefficients are 0. For this reason I estimate a second model omitting RANGE as an explan-

---

[14] In a previous version (Tsebelis 1999) I estimated three independent models: one the average number of significant laws, one estimating the error term, and one "correcting" for heteroskedasticity. The development of multiplicative heteroskedastic regression models permits simultaneous testing.

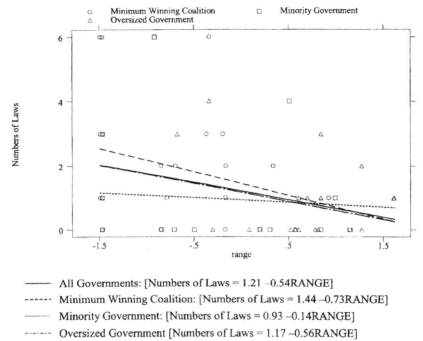

Figure 7.1. Number of important laws by ideological range of coalition.

——— All Governments: [Numbers of Laws = 1.21 –0.54RANGE]
------ Minimum Winning Coalition: [Numbers of Laws = 1.44 –0.73RANGE]
·········· Minority Government: [Numbers of Laws = 0.93 –0.14RANGE]
----·-- Oversized Government [Numbers of Laws = 1.17 –0.56RANGE]

atory variable from both equations and perform a likelihood ratio test that provides a chi^2 = 17.85, which gives a p-value of .0001.

More visual evidence is provided by Figures 7.1 and 7.2. Figure 7.1 presents the relationship between *LAWS* and *RANGE*. In this figure I have separated minimum-winning coalition governments (indicated by o in the figure) from minority governments (□ in the figure) and from oversized coalitions Δ in the figure). The reason for this distinction was explained in Chapter 4. The political logic in all these cases indicates that the parties in government are veto players. However, the arithmetic constraints are different between minimum-winning coalitions, where the support of all parties is arithmetically necessary, minority governments, where more votes are necessary, and oversized coalitions, where all the votes are not necessary. My expectation (in Chapter 4) was that the veto player argument will hold in an approximate way in the case of minority and oversized governments. The data overall confirm my expectations. I present four bivariate regression lines. The top line summarizes the relationship between laws and range occurring in minimum-winning coalitions. The relation-

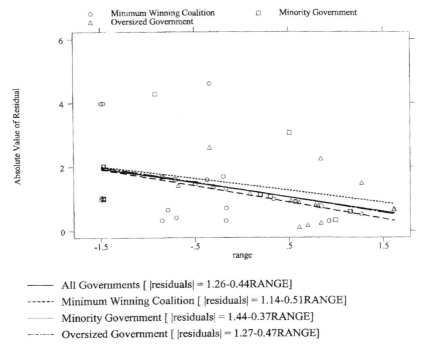

- All Governments [|residuals| = 1.26-0.44RANGE]
- Minimum Winning Coalition [|residuals| = 1.14-0.51RANGE]
- Minority Government [|residuals| = 1.44-0.37RANGE]
- Oversized Government [|residuals| = 1.27-0.47RANGE]

Figure 7.2. Residuals (absolute value) of important laws by ideological range of coalition.

ship is very strong and significant. The two intermediate lines summarize the overall relationship and the oversized coalitions. Both relationships are statistically significant. The last line represents minority governments and has a negative but very weak and not statistically significant slope. This result indicates that knowing the exact conditions of each of these minority governments, as Strom (2000) argues (see Chapter 3), would be preferable.[15] Comparison of Figure 7.1 with Figure 1.7 (used in Chapter 1 to indicate what to expect from empirical results) indicates the high degree of fit between theory and data (which also appeared in the regressions of Table 7.1).

Figure 7.2 gives a graphic representation of the absolute value of the residuals of an OLS regression of significant *LAWS* on *RANGE*. I selected the absolute value for this figure because the graphic of squared residuals is visually

---

[15] For example, it would be interesting to know whether support for government proposals was sought most of the time among the same parties, in which case the number of veto players increases.

misleading (it eliminates small residuals and exacerbates large ones). Again, I divided governments into minimum-winning coalitions, minority governments, and oversized coalitions, but this time there is no difference between the regression lines representing the whole dataset and each one of the two parts. We can see that the slope is negative and very significant, exactly as expected.

7.2.2. Test for Alternation and Government Duration

The models in this section are multivariate and introduce a series of control variables. According to my analysis, two additional control variables (*DURATION* and *ALTERNATION*) are expected to have positive signs. *ALTERNATION* (the difference between the midpoints of the current from the previous government) is one way to introduce a proxy for the status quo, in case legislation was introduced by the previous government. Of course, there is no guarantee that this was actually the case (see above).

Model 1 in Table 7.2 introduces both control variables in their linear form. Model 2 introduces the idea of a declining rate of production of significant laws by using the natural logarithm of duration as an independent variable. This model corroborates all the expectations generated by the veto players theory. This is why I subject it to three additional tests. The first test is to examine whether the findings hold for different subsets of the data. Models 2A, 2B, and 2C separate the different governments into minimum-winning coalitions (twenty-three cases), minority governments (fifteen cases), and oversized coalition (twenty-one cases), and retest the model for each of these categories. The second test is to introduce a series of control variables in order to test for spuriousness of the results. Model 3 introduces three plausible control variables: *AGENDA CONTROL, CORPORATISM*, and *LEFT IDEOLOGY* of the government. The existing literatures suggest these as alternative explanations for the findings. The last test is to rerun the model both with and without control variables as a negative binomial regression (given the fact that my dependent variable is a "count," the OLS coefficients may be biased).

As Table 7.2 shows, all the hypothesized relationships come out with the correct sign (negative for range, and positive for alternation and duration). On the basis of Model 2, one can say that the production of significant laws is affected negatively by the range of government, positively by the difference between current and previous governments (alternation), and that duration increases the number of laws but at a declining rate.

Models 2A, 2B, and 2C replicate the analysis for minimum-winning coalitions, minority governments, and oversized governments, respectively. All the

TABLE 7.2
Multivariate Models of Significant Legislation (linear and negative binomial)

Variable	Model 1	Model 2	Negative Binomial M2	Model 2A MWC[1]	Model 2B Minority	Model 2C Oversized	Model 3	Negative Binomial M3
Constant	−0.18 (0.26)	0.25 (0.24)	−0.89**** (0.26)	−0.27 (0.47)	0.29 (0.85)	0.81*** (0.36)	0.25 (0.25)	−0.9**** (0.27)
Range	−0.27* (0.17)	−0.33** (0.18)	−0.20* (0.15)	−0.63** (0.33)	−0.06 (0.50)	−0.57* (0.36)	−0.35** (0.19)	−0.24* (0.17)
Abs (Altern)	0.54*** (0.23)	0.65**** (0.23)	0.23* (0.16)	0.85*** (0.33)	0.73 (0.83)	−0.08 (0.42)	0.65*** (0.24)	0.25* (0.18)
Duration	0.35**** (0.06)							
Ln(Duration)		0.84**** (0.16)	0.83**** (0.16)	0.91*** (0.27)	0.73* (0.45)	0.84*** (0.23)	0.85**** (0.17)	0.83**** (0.17)
Agenda							−0.19 (0.80)	−0.09 (0.69)
Corporatism							0.01 (0.27)	0.07 (0.24)
Left							−0.01 (0.16)	0.01 (0.11)
N	59	59	59	23	15	21	59	59
R^2	0.525	0.504		0.635	0.299	0.493	0.506	
Adjusted R^2	0.499	0.477		0.577	0.108	0.404	0.449	
Pseudo R^2			0.205					0.207

[1] MWC: minimum-winning coalition
Standard errors in parentheses.
* $p < 0.05$.
** $p < 0.05$.
*** $p < 0.01$.
**** $p < 0.001$.
All tests are one-tailed.

signs of the coefficients are as hypothesized, but conventional levels of statistical significance are lost, except for the case of minimum-winning coalitions.[16]

Model 3 introduces three different control variables. The first of them is *AGENDA CONTROL*. Doering (1995b) has identified the importance of government agenda setting for both the quantity and quality of legislation pro-

[16] I thank an anonymous referee for the suggestion of subdividing the dataset. The division applied the standard criteria in most countries. However, in Germany I had to take into account the

duced in a country. In a nutshell, his argument is that government control of the agenda increases the number of important bills and reduces legislative inflation (few small bills). Doering defined agenda control in two different ways: qualitatively and quantitatively.[17] He hypothesized a positive relationship between significant laws and agenda control. However, Doering was discussing countries as units of analysis, and his measures (which I use) refer to countries. Consequently, the variance of significant legislation within each country cannot possibly be captured by Doering's variables. I will discuss his analysis more in detail in the next section.

CORPORATISM was the second variable introduced for control purposes. I introduced CORPORATISM both as a trichotomous variable (with Belgium, Germany, Luxembourg, and Switzerland as ambiguous cases) and as a dichotomous one (with the above countries considered corporatist). Like AGENDA CONTROL, it is considered constant by country. In this respect, I follow most of the literature on corporatism, despite the fact that contemporary research finds significant fluctuations in the variables that comprise the concept over time (Golden, Wallerstein, and Lange 1999).

In corporatist countries, the argument goes, peak associations of employers and unions negotiate the subjects covered by this article; and only if they do not agree does parliament step in and legislate or the government issues decrees. Because of this, corporatist countries (where government ranges are generally high) presumably produce less significant labor legislation. There are two problems with this argument. First, in corporatist countries legislation is produced whether the social partners agree or not. If they agree, the parliament or the government issues legislation or decrees confirming the agreement. If they disagree, the legislative institutions of the country decide on the disagreement. For example, at the end of the 1980s the problem in both Norway and Sweden was the need to cut wages to prevent unemployment from rising. In Norway, the social partners (unions and employers) agreed to a wage freeze and asked the social democratic minority government to put it into legislation so that it would be universally binding. The legislation was passed by parliament, while the independent unions (i.e., those not affiliated with the main confederation) complained that they were being victimized, wages had declined, and unemployment did not grow very much. In Sweden, at the same time, the social partners failed to agree to control wages, so the social demo-

---

Bundesrat if controlled by the opposition, in Portugal the president if his party was not included in the government, and in one case of a government decree in France I took into account the president of the republic. In all these cases the standard status of the government was altered to take into account the veto players theory: for example, in Germany a minimum-winning coalition government was coded as oversized if the support of an opposition-controlled Bundesrat was required.

[17] The qualitative measure of agenda control is the first of the indicators defined by Doering (see discussion in Chapter 3). The quantitative measure comes from my calculations in the same chapter and can be found in Table 4.1. In my analyses I used both measures with similar results.

cratic minority government introduced legislation to freeze wages. In the Swedish case, all the unions protested, the proposal was defeated, the government fell, wages continued to rise rapidly, and unemployment went much higher than in Norway. Second, if the argument were correct, one would expect less *overall* labor legislation in corporatist countries, not just less *significant* legislation. However, corporatist countries have more overall legislation in the area of working time and working conditions.

The third variable was the *ideology* of each government. Since the dependent variable is labor legislation, one may assume that left-wing governments produce more of it. In my view, this interpretation ignores the possibility of right-wing governments repealing labor laws, or undoing what left-wing governments have done. *LEFT IDEOLOGY* was measured exactly the same way as *RANGE* and *ALTERNATION*, so it varies by government and the empirical results will be conclusive.

As Model 3 indicates, none of the three control variables above has any impact on the results of Model 2. The additional three variables come out very close to zero and are completely insignificant. In addition, there is no increase in the R^2 of the model, and the adjusted R^2 shrinks. It is safe to say that statistically these variables do not explain anything (although conceptually one has to refer back to the discussion in the previous paragraphs to understand why it is so).

In order to make sure that these results are not generated because of peculiarities in any one country, I examined the points of highest leverage (the four cases—three points, but one of them is double—in the upper left quarter of Figure 7.1) in order to make sure that they do not reflect unusual situations. These four points represent governments of Belgium, Sweden, Greece, and the United Kingdom. In the case of the first two countries, the governments produced an extraordinary amount of laws because their range was unusually small. In the case of the second two countries, the rule was single party governments, and two of them (both comprised of two or more actual governments) produced a high number of significant laws. Even without these cases, the negative relationship between range and significant laws is preserved, although statistical significance is lost.

Finally, the negative binomial regression models do not alter in any way the conclusions of the previous models. Given that the interpretation of linear coefficients is easier and more intuitive, and given that additional control variables do not improve upon it, one should draw conclusions from Model 2. I caution the reader that the numbers will appear "small" because I am dealing with a single area of legislation. One would have to aggregate across different areas to find the overall effect.[18]

---

[18] In this aggregation, one would have to replicate the logic of this analysis, not extrapolate mechanically the results. For example, the positions of government parties on environmental issues should be considered in order to predict environmental legislation, not the left-right scale

Given that the coefficient of the natural logarithm of duration is positive, we can say that the effect of duration on government legislation is twofold. On the one hand, duration has a positive effect on legislation; on the other, the rate of law production declines with duration.

Let us examine the policy significance of these findings. The empirical findings taken together indicate that large range coalitions are unlikely to produce significant legislation, while small range coalitions and single-party governments may or may not produce such laws and decrees. In other words, policy stability is the characteristic of the first, while the *possibility* of significant policy change is the characteristic of the second. So, the findings of this section are that, depending on government composition (or on institutional structures that consistently produce single or multiple veto players), one can get either policy stability or the potential for policy change, but not both.[19]

7.3. Veto Players and Incremental Legislation

Having established the relationship between veto players, range, and significant legislation (lack of policy stability), we now turn to the incremental (non-significant) legislation and the total number of laws. My expectation has been that "ceteris paribus, significant and non-significant laws should vary inversely, because of time constraints. The ceteris paribus clause assumes that the parliament has limited time and uses it to pass legislation (either significant or trivial). If there are other uses of time like questions to ministers, general debates, etc., or if the time of meetings is itself variable, controls must be introduced for these factors" (Tsebelis 1995b: 104). In this section, the unit of analysis becomes the country instead of the government, because data at the government level are not available.

We have already discussed Doering's analysis of government agenda setting in parliamentary democracies in Chapter 4. Doering (1995b) has established the importance of government agenda setting for both the quantity and quality of legislation produced in a country. In a nutshell, his argument is that govern-

---

used here. It is therefore perfectly reasonable to expect that a government composed of parties close to each other on the left-right scale and that produces many significant laws on labor may produce few significant environmental laws if the veto players are far away from each other in the environmental policy dimension. Alternatively, one would have to perform a multidimensional analysis (Chapter 8).

[19] Unless a single-party government finds a technology to commit credibly: by appointing an independent agency and assigning jurisdiction, or by claiming that the status quo is its own ideal point. I am not going to discuss commitment technologies, but the bottom line is that multiparty governments have difficulty changing the status quo, while single-party governments do not (see discussion on taxation in Chapter 8).

ment control of the agenda increases the number of important bills and reduces legislative inflation (few small bills).

Doering (1995c) used actual legislative data to test his insights. The tests not only corroborated the intuition that government agenda control reduces legislative inflation, but they also eliminated other plausible explanations (including a country's population size, electoral barriers for party entry, number of parties in parliament, and additional legislation at the sub-national level) along the way. From a different perspective, then, Doering has come to the same conclusions as the veto players theory: as the number of significant laws increases, legislative inflation goes down; but for him, it is government control of the legislative agenda that connects the two.

In order to revisit Doering's findings I will use the composite measure of government control of the legislative agenda that I created in Chapter 4 out of Doering's seven indicators (see Table 4.1). However, everything I say holds also if one uses Doering's first indicator of government agenda control, or his quantitative index.

Table 7.3 introduces a series of variables for each country: the number of significant laws and decrees (the sum of such legislative instruments for the whole period under examination), the average number of laws per country (from Table 18.1 of Doering 1995a), an average number of veto players per country, a qualitative measure of veto players, as well as my index of government control calculated on the basis of Doering's seven indicators.

Some explanation of these data is necessary. For the number of laws per country variable, Sweden has two numbers: one taken from Table 18.1 of Doering 1995c, while the other is the average number of new laws, provided by Ingvar Mattson of the Department of Political Science of Lund University (Doering 1995c: 596). Apparently in Sweden they count each amendment as a separate law. Therefore the number in Doering's table, as he discusses, although technically correct, is inflated by comparative standards. In terms of veto players, I have used two different variables. One provides the average number of veto players for the period I examine. The other is a qualitative measure of veto players established the following way: countries with single-party governments receive a score of 1, countries with a mixture of one or two parties in government receive a score of 2, and countries with more than two parties in government receive a score of 3. These scores reflect the situation prevailing in these countries for a substantially longer period than the ten years we have been studying so far. The only country requiring additional explanation is Germany. The number 3 reflects the fact that, while the government coalitions since the beginning of the 1950s involve only two parties, the Bundesrat has been controlled by an opposing majority for significant periods of time.

Table 7.4 presents the correlation coefficients of the variables included in Table 7.3. The three parts depend on whether Sweden is included with 375 annual laws (Table 7.4, part A), with 56 such laws (Table 7.4, part B), or

TABLE 7.3
Number of Laws, Important Laws, Veto Players, and Government Control of
Legislative Agenda

Country	Important Laws (work time)	Laws/Year	Veto Players (qual)	Veto Players (numer)	Agenda Control (qual)	Agenda Control (numer)
Austria	3	121	2	1.79	−4	−0.044
Belgium	7	49	3	4.29	−4	−0.170
Denmark	5	165	3	3.57	−5	−0.106
Finland	4	343	3	3.89	−5	−0.148
France	8	94	2	1.57	−2	0.333
Germany	2	83	3	2.19	−4	−0.126
Greece	10	88	1	1	−2	0.280
Ireland	2	35	2	1.78	−1	0.519
Italy	1	264	3	4.70	−6	−0.219
Luxembourg	6	66	2	2	−3	−0.053
Netherlands	1	134	3	2.13	−7	−0.527
Portugal	5	69	2	2.34	−3	0.147
Spain	3	56	1	1	−4	0.221
Sweden	9	375 (56 new)	2	1.82	−5	−0.427
Switzerland	3	32	3	4	−3	−0.135
United Kingdom	6	62	1	1	−1	0.690

Number of laws and qualitative agenda control (with opposite sign) from Doering (1995).

excluded from the data set altogether (Table 7.4, part C). The reader can verify that the correlation between all laws and significant laws is negative in two of the three parts of the table, most notably the one that excludes Sweden. Thus in two out of the three parts, the expectation of negative correlation between significant and overall legislation is corroborated.

More interesting, however, are the relationships between veto players and the number of laws, as well as the relationship between veto players and agenda control by the government. Veto players correlated positively with the number of all laws, and negatively with the number of significant laws in all three parts

TABLE 7.4

Correlations among Veto Players, Agenda Setting, and Legislation

A. Sweden included with 375 bills/year

	Important Laws	Laws/Year	Veto Players (qual.)	Veto Players (ave.)	Agenda Control (qual)	Agenda Control (Table 4.1)
Important Laws	1.000					
Laws/Year	0.084	1.000				
Veto Players (Qual.)	−0.454	0.285	1.000			
Veto Players (Ave.)	−0.307	0.305	0.836	1.000		
Agenda Control (Qual.)	0.386	−0.594	−0.620	−0.490	1.000	
Agenda Control (Table 4.1)	0.213	−0.529	−0.704	−0.528	0.889	1.000

B. Sweden included with 56 bills/year

	Important Laws	Laws/Year	Veto Players (qual.)	Veto Players (ave.)	Agenda Control (qual)	Agenda Control (Table 4.1)
Important Laws	1.000					
Laws/Year	−0.278	1.000				
Veto Players (Qual.)	−0.454	0.436	1.000			
Veto Players (Ave.)	−0.307	0.506	0.836	1.000		
Agenda Control (Qual)	0.386	−0.552	−0.620	−0.490	1.000	
Agenda Control (Table 4.1)	0.213	−0.328	−0.704	−0.528	0.889	1.000

C. Sweden excluded

	Important Laws	Laws/Year	Veto Players (qual.)	Veto Players (ave.)	Agenda Control (qual)	Agenda Control (Table 4.1)
Important Laws	1.000					
Laws/Year	−0.235	1.000				
Veto Players (Qual.)	−0.461	0.430	1.000			
Veto Players (Ave.)	−0.279	0.496	0.835	1.000		
Agenda Control (Qual)	0.527	−0.606	−0.654	−0.534	1.000	
Agenda Control (Table 4.1)	0.424	−0.419	−0.791	−0.623	0.893	1.000

of Table 7.4. Similarly, as Doering has convincingly demonstrated, agenda control by the government is negatively correlated with legislative inflation. Finally, the most interesting finding is that the number of veto players is highly correlated with agenda control (again, in all parts of Table 7.4).

How can we interpret these findings? I think the positive correlation of veto players and lack of agenda control with the total number of laws and the negative correlation of the same variables with the number of significant laws point toward a difference in the very concept of "law" among countries. "Laws" in countries with many veto players and low government agenda control produce incremental changes of the status quo, while in countries with few veto players and significant government agenda control, they produce sweeping changes.

But why is the lack of agenda setting by the government correlated with the number of veto players? The reader should refer back to Figure I.1 in the Introduction, where I made the argument that many veto players lead to the lower significance of agenda setting, because the winset of the status quo is smaller, and so agenda control loses significance. Are the findings here in support of this proposition? The answer to this question is negative, because Doering's (1995a,b,c) indicators refer to the institutional structure of these countries, not on the frequency with which specific governments use such agenda control measures (to the extent they exist).

Is there any different argument for the correlation between veto players and government control of the agenda? In fact, is it a coincidental relation or a causal one? Several arguments can be made that it is not a mere correlation. While a causal argument attributing the existence of veto players to the lack of agenda control is difficult, a strategic argument going from agenda control to veto players is possible. In countries with strong government agenda control, party negotiations for coalition governments will end up in a minority government or a government with few veto players. Conversely, in countries without government agenda control, parties will form oversized government coalitions in order to control the legislature. On the other hand, a causal argument going from veto players to agenda control is straightforward: the existence of many veto players makes them incapable of passing through parliament the many and significant pieces of legislation required for agenda control. This argument considers agenda control to be a collection of significant pieces of legislation. Consequently, we expect *not to see it* in countries with many veto players. Finally, a third argument can be made: that veto players and agenda control have common origins. The same sociological and historical factors that fragment a country into many competing parties (none of which has a majority) make these parties sufficiently suspicious of each other, so that they reject the idea of allowing whoever is in government to have significant control over legislation.

Which one of the three explanations is closer to the truth? This is a major question for further investigation. In order to address this question, one would have to collect data on the adoption (and possible repeal) of the different agenda control mechanisms and analyze them in relation to the governments that produced them. In other words, one would have to replicate this study with agenda control as the subject matter.

Finally, how about the actual use of agenda control measures by different governments? The expectation introduced in this book (Figure I.1) is that more veto players reduce the significance of agenda control; consequently, governments with more veto players would make less use of such measures. Is there any empirical evidence to support this expectation? Again, the reference is in the work of Doering, who more recently expanded his research to the actual use of agenda control measures. Doering (forthcoming) examined some five hundred pieces of legislation from eighteen West European countries with multiparty governments (whether majority or minority) and found that they make less use of agenda control measures (13.7 percent) than single-party governments (20.7 percent).[20]

7.4. Conclusions

I have presented the implications of the veto players theory when parties are located in a one-dimensional space and analyzed data on significant pieces of legislation in sixteen Western European countries. All the relevant expectations of the theory presented in the Introduction and in Chapter 1 were corroborated by the data: the number of significant laws varies inversely with the range of governments that produce them and in direct proportion to the difference between ideological positions of the current and previous government. Duration of governments increases the number of significant laws, but with declining returns. In addition, the residuals of the above relationship are heteroskedastic and vary inversely with the range of the government coalitions. The reason for this relationship is that a wide range is a sufficient (but not necessary) condition for the absence of significant legislation.

The number of veto players is positively correlated with the number of overall pieces of legislation in a country. This generates the expectation that the very concept of "law" differs from one country to the next, with countries with a large number of veto players implementing more incremental legislation. The positive relation between veto players and total pieces of legislation and the negative relationship between veto players and significant pieces imply an overall negative relationship between total number of laws and significant pieces of legislation.

The conclusion from this analysis is that now the missing empirical link between veto players and a series of important features of parliamentary systems has been established. Many veto players with big ideological distances between them means that legislation can only be incremental. If an exogenous shock occurs, a government with many veto players with big ideological distances among them cannot handle the situation and cannot agree on the necessary policies (except if public opinion is unanimous on the subject). Finally, the relationship between veto players and agenda control that we iden-

[20] Recalculations from Doering (forthcoming): table 9.

tified here along with the relationship between agenda control and executive power identified in Chapter 4 leads to the conclusion that many veto players affect the relationship between government and parliament in Western European countries. Many veto players are correlated with lack of institutional agenda control by the government, and lack of agenda control means weaker governments and stronger parliaments. The reasons for the relationship between veto players and agenda control by the government have to be more thoroughly investigated in the future. Finally, few veto players lead to the use of the existing agenda control arsenal more frequently than many veto players, because the significance of agenda setting declines with the number of veto players since the winset of the status quo shrinks (and policy stability thereby increases).

8

Macroeconomic Policies

THIS CHAPTER DISCUSSES issues like deficits, budgets, inflation, and growth. A more appropriate title would have been "macroeconomic outcomes." The reason is that the phenomena covered in this chapter are the results not only of conscious government choices (like environmental or labor policies), but also of a series of other factors that escape the control of national governments. For example, unemployment policies decided by a previous government might under specific conditions strain the budget of a country, increase the deficit, increase inflation, and so on, without any action by the government in power. Similarly, an exogenous shock like the change in the price of oil may have an impact on unemployment without the interference of any specific government decision.

While in the previous chapter we were able to focus on government lawmaking and ignore the specific outcomes, here we will do the opposite. We will look at outcomes directly, and try to infer the effect of specific policy decisions (instruments) by introducing a series of control variables to eliminate as much of the noise as possible.

In this chapter there are two important results of the veto players theory as presented in the previous two parts. First, that policy stability does not refer only to legislation, but also to outcomes (states of the world). Second, that the veto players theory enables research not only on single dimensional phenomena, but also on multidimensional ones. Indeed, while most of the studies referred to in this chapter are in fact single dimensional empirical tests of the veto players theory, one particular phenomenon that we will study in this chapter, the structure of budgets, is multidimensional. So, this chapter provides a methodology for empirical testing of multidimensional models. This methodology can be used for the study of phenomena that cannot be reduced to a single dimension.

This chapter is based on existing literature and will be divided in three parts. The first focuses on budget deficits. The second and longest part addresses the composition of budgets. The last part reviews the effects of veto players on growth, taxation, and inflation.

8.1. Collective Action versus Inertia Explanation of Budget Deficits

In the late 1970s and 1980s, almost all OECD countries started trying to reduce the budget deficits generated by the oil shocks. Some of them stabilized their policies and reduced their deficits faster than others. The macroeconomics literature studied stabilization and produced a series of explanations that I will classify into two major approaches. The first (which I call "collective action") argued that the more parties participating in government, the higher the budget deficits, because each one of them wanted to serve its own privileged constituency, and as a result, increased spending (and deficits) was the only possible compromise among different government partners. The second (which I call "inertia") argued along with the thesis presented in this book that more government partners find it more difficult to *change* (reduce) the size of the deficit and stabilize. It is interesting to note that the first approach makes sharper predictions than the second: according to collective action, more government partners implies higher deficits (and debt), and fewer implies lower deficits and debt; however, inertia expects more government partners to slow down the pace of adjustments. Because the period under study was characterized by an attempt to reduce deficits, the empirical implications of the two theories were identical, and sometimes researchers do not pay attention to the underlying theoretical differences.

8.1.1. Collective Action Approach

The key notion in the collective action literature is the common pool problem. The essence of the common pool problem is that in a decentralized policymaking government, where each spending minister only has authority over his own portfolio, the cost of overspending is shared with other ministries. Therefore, each minister is motivated to overspend to please his constituency at the expense of other ministries. In other words, since each ministry internalizes only part of the cost of rising spending on their own goods, all of the groups have an incentive to spend more than the optimum so as to appropriate more resources for their benefits. Thus, individual rationality leads to a collective irrationality, where the resultant budget deficit is radically different from the cooperative solution. In sum, the collective action literature argues that the more dispersed the decisionmaking authority, the higher the budget deficit. The proposed solution, accordingly, is to completely centralize decisionmaking authority by delegating the decisionmaking power to an independent agent, such as a strong minister of treasury.

The collective action approach has received some empirical support. For example, in a panel study including twenty OECD countries from 1960 to 1995, Perotti and Kontopoulos (1998) found that government spending and public debt are significantly higher in countries where there are more coalition partners and spending ministries in the government. Roubini and Sachs (1989b) argue that coalition governments will have a bias toward higher levels of government spending relative to majority party government. Moreover, the idea of the common pool problem has also been widely studied in budgetary procedures. For instance, the empirical evidence in von Hagen and Harden (1995) and Hallerberg and von Hagen (1999) suggest that countries in which budgetary decisionmaking authorities are centralized are less likely to suffer from budget deficits.

8.1.2. Policy Inertia Approach

Unlike the collective action approach, which is based on an n-person prisoners dilemma, the policy inertia approach emphasizes the possibility that there may not exist a consensus to change an unsustainable status quo when there are too many parties in government. Alesina and Drazen (1991) first developed a "war-of-attrition" model of delayed stabilization and demonstrated the difficulty in reaching a collective decision to implement fiscal adjustments due to the disagreement among different social groups about how to distribute the fiscal burden. Spolaore (1993) extended the war-of-attrition model to coalition government and shows that a coalition government is more likely to delay fiscal adjustment than a single-party government. The rationale is that unlike the ruling party in a single-party government, which can easily shift costs to outside members, governing parties in a coalition government will likely disagree or veto any fiscal policy that is against their constituencies' interests. Accordingly, the policy inertia approach argues that delays in the adjustment or the elimination of existing deficits might result from struggles between coalition partners (or the social groups they represent) about who will bear the necessary costs/cuts in budget spending, even if these players agree that current debt requires adjustments. In short, the distributional struggle among different groups leads to deadlock in the policymaking process, which, in turn, delays the implementation of policing aimed at eliminating the budget deficit. Moreover, it predicts that delayed stabilization and prolonged deficits are more likely to occur in fragmented and polarized social/political systems.

The empirical evidence in favor of the policy inertia approach is strong but by no means unanimous. Roubini and Sachs (1989a) found that large deficits are positively associated with weak governments in OECD countries. Cosetti and Roubini (1993) and Alesina and Perotti (1995) expand Roubini and Sachs's structure model and confirm their finding.

With respect to American politics, Poterba (1994) and Alt and Lowry (1994) presented evidence on the effect of divided governments in the states. They considered the policy response to fiscal shocks and found that the adjustment is slower in states with divided control than in states with unified control. Their results are remarkably similar in spirit to those of Roubini and Sachs on OECD economies: in both cases, coalition or divided governments do not create budget deficits, but rather procrastinate the adjustment to shocks. Krause (2000) focused on the fiscal performance of the United States. He finds that the degree of ideological policy divergence among political institutions (the president, the House, and the Senate) plays a notable role in explaining fiscal budget deficits in the United States during the postwar period.

On the other hand, there is some empirical evidence that disputes Roubini and Sachs's findings. For example, Edin and Ohlsson (1991) only found a positive relationship between public debts and minority governments. Furthermore, de Haan and Sturm (1997) reexamined the findings of Roubini and Sachs (1989a, 1989b) and Edin and Ohlsson (1991) and found contradictory results: the growth of government debt and the level of government spending are not related to the Roubini-Sachs power dispersion index, nor to the variant thereof as suggested by Edin and Ohlsson.

Given that the set of countries studied by both the collective action and the stabilization literature aimed at reducing budget deficits, the empirical results of both theoretical approaches were identical. However, one particular study was able to produce an empirical result that contradicts the collective action literature. Robert Franzese (2002), who covered twenty-one countries over thirty-five years, came to the conclusion that multiple veto players delay changes to budget deficits regardless of whether these deficits were high (in countries like Italy) or low (in countries like Germany and Switzerland). Given the scope of Franzese's analysis, I will discuss it more in detail. First, Franzese tests seven different political economy theories of public debt. Second, he operationalizes the veto players variables in a precise way and in agreement with what I have described in this book. Third, he produces a particularly significant finding, which I describe below.

A. *Different political economy theories.* Franzese presents the following theories:

> 1. The government composition and delayed stabilization theories. In these theories he includes two different variations: the "influence" theory, according to which the parties in government exercise an influence proportional to their size, and the "veto-actor" theories, which are presented in this book.
>
> 2. The wealth and age distributions and the inter- and intra-generational transfer of debt.
>
> 3. The electoral and partisan political-budget cycles.
>
> 4. The strategic manipulation of debt to alter future government policies.
>
> 5. The multiple constituencies and distributive politics.
>
> 6. The tax structure complexities and fiscally alluded voters.
>
> 7. The central bank autonomy and reduction of debt financing.

Given that these theories are non-nested, that is, none can be expressed as a restriction of the other by setting some of the coefficients to zero, Franzese uses J-tests (Davidson and MacKinnon 1981) to compare their predictive power. The procedure for J-tests is the following: for two models $Z = f(X,*)$

and Z = g(Y,*), one estimates first Z = f(X,*) and includes its predictions $\hat{Z}$ in the estimation of the second Z = g (Y, $\hat{Z}$, *). If the coefficient of $\hat{Z}$ is nonsignificant, then the second hypothesis *encompasses* the first: there is no additional significant information covered by the first hypothesis. The procedure is repeated by reversing the two theories. It is possible that both theories encompass each other, or none of them encompasses the other. Thus the only conclusive test is when one of them encompasses the other but not vice versa. Given that the theories tested by Franzese discuss completely different aspects of budget deficits, it turns out that the most frequent comparative result is that each of the models does not encompass the others, or, to use Franzese's terms, "The data insist that each of the theories adds explanatory power to any of the others." There are, however, some exceptions, and I will present one of them in Franzese's terms (2002: 156):

> First, and most theoretically interesting, the data do *not* reject that the veto-actor conception of the weak-government model encompasses the influence conception, yet they easily reject the converse that the influence conception encompasses the veto-actor conception. Moreover, if one reads across the first two rows, the veto-actor conception more strongly rejects being encompassed by any of the others, while, if one reads down the first two columns, it is less strongly rejected as covering the others. Thus, Tsebelis' (1995) veto-actor conception of fractionalization and polarization clearly dominates the influence conception.

The reason for this clear result is that my model is more general than other competing explanations like influence, bargaining, or exclusive jurisdictions of ministers. Indeed, each of these theories imposes additional restrictions and comes to sharper predictions than veto players (see Introduction).

B. *Operationalization of veto players.* While most of the literature treats minority governments in an idiosyncratic way (some as a dummy variable [Edin and Ohlsson 1991, de Haan and Sturm 1997], some as a worse case of coalition governments [Roubini and Sachs 1989a, 1989b]), Franzese uses either the number or the distance of different veto players in a single dimension as his independent variables. As a result, his analysis is consistent with the arguments in this book, and his findings corroborate the veto players theory.

C. *Effects of "fractionalization" and "polarization."* These are the names that Franzese gives to the number of veto players and the range of the government coalition (in a single dimension). Franzese tested for both variables at the same time, and found that deficit adjustment is a negative function of the number of veto players, but does not depend on the range of government coalitions. Given that the two variables are correlated, it may be the case that each one of them would be significant if tested alone. It may also be the case that the underlying phenomenon is multidimensional (in this case the number of veto players may be a better proxy than the range of a coalition in a single dimension).

But the most interesting result is that when testing for the size of a deficit as a function of the size of debt (which in fact is nothing but accumulated deficits), he concludes that "standard deviation rises in fractionalization centered on the mean (i.e., = + 1.2 parties, from 1.5 to 2.7) raise deficits .2% of GDP at average debt, but the same NoP [number of parties] increase induces a .2% of GDP deficit *reduction* at low debt and a .55% of GDP increase at high" (2002: 176, emphasis in the original). In other words, Franzese finds that multiple parties in government preserve the status quo more effectively, whether this means that deficits will continue to be high (in countries like Italy) or low (in countries like Switzerland). This finding is evidence against the collective action theories and in favor of the inertia approaches. Given that both approaches were tested with data from a period when governments were attempting to reduce deficits, crucial experiments between the two approaches are very difficult to find, so Franzese's study is the only one with this additional attribute.

While the above literature focuses exclusively on the size of the deficit (with the exception of Alesina and Perotti 1995), one can focus instead on the composition of the budget and see how different items are financed as a function of the composition of the government. I will devote the major part of this chapter to this point, because the composition of budgets is by definition a multidimensional phenomenon, and, as a result, is likely to require multidimensional indicators for its study.

8.2. The Structure of Budgets

Veto players expects budgets to change from year to year at a slower pace as the size of government coalitions expands and their ideological distances increase. Along this line of argument, Bawn (1999b) focused on specific items in the budget of the Federal Republic of Germany form 1961 to 1989. She analyzed the budget into two-digit categories, and from these categories she identified items favored by the SPD and the CDU-CSU. In the first category she included spending on educational grants and loans, professional education, art and cultural education, labor market policy, sports, the environment, municipal community service, urban renewal, mining and manufacturing, and aid to East Germany. In the second, she included defense, non-university R&D, housing, improvements in agricultural structure, infrastructure investments, roads, rivers and harbors, aviation, and shipping (the last items on the grounds that they are infrastructure/business pork items). She also identified a series of ambiguous items, but these did not affect her analysis.

The Liberal Party was assumed to want to minimize spending throughout this analysis. As a result, on SPD items the preferences ranged from the Liberals (low) to the Christian Democrats (middle) to the Socialists (high), while on CDU-CSU items the preferences ranged form Liberals (low) to Socialists (middle) to Christian Democrats (high). Bawn's analysis identified the range of each one of the coalition governments and identified the items for which an increase or decrease in budget was to be expected with a change in government. For example, when the SPD enters the government in 1966, replacing the Liberals, budget items in the SPD list are expected to increase because the country moves from a coalition desiring low spending in these items to a coalition requiring high spending. On the contrary, when the SPD–CDU-CSU coalition is replaced in 1969 by the SPD-Liberal coalition, no change in the SPD budget items is expected (despite the fact that the SPD now controls the chancellorship). Bawn forms a series of expectations on the basis of this veto players analysis in a single dimension. Several of them are counterintuitive. All her expectations are corroborated in her empirical analysis.

König and Tröger (2001) essentially replicate Bawn's findings for a longer period of time, using estimated preferences of the different parties. Their approach is an improvement upon Bawn because instead of assuming that the Liberals want to minimize spending, they take them at their own word and estimate that they are willing to spend on some budget items. However, both Bawn's and König and Tröger's analysis cover only one country, and through the astute selection of budget items they reduce the policy space into a single dimension. Such a choice is impossible when one considers all the budget items. Tsebelis and Chang (2002) considered this problem.

For Tsebelis and Chang (henceforth TC), the composition of budgets is altered in two different ways. The first one is deliberate in the sense that the current government wants to increase or decrease the size of spending (the budget) and spend a higher or lower percentage of it in some area: for example, by increasing the defense budget, or by shifting expenses from defense to education. The second one is automatic, in the sense that existing legislation (whether introduced by the current or previous governments) has economic consequences: increasing unemployment affects the composition of the budget because of specific provisions in the social security legislation. Of course, the size of the budget change will depend on the specific provisions of legislation in each country.

In order to differentiate between the deliberate and automatic structural change of budgets, TC include a series of control variables in their study. First, they include inflation, unemployment, percentage of dependent population (individuals over sixty-five years old), and rate of growth because fluctuations in these variables may affect the social security component of the budget. Second, they include a series of country dummy variables, because legislation in one country may provide different solutions and have different effects on the country's budget. Their basic finding is that the deliberate change in the structure of budgets (i.e., government spending) in advanced industrialized countries depends on the composition of governments and the ideological distance between the previous and the current government. Specifically, the more diverse the government coalition (the bigger the ideological distances among parties), the less change occurs in the structure of budgets. In addition, the bigger the alternation, the more significant the change in structure. These findings are consistent with the findings in Chapter 7 but there is one significant difference: the TC study is multidimensional. Indeed, they consider the party positions in two different dimensions, and calculate "ideological differences" and "alternation" of veto players in a two-dimensional space.

According to Proposition 1.4 (and as Figure 1.7 indicates), if the unanimity core of a political system contains the unanimity core of another political system, changes in the status quo will be more difficult in the first case than in the second. In addition, given that budgets are determined by the government in place, it is easy to identify the position of the "status quo" as far as budgets are concerned. For the problem at hand, then, TC were able to test whether the possibility of change is a function of the position of the status quo. In fact, the further away the status quo is located from the preferences of the veto players, the bigger the possible departure from the status quo.

The dependent variable used in the TC study is the changes in the structure of budgets in advanced industrialized countries. The budget of each country allocates resources in a series of areas, so it was conceptualized as a vector in an n-dimensional Euclidean issue space. It consists of a sequence of percentages (in order to control for its size) allocated to different jurisdictions: (a_1, a_2, ..., a_n). Each year there is a different budget allocation, so TC indexed each sequence by the time it was selected. As a consequence, the difference between two budgets can be represented by the distance between the composition of the budgets of two successive years.

TC tested whether the differences in the annual composition of the budgets of each country were a decreasing function of the ideological distances of the existing veto players (ID), and an increasing function of the ideological distance between successive governments, which was called "alternation" (A) in Chapter 7. Note that ID is the multidimensional extension of what was called "range" in the previous chapter.

The reason that TC use *current* government characteristics instead of the characteristics of the government in power the previous year (which voted the budget) is because according to the literature, the current government has means to alter the existing budget. In particular, a comprehensive study of budget rules in European Union countries by Hallerberg, Strauch, and von Hagen (2001) identifies a series of ways a current government can amend the budgetary structure. First, finance ministers in most E.U. countries[1] can either block expenditure or impose cash limits. They also have the power to allow funds to be transferred between chapters, and the disbursement of the budget in the imple-

---

[1] This happens in eleven of fifteen E.U. countries. The exceptions are Finland, the Netherlands, Spain, and Sweden.

mentation stage has to be subject to finance ministers' approvals. Second, there is a set of formal rules that enable governments to deal with unexpected expenditure and revenue shocks. In particular, eleven of fifteen E.U. states grant governments the power to take necessary actions if they encounter unexpected fiscal shocks. For example, Denmark requires governmental action to correct the structure of the budget if either expenditure is higher than expectation or revenues are less than expected. Finally, most E.U. countries (with the exception of Finland, Greece, and Luxembourg) allow a carryover of funds into the next budgetary year. Hallerberg, Strauch, and von Hagen (2001) also note that the degree of governmental discretion over the current budget can be very substantial: in theory, the United Kingdom simply allows 100 percent of unspent funds to be moved forward into the following year.

Hallerberg, Strauch, and von Hagen's findings are replicated in presidential systems. In the study of state governments' budgetary policy in the United States, Alt and Lowry (1994) and Poterba (1994) suggest that it is the current government that determines the final formation of budget allocation. Their argument is that after a budget is passed, revenues and expenditures may diverge from expectations and lead to unexpected deficits. Under such a scenario, the current government can alter the budget decision so that the unexpected deficits can be avoided. Specifically, Poterba suggests that many state constitutions prevent state governments from running deficits, and states also vary in the policies that are available to eliminate a deficit and satisfy balanced-budget rules. For example, some states are allowed to borrow and close the current budgetary gap. Some states can also draw down their general fund balances to cover budget deficits. Similarly, Alt and Lowry argue that the states have a variety of balanced-budget laws that might influence fiscal policy, and some of the laws explicitly nullify unfunded expenditures.[2] Hence in the TC study each government is considered responsible for the budget realized during the year it was in power.

TC derived their dependent variable from the *Government Finance Statistics Yearbook* of the International Monetary Fund. In this dataset, all budgetary expenditures for each individual country are itemized into nine main categories: general public service, defense, education, health, social security and welfare, housing and community amenities, other community and social services, economic services, and others.

The independent variables were constructed exactly as in the previous chapter. In addition to the data concerning the first dimension, TC also used a second dimension from Laver and Hunt (1992), who scored parties on the

---

[2] Actually, TC tested both current and previous year's governments and did not find any association between previous government and current budgets, which can be explained because budgets change very slowly (at the margin) and current governments clearly have the means to impose such modifications.

basis of their "pro friendly relations to USSR vs. anti." Note that this dimension is different from the left-right dimension. In fact, the pair-wise correlation between the ideological distances based on these two dimensions in the dataset is only slightly above 0.5. However, parties scoring high in this second dimension are parties of the left.[3]

8.2.1. The Two-Dimensional "Ideological Distance" and "Alternation" Variables

On the basis of Proposition 1.4, we need to know whether the unanimity core of one government is included in the unanimity core of another. In a single dimension this is an easy task: one compares the length of the core of two coalitions (the "range," as we did in Chapter 7). In two or more dimensions, however, such a straightforward measure does not exist. For example, it is not true that if the unanimity core of coalition A covers a larger area than the unanimity core of coalition B, then A necessarily includes B (i.e., the relevant criterion according to Figure 1.6). For example, if a coalition has two distant members (which by definition means that its unanimity core is a straight line and therefore covers an area of zero), it can make decisions more easily than a coalition with three members located close to each other (which covers a small but positive area). As a result, TC approximated the ideological distances of different coalitions in two dimensions by using the range of these coalitions in each dimension, and calculating their average. For alternation, the selection of the indicator was easier because the position of the middle point of the range in each dimension was known, so the distance between two governments could be calculated by the Pythagorean theorem.[4] Note that this formula produces positive distances regardless of whether the successor government is to the left or to the right of the predecessor in the first dimension, or their relative positions in the second dimension.

It is interesting to compare this approach to the one used in Chapter 7. In Chapter 7 the problem was one-dimensional, and as a result it was possible to calculate range and alternation exactly. Here the problem is multidimensional, ideological distance (the equivalent of range) is calculated by approximation.

---

[3] Some examples from the TC dataset: in 1988 when the Schluter cabinet in Denmark experienced a government reformation from a coalition of the Conservatives, the Liberals, and the central Democrats to a coalition of the Conservatives, the Liberals, and the Radical Liberals, TC find that the ideological range in the second index changes from 1.6 to 5, while the ideological range in the first index only changes from 5.6 to 4.9. Similarly, in Australia in 1983, when the Fraser cabinet (which consisted of the National Party and the Liberal Party) was replaced by the Hawke cabinet (the Labor Party), the ideological position of government in the second index shifted from 12.59 to 7.29, while the ideological position in the first index only changed from 14.86 to 10.10.

[4] $A_{12} = \sqrt{A_1^2 + A_2^2}$, where A_1 and A_2 are alternation in the first and second dimension.

Indeed, there are multiple possible measures of the variable, and none of them captures the information required in Proposition 1.4 exactly. While it is more likely that a veto player configuration with higher ID score (as calculated by TC) will include one with smaller ID score, inclusion is not guaranteed. Multiple dimensions do not therefore, according to my approach, lead to "chaos" as in the social choice literature, but to a more complicated model that preserves the one dimensional intuitions, just like collective veto players in Chapter 2 led to a more complicated analysis that can be approximated quite well by the analysis of Chapter 1.

The first test TC performed was for negative effects of ideological distances on the change of budgets along with heteroskedastic outcomes (high variance associated with low ideological distances). They used multiplicative heteroskedastic regression (like in Chapter 7) and estimated two models, the first including ideological distance, and the lagged dependent variable (to take care of the time component) for the expected value of budget distance, and the ideological distance for the error term. As evident from Table 8.1, ideological distance has a negative coefficient both for the expected value of budgetary distance and the error term as predicted. The second model includes the same variables with the exception of ideological distance (in both equations). A likelihood-ratio test indicates that the probability that the expectation of negative coefficients in both equations is false is less than 6 percent.

TC then introduced two kinds of control variables to isolate deliberate budget modifications from automatic ones: first, they introduced (differences in) unemployment, growth, inflation, and the size of dependent population (individuals over sixty-five years old). Second, they introduced dummy variables for all countries in order to eliminate automatic modifications of the budget due to existing legislation. In addition, they introduced control dummies for the type of government (minimum-winning coalition, minority or oversized government). I remind the reader that on the basis of the discussion in Chapter 4, these variables are expected to have no effect, while other researchers (Strom [2000]) expect a negative sign from minority governments (since they require support from parties not in the government) and a positive sign for oversized coalitions (since they can dispense of the support of some government partners).

The results of estimation are summarized in Table 8.2, and are consistent with the predictions of the veto players theory: both coefficients of ideological distance and alternation in this model are significant and signed according to expectation. Moreover, the size of standardized coefficients of ideological distance (−0.17) and alternation (0.12) suggests that the effect of the veto players structure is not only statistically significant but also substantively important. The minority and oversized government dummies have no significance, as expected by veto players theory (and oversized even has the wrong sign). Dropping the type of government variables as well as the economic

TABLE 8.1

Simple Results on Budget Structure in Nineteen OECD Countries, 1973–1995 (Model Estimated by Multiplicative Heteroskedastic Regression).

	Model 1	Model 2
Dependent Variable: The Expected Value of Budget Distance		
Constant	0.2759****	0.2820****
	(0.0199)	(0.0201)
Lagged BD	0.1515****	0.1360****
	(0.0349)	(0.0351)
Ideological Distance	−0.0155	
	(0.0165)	
Dependent Variable: The Error Term of Budget Distance		
Constant	−2.5480****	−2.5243****
	(0.0769)	(0.0769)
Ideological Distance	−0.2004***	
	(0.0872)	
N	338	338
Prob $> x^2$	0.000	0.000

Likelihood-ratio test between Model 1 and Model 2: $\chi_2^2 = 5.74$

Probability $> \chi_2^2 = 0.0567$

Note: Standard errors in parentheses.
*$p < 0.1$ level
**$p < 0.05$ level
***$p < 0.01$ level
****$p < 0.001$ level
All tests are one-tailed.

variables $\Delta POP65$, $\Delta GROWTH$, ΔINF (which are also nonsignificant) and rerunning the regression to check for robustness presents exactly the same results (Model 2).

In conclusion, all the empirical evidence presented by TC validates the hypothesis that despite the factors that account for the automatic change of budgetary structure, the deliberate change of budgetary structure can be explained by governmental ideological distance and ideological differences between governments. Specifically, a government coalition is associated with more significant change in the budget if the members of this government are less ideologically diverse or if its ideological position is more divergent from the previous government. In other words, the budgetary structure tends to lock itself into the existing pattern in political systems with ideologically distant veto

TABLE 8.2

Multivariate Results on Budget Structure in Nineteen OECD Countries, 1973–1995 (Model Estimated by Fixed-Effect Cross-Sectional Time-Series Model with Panel Corrected Standard Errors)

	Model 1 Coefficient	Model 1 Standard Coefficient	Model 2
Lagged BD	0.0870** (0.0446)	0.1316**	0.0896** (0.0437)
Ideological Distance	−0.0547** (0.0277)	−0.1665***	−0.0500*** (0.0275)
Alternation	0.0375*** (0.0170)	0.1185**	0.0381*** (0.0172)
Δ unemployment	0.0360** (0.0208)	0.1008**	0.0361** (0.0209)
Δ age > 65	0.0041 (0.1416)	0.0018	
Δ Growth	0.0055 (0.0070)	0.0383	
Δ INF	0.0018 (0.0040)	0.0273	
Minority	−0.0432 (0.0879)	−0.0596	
Oversize	−0.0020 (0.0793)	−0.0024	
N	336		336
Adjusted R^2	0.6154		0.6200
Prob > x^2	0.0000		0.0000

Note: The estimated coefficients for country dummies are suppressed to facilitate the presentation. Panel-corrected standard errors are in parentheses.

*$p < 0.1$ level
**$p < 0.05$ level
***$p < 0.01$ level
****$p < 0.001$ level
All tests are one-tailed.

players; in contrast, the budgetary structure tends to be more flexible in political systems with ideologically similar veto players.

TC also investigated how the ideological distance and alternation affect budget structure on a disaggregated level. Their results, summarized in Table 8.3, suggest that the ideological distance and alternation also explain the change in

TABLE 8.3
Estimated Results for Each Budget Category

Budget Category	Ideological Distance	Alternation
General Public Services	−0.0852**	0.0040
	(0.0505)	(0.0266)
Defense	−0.0149	0.0111
	(0.0241)	(0.015)
Education	−0.1197**	0.0544**
	(0.0716)	(0.0271)
Health	−0.2340***	0.1160***
	(0.1033)	(0.0477)
Social Security and Welfare	−0.2724***	0.0672
	(0.1034)	(0.0574)
Housing and Community Amenities	0.0826	0.5096***
	(0.0953)	(0.0929)
Other Community and	−0.0119	0.0026
Social Services	(0.0126)	(0.0047)
Economic Services	−0.1804*	0.0612*
	(0.1306)	(0.0432)
Others	−0.1970	0.0018
	(0.1690)	(0.0852)

Note: Estimated coefficients for country dummies, change in unemployment rate and lagged dependent variable are surpressed to facilitate the presentation. Panel-corrected standard errors are in parentheses.
 * $p < 0.1$ level
 ** $p < 0.05$ level
 *** $p < 0.01$ level
 All tests are one-tailed.

each budget category well. In fact, there is only one of the nine budget items (housing and community amenities) with the wrong sign in the ideological distance variable (but it is not significant), and all the rest have the expected signs in both variables. Two of the eight remaining cases (defense and other community and social services) have the expected sign but no significance; and in all other cases both coefficients have correct signs and at least one of them is significant. Ideological distance significantly affects six of nine budget categories; and alternation has a significant effect on eight out of nine budget categories. In particular, they find that among these nine budget categories, the change of education, health, and social security are especially sensitive to both the effects of ideological distance and alternation.

Finally, TC replicate their model, checking for each one of the underlying dimensions separately, and find that the two-dimensional model has essentially the same performance as the first dimension, but outperforms the second dimension (see Table 8.4). Looking at each budget item in turn, the two-dimensional model presents improvement in one dimension (usually the second) in five out of ten cases, deterioration in four, and has no impact in one. These empirical results indicate that the improvement of the two-dimensional model is mainly conceptual over an analysis when using only the first dimension, and both conceptual and empirical in the second dimension.

8.3. Other Macroeconomic Outcomes

In this section I present three different studies with different dependent variables: inflation, taxation, and growth. The expectation of veto players theory is the same regardless of the dependent variable: significant changes of outcomes will be associated only with few and ideologically congruent veto players. Among the independent variables used in these studies, there is one (federalism) that is highly correlated with veto players. In addition, the arguments in these articles are either implicitly or explicitly related to the arguments made in this book. I will present these studies sequentially, and explain the relationship between their findings and the theory presented in this book.

A. *Federalism and Inflation.* The theoretical expectation generated from the analysis in this book is that changes in inflation will be lower in federal countries than in unitary ones. Indeed, as we saw in Chapter 6, federalism is associated with an increased number of veto players (*ceteris paribus*). Treisman (2000c) studied inflation in eighty-seven countries during the 1970s and 1980s. He was comparing three different expectations for the relationship between federalism and inflation generated by different theories (in his words, commitment, collective action, and continuity). The "commitment" theories expect lower inflation in decentralized countries, because the multiple actors involved in decisionmaking reduce the ability of a central government to inflate for political purposes. The "collective action" theories expect higher inflation in federal countries, because the multiple actors involved will engage in local fiscal free riding. What Treisman calls "continuity" theories is the veto players theory we have already described.[5] Treisman concludes early in the article that there is "strong support for the continuity hypothesis. In general, average inflation rates tended to rise during the 1970s and 1980s in both unitary and

---

[5] In fact, Treisman uses the veto players terminology frequently in this article.

TABLE 8.4

Comparison of Explanatory Power of Single- and Two-Dimensional Analysis

Budget Category	Ideological Distance in 1st Dimension	Alternation in 1st Dimension	Ideological Distance in 2nd Dimension	Alternation in 2nd Dimension	Ideological Distance in Two-Dimension	Alternation in Two-Dimension	Improvement Ideological Dimension 1st-2	Improvement Alternation 1st-2	Improvement Ideological Distance 2nd-2	Improvement Alternation 2nd-2
Total	***	***	*	***	**	***	↓		↑	
General Public Services	**	*	C	*	*	*	↓		↑	
Defense	C	**	C	**	C	C		↓↓		↓↓
Education	**	**	C	***	**	**			↑↑	↓
Health	***	****	**	****	***	****			↑	
Social Security and Welfare	***	*	***	C	***	*				↑
Housing	W	C	W	*	W	C				↓
Other Community and Social Services	*	C	C	C	C	**	↓	↑↑		↑↑↑
Economic Services	**	*	C	**	*	***	↓	↑↑	↑	↑
Other	C	**	**	*	*	C	↑		↓	↓

Notes: W denotes "wrong sign." C denotes "correct sign."

*p < 0.01   **p < 0.05   ***p < 0.01

↑ denotes results improving by one step (from W to C, * to ** etc.).

↑↑ denotes results improving by two steps (W to *, * to *** etc.).

↑↑↑ denotes results improving by three steps (C to *** etc.).

↓ denotes worsening results.

federal states. Although there was a general upward drift, the rise was less in federations with low inflation in the previous period compared to similar unitary states, and the rise was greater in federations that started from high inflation compared to similar unitary states" (Treisman 2000c: 844). The rest of the analysis aims at identifying the mechanisms for accounting for these outcomes. According to Treisman, there are two major reasons. First, "Federal structure, by increasing the number of veto players required to change the system of control over central bankers, tends to lock the degree of central bank independence, whether high or low" (Treisman 2000c: 851). Second, political systems differ in the degree to which imbalances are pushed from the local to the regional and then the national level (which Treisman calls "fiscal conductivity"). "Decentralization . . . appears to reduce change in the degree of conductivity, whether high or low" (Treisman 2000c: 853).

B. *Taxation and Veto Players*. According to the theory presented in this book, any significant change in taxation will be possible only with few veto players. Hallerberg and Basinger (1998) studied the change in taxation that occurred in OECD countries in the late 1980s. All OECD countries reduced taxes for the highest income individuals, and for enterprises. Considering the size of each one of these two reductions as a dependent variable, Hallerberg and Basinger try to identify the cause of this change. In their analysis they consider a series of variables from the economic literature that should have an impact on theoretical grounds. First, they include capital mobility, since countries may be forced to lower their tax rate to prevent capital flight as capital becomes more mobile. Second, they take into account trade dependence since open economies tend to be more sensitive to changes in tax rates than closed economies. Finally, they also control for inflation and economic growth. From the political science literature the possible relevant variables were veto players (included in their analysis as a dummy variable) and partisanship, the latter because practically all political science literature argues that right-wing parties reduce taxes for high-income brackets and corporations, while the left raises taxes with these two groups as its privileged targets.

Only two of these variables produced consistent results for both tax reductions (the personal and the corporate one): veto players and real growth. Hallerberg and Basinger interpret their veto player result as follows: "The findings with regard to veto players were extremely encouraging. A move to two or more veto players from one veto player reduces the change in corporate rates by 18.4 points and reduces the change in the top marginal income tax rate by 20.3 points."

The use of a dummy variable by Hallerberg and Basinger (1998) is consistent with the argument presented here. As we saw in Chapter 7, in a single dimension what matters is the ideological distance among coalition partners.

While single-party governments have by definition range of zero, the range of two or multiparty governments is not necessarily related to the number of partners.

C. *Growth and veto players.* The theory I present in this book does not make any predictions about a relationship between veto players and growth. As stated in the Introduction, the underlying assumption of many economic arguments is that many veto players create the possibility for a political system to "commit," not to alter the rules of the economic game (like suddenly confiscate wealth through taxation). Conversely, the underlying assumption of most political analyses is that political systems should be able to respond to exogenous shocks. I have connected the two arguments and said that "high level of commitment" is another way of saying "inability for political response." It is not clear whether many veto players will lead to higher or lower growth, because they will "lock" a country to whatever policies they inherited, and it depends whether such policies induce or inhibit growth.

Witold Henisz (2000a) tested the standard economic argument, that many veto players create a credible commitment for non interference with private property rights which "is instrumental in obtaining the long term capital investments required for countries to experience rapid economic growth" (Henisz 2000a: 2–3).

The careful reader will recognize that this argument adds one important assumption to my analysis: that more credibility leads to higher levels of growth. Henisz (2000a: 6) recognizes that more stability might also lock in a bad status quo: "The constraints provided by these institutional and political factors may also hamstring government efforts to respond to external shocks and/or to correct policy mistakes. . . . However, the assumption in the literature and in this article is that, on average, the benefit of constraints on executive discretion outweigh the costs of lost flexibility."

For the empirical test, Henisz (2000a) creates a dataset covering 157 countries for a 35-year period (1960–95). He identifies five possible veto players: the executive, the legislature, a second chamber of the legislature, the judiciary, and federalism. He constructs an index of political constraints, taking into account whether the executive controls the other veto players (legislature, judiciary, state governments) and the fractionalization of these additional veto players, and averages his results over five-year periods. He then reexamines Barro's (1996) analysis of growth introducing his new independent variable. His results are that the "political constraints" variable has additional explanatory power and its results are significant: a standard deviation change in this variable produces between 17 and 31 percent of a standard deviation change in growth.

Henisz's independent variable is conceptually very closely correlated with veto players, and covers an overwhelming number of countries. However, the empirical correlation between "political constraints" and either the number or the distances among veto players is questionable. For example, the judiciary does not always have veto power (see Chapter 10), and federalism seems to be double-counted because it is included in the second chamber of a legislature. In addition, legislative constraints are included while taking into account *all* parties in parliament. Such an approach may be correct for presidential systems with coalitions created around specific bills; but in parliamentary systems the government controls the legislative game (as discussed in Chapter 4) because it is based (at least most of the time) on a stable parliamentary majority. As a result, opposition parties impose no constraints on legislation.

These different rules of counting produce significantly different assessments of countries. For example, Henisz finds that Canada has very high political constraints, while in this book the classification is very different (the second chamber representing also local governments is weak or controlled by the same party as the first, and the judiciary is not so strong). Similarly, Germany and Belgium are considered to have very high "political constraints," while in my analyses Germany has an intermediate range of veto players (only when the Bundesrat is controlled by the opposition is the ideological distance of veto players high).

In sum, the big advantage of Henisz's dataset is that it covers the greatest number of countries reported in this book; the disadvantages are that some constraints are introduced without reflecting the actual decisionmaking process, and that while a plausible mechanism (according to which constraints affect credibility of commitments, affect investment, and affect growth) is identified, only the first and last steps of the process are shown to be correlated.

8.4. Conclusions

This chapter discussed empirical studies of a series of macroeconomic outcomes. All seem to be correlated with the structure of veto players in an important way: the more veto players and/or the more distant they are, the more difficult the departure from the status quo. Indeed, budget deficits are reduced at a slower pace (when their reduction becomes an important political priority), the structure of budgets becomes more viscous, inflation remains at the same levels (whether high or low), and tax policies do not change easily. All these results indicate high stability of outcomes. In addition, reviewing the literature, we encountered the empirical corroboration of an outcome expected in the economic literature: the existence of many veto players may reduce the political risks associated with an active government, increase investment, and lead to higher levels of growth.

Most of the analyses discussed in this chapter use either some measure correlated to veto players (like Treisman's [2000c] federalism, Hallerberg and Basinger's (1998) veto dummy) or a one-dimensional indicator (Bawn 1998, Franzese 2001). One study however, Tsebelis and Chang (2002), makes use of the multidimensional analysis presented in the first part of this book.

PART IV

SYSTEMIC EFFECTS OF VETO PLAYERS

IN THIS LAST PART I discuss the structural outcomes of policy stability. Why should we care if it is easy or difficult to change the status quo? As stated in the Introduction, one way of conceiving policy stability is as a credible commitment of the political system not to interfere in economic, political, or social interactions and regulate them. Another way is to conceive policy stability as the inability of the political system to respond to changes occurring in the economic, political, or social environment. Both these aspects are intrinsically linked and inseparable. Some analysts may prefer one way of thinking to the other, until the moment that institutional structure, praised for its ability to make credible commitments, is unable to respond to some shock, or the political system with admirable decisiveness is unable to make credible commitments. The argument so far has been that particular institutional structures will produce specific levels of policy stability, and it is not possible to have credibility some of the time and switch to decisiveness when you need it. Deciding on an institutional structure locks the situation to a certain level of policy stability. But what are the results of different levels of policy stability?

Policy stability has multiple effects. First, in presidential regimes, if policy stability is high, regime instability increases (as we saw in Chapter 3): it is possible for the president or the military to turn against the democratic institutions that are unable to solve the problems of the country. In the following three chapters we examine in more detail other results of policy stability.

The first result of policy stability that we study in Chapter 9 is government *instability* in parliamentary democracies. As we have seen, parliamentary systems have the flexibility of government change when there is a political impasse. The government decides to challenge parliament with a question of confidence and loses or resigns because it cannot pass its legislation through parliament, or the parliament that disagrees with the government removes it from power. A significant disagreement between government and parliament leads to a new government coalition that may (or may not) resolve the political impasse. What is interesting in this story is that what is perceived as "political impasse" by the players is what we have called policy stability throughout this book. Consequently, policy stability increases the probability of replacing governments, to be referred to henceforth as government instability.

Chapter 9 addresses the question of government survival. While most theoretical and empirical analyses explain government instability by characteristics prevailing in the parliament of a country, veto players theory focuses on the composition of governments to explain government survival. As has been demonstrated in the work of Warwick (1994), explanations based on government composition are more accurate empirically. What this chapter shows is that this analysis is consistent with the veto players framework introduced in this book. I demonstrate that the veto players theory combined with a theoretically informed understanding of the concept of "status quo" can account for all the puzzling findings of the empirical literature.

Chapter 10 deals with the independence of bureaucracies and the judiciary. I explain why policy stability leads to higher independence of these two branches, and present empirical evidence corroborating the expectations. I compare my findings for both bureaucrats and judges with other theoretical or empirical work. If different theories generate different expectations, I explain the reasons for the differences and look to the empirical evidence for corroboration.

Chapter 11 applies the veto players theory to an unusual case: the European Union. According to Alberta Sbragia (1992: 257), the European Union is "unique in its institutional structure . . . neither a state nor an international organization." The European Union has also changed its constitution several times in the last fifteen years. These peculiarities have led students of the European Union to characterize it as a "sui generis" system (Westlake 1994: 29; Nugent 1994: 206). Finally, E.U. institutions include very complicated provisions. Decisions in the Council of Ministers are made by a triple majority, while two more institutions, the European Parliament and the European Commission, participate in the decisionmaking process quite frequently as veto players. For these reasons, I consider a successful analysis of this fluid and unusual system as a demanding test for the theory in this book. Should veto players analysis provide us with interesting and accurate insights about the European Union, the theory will have gone through a quite demanding test. The reader will see that the structure of the legislative process has changed several times, shifting power among the main institutional actors. In addition, these changes have affected the role of other actors, like bureaucracies and the judiciary, exactly the same way as in other countries, as the first half of this book has led us to expect, and exactly as Chapter 10 demonstrates.

9

Government Stability

As WE SAW IN CHAPTER 4, government stability is an important variable for the study of parliamentary systems. For example, Lijphart (1999: 129) considers government duration as a proxy for "executive dominance" and differentiates his approach from what he calls the "prevalent" point of view according to which "cabinet durability is an indicator not just of the cabinet's strength compared with that of the legislature but also of regime stability." Huber and Lupia (2000) argue that government stability increases ministerial efficiency because a minister expected to stay in place will be respected by the bureaucracy.

Actually the formation of government coalitions and the duration of the corresponding governments has probably been one of the most prolific branches in the literature of politics in advanced industrialized democracies. Starting with the work of Riker (1962), coalition theorists discovered the significance of "minimum-winning coalitions"[1] and then proceeded to define a series of other concepts useful for the study of coalition formation: "minimum size," "minimal range," "minimum connected winning," "policy viable."[2] Empirical work on the durability of different governments flourished (Dodd 1976, Sanders and Herman 1977, Robertson 1983, Schofield 1987, Laver and Schofield 1990, Strom 1988, King et al. 1990, Warwick 1994). Some of this work was based on the "numerical" composition of different governments (number of seats they controlled, majority or minority status); other parts included the policy positions of parties (either all of them, or only the ones composing the government); most of it included additional information relevant to government formation (whether the government had to receive an investiture vote from parliament, how many attempts at government formation were made before a successful government).

In this chapter I review this literature, point out the latest findings, and confront it with the main expectation generated by the veto players theory: that policy stability leads to government instability. In order to be able to generate specific predictions from the theory, I discuss in depth a fundamental (in game theoretic models) but elusive (in empirical work) concept: the "status quo." I further develop the difference between policies (such as the ones studied in Chapter 7) and outcomes (such as the ones in Chapter 8), and explain

---

[1] Coalitions that stop controlling a majority of seats in parliament if they lose a party member.
[2] See Lijphart (1999: 91–96) for definition and discussion of all these concepts.

why what used to be a satisfactory situation in a country in the past may now require significant changes. From this starting point I study the implications for government survival. Governments are the actors who are responsible for such adjustments, and since their composition affects their capacity to act, it ultimately affects their probability of survival. As a result of this analysis, government duration in parliamentary regimes will be linked to the configuration of veto players. Once this link is established, I revisit Lijphart's analysis of the connection between government duration and executive dominance introduced in Chapter 4, and explain why government duration empirically correlates with executive dominance despite the fact that there is no logical connection, as we saw in Chapter 4.

This chapter is organized into three parts. The first part reviews the literature on government duration and examines whether it depends on characteristics of the parliament or the government of a country. The second uses the theory presented in this book to explain the empirical findings. The third uses the findings in previous chapters of this book to explain why government duration correlates with executive dominance, despite the lack of logical connection.

9.1. The Literature on Government Stability

Most of the literature on government duration correlates it with parliament characteristics, like the number of parties and their ideological distances from each other. More recent analyses focus on government characteristics. In this section I compare and contrast the two approaches, but I start by explaining what the literature measures when it discusses "government stability."

1. *Government stability.* While many authors have written about government stability, they have not applied the same defining conditions for what a government replacement is. For example, different authors do not agree if the situation where a government is replaced by another with the same party composition should be counted as a single government or two different ones.

More precisely, there are four different criteria used in the literature: whether the party composition of a government changes, whether there is a formal government resignation, whether there is a change in prime minister, and whether there is an election. While all authors accept the first criterion, variations exist with respect to all the others. Dodd (1976) and Lijphart (1984) accept only the first criterion as a necessary and sufficient condition for the change in government. The second most frequently used criterion for government termination is an election. Laver and Schofield (1990: 147) justify this criterion because an election changes party weights in parliament, and consequently modifies the bargaining environment where coalition formation takes place. The other two criteria have serious drawbacks for comparative analysis:

formal resignation is required in some countries and not in others, and resignation of a prime minister may or may not be for political reasons, so there is wider disagreement with respect to these two criteria.

Which one of these criteria is the most appropriate? I think that every author selects a criterion that makes the most sense on the basis of his view of how the process works. For example, if the view is that government composition depends on the relative power of different parties, inclusion of elections as a criterion is a very reasonable choice. If it is perceived that most prime ministers' resignations are political events, even if actors involved are claiming that they resign "for personal reasons," inclusion of prime minister resignation makes sense, too. In Chapter 7 I adopted the Lijphart (1984) and Dodd (1976) criterion of party composition of governments by creating a list of "merged" governments but replicated the calculations with the more traditional definitions with the same qualitative results. Lijphart (1999) averaged the duration results generated by his own criterion with the criteria applied by most of the literature and used "average duration" generated this way to calculate his "executive dominance" index. We return to that point in the last section of this chapter.

2. *Parliamentary features affect government stability.* No matter what the criterion of duration, it is usually correlated with parliamentary characteristics. For example, even in the initial impetus for the development of coalition theories (Riker 1962, based on cooperative game theory), a series of "policy blind" models were assuming that the coalitions formed would be "minimum winning" in parliament so that ministerial portfolios would not be allocated to parties that were not needed for a majority in parliament.

Subsequently, policy position criteria were introduced, and the underlying model revolved around improving one's position in the cabinet. Most of the time this meant increasing a party's portfolio share, although some analysts like De Swaan (1973: 88) maintained that "an actor strives to bring about a winning coalition in which he is included and that he expects to adopt a policy that is as close as possible . . . to his own most preferred policy."

The implicit or explicit argument in all the approaches was that different parties will force a government to resign when they have a good chance to be included in the next government and obtain a better position. As a result, the characteristics of the *parliament* that produce the governments enter into play. If a party is centrally located in the parliament, if it is large, if other parties are dispersed or clustered, all these indicators are good predictors that a party will be included in the next government. Here are the variables affecting government duration on the basis of this literature: the number of parties in the political system (Duverger 1954), the "effective number of parties" in a system, the presence of anti-system or other "extreme" parties, the degree of ideological polarization or "cleavage conflict" (all these conditions make it more difficult to form and maintain governments). Finally, a formal investiture requirement eliminates some governments that might have survived for a while otherwise (Laver and Schofield 1990: 147–48). With respect to characteristics of the government itself, the results of empirical analyses indicated that "minimum winning" status increased government longevity, while Sanders and Herman (1977) and Schofield (1987) did not find evidence that ideological compactness of the government affected its longevity.

All these approaches, according to Laver and Schofield (1990: 155), leave "two important loose ends. . . . The first is that there is considerable unexplained variation between systems in the average duration of cabinets. The second is that the duration of cabinets seems to be unrelated to policy matters, despite the fact that party policy greatly enhances our ability to explain the formation of governments in the first place." In order to address these two problems, Laver and Schofield introduce "bargaining environment" as an independent variable. They show that in a single dimensional policy space (left-right), one can divide different countries into unipolar centrist, unipolar off-center, bipolar, and multipolar. They then demonstrate that countries with a centrist unipolar bargaining system (like Luxembourg and Ireland), or with a bipolar system (like Austria and Germany), have governments that last significantly longer than countries with multipolar bargaining environments (like the Netherlands, Finland, Italy); countries with unipolar (off-center) systems (like Norway, Sweden, Iceland) have intermediate levels of government longevity. Laver and Schofield (1990) were one of the last "deterministic models"[3] of government duration, and they pushed the method as far as it has reached.

The deterministic approach was criticized by the "events approach" models that are based on the idea that actual dissolutions of governments are caused by random events that could not have been anticipated by the actors (Browne, Gleiber, and Mashoba 1984). The initial attempt of the events approach was not to focus on the causes of government duration, but to explicitly model its randomness. Events models focused on the conditional probability that a government will be terminated given that it had survived for a certain period of time. This conditional rate of termination (hazard rate) assumed to be constant across countries became the dependent variable in most of the analyses, but the empirical results were poor: hazard rates were different across countries (the only exceptions were Belgium, Finland, Italy, and Israel).

King et al. (1990) were the first to present a model that unified the two approaches. It included the causal arguments of deterministic approaches along with the superior methodology of the events approach: the model made hazard rates a function of the characteristics studied by the deterministic models. In other words, the new model was assuming that governments fall as a result of random events, but the capacity of different governments to survive was a

---

[3] Deterministic models are those that assume government duration to be a function of the independent variables included in the model.

function of different characteristics prevailing in the party system of the country. The results of this unified model indicate that fragmentation of the party system and polarization of the opposition are the regime attributes most strongly associated with cabinet duration.

As a result of these findings, Laver and Schofield (1990: 161) conclude "that the fragmentation and polarization of the party system appear as the important variables in an analysis that controls for a wide range of matters and even takes account of the impact of random shocks. These, of course, are the variables we identified as being important parameters of the stability of the bargaining system and therefore liable to have an impact on cabinet stability."

In conclusion, the introduction of more advanced methodology did not alter the conclusions of the coalition literature by 1990: the two main characteristics that affect government survival in parliamentary systems are features of the party system of a country: fragmentation and polarization. Both these variables represent characteristics determined by the *parliament* that selects the different governments, and both have to do with the bargaining environment prevailing in this parliament.

3. *Government features affect government stability.* Several years later, Paul Warwick (1994) presented a serious criticism of the above results, and an alternative specification of the underlying model. He moved the explanation of government survival from the parliament to the *government*. He criticized both the parliament polarization variable and the parliament fragmentation variable, and replaced them with similar variables describing governments.

With respect to polarization, Warwick argued that it did not necessarily affect the complexity of the bargaining environment. In fact, it had the opposite effect: "Laver and Schofield believe that the polarization variable reflects the overall complexity of party positions in the party system; the more complex this array, the more vulnerable the distribution of bargaining power to slight perturbations. But what the variable actually measures is the proportion of parliamentary seats held by extremist parties, and since extremist parties are normally considered unsuitable coalition partners by prosystem parties—"noncoalitionable," in Laver and Schofield's (1990: 200–201) terms—their presence should narrow the range of coalition alternatives, other things being equal" (Warwick 1994: 46). Warwick presents an alternative explanation of polarization: "Given the noncoalitionable status of extremist parties, governments formed in such systems usually must either encompass an ideologically diverse array of prosystem parties and/or settle for being minoritarian; either way, they are vulnerable to early collapse or termination. Apart from accounting for the sign of the polarization coefficient, this explanation has the advantage of locating the proximate cause of government survival in a particular government attribute, rather than associating it with a general feature of the larger parliamentary environment" (Warwick (1994: 47)).

With respect to fractionalization, Warwick argued that the measure should reflect the situation inside the government: "King et al.'s interest in size or fractionalization extended only to the size of the party system; they never tested the size of government. Once government size is taken into consideration, however, it eliminates the significant role played by effective party system size, indicating that large party systems tend to experience greater instability because the governments they produce are themselves large. This refinement on the King et al. model implies that if there is validity to the bargaining-environment idea, it is the bargaining environment within the government that matters, not the larger parliamentary bargaining environment" (Warwick 1994: 47).

Warwick introduces the variable "ideological diversity," similar to what I called "range" in Chapter 7 and "ideological distances" in Chapter 8. It measures the ideological diversity of the government coalition on the basis of a series of indicators including left-right, clerical-secular, and regime support. The introduction of this variable turns polarization (the size of extremist parties) into an insignificant independent variable for majority governments. For minority governments the opposite is true: while the ideological diversity of the government is not significant, polarization is. Warwick (1994: 66) explains the difference as follows: "Although polarization shows a highly significant impact on government survival in both majority and minority situations before ideological diversity is introduced (Models 1 and 3), a comparison of Models 2 and 4 shows that it survives the introduction of ideological diversity index only in minority government situations. Correspondingly, the significant effect conveyed by the ideological diversity index is confined to majority governments."

To summarize the arguments: Most of the literature up to 1990 explained government duration in parliamentary democracies on the basis of characteristics of the party system, mainly ideological diversity and fractionalization. The reason they focused on prevailing characteristics of the parliament was that parties would determine their behavior on the basis of their probabilities of being included in the new government, and these probabilities are determined by characteristics of the party system. Warwick (1994) performed crucial experiments and introduced both characteristics of the parliament and of the government. The result was that the number of parties in parliament was replaced by the number of parties in government, which itself was replaced by the ideological distances between parties in government for majority governments. For minority governments (which are usually single-party governments), the ideological diversity of parliament remains a strong explanatory variable. Warwick interprets his findings as indicating that what determines survival is bargaining *within* governments. I now review these findings on the basis of veto players theory.

9.2. Veto Players and Government Stability

So far in this book I have presented results on the basis of spatial models without being specifically concerned about the position of the status quo. At the theoretical level (Chapters 1 and 2) I generated propositions that held for every position of the status quo, while at the empirical level I used two short-cuts. In Chapter 7 I explained why it was difficult to identify the status quo and used the position of the previous government as a proxy. In Chapter 8 I used the same approximation but the justification was more appropriate, since it is quite frequent that the default solution for not voting a budget on time is the automatic or quasi automatic adoption of the previous year's budget.

I explained that any attempt to include the status quo in empirical work has to be a posteriori, such that the status quo is defined only *after* the new legislation passes. The reason is that new legislation in an area (e.g., social security) may or may not include provisions modifying several bills. For example, the new social security bill may include provisions about mental health. This subject may have existed in other pieces of legislation, or it may not have been addressed legislatively in the past. If such provisions are included in the new bill, then the status quo is determined not only by the provisions of the previous social security bill, but also by the provisions of other bills specifying the appropriate definitions and conditions related to mental health. If mental health is not included in the new bill, then the status quo should not include provisions on mental health. In addition to the difficulties of identifying the specific policy position of the status quo discussed in the previous paragraph, there are more serious theoretical problems with the concept that are related to the issues of government duration.

The "status quo" is an essential element of every multidimensional policy model, like the ones I have presented throughout this book. One first assumes the positions of the status quo and the ideological preferences of different actors, and then identifies how each of these actors are going to behave. While the concept of "status quo" is essential in all theoretical models, little attention has been paid to how the concept corresponds to actual political situations. Usually models assume a policy space, complete information, and stability of the status quo, just like all the models I presented in Part I. Such models may be sufficient when discussing simple situations like legislation in a specific policy area. However, they are inadequate when one discusses more complicated issues like government selection or government survival.

I want to introduce two elements of uncertainty that will be essential in understanding the mechanism of government selection and duration. The first element is the uncertainty between policies and outcomes; the second is uncertainty over time. Let me analyze each of these elements.

Uncertainty between policies and outcomes. Several models have assumed that there is uncertainty between policies and outcomes (Gilligan and Krehbiel

1987, Krehbiel 1991). According to these models, actors have preferences over outcomes but have to select policies. The modeling implication is that actors are located on the basis of their preferences in an outcome space, but they cannot select outcomes directly. They have to select policies, which include a random element in them. Only some experts have specific knowledge of the exact correspondence between policies and outcomes, and as a result decisionmakers have to extract this information from them (I say "extract" because experts may not want to reveal it and act strategically). However, these models do not study any further variations in outcomes; once a policy is selected it always has the same outcomes. But this is a simplification that has been disputed by the "events approach" to coalition formation.

Uncertainty between current and future outcomes. The "events approach" highlighted the fact that unexpected events might challenge governments and divide the coalitions that support them. The reason that these events are unexpected is because they are either exclusively determined by happenings in the environment or jointly determined by such happenings and the policies of governments. However, such outside events modify the position of the status quo in the outcome space even if the policy does not change. For example, when there is an oil crisis, the government budget (which could have been a perfect compromise at the time it was voted) appears completely inadequate because the price of energy increases dramatically. Such variations of outcomes (while policy remains constant) are additional sources of uncertainty. The uncertainty between policies and outcomes was dealt with at the time of the vote of the budget, but now the same policy produces very different outcomes than before.

Similarly, import or export policies may have different results when a trade partner modifies some component of his behavior, or when outside conditions change. If a country is dumping its products in the international market, or if it is exposed to, say, radioactivity because of a nuclear accident, trade restrictions may become necessary, while such measures were not even considered before.

If parties know that they are going to be confronted with both kinds of uncertainty, how are they going to address the situation when forming a government? First they will consider the distance between coalition partners a very significant factor to be taken into account. Reducing the distances between veto players enables governments to produce a policy program *before* they form *and* respond to *subsequent* exogenous shocks.

How would negotiations among potential veto players take place? Figure 9.1 presents an *outcome* space with three potential veto players. They would discuss their government program and include in it all the cases where the outcomes (produced by existing policies) are far away from their preferences. For example, if the status quo was in the position SQ, they would move it in some point within W(SQ), and if it were at SQ1, they would move it inside

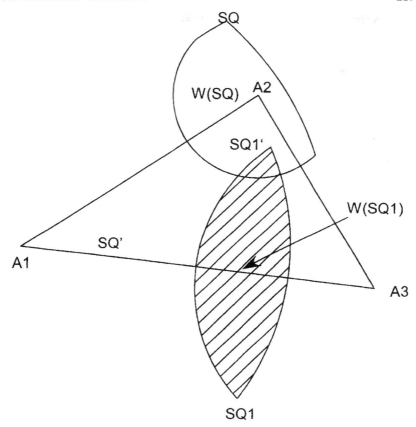

Figure 9.1. Different effects of shocks on government coalitions.

W(SQ1). They would be able to include more items in the government program the further away the status quo is and the closer they are to each other, as we have seen in the first part of this book. In particular Figure 1.6 and Proposition 1.4 demonstrate that (transaction costs aside) what matters is not the number of veto players but the size of their unanimity core.

Suppose that some exogenous shock replaces an existing outcome. The underlying assumption in the "events approach" literature is that the size of the shock matters, and some of them are too big for certain governments to handle. I will show that this is an inaccurate way of thinking about the problem. In my model there are two possibilities: this movement can be "manageable" or "nonmanageable." By manageable movement I mean a replacement of SQ that either is very close to the government program (the shock in effect simulates government policy, so no further action is necessary), or the new SQ moves away from its previous position, so that the government program is still included in W(SQ). In Figure 9.1, moving the status quo from SQ1 to SQ1' or vice versa is a manageable situation, because the coalition can respond by leaving SQ1' or moving back to SQ1', as the case may be. What is of interest in this example is that the size of the shock is not necessarily related to whether the situation is manageable. It is possible that large shocks are easily manageable.[4]

By contrast, the situation is nonmanageable if the change in status quo has made an agreement among veto players impossible. For example, if SQ is moved to SQ' in Figure 9.1, an agreement to go back to whatever solution was included in the government program (it had to be within W(SQ)) is impossible. Again, nonmanageable situations are not necessarily the result of large shocks.

What are the implications of this analysis for government formation and duration? For government formation, if there is a cluster of parties that are close to each other and they have a majority of seats in parliament, they are likely to become the government coalition. If there is no such cluster, either a majority government will form out of parties with larger differences, or a minority government will form. Minority government will be more likely to form when the opposition is divided (otherwise the government could have been formed by the opposition also). These expectations are confirmed by the empirical analysis of Martin and Stevenson (2001: 41), who find that "any potential coalition is less likely to form the greater the ideological incompatibility of its members, regardless of its size." They also find that the probability of formation of minority governments increases when the opposition is divided.

In terms of government duration, Warwick has performed all the crucial tests implied by the above analysis: he has demonstrated that the standard variables measuring parliamentary characteristics (fractionalization and polarization of the party system) are replaced by the ideological distances of parties in government, except for minority governments where parliamentary polarization has a significant impact.

Finally, one additional reason why polarization of parliaments may have an independent impact on government survival is what was discussed in Chapter 6 under the title "qualified majority equivalents." The existence of anti-system parties essentially increases the required majority for political decisionmaking from simple to qualified majority, and as a result reduces significantly the winset of the status quo.

---

[4] For example, if the new position of SQ is covered (see definition in Chapter 1) by the old one, the situation is manageable. The result is consistent with Lupia and Strom's (1995) analysis. They have also included electoral expectations of the different parties in order to determine whether there will be an election or not. A common conclusion of both our analyses is that there is no direct correspondence between the size of the shock and government termination.

9.3. Government Stability and Executive Dominance

On the basis of the previous discussion, government duration is proportional to the government's ability to respond to unexpected shocks, and this ability is a function of the veto player constellation: the size of the unanimity core of the veto players (Proposition 1.4). According to my explanation there is no logical relationship between government duration and executive dominance as argued by Arend Lijphart (1999) (see discussion in Chapter 4).

However, in Chapter 4 I only argued that government duration and executive dominance were logically independent, and left their high correlation (the basis of Lijphart's argument) unexplained. Now I come back to examine the reasons for the correlation between government duration and executive dominance. My argument is that it is a spurious correlation, and I will explain which way the causal arrows go.

In Chapter 4 I presented evidence that executive dominance is a function of government agenda-setting powers. Indeed, while every parliamentary government has the possibility of attaching a question of confidence to any particular bill, or, equivalently, to make the commitment that if a particular bill is defeated it will resign, this is a weapon of high political cost and cannot be used frequently. Of more everyday use are institutional procedures that restrict the amendments on the floor, and the more of those weapons the government controls, the more it can present "take it or leave it" questions to the parliament, and the more it has its legislation accepted as a result. Hence, Chapter 4 established a causal relationship between government agenda setting and one of Lijphart's variables: executive dominance.

The current chapter establishes a causal relationship between veto players and the other variable used by Lijphart in his analysis: government duration. The argument was that the closer the veto players, the more they are able to manage policy shocks, and consequently the longer the duration of the government. In fact, my argument moves one step further and makes predictions about government formation: the closer different potential veto players, the higher probability that they will form a government.

What needs to be established is a relation between veto player and government agenda control. But this issue was addressed in Chapter 7. There I pointed out the strong correlation between the two variables at the national level, and provided the reasons why this correlation is not accidental. I was not able to establish the direction of causation, but I pointed out three different arguments that can account for the relationship. The first was a causal argument going from veto players to government agenda setting: multiple veto players cannot introduce important legislation, and therefore countries with coalition governments have not been able to introduce such agenda-setting rules. The second was a strategic argument going from agenda-setting powers to veto players: if

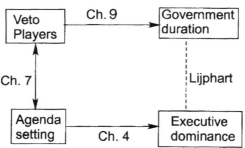

Figure 9.2. Causal relationships between VPs, government agenda setting, government duration, and "executive dominance."

agenda-setting powers are present, coalition negotiations are easier because governments can do what they want with bare majorities or even with a minority of votes. The third was historical, that the same sociological reasons that generated multiple veto players also made them suspicious of each other, so that they refuse to provide agenda-setting powers to the winners of the coalition formation game. Whichever argument is empirically corroborated provides the direction of the causal relationship. For the time being this is an open question. This is why in Figure 9.2 I have included an arrow pointing in both directions between veto players and agenda-setting power.

As this figure indicates, in different parts of the book I examined the relationships between the different variables, and established the causal links between agenda setting and executive dominance (Chapter 4), veto players and government duration (Chapter 9), and veto players and agenda setting (Chapter 7). Figure 9.2 thus traces the origins of the correlation between government duration and executive dominance.

9.4. Conclusions

Government formation and duration in parliamentary democracies has been a subject of numerous studies. While the empirical literature had identified party system characteristics as the defining variables of government duration, veto players focuses on the composition of governments. The crucial experiments performed by Warwick demonstrate that government characteristics, particularly the ideological distances among parties in government, are better explanatory factors of government duration than parliamentary (or party system) characteristics. In addition, Warwick demonstrated that the ideological distances among parties in government are better predictors of government duration than the number of parties in government, a result that is directly presented in Figure 1.6 (and Proposition 1.4).

As a result, the prediction of veto players theory that government duration is a function of the constellation of veto players is corroborated. In addition, the distances among parties are good predictors of government formation, which is consistent with the idea that parties are implicitly or explicitly using reasoning consistent with veto players analysis when they participate in the government formation process. Finally, since government duration is not an indicator of executive dominance as I argued in Chapter 4, I explained why these two variables had a strong correlation between them.

In the Introduction I referred to A. Lawrence Lowell's (1896: 73–74) "axiom in politics": "the larger the number of discordant groups that form the majority the harder the task of pleasing them all, and the more feeble and unstable the position of the cabinet." The first two sections of this chapter demonstrated that, one hundred years later, we confirm half of this axiom (the part about veto players and government instability). The other half may or may not be correct, depending on the interpretation of the word "feeble." If "feeble" means a cabinet that cannot make important shifts in policy, it is exactly what the second and third parts of this book have demonstrated. But if it means lack of "executive dominance," it is based on a spurious correlation, as the last section of this chapter indicates.

10

Judiciary and Bureaucracies

IN THE INTRODUCTION I connected the legislative game and the capacity of political actors to change the status quo with the independence and significance of the judiciary and bureaucracy in a country. The reasoning was simple: both the judiciary (when making statutory interpretations) and the bureaucracies can be legislatively overruled if they make choices the (legislative) veto players disagree with, so they are likely to avoid such choices. In fact, both the judiciary and the bureaucracy will try to interpret the law according to their point of view (or perhaps interests) while eliminating the possibility that they will be overruled. High policy stability will thus give more discretion to both bureaucrats and judges.

In game theoretic terms I describe a sequential game where the bureaucrats or judges make the first move (interpret the existing laws) and the veto players make the second (decide to overrule or not and how). This description can be found in the literature quite frequently.[1] I am discussing only the mechanism of legislative overrule, and I am not addressing other factors (like length of tenure) that presumably also affect independence.

In this chapter my goal is to discuss this literature and present empirical evidence corroborating the expectations. It should be noted that we are in the beginning of the empirical search, and we have advanced more on judges in a comparative perspective than on bureaucrats. The empirical analysis will therefore depend either on indicators developed as proxies or assessments by experts that sometimes turn out to be conflicting. My presentation will be in three parts: the first presenting the decisionmaking problem of the first mover when he chooses with the possibility of being overruled, the second applying the model to the judiciary, and the third to bureaucracies.

10.1. How to Avoid Legislative Overrule

Let us assume that there are three legislative veto players. The triangle 123 that they define is their core, the set of points that they cannot agree to change.

---

[1] Gely and Spiller (1990), Mikva and Bleich (1991), Ferejohn and Weingast (1992a, 1992b), Eskridge (1991), Cooter and Drexl (1994), and Bednar, Ferejohn, and Garrett (1996) about judges; McCubbins, Noll, and Weingast (1989), Hammond (1996), Hammond and Knott (1999) about bureaucrats.

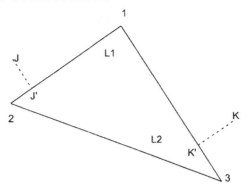

Figure 10.1. Selection of a policy within the core by first mover (bureaucracy or judiciary).

Consequently, if the first mover selects one of the points of the core, there will be no legislative overrule. Figure 10.1 presents three different possibilities. In the first two cases the first movers' ideal points J and K are outside the legislative core and they select the closest core point to them (J' and K', respectively). Despite the fact that these two choices are significantly different from each other, the veto players are incapable of changing either of them. In the third case, the first mover is located inside the legislative core but changes her mind and moves from point L1 to point L2. Since the first mover is inside the core, she can select her own ideal point.

These idealized stories are close to political realities. Think about the following cases: in the United States (a country with three veto players) the Supreme Court decided on several extremely important issues that in most other countries would have been the prerogative of the legislative branch. Desegregation and choice come immediately to mind. But tobacco and guns may join the list of political decisions delegated to courts because the political system is unable to legislate on the issue.

As an example of the change in mind of the first mover, consider the issue of sexual harassment where the burden of proof requirements changed. In the past the victim needed to show that as a result of the behavior of a superior or co-worker she was very disturbed, she lost days of work, she visited doctors, and so on. After the *Harris v. Forklift Systems* (1993) decision,[2] any behavior that would have disturbed an average person was defined as sexual harassment.

However, the model I present here is very simple, and the theoretical argument needs to be buttressed (on top of the supporting stories). The first question is what happens if the veto players are not individual but collective, the dimen-

[2] I thank Eugene Volokh for the reference.

sionality of the policy space high, and, as a consequence, there is no core as in Figure 10.1. No point is then invulnerable from a legislative overrule. Does this mean that the first mover (judiciary or bureaucracy) has no agenda-setting power? Not exactly.

In the case of absence of a legislative core, the winset of the status quo is not empty but, as demonstrated in Chapter 2, it can be quite small for certain positions of the status quo. A bureaucratic or judicial decision that has such a small winset may not be worth the effort of legislative overrule. Indeed, there are serious transaction costs for every legislative decision: one may, for example, take the initiative to present a bill, put together a coalition to support it, or eliminate opponents who may have a different opinion by buying them out or by solidifying allies. If the difference between the judicial or bureaucratic decision and the outcome a particular veto player is likely to obtain is not big enough, such an enterprise may not be worthwhile.

The discussion of existence of the core brings us to another interesting point: the legislative overrule may require different majorities, in which case the legislative core may have significant size. For example, in the United States, Supreme Court decisions may be constitutional rather than statutory interpretations. After President Clinton signed the Freedom of Religion Act into law (an act that he had practically initiated and commanded almost unanimous support in both houses of Congress), the Supreme Court decided that the law violated the Constitution because it was legislating in an area that was the jurisdiction of the states. All the proponents of the law changed their course of action and decided to introduce fifty such laws, one in each state, rather than try to modify the constitution. The reason is that very few people think that a modification of a Supreme Court constitutional decision can come in any other way but from a change in the Court's collective mind (the only way to change *Roe v. Wade* is either to wait for the Court to change its mind, or with a constitutional amendment).[3]

There are two more objections concerning the above simple game-theoretic account raised in the literature. The first is that given that the first movers in the game presented above will be able to select a policy close or identical to their own ideal point, what will the legislative branch do to prevent this event from materializing? There is extensive literature arguing that legislation will be more restrictive when there are many veto players (e.g., McCubbins, Noll, and Weingast 1987, 1989; Moe 1990; Moe and Caldwell 1994; Epstein and O'Halloran 1999). I will demonstrate that my analysis only appears to contradict this argument. The second is that there may be significant differences between parliamentary and presidential systems with respect to delegation of powers: veto players in presidential systems, according to some (Moe 1990; Moe and Cald-

---

[3] I will make the point that constitutional interpretation may turn the Court into an additional veto player in the following section.

well 1994; Strom 2000; Ackerman 2000), have explicit assignments to oversee the bureaucracy, while parliamentary veto players practice oversight collectively. As a result, this view contends that political systems differ from each other not because of the number of veto players but because of regime type.

It is interesting to note that these objections have been raised only about bureaucrats and not about judges. To my knowledge, while many American researchers have made the argument that more detailed legislation is designed to restrict the role of bureaucrats, none has made the same argument about the role of judges.[4] Similarly, the difference between presidentialism and parliamentarism has appeared in the literature on bureaucracies and not in the literature about the judiciary. Given that my presentation on bureaucracies and the judiciary was symmetric, I do not know the reason for this differential treatment in the literature. However, I will respect it, and address these points in the third section on bureaucracies.

10.2. Veto Players and the Judiciary

10.2.1. Traditional Theories of the Judiciary

The usual distinction in comparative law is between countries with traditions of common law and civil law. In common law countries (the United Kingdom, and all its ex-colonies such as the United States, Australia, New Zealand, Ireland, and Malta), "laws" are seen less as the acts of parliament and more as the accumulation of decisions and interpretations of the judges. The central rule in common law countries is *stare decisis* ("let the decision stand"), the Latin words for the importance of precedent. Decisions made by previous judges in similar cases are binding for a judge. As a result, judges create the law as well as apply and interpret it.

In countries that follow the civil law tradition, the foundation of law is a comprehensive and authoritative legal code. It is upon this code that legislatures build a superstructure of statutes. The most frequently used of such codes is the Napoleonic Code (used in France, Belgium, Greece, Luxembourg, Netherlands, Italy, Spain, and Portugal). A second such code is the German Civil Code (used in Germany, Norway, Sweden, Finland, Denmark, and Iceland). In civil law countries the judges interpret the law; they do not make it.

---

[4] For a European exception see Fritz Scharpf (1970), who has made precisely this argument about the German legislature. His point is that German law is very detailed for a series of reasons, among which are the restraint of judges (who decide on both procedural and substantive grounds) as well as the restraint of state bureaucracies (who are independent from the federal government). In Scharpf's analysis, American courts do not have substantive review of bureaucratic decisions, and there are federal bureaucracies. These differences may account for the absence of the argument that detailed legislation restricts judges in the United States.

According to this classic distinction, the role of the judiciary should be more important in common law countries. However, more recent analyses indicate convergence of the two systems. Gallagher, Laver, and Mair (1995: 62) cite a series of authors who explicitly discuss convergence (Waltman and Holland 1988: 85), or describe the behavior of the judiciary in civil law systems in terms of "precedent" and discuss "statutes" in common law systems.

Convergence theories agree with the analysis in the first section of this chapter. According to the veto players theory, what matters for the independence and significance of the judiciary is not the legal system of a country, but whether courts are constitutional or not and the difficulty of the political system to overrule a statutory or constitutional interpretation.

We already discussed the issue of statutory interpretation as a matter of policy stability of the corresponding political system; let us now focus on the question of constitutional interpretation. This is a major issue, because if courts can interpret the constitution and base their decisions on it, they cannot be overruled by the political system. The only exception would be by a modification of the constitution, which would mean that the judiciary of a country would be a veto player, since a decision by the judiciary could invalidate a law.

10.2.2. Are Judges Veto Players?

While it is clear that the judiciary of a country is not a veto player when performing statutory interpretations because it can be overruled by legislation, the opposite is true with respect to constitutional interpretation. Indeed, a rejection by a constitutional court is sufficient to abrogate legislation approved by the legislature. Some countries like France have *a priori and abstract* review of legislation, invalidating laws on constitutional grounds before they are applied. In this case, the Conseil Constitutionel of France acts as an additional chamber of parliament and can abort whole pieces of legislation or parts of them just before this legislation is signed into law by the president of the republic (Stone 1992).

Stone-Sweet (2000) argues that the introduction of scrutiny by constitutional courts has profoundly altered the role of both courts and legislatures, and has introduced a constant interaction between the two institutions. According to this interaction the legislatures are always aware that their actions can be overruled by constitutional courts, and sometimes even ask the courts for instructions in order to immunize their decisions from judicial abrogation. According to Stone-Sweet, as courts become increasingly more elaborate in different areas, the discretion of legislatures is reduced. As a result, we are in the process of the formation of a government of judges. Volcansek (2001) makes similar arguments in the Italian case, and explains how and why the Italian constitutional court has intervened on the questions of divorce and executive decrees.

The essence of these arguments is correct: constitutional courts can abort legislation, and consequently they are veto players. However, the conclusions and predictions about governments of judges seem exaggerated. Why? My answer is based on the discussion of the absorption rule in Chapter 1. While constitutional judges are veto players, most of the time they are absorbed.

As we discussed in Chapter 1, for a veto player to make a policy difference it has to be located outside the unanimity core of the other existing veto players (see Proposition 1.3). I will argue that constitutional courts very often are located inside the unanimity core of the other veto players. The main reason is the appointment process to the highest positions. The only major country without any restrictions to a purely politicized appointment process is France, where the nine members of the Conseil Constitutionel are appointed by the president of the republic (three), the president of the National Assembly (three), and the president of the Senate (three) without any specified qualifications or approvals.

In the United States the president's nominees have to be approved by the Senate. In Italy one-third of the members of the Constitutional Court (five) are appointed by the president of the republic, one-third by the judiciary, and one-third by the parliament by a two-thirds majority in a joint session of the Chamber of Deputies and the Senate; all appointments have to be judges with twenty years experience or tenured law professors. In Germany eight members are elected by the Bundestag, and the other eight by the Bundesrat with a two-thirds majority; all members must be qualified to be federal judges (and six of the sixteen must actually be federal judges). In Spain two of the twelve judges are appointed by the government, two by the judiciary, and four by each chamber of parliament by a three-fifths majority; their judicial competence must be well known (Stone-Sweet 2000: 49).

The restrictions imposed upon the selection of members of the highest institution of the judiciary eliminate extreme positions, and practically guarantee that the median of the court will be centrally located in the policy space. However, the means used by American political scientists and judicial scholars to study the U.S. Supreme Court are unavailable for other courts because deliberations are secret and most of the time dissents (if any) remain unknown and certainly are not signed and published.

The above account generates another question: how is it possible for constitutional courts to ever veto legislation under these conditions? That is, under what conditions is the median of the Supreme Court not included in the unanimity core of the existing veto players? I will provide two plausible answers to this question, and remind the reader that plausibility is the most one can expect unless the black box of judicial deliberations opens.

First, judges are selected for competence and for their (known) policy positions. Some of their positions may be unknown because they have not deliberated on every issue, and some positions may be considered secondary so that they are not subject to litmus tests. One of these issues may become important or controversial, like gay marriages or euthanasia, and the Supreme Court may be in disagreement with policymakers, but this was not the criterion of selection in the past. In fact, this is likely to be a new dimension that cuts across party lines.

Second, a veto by the Supreme Court should not necessarily be considered as opposition to government action. It may be the expression of *procedural preferences* (Rose-Ackerman 1990; Ferejohn and Weingast 1992a), like the introduction of technical restrictions. The court may be indicating to the government that this particular way of reaching its goal violates the constitution, so a different course of action is necessary. Stone-Sweet (1992) provides several examples when the French parliament asked the Constitutional Council to provide specific wording so that legislation would survive the court's constitutional scrutiny. Finally, courts through their own interpretation of the law might also provoke new, more desirable legislation. This is the way Van Hees and Steunenberg (2000) explain the famous decision by the Dutch Supreme Court permitting euthanasia under the specific conditions that occurred in the case under review, which then provoked additional legislation on the issue.

In conclusion, judges are not veto players when they make statutory decisions. They are veto players when they make constitutional interpretations, but most of the time they are absorbed by the existing political veto players. The only exceptions would be if the existing veto players are located in extreme policy positions (the case of France under the first Mitterrand government [1981] comes to mind where the government wanted to implement a series of significant policy changes while the constitutional court had been appointed by right-wing governments), or if new issues come under consideration. In these cases, constitutional courts should be counted as additional veto players. However, given the black box that contains decisionmaking by the judiciary, it would be impossible to attribute this to veto player policy positions. As a result, I have not included the judiciary (not even in the form of constitutional courts) as a veto player in my accounts in this book.

10.2.3. Empirical Evidence

If the judiciary is not an additional veto player, then we can study judicial discretion as a dependent variable. As I have argued in this chapter, political systems that exhibit policy stability will also have independence of the judiciary. Is there any empirical evidence to support this claim? Several empirical studies have tried to measure independence of the judiciary. Some of them have tried to test predictions similar to the ones introduced in this book.

Lijphart has introduced a measurement of strength of judicial review "based first on the distinction between the presence and absence of judicial review and, second, on three degrees of *activism* in the assertion of this power by the courts" (1999: 225–26; emphasis added). He also determines the difficulty by which the constitution of a country is amended (by higher than a two-thirds majority, by "two-thirds or equivalent," "between two-thirds and ordinary majorities," and by ordinary majorities). He scores the thirty-six countries he studies on the basis of these two variables and finds that "judicial review" has a moderate but statistically significant correlation with constitutional rigidity.

Similarly, Nicos Alivizatos (1995) has introduced a fourfold typology of what he calls "judicial politicization," the extent to which judges "influence the decisionmaking process." For this purpose he determines a dependent variable on whether a country has a constitutional court or not, and whether the judges are considered activists or not.[5] Countries with a constitutional court and activist judges are scored as four, countries with a constitutional court and non-activist judges are scored as three, countries with no constitutional court but active judges are scored as two, and countries without a court or judicial activism are scored as one. He introduces a series of possible independent variables to assess what causes "judicial politicization." First, he classifies countries as decentralized or not (actually using three categories, one for federal countries, one for de facto federalism, and one for unitary countries); second, he assesses the degree of left-right polarization (in two categories); third, he introduces a qualitative variable expressing veto players (scored one for single party, three for multiparty, and two for mixture of the two); fourth, he introduces a variable assessing parliamentary anomalies (civil wars or dictatorships); fifth, a variable indicating degree of integration in the European Union (at the time some countries were members, some were about to become members, and others were not). He finds that the decision to have a constitutional court depends mainly on two variables: whether the country is federal and whether in the past there were parliamentary anomalies. "Judicial politicization" on the other hand depends on decentralization, polarization, and veto players (at p levels less than .05).

Finally, Cooter and Ginsburg (1996) have used a scale of "judicial discretion" generated by a series of experts. A second and far more creative way of assessing judicial discretion is through the move to restrict liability. "We found that courts with high predicted daring were willing to innovate in this area of private law more than other courts. Courts with low predicted daring, by contrast, were content to wait for legislative adoption of the new standard." In fact, the two authors classify different countries on the basis of whether the courts introduced strict liability standards before the legislature, or whether they simply reversed the burden of proof from the plaintiff to the defendant, or waited for the legislature to change the law.

---

[5] To use the author's specification: "depending on whether their courts have actually given unambiguous signs of judicial activism as opposed to judicial self-restraint."

Cooter and Ginsburg use two independent variables. The first is "the number of legislative vetoes" that is determined the following way: "In unicameral parliamentary systems, where the government is formed by the majority coalition in the legislature, there is essentially one veto on legislation. . . . Other systems have two vetoes on new legislation. Such would be the case in either a bicameral parliamentary system (as in Germany), or an essentially unicameral parliamentary system with a strong president (as in France)." The second independent variable that they use is the duration of government coalition as "a simpler indicator of party dominance" (1996: 299). They find that both these independent variables affect judicial discretion, whether measured by the judicial expert assessments or by the strict liability test.

The careful reader may have already identified problems with each one of the two independent variables used by Cooter and Ginsburg. The variable "number of vetoes" uses what I called the "numerical criterion" in Chapter 1. I stated there that this is a questionable basis for comparative statics across countries. It ignores differences in the ideological positions of different veto players, which may be very important from one country to another. In addition, the particular scores do not adequately reflect the institutions of the different countries. For example, France is scored with two, although the president has no veto power; the Netherlands or Austria with two, although their respective upper chambers are very weak (in fact, Austria's is weaker than the United Kingdom's, which is scored as one veto). Israel and Denmark received a score of one because they are unicameral, despite the fact that they usually have coalition governments. The variable "duration" as a measure of dominance of one sort or another has been criticized in the third section of Chapter 4, so I do not repeat my objections here.

These studies have used different ways of measuring judicial independence and have correlated it with different independent variables, some of which were connected with veto players, some of them not, and yet others supposedly connected but incorrectly so. I will use the independent variables in each of these studies: *judpol* for Alivizatos's "judicial politicization," *judrev* for Lijphart's "judicial review," *experts* and *strict liability* for Cooter and Ginsburg's two different measures of judicial independence. I will correlate these variables with the qualitative measure of veto players introduced in Chapter 7. I have extended this measure for the countries covered by Cooter and Ginsburg, but not for the thirty-six countries of Lijphart. Some of the tests will therefore cover the eighteen countries in the Alivizatos dataset, some the twenty countries of Cooter and Ginsburg, and others all twenty-four countries included in the table.

Table 10.1 introduces the data to be analyzed. The missing data are generated because Alivizatos covers only West European countries, while Cooter and Ginsburg have a significant intersection with these countries but cover other countries as well. Only Lijphart covers all twenty-four countries. Table 10.2 produces the Pearson correlations as an easily interpretable measure of

TABLE 10.1
Judicial Independence

Country	Judpol	Judrev	Experts	Strict Liability	Decentralization	Politicization	Veto Players	Duration
Australia		3	2.33	1	3	1	2	9
Austria	3	3		2	3	2	2	8
Belgium	3	3	3.5	3	3	1	3	4.8
Canada		3	2.33	2	3	1	2	8
Denmark	1	2		1	1	1	3	8
Finland	1	1		1	1	1	3	4.8
France	4	3	3.7	3	1	2	2	6.8
Germany	4	4	3.46	2	3	2	3	6.3
Greece	2	2			1	2	1	
Iceland	1	2			1	1	3	
Ireland	2	2		1	1	2	2	6.4
Israel		1	4.5	2	1	2	2	2.4
Italy	4	3	3.33	2	2	2	3	1.3
Japan		2	2.17	1	1	1	1	9.4
Luxembourg	1	1		3	1	1	2	4
New Zealand		1	2	1	1	1	1	6
Norway	1	2		1	1	2	2	4
Portugal	3	2			1	2	2	
Spain	3	3	2	1	3	2	1	6
Sweden	2	2	2.5	1	1	2	2	4.2
Switzerland	2	1			3	1	3	
Netherlands	2	1	4.2	2	1	1	3	2.5
United Kingdom	2	1	2.1	1	2	2	1	8
United States		4	4.42	3	3	1	3	6.9

TABLE 10.2
Correlations between Independent Variables with and without Australia, Canada, Israel, and the Netherlands

	10.2A				10.2B			
	Judrev	*Experts*	*Strict Liability*	*Judpol*	*Judrev*	*Experts*	*Strict Liability*	*Judpol*
Judrev (Lijphart)	1.000				1.000			
Experts	**0.12611**	1.000			**0.6446**	1.000		
Strict Liability	0.4003	0.7912	1.000		0.5286	0.9132	1.000	
Judpol (Alivizatos)	0.8660	**0.3259**	0.5547	1.000	0.8346	**0.7603**	0.6471	1.000

Note: Correlations among different indices are similar whether the four countries are included or not, with few exceptions (noted in bold).

the association among the different independent variables. The reader can verify that while Lijphart's data correlate very well with Alivizatos's assessments in the subset of West European countries, they have significant differences with the expert judgments when we go to countries outside Europe. In particular, Israel is classified as a very weak judiciary by Lijphart (one) and very strong by the expert reports (4.5, even higher than the U.S. Supreme Court), while Australia and Canada are coded as very independent in Lijphart (three), but not strong by the expert reports (2.33). Finally, another country of disagreement is the Netherlands, where the judiciary is considered very independent by the experts, not at all by Lijphart, and intermediate by Alivizatos. These remarks are made to indicate that even experts disagree with some assessments. It is possible that these disagreements are based on different underlying properties of the variable that each one of them examines (as the different names they use indicate). If one eliminates these four countries of disagreement, the correlations between the expert judgments become significantly higher. Given the scarcity of countries and data, I do not intend to drop the countries where experts disagree from the empirical tests.

Table 10.3 presents the relationship between the different measures expressing the independence or importance of the judiciary and the corresponding dependent variables, one of which is always a qualitative expression of veto players. While all the literature under review uses OLS estimation, the technique is inappropriate given that the dependent variable is composed of only three or four groups of countries. In the estimations that follow I use an appropriate ordered probit technique whenever the dependent variable has discrete

TABLE 10.3
Judicial Independence as a Function of Veto Players

Independent Variable		Judpol (Alivizatos)	Judrev (Lijphart)	Strict Liability	Strict Liability	Strict Liability	Experts	Experts	Experts	Judpol (Alivizatos)
Dependent Variables	Veto Players (z or t)	1.292** (0.6305)	0.4117 (-0.3484)	0.8022** (0.4311)	0.8145** (0.4207)	0.7952** (0.4432)	0.9652**** (0.2125)	0.7212*** (0.2456)	0.8514**** (0.2143)	0.6308** (0.3011)
	Polarization (z or t)	3.2597**** (1.0628)	0.9319** (0.5199)	-0.068 (0.5555)	—	—	0.1392 (0.3288)	—	—	1.6745**** (0.4522)
	Decentral-ization (z or t)	0.9234*** (0.3632)	0.9837**** (0.3045)	0.2959 (0.2894)	0.2954 (0.2893)	—	-0.3155* (0.1848)	—	—	0.5093*** (0.1939)
	Duration (z or t)	—	—	—	—	-0.0437 (0.1245)	—	-0.0866 (0.0812)	—	—
Number Observations		18	24	20	20	20	14	14	14	18
PseudoR² or Adjust. R²		0.371	0.234	0.136	0.136	0.113	0.579	0.537	0.532	0.556

Notes: Columns with the independent variable marked by *** use OLS estimates. Standard errors are in parentheses.

* $p < 0.10$
** $p < 0.05$
*** $p < 0.01$
**** $p < 0.001$
All tests are one-tailed.

values. The last four columns of Table 10.3 present OLS estimations because the dependent variable is continuous. For comparison purposes I have estimated the data generated by Alivizatos twice: once by the correct procedure (ordered probit) and once by the traditional one (OLS). Note the difference in pseudo R^2 of the probit estimation in the first row from the adjusted R^2 of the OLS technique in the last.

I have estimated different models. In each case I started by including two variables: veto players and political decentralization. I discussed the "veto players" variable in Chapter 7. The variable decentralization is measuring whether a country is unitary, federal, or in between. I have included this variable because the judiciary in federal countries may be asked to adjudicate conflicts among different levels of government, so there is an additional source of significant decisions to be made by the judiciary. In fact, as we saw in Chapter 6, the independent judiciary is considered by some authors (Bednar, Eskridge, and Ferejohn 2001) as a condition for federalism. Like some of the literature (Alivizatos) I have added the variable "polarization." This is essentially a qualitative version of the variable "alternation" that was used in Chapters 7 and 8. However, it is not clear that this variable will have a positive or negative effect on the role of the judiciary. It can be argued that the judiciary will moderate extremes of different governments, or that it will be intimidated by the prospect of being overruled. As a matter of fact, Alivizatos's variable comes out positive or negative depending on the model. When it comes out nonsignificant, I reestimate the model by dropping "polarization." In the case of the two independent variables from the Cooter and Ginsburg article, I also integrated a model including the variable "government duration" because according to the authors' expectations it should be significant. It turns out that it was not. Finally, I do not include in the table tests of the judicial system (civil law versus common law), because none of them comes out statistically significant, and some of them even have the wrong sign.

The results presented in Table 10.3 lead to the following conclusions. In all the models except for two the statistical significance of veto players is high (above .05 in one-tailed tests). The two exceptions are the one using Lijphart's independent variable with no statistical significance,[6] and the one testing Cooter and Ginsburg's hypothesis on the basis of strict liability data (significance at the .10 level).

In addition, most of the time decentralization is statistically significant. On the other hand, polarization does not appear to be significant except for Alivizatos's indicator and comes out several times with a different sign. Consequently, the empirical evidence corroborates the expectation that independence of the judiciary increases as a function of veto players. In addition, most of

---

[6] Even with Lijphart's variable, the z-statistic doubles when one drops the four countries where the legal experts significantly disagree with Lijphart's scoring.

the time there is empirical support for the idea that federal countries will have more independent judiciary than unitary ones. There is no evidence that the judicial system of a country (common versus civil law) or the polarization of political forces in it affect judicial independence.

10.3. Veto Players and Bureaucracies

In this section I first discuss the different arguments about bureaucracies presented in the literature. I single out and focus in particular on two arguments that come to different expectations from the theory presented in this book. The first has to do with the independence of bureaucracies, whether it increases or decreases with veto players; the second with the independent variable that explains bureaucratic independence: is it veto players or regime type?

10.3.1. Theories of Bureaucracies

Mathew McCubbins, Roger Noll, and Barry Weingast have written a series of articles that compose probably the most influential study of administrative law. In two of the most important (McCubbins, Noll, and Weingast 1987, 1989), the authors (henceforth "McNollgast") focus predominately on how legislatures create administrative law that effectively restricts the bureaucracy to performing the duties prescribed by the enacting coalition. The basic problem according to them is *moral hazard*, the possibility for bureaucracies to choose policies that differ from the preferences of the enacting coalition.

In order to avoid moral hazard, legislatures can create administrative law, which has three major characteristics: First, the enacting coalition should create for the bureaucracy an environment that mirrors the politics at the time of enactment. Second, they should stack the deck in favor of the groups that are the most affected and the most favored by the coalition. Third, agency policies should exhibit an autopilot characteristic: they should enable policy changes as the preferences of the interested groups change.

This analysis has certain consequences for the model developed in the first part of this chapter. Given that the first movers in the game I presented above will be able to select a policy close or identical to their own ideal point, the legislative branch will *stack the deck* to avoid this possibility. McNollgast (1987, 1989) argue that no political actor will enter an agreement unless their interests are protected, and as a result, legislators will seek to create such protection to themselves when they write administrative law.

On the basis of the arguments and findings of this literature, Terry Moe (1990) and David Epstein and Sharyn O'Halloran (1999) have argued that legislation will be more cumbersome when the legislative body is more divided because they will try to lock into the legislation the intents of the coalition that produced it, leading to a reduction of the independence of bureaucracies. This argument seems to contradict my account, and so I address it in detail.

My argument is based on what may happen *after* the bureaucratic decision (*ex post*), while the McNollgast arguments are based on what the legislature will do beforehand (*ex ante*). I expect, that keeping legislation constant, bureaucrats and judges will be more independent from government when there are many veto players. McNollgast's "deckstacking" argument *does not keep legislation constant*; in fact, the essence of this argument is to compare the different kinds of legislation produced under different veto player configurations. In addition, the "deckstacking" argument concerns independence of bureaucrats *from the coalition enacting legislation*. These are two different arguments; let me take them one at a time.

First, let me give my own expectation for administrative legislation as a function of veto players. Given the freedom of courts and bureaucrats to interpret legislation freely when there are multiple veto players, these veto players will prefer to restrict them *ex ante*, that is, would like to include procedural restrictions inside the legislation itself (exactly as McNollgast argue). Would they be able to do so? It depends on their preferences for this kind of legislation. If their preferences are similar then they will be able to do so. If, however, they have preferences as to how to tie the hands of different bureaucrats (one party wanting to empower citizens to blow the whistle, the other to have strong and independent monitoring agencies, to use a well-known example [McCubbins and Schwartz 1984]), there may not be agreement. Thus, in case of multiple veto players the actual prediction depends on the preferences of the existing veto players. On the other hand, single veto players can overrule bureaucrats or judges at any time (assuming no transaction or political costs). As a result, such governments would not care about introducing additional restrictions into legislation.

This argument expects cumbersome bureaucratic legislation to be *sometimes* the outcome of multiple veto players, while simple legislation to be *always* the outcome of single veto players. In other words, multiple veto players are a necessary but not sufficient condition for cumbersome bureaucratic legislation. As a result, on average, one would expect more cumbersome legislation in the case of multiple veto players (as McNollgast predict), but would also expect higher variance in the case of multiple veto players, exactly as the argument presented in Chapter 1 specifies (see Figure 1.7). Huber and Shipan (2002) and Franchino (2000) have found different average levels of restrictive legislation, but have not tested for the variance component of this argument.

My second point is that the deckstacking argument is about bureaucratic independence from the enacting coalition, while I am interested in independence from government, or from the political principals at the time of the decision. It may be the case that the enacting coalition was successful in restricting bureaucrats through ex ante restrictions built into law, but if this coalition is replaced, then the new principals will not be able to force the bureaucrats to obey their wishes. In order to do that they may have to change the law, and a multiple veto player coalition may be unable to do so.

The distinction between enacting and current coalition may not be significant in the United States, because divided government has been the rule for decades, and, given supermajoritarian restrictions in the Senate (Chapter 6), even the periods of one-party government almost disappear. However, in other countries one cannot eliminate the distinction between enacting coalition and coalition in power, and it is independence from the current political leadership that defines bureaucratic or judicial independence.

In conclusion, my argument is that, keeping legislation constant, bureaucratic independence from current veto players increases with the number and distances among veto players. In addition, legislation becomes more cumbersome on average (although the variance of this prediction is a function of veto players). Under the same conditions, the deckstacking argument expects more cumbersome legislation, and less independence of bureaucrats from enacting coalitions. The two arguments are different from each other and not incompatible.

The second issue raised by the literature on bureaucracies is whether there are specific problems of multiple principals associated with the presidential regime as opposed to veto players. There are several articles that make the claim that parliamentarism has a unity of direction of bureaucracies compared to presidentialism. The argument has been made by Moe and Caldwell (1994), who compare the British and the American system, by Ackerman (2000), who criticizes the bureaucracies of the United States, and by Strom (2000), who analyzes not just bureaucracies but more generally the delegation characteristics of parliamentary systems. Out of these three pieces, the first two make arguments that do not identify the causal connections. It is indeed possible that the U.S. system presents problems of unity of direction of bureaucracies (as both Ackerman and Moe and Caldwell claim) and that the British system has unity of direction (as Moe and Caldwell argue), but the reason for these features is the distinction between single and multiple veto players, not the difference in regimes. This argument, however, cannot be made about Strom, who explicitly compares the two systems and addresses the veto players argument, so I focus on his presentation and address the question of bureaucratic independence on the basis of his analysis.

According to Strom, the major characteristic of a parliamentary regime is the simplicity of its structure of delegation. Indeed, from elections to selection of prime minister to the selection of ministers to the instructions to bureaucrats, the whole political life is a series of delegations from individual or collective principals to individual or collective agents. By contrast, delegation in presidential systems, ignoring the issue of individual or collective actors, takes place from single principals to multiple agents (the people select multiple institutions), from multiple principals to single actors (the different legislative institutions delegate to single agencies), or from multiple principals to multiple agents (sometimes the legislative institutions may have different agencies compete for some particular task).

However, this is the ideal type representation of the two systems, and Strom recognizes that reality may come in different shades (in fact, he acknowledges that some of these shades are determined by the veto players theory). I want to expand on these points and argue that the single chain of delegation is a simplification. This simplification may be important in order to highlight characteristics of presidentialism, like the explicit supervision of bureaucracies by the different principals, compared to the absence of similar hearings in parliamentary systems; however, it ignores decisionmaking inside the government, which, in case of multiparty governments, may be a single principal only in a very abstract and black box–like way.

Let us try to open the black box of government: according to Strom, the prime minister delegates to the ministers, and the ministers delegate to the bureaucrats, so the bureaucrats are part of the single chain of command. So, in the idealized version of Strom's argument, the prime minister ultimately determines the behavior of bureaucrats.

Compare this point of view with the Laver and Shepsle (1996) argument of ministerial jurisdictions discussed in Chapter 4. According to these authors, the minister decides what the bureaucrats are going to do. Not so, Thies (2001) would claim; he presents evidence of governments being composed of different parties not only across but also within ministries, so that the vice ministers are of different parties from the minister in order to keep him in check. In Thies's point of view, the chain of command is not unambiguous.

Let us now present a different point of view presented by Mark Hallerberg and Jürgen von Hagen (1999), who claim that with respect to budgets some countries delegate ultimate authority to the minister of finance in order to keep the budget at the level decided by the government. Hallerberg and von Hagen present the institutional structures of different countries and demonstrate that in several delegations of significant policymaking, powers belong to the minister of finance. Here the chain of command involves the minister and the minister of finance (it could involve the prime minister, too).

However, as the minister of finance may play a key role on economic issues, other ministries may also participate in decisionmaking relevant to their jurisdictions. For example, it does not seem plausible that in an international conference on the environment, national delegations would include bureaucrats from the ministry of the environment without representatives of the ministry of foreign affairs. In preparation of documents on women's health, bureaucrats from health and labor, for example, are likely to be involved.

Enter Wolfgang Mueller (2000) and his analysis of parliamentary systems as involving *parties* in every step of the delegation process. In Mueller's account, parties are more present in the formation of government, less in the process moving from government to individual ministers, while interference in the delegation from ministers to civil servants is illegitimate: "Civil servants should merely implement general rules and should do so impartially" (Mueller 2000: 311). Note that Mueller's point here is normative (he tells us what should be happening, not what is happening); be that as it may, it seems to severely limit the delegation principle at the level of bureaucracy.

My argument is that when we try to open the black box of delegation, several plausible theories emerge and each one of them identifies a different stream from "government" to "bureaucrats." It may be from the minister to bureaucrats directly (Laver and Shepsle), or it might involve other actors: the prime minister (Strom), minister of finance (Hallerberg and von Hagen), or other ministers or parties. My theory is the only one that encompasses all these possibilities without taking sides. It merely states that if things are important, any government actor involved will want his point of view respected, so the outcome will be acceptable by all of them. This is a minimalist position and does not take sides. It may be that the outcome will be located closer to the minister or the prime minister or to any other of these actors. More likely, skillful bureaucrats will play each one of the principals against the others.

As argued in Chapter 4, it is true that presidential and parliamentary systems differ in several dimensions (who controls the agenda, whether coalitions are fluid and address policies or are rigid and form governments). Strom's arguments add interesting variations on the theme of delegation: that in parliamentary systems the ex ante selection of agents is more effective; that in presidential systems the ex post controls are institutionalized; that parliamentarism is characterized by more indirect delegation and accountability (since there are additional stages involving government selection). However, focusing on bureaucracies, the conclusions are based on the "ideal type" (or according to Strom, the "maximalist") model, which ignores decisionmaking in government and replaces it by the principle that "civil servants have a single principal, their respective cabinet minister" (Strom 2000: 269). If we see that bureaucrats in coalition governments have multiple principals, then the more principals they have the more they can play them one against the other, and the more their independence increases.

10.3.2. Empirical Evidence

A series of empirical studies have tested the deckstacking argument of McNollgast and found supportive evidence for it. Huber and Shipan (2002), corroborated the argument with data from labor legislation in two different instances:

on the one hand American states, and on the other European countries. They found that more veto players lead to more restrictive legislation. Similarly, Epstein and O'Halloran (1999) corroborated the argument in several occasions with U.S. data. Franchino (2000) analyzed E.U. legislation and found out more extensive delegation to the European Commission (bureaucracy) when legislation is adopted by qualified majority in the Council of Ministers than when it is adopted by unanimity.

There is then a significant amount of evidence that deckstacking occurs, and that countries with multiple veto players have more cumbersome bureaucratic legislation. Is there any evidence that when legislation is fixed, bureaucrats interpret it in a more independent way when the number of veto players increases?

This is a much more difficult proposition to demonstrate, because in order to run convincing tests one would have to include the preferences of bureaucrats as part of the analysis. Identifying the preferences of bureaucrats on different issues imposes an almost insurmountable problem for the analysis. However, there is one case where we can assume the preferences of bureaucrats as known and see whether results approximate more or less such preferences. The case is the question of central bank independence.

Here is my argument. Central banks have been assigned duties related to monetary policies, exchange rates, and inflation. The literature on central banks and their significance is vast and will not be reviewed here.[7] A series of articles in economics have measured the independence of this particular branch of the bureaucracy. I examine the part of this literature that connects central bank independence (CBI) to the predictions generated by the theory presented in this book. In particular I examine whether central banks can exercise more independence when there are many (and more distant) veto players.

There are two streams in the empirical literature. The first uses CBI as a dependent variable and correlates it with institutional characteristics of countries (Bernhard 1998; Lijphart 1999; Moser 1999; Hallerberg 2001a, forthcoming). The second correlates central bank *behavior* with institutional characteristics (Lohmann 1998; Keefer and Stasavage 2000, forthcoming). Let me discuss each one of these streams separately.

Veto players and CBI. While the papers on the effects of CBI are abundant in the economics literature, very few of them have treated CBI as a dependent variable. The overwhelming majority look at the effects of CBI on a series of other variables, or on the robustness of different indicators of CBI.

The existing CBI measures use some combination of institutional characteristics to assess the independence of central banks. They involve appointment and length of tenure of the bank's governor, whether the bank participates in the formulation of monetary policy, whether price stability is the major objec-

---

[7] See Berger et al. (2001) for a review covering more than 150 articles.

tive for the bank, and whether the bank lends money only to the government. Positive answers to the above questions indicate higher CBI.

William Bernhard (1998) examined the CBI of eighteen industrial democracies in the 1970–90 period and correlated it with a series of institutional characteristics. He used three different indices of CBI generated by Grilli et al. (1991), Alesina and Summers (1993), and Cukierman (1991), but he reports results only on the basis of the average of all three. Among his independent variables were the Alford index (an indicator of class voting), strong bicameralism, a combination of polarization, coalition government, and legislative institutions that he called "threat of punishment." He found that all his variables were statistically significant.

Similarly, Lijphart (1999) examined several different CBI measures and correlated them with two different variables: federalism and executive dominance. Both these variables are correlated with veto players (see Chapter 3, which explains the positive correlation between veto players and federalism and Chapters 4 and 7 that clarify the negative correlation with executive dominance). He found that there is a strong correlation of CBI with federalism but no correlation with executive dominance.

Moser (1999) created a trichotomous variable, which he called "checks and balances," and examined all OECD countries. His argument is that high checks and balances will generate independent banks because it will be difficult for the political system to modify the charter of the bank. He found strong corroborating results. However, Moser's classification has been criticized as inconsistent. For example, Hallerberg (forthcoming) argues:

> The states Moser classifies as having strong checks and balances (Australia, Canada, Germany, Switzerland, and the United States) are the same OECD states Lijphart (1999) classifies as truly federalist states. Yet one of them, Canada, should not be a case of "strong checks and balances" according to Moser's own classification scheme, which emphasizes that chambers must have equal power and have different procedures to elect them for the checks to be strong. . . . More generally, on Lijphart's federalism scale from one to five, Moser's "strong checks and balances" states all score a five, while the average of the remaining states is just 1.9.

I agree with this assessment and in addition find that other countries like Portugal, Greece, Finland, and Iceland are misclassified in the intermediate category.[8] I infer from this account that Moser's result provides some additional evidence that federalism (but not the existence of partisan veto players) is correlated with CBI.

---

[8] Portugal has a president with veto powers, so it should be included in the countries with strong checks and balances, while the other countries have a government that agree with the parliament, so they should be classified as weak checks and balances.

Finally, Hallerberg (forthcoming) provides a series of reasons why both overall veto players and federalism should increase central bank independence.[9] According to his argument, unitary states with single-party governments prefer both dependent central banks and flexible exchange rates; unitary states with coalition governments prefer (moderately) independent central banks and fixed exchange rates; federal systems with a single-party government (like Canada) prefer (moderately) independent central banks and flexible exchange rates; and multiparty governments in federal states prefer independent banks and flexible exchange rates. Hallerberg finds strong empirical evidence for all his predictions, both on the independence of central banks variable and on the exchange rate regime.

Hence some of the empirical research (Bernhard 1998; Hallerberg 2001) identifies both institutional and partisan veto players as correlated with CBI, while others find the correlation valid only with institutional veto players (federalism). In order to see whether there is a distinction between the two, I used Bernhard's (1998) four CBI indices and correlated them with both federalism and veto players.

Table 10.4 replicates Bernhard's (1998) data on CBI, and Table 10.5 uses these data to estimate the effects of veto players and federalism. Table 10.5 indicates that both federalism and veto players have independently high correlations with CBI. However, how can we interpret these correlations? All CBI indices are mainly institutional variables, describing what is written in the laws of the corresponding countries. Nevertheless, the laws are not always specific in all the questions the coding requires. If answers to questions are provided not by laws alone but also by prevailing practices, then the indicator is not a purely institutional measure.

Depending on whether the CBI indices involve behavioral characteristics or are purely institutional, the interpretation of the empirical findings changes. The first possibility is that the measures involve also behavioral characteristics. In this case, the evidence in Table 10.5 corroborates the veto players theory: the more veto players, the more independent this particular bureaucracy. I do not have an answer to why federalism in all empirical studies has an independent impact on CBI. One possible answer would be that in some countries (e.g., Germany, the United States), states participate in the appointment of board members of the central bank. However, this is not a universal practice.

The second possibility is that the CBI measures represent purely institutional characteristics. In this case, CBI is not an answer to the question, "If legislation is held constant, which central banks are more independent?" the question addressed in the first section of this chapter. The question pertinent to the CBI data would be, "Why do lawmakers in some countries prefer higher levels of central bank independence?" and the theory presented in this book provides no

[9] See also Clark and Hallerberg (2000).

TABLE 10.4
Central Bank Independence

Country	Decentral-ization	Veto Players	Grilli et al. (1991)	Alesina and Summers (1993)	Cukierman (1991)	Total
Australia	3	2	0.6	0.5	0.31	0.47
Austria	3	2	0.6	0.625	0.58	0.6
Belgium	3	3	0.47	0.5	0.19	0.39
Canada	3	2	0.73	0.625	0.46	0.61
Denmark	1	3	0.53	0.625	0.47	0.54
France	1	2	0.47	0.5	0.28	0.42
Germany	3	3	0.87	1	0.66	0.84
Ireland	1	2	0.47	0.625	0.39	0.49
Italy	2	3	0.33	0.45	0.16	0.33
Japan	1	1	0.4	0.625	0.16	0.4
New Zealand	1	1	0.2	0.25	0.27	0.2
Norway	1	2	0.44	0.5	0.14	0.4
Spain	3	1	0.33	0.375	0.21	0.31
Sweden	1	2	0.44	0.5	0.27	0.4
Switzerland	3	3	0.8	1	0.68	0.83
Netherlands	1	3	0.67	0.625	0.42	0.57
United Kingdom	2	1	0.4	0.5	0.31	0.42
United States	3	3	0.8	0.875	0.51	0.73

Source: Bernhard 1998.

answer. The answer requires a "genetic" kind of argument.[10] Hallerberg (forthcoming) is, to my knowledge, the only article providing reasons why different kinds of governments (federal versus unitary) *and* different configurations of veto players (single versus multiple) would have different preferences and generate different outcomes in terms of CBI and exchange rate regimes. His argument is completely independent from the argument presented in this book.

[10] This would be an argument like the one presented by Alivizatos (1995) with respect to constitutional courts (see previous section), that *ceteris paribus* such courts are likely to be present in countries with serious human rights violations in their past.

TABLE 10.5

Different Measures of Central Bank Independence (CBI) as a Function of Veto Players and Decentralization

CBI	Grilli et al. (1991)	Alesina and Summers (1993)	Cukierman (1991)	Total CBI
Veto Players	0.126***	0.1316***	0.0842**	0.1161***
(t)	(0.0423)	(0.0508)	(0.0475)	(0.0423)
Decentralization	0.0751**	0.0535*	0.0592*	0.0632**
(t)	(0.0343)	−0.0412	(0.0385)	(0.0343)
Contant	0.1073	0.2025	0.0586	0.1193
	(0.1057)	(0.127)	(0.1188)	(0.1058)
N	18	18	18	18
Adj-R^2	0.479	0.334	0.232	0.414

Note: Standard errors are in parentheses.
* $p < 0.10$.
** $p < 0,05$.
*** $p < 0.01$.
All tests are one-tailed.

Veto players and Central Bank behavior. Let us now move to a more precise expression of independence: the behavior of the bank. Is this behavior affected by the political environment under which the bank operates? In an important empirical article, Susanne Lohmann (1998) tested a series of theories related to the actual performance of the German Bundesbank. Her conclusions were that "the *behavioral* independence of the German central bank fluctuates over time with the party control of federalist veto points" (Lohmann 1998: 401).

In order to reach this conclusion, Lohmann examines five competing hypotheses: first, that the central bank has full independence and is composed of technocrats; second, that the central bank has no independence (in which case, it does not matter what it is composed of); third, that the central bank has full independence and is composed of partisans; fourth, that it has partial independence and is composed of partisans; and fifth, that it has partial independence and is composed of technocrats. Each of these combinations of composition and level of independence produces a different time trajectory of money growth as a function of the composition of government and the timing of elections: left-wing governments want expansion of monetary growth; partisan banks try to help a government of their party and hurt an opposed government particularly at the time of elections, while technocrats behave the same way regardless of who is in power; independent banks are not affected by approaching elections, while non-independent banks are.

In order to test all her hypotheses, Lohmann introduces a series of variables: economic (monetary growth, GNP growth, inflation, exchange rates), institutional economic (Bretton Woods, European Monetary System), electoral cycles, government composition, upper house (Bundesrat) composition, central bank composition (who appointed the different members), and chancellor popularity. Her results support the following two conclusions: "German monetary policy is subject to electoral pressures. There is no evidence that partisan preferences are influential via the power of appointment. The Bundesbank Council is stuffed with partially independent technocrats whose independence decreases with the partisan support for the federal government in the Bundesrat. . . . The auxiliary hypothesis that the Bundesrat veto point protects the Bundesbank's independence is the only hypothesis that is consistent with the evidence compiled in both the case study and the regression analysis" (Lohmann 1998: 440).

Lohmann's findings are consistent with the theory presented in this book. However, as she notes, the composition of the Bundesrat in Germany is correlated with government popularity, so the institutional measures might in fact reflect the ability of government to control monetary policy. This is a problem of co-linearity that cannot be resolved with a dataset covering one country and forty-five years.

However, two more recent studies (Keefer and Stasavage 2000, forthcoming) have much more expanded datasets. Philip Keefer and David Stasavage (2000: 17) develop an economic model that leads to the following three predictions: "1. The presence of a legally independent central bank should have a negative effect on inflation only in the presence of checks and balances. 2. Political interference, such as replacement of central bank governors, is less likely when checks and balances are present. 3. The presence of a legally independent central bank has a more negative effect on inflation when different branches of government have divergent preferences over inflation." All three predictions are consistent with the theory developed in this book. In fact, Keefer and Stasavage's Proposition 3 is testing not simply the number of veto players but also their ideological distances (see Proposition 1.4 of Chapter 1).

To test their predictions, Keefer and Stasavage use a dataset including seventy-eight countries over twenty years (for the 1975–94 period). Their dependent variable is inflation. Their independent variables include central bank independence and a series of institutional variables. They use as indicators of central bank independence both the "legal independence" measuring a series of institutional indicators (see the previous section) and turnover rates of the governors of the central bank (a variable that is considered in the literature to reflect better the actual independence in developing countries). Their institutional variables can be found in a database on political institutions assembled by Beck et al. (1999). The variable "*checks*" is "based on a formula which first counts the number of veto players, based on whether the executive and legislative chamber(s) are controlled by different parties in presidential systems and on the number of parties in the government coalition for parliamentary systems" (Keefer and Stasavage 2000: 19). *Polarization* is measured "according to whether data sources indicated parties (the four biggest ones) as having an economic orientation that was left, center or right . . . the maximum difference between those entities that comprise the *checks* indicator explained earlier. This maximum constitutes the *political polarization* measure" (Keefer and Stasavage 2000: 20).

The reader can verify that the method used for the identification of institutional variables is quite closely connected to the methods used in this book. The biggest difference is that ideological positions of different veto players are not accurately identified, which is compensated by their sample size. Keefer and Stasavage use interactive variables (CBI* veto players) in order to test whether institutions matter. In their analysis they find that central bank independence has no effect on inflation when it enters linearly (a result reported quite frequently in the literature), but the coefficients of the interactive terms are negative and significant. They conclude: "More concretely, in a parliamentary system with three party governing coalition . . . a one standard deviation increase in legal central bank independence would be predicted to reduce annual rate of inflation by approximately 20 percent. In contrast, in a parliamentary system with a single party majority . . . the predicted change in inflation would be close to zero. . . . This suggests an explanation for Cukierman, Webb, and Neyapti's (1992) finding that CBI is significantly and negatively correlated with inflation in advanced industrial countries but not in developing countries: developing countries, on average, have lower levels of checks and balances" (Keefer and Stasavage 2000: 23). When the variable "political polarization" is included in the regressions, the results indicate that "checks and balances make the biggest contribution to central bank effectiveness in more polarized societies" (Keefer and Stasavage 2000: 33).

10.4. Conclusions

In this chapter I have developed a simple model that generates the expectation that for any given legislation, the independence of bureaucrats and the judiciary will be positively related to the veto players (number and distances among them) that control the legislative process. This model was then tested with existing data on judicial and bureaucratic independence.

At the theoretical level I made the distinction between countries with or without constitutional courts. I argued that constitutional courts are additional veto players (since for all practical purposes they cannot be legislatively overruled). However, because of the rules of selection of these courts, most of the time they are absorbed as veto players by the existing political ones. The empirical findings about judges were based on four different indices of judicial independence generated by combinations of some twenty advanced industrialized countries, and corroborated the expectations of the model of the first section.

With respect to bureaucracies I made the distinction between institutional and behavioral independence in order to differentiate the argument presented in this book from the standard arguments in the literature. I was able to identify a case (central bank activities) where the expectations generated from my argument could be tested. Examining empirical evidence I found that central bank independence is correlated with both veto players and federalism. I argued that, most likely, CBI is an institutional variable and as a consequence the theory presented in this book cannot account for the reasons that central banks are more independent in countries with many veto players. However, focusing on behavioral independence (in the fight against inflation), I presented evidence that the expectations generated in the first part of this chapter are strongly corroborated by a dataset covering a large number of countries.

11

Veto Players Analysis of European Union Institutions

THE EUROPEAN UNION fascinates observers and scholars because it is a unique object of study. The institutional structure of the European Union is new, and, as a result, a series of neologisms has been invented to describe it. It is "neither a state nor an international organization" (Sbragia 1992: 257); "less than a Federation, more than a Regime" (W. Wallace 1983: 403); "stuck between sovereignty and integration" (W. Wallace 1982: 67); "institutionalized Inter-governmentalism in a supranational organization" (Cameron 1992: 66); the "middle ground between the cooperation of existing nations and the breaking of a new one" (Scharpf 1988: 242). Some scholars have even seen advantages in the situation: Sbragia (1992: 258) approvingly quotes Krislov, Ehlermann, and Weiler, claiming: "The absence of a clear model, for one thing, makes ad hoc analogies more appropriate and justifiable. If one may not specify what are clear analogies, less clear ones may be appropriate."

In this chapter, instead of using analogies (appropriate or inappropriate), I apply the veto players theory and examine the logic and the outcomes of decisionmaking generated by the different legislative procedures adopted in successive treaties, and compare my conclusions with other institutional analyses. As a result, this chapter has three important characteristics: first, it studies several different institutional structures that prevail in the same territory; second, it advances the application of the veto players theory, because the E.U. institutions are quite complex: they involve three legislative institutions, each of them deciding by different formal or actual majorities, and the right to set the agenda sometimes includes restrictions, sometimes is shared, and sometimes shifts among actors; third, because the study of E.U. institutions and policies has progressed further than case studies, the predictions of different theories are sharper, and the data collected enable comparisons on a relatively solid basis. In short, this chapter makes comparisons across different institutional settings (that involve the same geographic area), pushes theory to cover more complicated institutions, and uses empirical tests to corroborate more detailed empirical predictions than any of the previous chapters.

The chapter is divided into four parts. The first part discusses some of the issues studied in the literature on the European Union. We will see that different parts of the literature focus on the national or supranational composition of different institutions, and they consider these institutions as the framework within which rational actors pursue their goals, or as shaping the preferences and identities of these actors. The second part describes what is considered throughout this book to be the basis of an institutional approach to politics, the legislative system of the European Union. The European Union has adopted a series of different legislative procedures. These procedures are quite complicated and significantly different from other political systems (whether presidential or parliamentary) so that one cannot assume that the reader knows what exactly they permit and what they rule out. The third part analyzes the anticipated distribution of power among the legislative institutions (the European Commission, Council of Ministers, and European Parliament), as well as implications of legislative rules on bureaucracies and the judiciary. The last part looks at available empirical evidence to assess the validity of different institutional theories.

11.1. E.U. Literatures

The literature on the European Union is extensive. probably due to the fact that the European Union is one of the few examples of ongoing real-scale institutional development where observers and actors alike look at the effects of institutional provisions and design the next step. It is impossible to summarize this literature in a few pages. I refer the interested reader to reviews synthesizing the literature. Some of these (Hix 1994) multiply the different streams of thought, dividing not only into approaches based in international relations and approaches based in comparative politics, but also into pluralist, realist, structuralist, sociological, and rational choice. Others (Pollack 2001; Aspinwall and Schneider 2000) merge different approaches and divide studies into rational and constructivist.

It is true that most of these studies adopt a rationalist framework that assume that institutions are rules within which actors develop their choices in order to achieve the best outcome.[1] I narrow my discussion in this section to such studies, in particular intergovernmentalism, neofunctionalism, and institutional analysis and explain their differences. I focus on the institutional analysis literature in the last three parts of this chapter.

---

[1] Other studies adopt a constructivist framework, considering that institutions shape identities and preferences of actors as well. Thomas Christiansen, Knud Erik Jorgensen, and Antje Wiener (1999: 529) have expressed the essence of the approach as follows: "European integration itself has changed over the years, and it is reasonable to assume that in the process agents' identity and subsequently their interests have equally changed. While this aspect of change can be theorized within constructivist perspectives, it will remain largely invisible in approaches that neglect process of identity formation and/or assume interests to be given exogenously." I will not deal with such approaches here, because as Moravcsik (1999) argues, most of them have failed to construct distinctive, testable hypotheses.

At the risk of oversimplifying, intergovernmentalists focus on treaty bargaining, and treat the European Union's institutional structure as the dependent variable. Moreover, this structure is conceived in general terms—such as Moravcsik's (1998) focus on E.U. institutions as credible commitments to integration—rather than analyzed in terms of the detailed interactions among the European Union's four primary institutions and their likely effects on policy. However, the laserlike focus of intergovernmentalism on treaties requires a prior study of everyday E.U. realities that are generated (or likely to be generated) by the institutions that were generated by the previous treaties. As we will see, the European Union has changed its institutional structure very frequently, and as a result the influence of different actors as well as policy outcomes may vary over time.

For neofunctionalists, in contrast, the European Union's institutions are not independent variables, but actors: the European Commission, European Court of Justice (ECJ), and European Parliament (EP) undertake actions that affect the direction that European integration takes. More specifically, neofunctionalist theory argues that integration in Europe is proceeding because "actors in several distinct national settings are persuaded to shift their loyalties, expectations and political activities towards a new center, whose institutions possess or demand jurisdiction of the pre-existing national states" (Haas 1961: 366–67). The motor behind this process is "spillovers," that is, situations where "a given action, related to a specific goal, creates a situation in which the original goal can be assured only by taking further actions, which in turn create a further condition and a need for more, and so forth" (Lindberg 1963: 9). As a result, neofunctionalists eschew analysis of the strategies available to different actors and the constraints under which they operate. That is, they do not analyze institutions in terms of generating particular equilibrium outcomes.

Garrett and Tsebelis (1996) and Tsebelis and Garrett (2001) have differentiated the institutionalist approach from both intergovernmentalism and neofunctionalism by discussing the most representative recent works in each one of these research programs. I do not repeat their arguments here, except for the major point presented in Table 11.1.

The table presents the two dimensions that differentiate among these three major streams of research. The first is whether one focuses alone on interactions among member governments as defining the integration process. Here, the institutional approach is closer to neofunctionalism than intergovernmentalism. It avoids the—inappropriately—myopic focus of intergovernmental analyses on treaty revisions by paying close attention to the multitude of clearly important directives, regulations, and court decisions that influence the course of European integration from day to day.

The second dimension concerns the question of whether the course of European integration is the product of intentional choices by (and strategic interactions among) the relevant actors. For neofunctionalists, the law of unintended

TABLE 11.1

Three Approaches to European Integration

	Intergovernmentalism	Neofunctionalism	Institutionalism
Are governments the only (important) actors?	Yes	No	No
Unintended consequences?	No	Yes	No (under complete information)

consequences (spillovers) is the basis of the analysis. For intergovernmentalists, in marked contrast, the governments that sign treaties are not only in the driver's seat, they also know exactly where they are going.

The position of institutional analysis on this issue is more qualified. If actors operate under complete information (i.e., they know all relevant information about each other), they will design institutions that best promote their preferences—subject to the constraint that every other actor will behave similarly. Nonetheless, even under conditions of complete information, institutional analysis suggests a different type of research on treaty bargaining than is typical in intergovernmentalism.

Intergovernmentalism treats the European Union's institutional structure as a dependent variable; it is the product of treaty bargaining. Institutional analyses, however, argue that the study of institutional outcomes is logically prior to the analysis of institutional choice. To use Shepsle's (1986) terminology, one has to understand "institutional equilibria" before moving to the analysis of "equilibrium institutions." The fact that intergovernmentalists typically eschew the "institutions as independent variables" analysis significantly lessens their ability to understand institutional choice. Even if intergovernmentalists are right to assume that treaty bargaining takes place under complete information, the fact that they pay more attention to stated policy objectives rather than the institutions created to implement them is a serious weakness in this mode of analysis.

But how appropriate is the complete information assumption for treaty bargaining? I think that reality is somewhere in between the black and white of the neofunctionalism-intergovernmentalism divide. The complete information assumption is a strict one. As the reader will see, I use it only in the final stages of the European Union's complex procedures after actors have exchanged information. With respect to implementation and adjudication, the fact that the Barber Protocol was written into the Maastricht Treaty to countermand an ECJ decision is good evidence that the ECJ does not always accurately predict the reactions of member governments (Garrett, Kelemen, and Schulz 1998).

In the case of treaty bargaining, the threshold for complete information is even higher—because the governments are making decisions that will have long chains of effects into the indefinite future. If they do not know all relevant information about each other, or if they operate under cognitive pressures that restrict their ability to behave perfectly rationally, or if they expect with some probability that shocks in the political environment will change the endowments of other actors, the strict complete information assumption is unlikely to be very helpful.

But as an empirical matter, it is worth asking how much of the evolution of the European Union since the mid-1980s that we see in the next section was anticipated by the member governments during the treaty-making processes, and how much was unintended. If one focuses on debates about reducing the democratic deficit through the reform of the European Union's legislative procedures—one of the most important features of European integration in the past twenty years—the balance seems to fall in favor of the complete information assumption. By and large (but, as we will see, not in all aspects), the institutional modifications introduced had the intended effect of reducing the Commission's role and increasing that of the EP.

In sum, the purported "law of unintended consequences" has empirically been riddled with many more exceptions than most commentators on European integration suggest. Thus, focusing on the formal institutional interactions in the European Union not only helps explain how the European Union has operated in different epochs; it also gives us important insights into how the member governments have decided to pool their sovereignty in the integration process.

11.2. Legislative Procedures in the European Union

There are four major institutional actors in the European Union: the Council of Ministers, the European Commission, the European Parliament, and the European Court of Justice.[2] Three of these actors (all but the ECJ) compose the legislative branch of the European Union. The interaction among them has been defined by a series of treaties starting with the Treaty of Rome in 1957 and going on to the Treaty of Nice (2001). A new European Intergovernmental Conference has already been scheduled for the year 2004.

The Intergovernmental Conferences that introduced or altered legislative politics in the European Union are the following: The Treaty of Rome (1957), the Luxembourg Compromise (1966), the Single European Act (1987), the Maastricht Treaty (1991), the Treaty of Amsterdam (1997), and the Treaty of

---

[2] To these four one should add the European Central Bank, created by the Maastricht Treaty (1991).

Nice (2001). In some sense, the European Union has been constantly fine-tuning its political institutions: six revisions in its forty years of history, and four of them in the last fifteen years. I focus on this fast-paced revision period that began in 1987 and produced an institutional innovation every three years. But a short historical introduction is called for first.

11.2.1. From the Rome Treaty to the Luxembourg Compromise

The Treaty of Rome (1957) was the codification of a compromise between the federalist and anti-federalist elements of the European Union (at the time, European Economic Communities [EEC]). The institutions designed in this treaty phased in a new legislative procedure called "consultation." The Treaty of Rome specified that the unanimous decisionmaking in the Council would be replaced by a qualified majority decisionmaking in some areas in 1966 (as the third stage of integration began; EEC Treaty, Art. 8, points 3–6). In fact, according to the consultation procedure, a proposal by the Commission would require a qualified majority in the Council to be accepted, but unanimity to be modified. This decisionmaking mode, which provided the Commission with the authority to make proposals that were more difficult to reject or modify, has been preserved in subsequent treaties, and is discussed in detail in the next part.

However, the specifications of the Rome Treaty were not applied in 1966 because of the objections of the French government to the qualified majority provisions. The French began to raise such objections shortly after General de Gaulle came to power in 1958. De Gaulle was a known opponent of supranationalism, but he very much supported intergovernmentalism and the close cooperation of independent sovereign nation-states (de Gaulle 1960 and 1971: 189–91). Following the Treaties of Rome, de Gaulle made several attempts to have his ideas accepted by his European allies. The first two, under the name of Fouchet Plans I and II, failed, while the third, known as the Luxembourg Compromise, was successful.

In 1966, de Gaulle succeeded in achieving a de facto end to majority voting that was to last until 1987. The battle that led to the Luxembourg Compromise began over a proposed plan by the Commission to fund the newly agreed Common Agricultural Policy (CAP). The Commission proposed an amount that exceeded the needed amount significantly, and the Commission's proposal suggested that this "extra" income could be used to finance projects other than those already accepted by the governments. In addition, the proposal called for increasing the budgetary powers of the EP and indirectly the Commission (Tsebelis and Kreppel 1998: 60–63).

De Gaulle seized the opportunity and in a 1965 press conference argued that the episode illustrated a Commission attempting to exceed its powers to the detriment of the national sovereignty of the member states. Beginning in July 1965, after an inconclusive Council meeting over the impending budget crises, France began its so-called "empty chair" policy. In effect, France boycotted the European Community for seven months, causing a profound crisis that in the end was resolved only through the Luxembourg Compromise. The compromise itself had nothing to do with the financial proposals, which had purportedly inspired the crisis. Instead, the compromise dealt solely with the issue of majority voting in the Council, which was due to come into effect that same year. The compromise was an "agreement not to agree" (Marjolin 1980: 56–59). The text of the compromise reaffirmed the desire of the other five members of the European Community to move forward with majority voting, although they were willing to delay decisions "when issues very important to one or more member countries were at stake." The French, however, stated their view "that, when very important issues are at stake, decisions must be continued until unanimous agreement is reached" (Extraordinary Session of the Council, January 18, 1966, EC Bulletin, 3/66, part b, paragraphs 1–3). This divergence of opinion was noted by all six member states, and an agreement was reached that this difference of opinion should not hamper "the Community's work being resumed in accordance with the normal procedure" (EC Bulletin 3/66, part b, paragraph 4).

The effects of the compromise were deep and enduring. Although initially the other five member states opposed the requirement of unanimity, they came not only to accept it, but also to support and protect it against a series of attempts to regain majority voting. The Luxembourg Compromise heralded "a change of ethos, at first rejected by the Five, but later, especially after the first enlargement, eagerly seized upon by all" (Dinan 1994: 59).

11.2.2. The Cooperation Procedure

The Luxembourg Compromise effectively governed the legislative process in the European Union until the ratification of the Single European Act (SEA) in 1987. The SEA introduced the "cooperation procedure" among the three legislative institutions, the Commission, the Council, and the EP (directly elected since 1979).

The cooperation procedure did not cover all areas of E.U. legislation. It applied to some ten articles of the Treaty of Rome and constituted between a third and a half of parliamentary decisions (Jacobs and Corbett 1990: 169). The procedure entails two readings of each piece of legislation (initially introduced by the Commission) by the EP and the Council. The Council makes the final decision either by qualified majority or by unanimity. In the abstract, the procedure is reminiscent of a navette system between the two houses of a bicameral legislature where the upper house (the Council) has the final word.[3]

The legislative process begins with the submission of a Commission proposal to the EP. At the same time, the Council may begin deliberating but cannot reach a decision until it receives the EP's position. The EP in the first reading may accept, amend, or reject the proposal; it may also withhold its opinion by referring the legislation back to committee, thereby effectively aborting the proposal. Once the EP decides, the proposal goes back to the Commission members, who may revise the initial proposal to accommodate the EP. The Commission presents the proposal as amended to the Council. The council members adopt a "common position" by qualified majority (at the time, with 12 members, 54 of 76 votes) if they agree with the Commission proposal, or by unanimity if they effectively amend the proposal. No time limits on deliberation exist in this first reading of the proposal. It is therefore obvious that any of the institutions can effectively abort legislation at this stage of the process.

Once the Council adopts its common position, the second reading of the proposal begins. The Council sends its common position back to the EP, along with a full justification of the reasons why it adopted this position. The full justification of the position of the Council and the Commission is required by Article 149(2b) of the Single European Act. However, in the early phase of application of the procedure, the Council provided extremely sketchy reasons or even no reasons at all. In one case, it even apparently failed to notice that the EP had tabled amendments to the Commission proposal (Bieber 1988: 720). The EP formally protested, its president declaring on October 28, 1987, that "as a minimum, the Council should provide specific and explained reactions to each of Parliament's amendments" (Jacobs and Corbett 1990: 173). On November 18, 1987, the EP threatened the Council with legal action in two resolutions (Bieber 1988: 720). As a result, the Council altered its approach and provided an account of its point of view on each of the substantive issues raised by draft legislation (Jacobs and Corbett 1990: 173).

The EP then has three months to select one of three options: to approve the common position of the Council (or, equivalently, take no action), in which case the Council adopts the proposal; to reject the common position by an absolute majority of its members (at the time 260 votes); or to amend the common position, again by an absolute majority of its members. In this second round, time is of the essence. The clock starts when the president of the EP announces that she has received all relevant documents in all nine official languages.

---

[3] See Chapter 6. For a detailed discussion of the navette system across countries, see Tsebelis and Money (1997).

The Commission may or may not introduce legislation rejected by the EP to the Council; if such legislation is introduced, the Council can overrule the rejection by unanimity. Amended legislation is presented to the Commission, which within a month must revise the proposal. Parliamentary amendments that are accepted by the Commission can be adopted by the Council by qualified majority (54 of 76), whereas any other version requires unanimity in the Council. If the Council fails to act within three months (four, with the agreement of the EP), the proposal lapses.

Once discussion is initiated by a Commission proposal, there are no restrictions on the amendments that the EP can introduce in its first reading. In the second reading, parliamentary rules specify that amendments have to be only on those parts of the text that have been modified by the Council, and that seek to adopt a compromise with the Council or to restore the EP's position in the first reading (Bieber 1988: 722).

There is, however, a very important restriction on the EP's second reading amendment power. Amendments require absolute majorities to be adopted. In practice, the 260 required votes constitute a two-thirds majority of members present. Moreover, given that MEPs of the twelve member countries at the time were organized into more than ten (crossnational) parliamentary groups and that voting alignments occurred more frequently by political group and less frequently by country, and given too that voting discipline is weak, 260 votes is equivalent to a qualified majority requirement, as we saw in Chapter 6.

To summarize, according to the cooperation procedure, in its second reading the EP may make a proposal by an absolute majority of its members, which, if adopted by the Commission, may be accepted by a qualified majority (54 of 76) of the Council, but requires unanimity of the Council to be modified. This proposal may be anywhere between the EP's and the Council's first reading of initial legislation, including a reiteration of the EP's previous position. This is what I have called "conditional agenda-setting power of the EP" (Tsebelis 1994); I analyze its strategic properties in the next section.

11.2.3. The Codecision I Procedure

The Maastricht Treaty introduced a new decisionmaking procedure, which was named (in the literature and everyday debates, not in the treaty itself) "codecision." This procedure essentially adds some new stages to the cooperation procedure after the second reading of legislation by the EP. If in its second reading the Council disagrees with any of the parliamentary amendments, the text is referred to a conciliation committee, composed of an equal number of members of Council and parliamentary representatives. If the committee comes to an agreement, it has to be approved by a majority in the EP and a qualified majority in the Council in order to become law. If there is no agreement, the initiative reverts to the Council, which may reintroduce its previous position, "possibly with EP amendments," by qualified majority or unanimity (depending on the subject matter). Unless an absolute majority of the members of the EP disagrees, the law is adopted.

A comparison of the two procedures indicates several major differences. First, parliament has an absolute veto power in the codecision procedure, but needs an alliance with the Commission *or* at least one member of the Council in order to have its veto sustained in the cooperation procedure. Second, at the end of the codecision procedure, it is the Council that makes a "take it or leave it" proposal to the EP. Third, in the codecision procedure, disagreement even over a single parliamentary amendment triggers the conciliation procedure, while in the cooperation procedure the Council could modify only those parliamentary amendments accepted by the Commission that had unanimous Council agreement (leaving the others intact). Fourth, according to the codecision procedure, in certain areas (including culture and framework programs in Research and Development) decisions by the Council in the joint committee as well as in the final stage can only be made by unanimity. Fifth, in the conciliation stage of the codecision procedure the Commission is present, but its agreement is not necessary: if the EP and the Council come to an agreement, the position of the Commission is irrelevant.

11.2.4. The Codecision II Procedure

The EP intensely disliked the last steps of the cooperation I procedure: the fact that a disagreement in the conciliation committee did not mean the rejection of a bill, but enabled the Council to revert to its previous "common position," possibly including EP amendments. The EP's point was adopted in the Amsterdam treaty, where it was recognized that a failure of the conciliation committee to reach an agreement implied rejection of a bill. It is interesting to study how the EP was able to impose its will on the governments that signed the next Treaty.

In order to make its preferences clear, the EP adopted a set of new rules after Maastricht. One of these rules (#78) specified the reaction of the EP if there was no agreement in the conciliation committee:

1. Where no agreement is reached on a joint text within the Conciliation Committee, the [European Parliament] President shall invite the Commission to withdraw its proposal, and invite the Council of Ministers not to adopt under any circumstances a position pursuant to Article 189b(6) of the EC Treaty. Should the Council nonetheless confirm its common position, the President of the Council of Ministers shall be invited to justify the decision before the parliament in plenary sitting. The matter shall automatically be placed on the agenda of the last part-session to fall within six or, if

extended, eight weeks of the confirmation by the Council. . . . 3. No amendments
may be tabled to the Council text. 4. The Council text as a whole shall be the subject
of a single vote. Parliament shall vote on a motion to reject the Council text. If this
motion receives the votes of a majority of the component Members of Parliament,
the [European Parliament] President shall declare the proposed act not adopted.

Rule 78 was applied only once, in the case of the draft directive on open
network provision in voice telephony (ONP). On another occasion when a
joint text could not be agreed upon in conciliation (on the draft directive on
investment firms and credit institutions in 1998), the Council decided not to
reaffirm its common position.

Hix (forthcoming) has inferred that "this vote revealed that Rule 78, backed
by the EP leadership's institutional preferences, was in fact a credible threat. . .
This strategy paid off, as it established compromise in the conciliation committee as the actual game equilibrium." On the basis of his analysis, Hix (forthcoming) concludes that the Amsterdam Treaty simply recognized a de facto
reality, that there was only one way to get any piece of legislation to be accepted: have it proposed by the conciliation committee to both the Council
and the EP (see also Corbett 2001a). However, the elimination of the last
stage of the codecision I procedure was not a trivial matter, as Moravcsik and
Nicolaïdis (1999) demonstrate. Until the last minute, several governments
were against the elimination of the last step of this procedure.

I discuss the difference between the two versions of codecision in the next
section, and look at some of the empirical implications of this analysis in the
last section of this chapter.

11.2.5. Extending Codecision II and the Qualified Majority Requirement

The Treaty of Nice extended the areas of applicability of the codecision II
procedure, but at the same time increased the qualified majority threshold. The
qualified majority required at Amsterdam (for a fifteen-member European Union) was 62 of 87 votes in the Council (q = .7126). Nice (among
other things) altered the weight of different countries in the Council. For
example, the five largest countries had 48 of 87 votes (55 percent) until the
Treaty of Amsterdam.[4] They now receive 143 of 237 (60 percent).[5] However,
the most interesting change that will occur in the future is that along with the
enlargement of the European Union to twenty-seven members (by expansion
to Eastern Europe), the required qualified majority threshold will be 253 of
345 (q = .7333).

---

[4] Germany, France, the United Kingdom, and Italy had ten votes each, and Spain eight votes.
[5] Germany, France, the United Kingdom, and Italy have twenty-nine votes each, and Spain
twenty-seven votes.

However, this official increase in threshold is underestimating the situation. The actual requirement specified in Article 205(4) of the Nice Treaty is a triple majority: besides the qualified majority threshold, a Council decision has to be supported by a majority of the member states, and if a member state requires, it has to be supported by members totaling 62 percent of the E.U. population (Yataganas 2001). All these restrictions raise significantly the qualified majority threshold for Council decisionmaking, and as I demonstrated in Chapter 2, increase policy stability. I analyze these modifications in detail in Section 11.4.

11.3. Veto Players Analysis of Legislative Procedures

We now study the implications of these complicated decisionmaking rules both in terms of the distribution of legislative power among the three different institutions and in terms of the consequences on the decisionmaking discretion of other actors, like the ECJ. Therefore, this section is divided into two parts: the legislative consequences of decisionmaking procedures, and the effects on bureaucracies and the judiciary.

11.3.1. Legislative Consequences of Decisionmaking Procedures

In all legislative procedures, agreement among the different institutions is sought. What differs is who is the institutional actor in charge of formulating the possible agreement (agenda setter) and what happens if such an agreement cannot be achieved (who has veto powers).

In order to address these questions, I focus on the last stages of each procedure. The reason that I focus on the last stages is that any rational actor when called upon to decide will look down the road at the possible consequences of his actions, and will make the decision that will make him better off in subsequent stages of the game (and of course the final stage).[6] If all the actors knew each other's preferences and payoffs (the game theoretic term for such a situation is "complete information"), this way of thinking would lead to an immediate end of the legislative game: the Commission would propose a bill that would be accepted by all other actors. Indeed, the Commission would never make a proposal that would be ultimately rejected, and the other players would not raise objections if they knew they would not win in a confrontation. Given, however, that all these procedures unfold with moves and countermoves by each actor, that cooperation reaches the second reading, and that codecision goes to conciliating committee meetings, the most reasonable assumption to

---

[6] This is called "backwards induction" in the game theoretic literature.

make is that the different players do not operate in the ideal world of "complete information." Let us look at the last stage of each one of the procedures.

The last stage of the cooperation procedure is clear: the EP proposes a series of amendments, and the Commission incorporates all, some, or none of them into the final report it submits to the Council. The Council accepts the Commission's proposal by qualified majority, or modifies it by unanimity. In other words, it is more difficult for the Council to modify a parliamentary proposal (provided it is accepted by the Commission) than to accept it. "This procedure *may* enable EP to offer a proposal that makes a qualified majority of the Council better off than any unanimous decision. *If* such a proposal exists, *if*[7] the EP is able to make it, and *if* the Commission adopts it, then the EP has agenda-setting powers. If, however, these conditions are not met, the EP loses its agenda-setting power. This is why I characterize EP's agenda power under the cooperation procedure as conditional" (Tsebelis 1994: 131).

I will provide an example of how the EP can make use of its conditional agenda-setting powers. I will start with a one-dimensional policy space and then move to a two-dimensional space where the results differ.

The Council is represented by seven members (so that the required qualified majority can be approximated by five of the seven members). The underlying dimension is integration, so that the EP and the Commission are to the right of the country members, while the status quo is to the left. The strategic calculations of the EP are as follows: it has to offer five members of the Council a proposal that will make them better off than anything that the Council can decide by unanimity (see Tsebelis 1994, 1997).

Other researchers (Steunenberg 1994; Crombez 1996; Moser 1996) argue that even if the EP behaves in the way described by Tsebelis (1994) in the second round, one of two things would have happened in the previous round: either the Commission would have liked some of the amendments and made them on its own, or, the EP would have known that the Commission would reject its amendments and consequently not offer them. Thus, the EP should not be making amendments, either because its opinion is already incorporated in the text or because any changes would be rejected. In Figure 11.1, the Commission and the EP have similar preferences, so the Commission should start the procedure by making the proposal X. Either the EP would understand that no improvement is possible or, if it offered a different proposal (say, its own ideal point), the Commission would reject the amendment. Crombez (1996: 218) puts it succinctly: "Proposition 3: Under the Cooperation procedure the Parliament's opportunity to amend the Council's common position does not affect the equilibrium policy." As a result, they expect an impotent EP, and argue that the agenda-setting power is with the Commission. This is a difference in the identity of the agenda setter.

---

[7] The reader is reminded that 260 votes are required for a proposal.

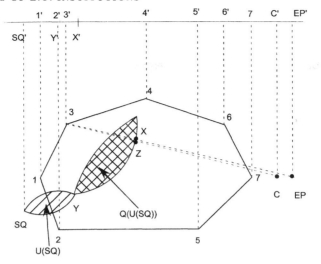

Figure 11.1. Conditional agenda setting in one and two dimensions.

Be that as it may, there is a second difference between my analysis and the expectations of Crombez (1996), Steunenberg (1994), and Moser (1996). They believe that the agenda setter will make a proposal that makes a qualified majority better off than the status quo, while in my analysis the proposal will make a qualified majority better off than anything that can be promoted in the Council by unanimity.

Figure 11.1 presents the differences of the two arguments. According to my argument, the Council can unanimously modify the status quo and select anything in the SQ'Y' area. Consequently, if the EP offers X', a proposal that member 3' barely prefers over Y', it will be accepted by the Commission and members 3', 4', 5', 6', and 7' of the Council. According to Crombez (1996), Steunenberg (1994), and Moser (1996) the winning proposal will be located close to point 4' (it is the symmetric of SQ with respect to the pivotal member of the Council: 3'). In addition, the winning proposal will be made by the Commission, and the EP will make no amendment, because it cannot improve its situation (any amendment to the right of the Commission will be defeated, and any amendment to the left is less preferred).

A third direction of research is adopting an intermediate position. Bieber, Pantalis, and Schoo (1986: 791) argued, "With regard to the European Parliament, the Single Act is an inconsistent document: Where it increases the EP's powers of participation in decisionmaking the practical effect is either very limited or diminished because the exercise of the powers is conditional on the *attitude* of the Council and the Commission." Similarly, Fitzmaurice (1988: 391) argued that "despite the appearances of a co-decision model, the Council virtually retains the last word." Jacobs (1997: 6) explicitly criticizes the first approach by making two arguments: first, that there is a tendency for the Council to decide unanimously, and second, that the Commission has the tendency to "either side with, or at least not go against the most powerful actor, the Council, in the final stages of the procedure . . . even if it has supported Parliament amendments in first reading."[8] A similar argument is made by Corbett (2001a: 376): "Parliament's powers under the cooperation procedure to formulate a 'take it or leave it' position toward Council depend on so many conditions that, in practice, it does not usually apply." Finally, Lodge (1987: 23) claims that the EP's limited power stems from the threat to block decisions, which can occur "in an alliance with one or more member states prepared to thwart the attainment of the necessary majorities (qualified or unanimous) unless EP's views and amendments were accommodated."

Tsebelis (1997) addressed the criticisms of the other two approaches by arguing that some of the no-impact or limited impact theories are based on unrealistic assumptions of complete information and single dimensionality of the issue space. Once these assumptions are relaxed, successful EP amendments are possible. Tsebelis enumerates several such examples. For instance, the Commission may be willing to compromise with the EP because it acts as an "honest broker" or to avoid friction. But, because of incomplete information about the EP's preferences, the Commission may wait to observe the degree of the EP's resolve first (indicated, for example, by a strong majority or the assignment of a highly competent rapporteur) and then adopt these amendments. Tsebelis also argues that the Commission may adopt EP amendments if the latter are introduced in a new dimension. The lower half of Figure 11.1 indicates how the introduction of a new dimension may make the Commission better off than its own initial proposal.

Suppose that the Commission started with a one-dimensional representation of the problem, and made the proposal X'. The EP can now introduce an amendment on a different dimension and generate a two-dimensional policy space. In this space, the preferences of the Council are presented by the numbers 1–7, while the EP and Commission (point C) positions are indicated to the right. Again, the EP has to make the following calculations: find what the Council can do unanimously (anything in the area U(SQ)), and make a proposal that makes five members better off than anything inside the area U(SQ). This is denoted by the cross-hatched area Q(U(SQ)) in the figure. Out of all the points in Q(U(SQ)), the EP selects the point closest to its own position,

[8] Strictly speaking, Jacobs's argument is not a refutation of Tsebelis's (1994) thesis: the "conditional agenda setting" argument is predicated upon acceptance by the Commission, and absence of unanimity in the Council. He does not make any prediction about how often these conditions will be obtained. However, if these conditions are rarely met, conditional agenda setting becomes less empirically relevant. For this reason we will examine Jacobs's claims empirically below.

while the Commission has the choice of modifying this amendment slightly to Z or (if transaction costs are high) accepting it exactly the way it was written by the EP. The top and bottom of Figure 11.1 indicate that the Commission prefers the proposal in a two-dimensional space (whether X or Z) to its own one-dimensional proposal.

Hence the EP, by introducing an amendment in a different dimension, generates a different strategic situation both for the Commission and the Council. For the Council, the new situation is generated by the difference in opinion between members 2 and 3 along the new dimension. Because 2 and 3 have significant differences in the two-dimensional picture (but not in the one-dimensional projection), member 3 is willing to make many more concessions to the Commission and the EP than before. The Commission prefers the EP's amendment because it makes the Commission significantly better off compared to its initial proposal. As a result, the EP does make a proposal and its proposal is accepted (unlike the results in single-dimensional, complete information models).

Figure 11.1 simplifies the decisionmaking procedure in a significant way. It assumes that the EP is a unified player, which for a parliament representing fifteen nationalities and twelve ideologies is a heroic simplification indeed. However, as Chapter 2 has demonstrated, the results do not change significantly if one replaces the false unified player assumption with the more realistic "cooperative decisionmaking" assumption. Tsebelis (1995c) makes the case that because of the organization of the EP, and in particular because of the "rapporteurs" of the different bills, cooperative decisionmaking is a reasonable assumption.

This is the second time that we find concrete cases where multidimensional models lead to different results from single dimensional ones, and therefore the case has to be made that decisionmaking is in one dimension for the conclusions to follow.[9] These examples make a strong case in favor of the veto players theory, based on multidimensional policy spaces. We will see whether empirical evidence corroborates these expectations in the next section.

The codecision I procedure has two major differences. First, it eliminates the Commission from the last round of negotiations, and as a result reduces the influence of the Commission on legislation. The legislative influence of the Commission is not eliminated altogether, as some researchers have argued (Crombez 1997). The reason is that the Commission can make a proposal in the beginning of the process that will be accepted by the other two actors (the reader is reminded that the legislative process starts with a Commission proposal, so the Commission has an agenda-setting role).

Second, there are two possible endings of codecision I, depending on the outcome of the negotiations in the conciliation committee: (1) If the concilia-

---

[9] The other was in the discussion on "pivotal" or "supermajoritarian" politics in Chapter 6.

tion committee comes to an agreement, this agreement is introduced to both the Council and the EP; it is adopted if it receives a qualified majority in the Council, and a majority in the EP; it fails otherwise. (2) If the conciliation committee fails to reach an agreement, the Council can make a proposal to the EP; this proposal is considered accepted unless an absolute majority of the EP votes against it, in which case it fails. The content of the proposal is the position "to which it agreed before the conciliation procedure was initiated, possibly with amendments proposed by the EP" (Article 189b(6) of the Maastricht Treaty). Depending on which process is selected, the identity of the agenda setter differs. In the first case, it is the conciliation committee itself (i.e., a combination of the Council and the EP), while in the second it is the Council alone.

The codecision II procedure eliminates the second path of codecision I, and considers the failure of the conciliation committee to reach an agreement equivalent to the termination of a bill. There are two different interpretations of codecision I and codecision II. According to the first, powers shifted away from the Council from codecision I to codecision II; according to the second, this difference is only in the formal rules, but not in reality.

In a series of articles (Garrett 1995b; Tsebelis 1997; Garrett and Tsebelis 1996, 1997), Geoffrey Garrett and I have made the argument that since the Council essentially decides which of the possible two endings of codecision I will be selected (the Council can lead the conciliation committee to reach an agreement or not), in codecision I the Council can ultimately make a take-it-or-leave-it offer to the EP. The transition from cooperation to codecision entailed the EP's exchanging its conditional agenda-setting power for unconditional veto power. The impact of the exchange of conditional agenda setting (cooperation) for unconditional veto (codecision I) varies with the relationship between the EP's preferences and those of members of the Commission and the Council. If the EP and the Commission have similar positions (and so long as the members of the Council have different preferences themselves), the swap of the conditional agenda setting under cooperation for the unconditional veto of codecision I was a bad deal for the EP—and for the pro-integration agenda. If on the other hand the Commission disagrees with the EP, or if the Council is unanimous, the EP has no conditional agenda-setting powers, and consequently it is better off with a veto.

A different argument is presented by Corbett (2001a) and Hix (2001). They argue that because of the adoption of Rule 78 by the EP (see discussion above), the EP had de facto modified the rules of the interaction, and eliminated the possibility of the Council to make take-it-or-leave-it offers to the EP. Consequently, codecision II simply recognized what was already in practice since codecision I.

Regardless of this difference, there is wide agreement that under codecision II the EP is a co-equal legislator with the Council. The reason is that the Council can no longer overrule the EP (not even unanimously, as in cooperation) and no longer can it present take-it-or-leave-it proposals to the EP (as was the case under the Maastricht Treaty). Rather, the Council and the EP must bargain on equal footing over the final legislative outcome, with no a priori bargaining advantage inherent to either institution.

Thus the only difference remaining in the literature on codecision I and codecision II is whether there was a significant shift of power in favor of the EP in Amsterdam, or whether this shift had already been achieved unilaterally with the adoption of Rule 78. We will return to this point in the last section of this chapter.

The Nice Treaty modified the majority requirements of the codecision procedure, and introduced a triple majority in the Council. This modification is equivalent to increasing the number of veto players in the system.[10] As a result, decisionmaking in the European Union becomes more difficult, and policy stability increases.

What is interesting to note in these discussions is that different analyses disagree with respect to "nominal" or "actual" rights of different institutions, whether decisions are made under complete or incomplete information, in one or multiple dimensions. Some readers may find these questions important, and others too technical. For the latter, I have to point out that E.U. institutions are complicated, and these details have significant consequences on the distribution of power and on policy outcomes. Be that as it may, the more general picture is that the questions asked and the inferences made in all these pieces of literature are on the implicit or explicit basis of questions studied by the veto players theory: who are the veto players, how do they decide, who controls the agenda, and how much.

11.3.2. Legislative Procedure Consequences on Bureaucracies and the Judiciary

Legislative decisionmaking in the European Union has changed in several dimensions: it started by unanimous decisions by the Council, then moved to a qualified majority inside the Council along with agreement of the other two institutional legislators (the Commission and EP), then it moved (and remains today) into a codecision stage where an agreement by the EP and the Council are sufficient for decisions to be adopted.

All these changes have effects on the number and the ideological distances of veto players, and as a consequence and for the reasons we have seen in

---

[10] More accurately, it will increase the distances among existing veto players. If additional veto players have smaller distances from the existing ones they will be absorbed, and if they are further away from the existing ones they will not be absorbed.

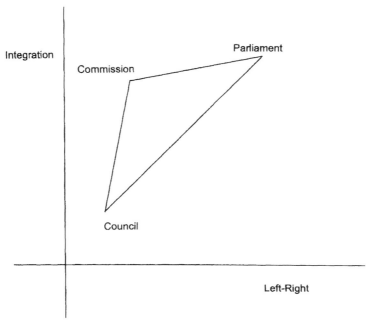

Figure 11.2. EU institutions in two dimensions.

Chapter 10 they are likely to affect the discretion of bureaucrats and judges. Since the legislative procedures are quite complicated, we will have to look at the identities and distances of veto players more closely. I will start with a more realistic representation of policy dynamics in the European Union than the simplistic version I started with in Figure 11.1. I will make use of a two-dimensional figures (Figures 11.2 and 11.3) for at least two reasons: first, as I have argued, because a one-dimensional approximation may be misleading, and second, because many important policy disputes in the contemporary European Union appear to take place in an at least two-dimensional issue space. One dimension describes their preferences for more regional integration; the other is more akin to a traditional left-right cleavage (most notably on regulatory matters) (Hix 1999; Kreppel and Tsebelis 1999). The analysis that follows is based on an article by Tsebelis and Garrett (2001).

   The locations of the actors in Figure 11.2 represent plausible general preference configurations in these two dimensions. In both cases the Council and the EP are likely to be the more "extreme" actors, whereas the Commission is likely to be positioned somewhere in between them. On the left-right dimension the Commission is more likely to be closer to the national governments that appoint the commissioners; on the integration dimension, however, the Commission and the EP are more likely to be allied as pro-Europe actors.

What emerges from these assumptions is that the locations of the three actors represent the corners of a triangle. Theoretically, this is the most general representation of all cases in which the three actors can have any position with respect to each other—except where two of them have identical positions,[11] or where one of them is located exactly on a straight line connecting the central points of the other two. It should be emphasized, therefore, that the analytic thrust of this analysis holds regardless of the relative position of actors.

Let us now rotate Figure 11.2 by 45 degrees (for presentational purposes only), and incorporate the fact that all three institutional actors are in fact multimember bodies deciding by simple, absolute, or qualified majorities (Figure 11.3). I present the preferences of a parliament made up of nine members to characterize what is a de facto supermajority threshold for voting in the EP under the absolute majority requirements for passage in the second reading of legislative bills. I incorporate this restriction into the model by requiring a majority higher than five-ninths for a bill to be adopted. Thus in Figure 11.3 there is no majority to the left of line E1E5, no majority above line E3E8, and so on.[12] As a result of this de facto supermajoritarian requirement, there are some points located centrally in the EP that cannot be defeated by the required qualified majority. The Commission is presented with three members, deciding by a majority of its members (two of the three), since this is the formal decision rule for the College of Commissioners. Finally, again I analyze a seven-member Council where five of its members represent the required qualified majority for decisionmaking.

The central feature of Figure 11.3 is its description of the "core" of the European Union's legislative institutions under the various legislative procedures. The core of a legislative rule is the set of outcomes that cannot be overruled by the application of that rule. The core of the European Union's different legislative procedure describes the discretionary space available to the Commission in the implementation of legislation, and to the ECJ in statutory interpretation. As I have demonstrated in Chapter 2, the propositions that follow generalize to more than two dimensions, even if the core does not exist.[13] It also assumed that the outcome of legislative interactions—in the long run—will select points inside the core. Indeed, no matter what the deci-

[11] This was the case I presented in Figure 11.1. Even in the two-dimensional figure, the Commission and the EP had almost identical positions.

[12] Since there are only five points in the specified directions and the requirement is more than five-ninths of the votes. The qualified majority requirement increases the size of the core, but is not necessary for the arguments that follow (Tsebelis and Yataganas 2002).

[13] The core formally ceases to exist if one sufficiently increases the dimensionality of the policy space. However, we have seen in Chapter 10 that one can make similar arguments on the basis of veto players even when the core ceases to exist.

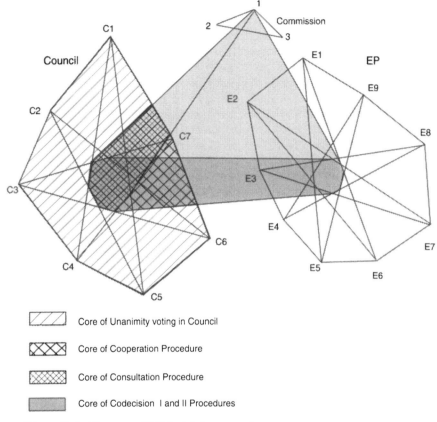

Figure 11.3. The core of EU legislative procedures.

sionmaking rule is, some point inside the core can always defeat any point outside the core. Thus, in equilibrium, we would expect the legislative status quo to be inside the core, even if at particular times the actors cannot agree to such a move.

Let us begin by briefly reinterpreting political dynamics where the Council decides by unanimity. In such cases, a unanimous Council is required for a change of the legislative status quo. Any point inside the C1 . . . C7 heptagon cannot be modified by unanimity because at least one member of the Council would object to any change in the status quo. The hatched area in Figure 11.3 (regardless of its shade) is thus the core of unanimity-based legislative procedures (and for treaty revisions). Turning to discretion, the Commission and the ECJ could therefore effectively implement or interpret a given piece of legislation (the status quo) in any way they wish—so long as the ensuing policy outcome remains within the core. This would be true even if the Commission's implementation or the ECJ's interpretation were inconsistent with the Council's intent when it passed the legislation.

The final observation concerns the spatial location of actors. It is obvious that preference convergence (e.g., if C1-C7 were clustered more tightly under unanimity, or if the distances among the Council, EP, and Commission shrank) would reduce the core and hence the scope of discretion in implementation and adjudication as well. Increasing heterogeneity would have the opposite effect. In the context of the European Union, adding new members might be expected to increase heterogeneity in some cases (the southern accessions and, in the future, those from Eastern Europe),[14] but decrease it in others (Austria, Finland, and Sweden, on many issues). Moreover, there might be reasons to expect the distance among the institutions to be reduced, for example, if citizens come to hold their MEPs more accountable (and then vote the same way in national and EP elections).

Here I will hold preferences constant and analyze differences in the cores of E.U. legislation—and hence the scope for bureaucratic and judicial discretion—in terms of the procedures used to aggregate the preferences of legislative actors. Legislation can pass under the consultation and cooperation procedures in two ways. A decision can be taken with an agreement of the relevant actors, or by unanimity in the Council (acting alone). For consultation, the "relevant actors" are a qualified majority of the Council and a majority of the Commission. For cooperation, an absolute majority of the EP should be added to this list. Figure 11.3 has already shown the unanimity core of the Council. What constraints does the alternative rule (agreement of Commission for consultation, or the Commission and the parliament for cooperation) impose on policy discretion?

I concentrate on the cooperation procedure because of the additional complexities generated by the participation of the EP in legislation. Recall that we are assuming that the absolute majority requirement in the EP creates a de facto supermajority threshold of more than five-ninths. In Figure 11.3, the five-ninths core of the EP can be identified. Following the procedure described in Chapter 6, I connect each EP member with another so that three members are on one side of the line and the other four members are on the other side. Such lines are the pairs E1E5, E1E6, E2E6, E2E7, and so on. These lines define a polygon inside E1 . . . E9. This is the EP's core under absolute majority. Call this specific set of outcomes the "five-ninths EP core." It is obvious that the EP cannot modify anything located in that core—even if it could act alone, without the support of the Council or Commission. The reason is that there is a majority of more than five-ninths against moving away from any particular point of this nine-sided polygon. Similarly there is a core for the Council when it decides

[14] Bednar, Ferejohn, and Garrett 1996.

by five-sevenths QMV. As Figure 11.3 indicates (and for similar reasons as for the EP), this "QMV core" is a heptagon located inside C1 . . . C7.

The lightly shaded area of Figure 11.3—connecting what turns out to be the decisive commissioner (#1) with the extreme points of the EP's five-ninths core and the Council's QMV core—is thus the core of legislation requiring a qualified majority in the Council, an absolute majority in the EP, and a simple majority in the Commission.

But this is not the core of the cooperation procedure because a unanimous Council can also pass legislation. The core of cooperation is thus defined as the intersection of the unanimity core of the Council (the hatched area) and the interinstitutional core (the shaded area). In the figure, the crosshatched area denotes this cooperation core. Note that this area is always smaller than the Council's unanimity core (which readers will recall defines the room for policy discretion under the Luxembourg Compromise, treaty revisions, and legislation still subject to unanimity voting).

It is easy to calculate the consultation core, which is simply a subset of the cooperation core—since the salient difference between the two procedures is that the agreement of the EP is not required. This consultation core is represented in Figure 11.3 by the most heavily hatched area (regardless of shade).

If the Commission or the ECJ wants to make a decision that will not be overruled under the cooperation procedure, they can implement and interpret legislation anywhere within the crosshatched area. How big this area is, of course, depends on the relative position of the Commission and the EP with respect to the Council (and the cohesion of individual actors' preferences in these institutions). If, for example, the Commission were located close to E3, the core would shrink. One may think that given the selection mechanism for the Commission (that requires approval by both the Council and the EP), this is the most realistic position of the three actors most of the time. The core would expand, however, if the Council was located between the Commission and the EP.

Both versions of codecision specify that at the end of the legislative game, an agreement by a qualified majority of the Council and an absolute majority of the EP can overrule other actors. In particular, they can bypass the Commission. Consequently, the heavily shaded area of Figure 11.3 that connects the five-ninths EP core and the five-sevenths Council core represents the core of codecision (I and II). The greater the policy differences between the Council and the EP (and the greater the preference dispersion inside these institutions), the greater the size of the core, and hence the greater the discretion available to the Commission in policy implementation and the ECJ in statutory interpretation.

Figure 11.4 focuses on the effects of the Nice Treaty. As I discussed in Section 11.2, the qualified majority threshold slightly increased, and the preferences of the new countries are likely to be less homogeneous than those of the

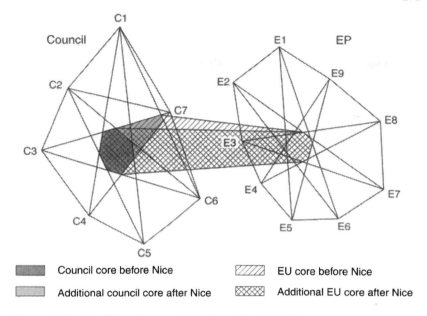

Figure 11.4. After Nice, the core of the Council and the EU expands.

current fifteen members. Both these changes tend to increase the core of the Council. However, here I will focus on the other two modifications, the requirement that legislation be supported by a majority of the countries members and the requirement that winning proposals should be supported by countries totaling at least 62 percent of the E.U. population. Figure 11.4 starts from the core of the codecision procedure before Nice (as presented in Figure 11.3), and compares it with the core after.

Because of the required triple majority in the Council, some of the qualified majority dividers under Amsterdam are replaced. For example, let us assume that C2C6 in Figure 11.4 does not fulfill one of the two additional requirements. In order to calculate the qualified majority core of the Council, this line has to be replaced by the actual qualified majority dividers. Let us consider that these lines are C2C7 and C1C6.[15] Recalculating the core of the Council under these assumptions indicates that it expands as Figure 11.4 indicates. As a result, the core of the E.U. legislative procedures expands also.

Why did the member states of the European Union select such a convoluted process? Tsebelis and Yataganas (2002) trace the Nice negotiations and dem-

[15] These lines should go further away from the center of the yolk in order to fulfill the additional requirements. It is possible that even these lines would not fulfill the additional requirements, and one would have to move to the lines C2C1, C1C7, and C6C7. In this case the difference between Amsterdam and Nice would be even more pronounced than the one I am about to describe.

onstrate that the large countries were essentially satisfied by the qualified majority decisionmaking in the Council, while the small countries wanted to introduce a requirement for a majority of countries in order to increase their weight in the Council. The terms of this debate take us back to the differences between Condorcet and Madison with respect to qualified majority and bicameralism as discussed in Chapter 6. Instead of resolving the issue, Nice adopted all possible criteria, resulting in an overwhelming expansion of the legislative core.

There is one more expectation resulting from the Nice Treaty that we should underline. Because the core of the Council expands, policy stability in the Council increases, and consequently it is more difficult for the Council to change the status quo or its previous position. As a result, in the conciliation committee of codecision, it will be more difficult for the EP to make the Council alter its previous positions, which implies at the institutional level a shift of power toward the Council (see Figure 6.3 and the discussion around it).

In conclusion, the Nice Treaty expands further the size of the Council core and the E.U. core. The result of these modifications is a shift of legislative power in favor of the Council, and an increase in the discretion of the Commission and the ECJ resulting from the reduced capacity of the European Union to legislate. It is important to note that in the above discussion, just like in Chapter 10, "discretion" refers to the behavior of the Commission and the ECJ, not to the institutional rules regulating their activities.

On the subject of institutional rules regulating bureaucratic behavior, Franchino (2000) has argued that when the legislative branch cannot overrule bureaucratic behavior (when the core of the European Union is large), then they will be more restrictive *ex ante*—they will write the legislation so as to reduce Commission discretion. I have discussed this point in Chapter 10.

11.4. Empirical Evidence

The institutional literature I reviewed shares several important assumptions with this book. All the authors consider institutions as constraints for the behavior of the different actors. As a result, they expect outcomes to be dependent on the institutions under which they were produced. However, given the complexity of E.U. institutions, they frequently come to different predictions with respect to specific procedures or outcomes. Let me present some of these differences as questions.

Question 1: Does the EP have conditional agenda-setting powers under cooperation? I have argued that it does (Tsebelis 1994), while other researchers (Crombez 1996; Steunenberg 1994; Moser 1996) contend that these powers belong to the Commission.

Question 2: Regardless of who has agenda-setting powers, will the outcome in the qualified majority winset of the Council be $(Q(SQ))$, as Crombez (1996), Steunenberg (1994), Moser (1996) expect, or only in the points that command a qualified majority over everything that the Council can do unanimously $(Q(U(SQ)))$, as I have argued (Tsebelis 1994)?

Question 3: Is there a difference in the influence the EP has between cooperation and codecision I? Is this difference in favor of the EP when it has the Commission on its side and is not confronted with a unanimous Council (that is, when it has conditional agenda-setting powers)? Garrett and Tsebelis (Garrett 1995b; Tsebelis 1997; Garrett and Tsebelis 1996, 1997) have provided an affirmative answer, while the conventional wisdom is that the EP gained power across the board with codecision I (see Crombez 1996, Corbett 2001a, and Scully 1997, among others).

Question 4: Has the Commission lost agenda-setting powers under codecision I (Crombez 1997), or have these powers simply been reduced compared to cooperation (Tsebelis and Garrett (2001)?

Question 5: Do the Commission as a bureaucracy and the ECJ as the judiciary have constant powers, do their powers increase over time (as neofunctionalist theories argue), or do their powers vary as a function of legislative procedures?

These questions about the way E.U. institutions operate are much more precise than other questions asked in this book. These differences of results are an indication of how far the collective enterprise of research can go when there is a group of people participating in the same research program. How can we corroborate one of the answers in each of these questions?

There have been hundreds of empirical studies on the European Union. In fact, there are at least two journals dedicated exclusively to the subject,[16] but these publications tend to focus on case studies. Such studies may provide very important insights, but it is not clear whether the conclusions are general or hold exclusively in the set of cases they study. Also, the explanations proposed may be correct, but it is not clear how the same variables would be measured in different cases. Instead of trying to extrapolate from such studies, I will describe the results from two different statistical analyses and relate them to the questions I enumerated, one from Thomas König (1997) and the other by Tsebelis et al. (2001).

König (1997) combined two different data sources related to a set of seven bills: on the one hand, a list of issues debated in the Council upon the discussion of these bills; on the other, expert assessments on the positions of the different countries, the Commission, and the EP on all the issues discussed in

---

[16] For example, *The Journal of Common Market Studies* and *European Union Politics*, not to mention *European Journal of Political Economy, European Journal of Political Research*, and *West European Politics*, which also publish articles on the politics of different European countries.

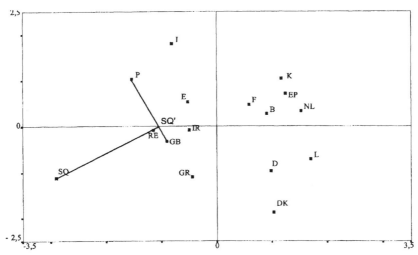

Figure 11.5. Council preferences and voting outcomes under unanimity.

Council. As a result, he was able to locate the position of actors, the status quo, and the outcome of several bills in a high dimensional space (he identified seventy-eight issues or dimensions). He then used multidimensional scaling to reduce the dimensionality of space and present the outcomes in two dimensions. He presents the following two figures (König 1997: 187, 189).[17]

Figure 11.5 presents the average legislative outcome under decisions that required unanimity in the Council. Figure 11.6 presents the average legislative outcome obtained under cooperation. I have used König's figures and introduced additional straight lines in order to calculate the predictions of the literature and compare them with the actual outcomes.

In Figure 11.5 I have drawn a straight line connecting the preferences of the two countries located closest to the status quo (Great Britain and Portugal). Given that all the countries are veto players (under unanimity rule), they will all be better off by replacing SQ by its projection on the unanimity core. The reader can refer to Figure 10.1 for a similar argument with respect to bureaucrats or judges. With respect to legislative studies, this is not an uncommon argument. In particular, in the E.U. literature the common belief was that under unanimity the prevailing outcome was "the least common denominator" (Lange 1992). König's study corroborates this expectation.

Before analyzing the results of Figure 11.6, let me compare it with the theoretical picture I presented in Figure 11.1. First, notice the location of the status

[17] I thank Thomas König for providing me with the electronic version of these figures, which permitted subsequent graphic elaborations on my part. Because of their origin the figures have German characters (D for Germany, K for Commission).

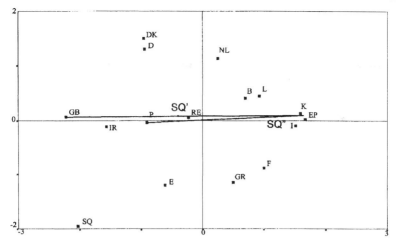

Figure 11.6. Council preferences and outcomes under cooperation procedure.

quo, the Council members, and the EP and Commission. In both cases, the theoretical and the empirically constructed, the status quo is located to the left, outside the unanimity core of the Council, while the Commission and the EP are located on the other side and close to each other. The empirical picture very clearly corroborates a division among these actors as expected along the integration dimension.

In Figure 11.6 I drew two lines, one connecting the ideal point of Great Britain and another connecting the ideal point of Portugal with the Commission (K) or the EP (P) (given their proximity it does not matter). The reason I drew these lines is to identify the location of a winning proposal by the EP and the Commission to the Council. According to Tsebelis (1994) and the argument I presented in the previous section, the EP identifies all the outcomes that can defeat the status quo by unanimity, and identifies the set of points that will make a qualified majority (q = five-sevenths) better off than anything the Council can do unanimously (U(Q(SQ))). In Figure 11.6 there are no such points, so the EP will select the point it prefers from the unanimity set of the status quo (U(SQ)).[18] Which is the most preferred point in (U(SQ))?

On the line connecting Great Britain (at the extreme left) with the EP and the Commission (given that their ideal points are very close to each other, I drew a line passing between these two points) I selected a point SQ' so that the distance SQ'GB is the same as the distance SQGB. This is the ideal point for

[18] On that point, Tsebelis (1994) was mistaken to claim that under these conditions the EP will not have a winning proposal, because it can select the point in U(SQ) that it prefers instead of leaving the Council to decide on its own.

the EP and the Commission among all the points of U(SQ). Indeed, the point SQ1 belongs to U(SQ) since GB is indifferent between it and SQ, and all other countries prefer it over SQ; in addition, the Commission and the EP cannot do any better because if they select a point closer to them, GB is going to veto it.

In order to identify the Commission proposal following Crombez (1996), Steunenberg (1994), and Moser (1996), we have to find the most preferred point by the Commission inside the qualified majority (q = five-sevenths) preferred set of the status quo Q(SQ). This point can be identified if the Commission makes a proposal to the qualified majority that has preferences as close as possible to its own, that is, if it ignores Great Britain (GB with 10 votes), Ireland (IR with 3 votes), and Spain (ES with 8 votes) and concentrates on the other 66 (= 87 − 21) votes of the Council.[19] In fact, the Commission has to make Portugal indifferent between the status quo and its own proposal, so it proposes SQ″. This is the best for the Commission point inside Q(SQ), since all countries with the exception of Great Britain, Ireland, and Spain prefer it to the status quo, and any point closer to the Commission would be vetoed by Portugal.

A comparison between the two predictions SQ′, SQ″, and the actual outcome RE indicates that SQ′ is closer to RE than SQ″. Thus my predictions are corroborated by König's (1997) data. A problem with König's data set is its size: it contains few bills with several hundreds amendments. One would prefer to have additional data, but I think this problem will be addressed in the future by König and his collaborators. Another problem is that Figures 11.5 and 11.6 aggregate different bills. In a more recent article (König and Pöter, 2002), the authors address this problem: the data are disaggregated by a bill, a new bill is added, along with a dimension-by-dimension method of comparison of the different theories. The disaggregation produces essentially the same results as the ones reported above. The one new case produces results far away from my predictions and approximates the expectations by Crombez (1996), Steunenberg (1994), and Moser (1996) better. The dimension-by-dimension comparison does not discriminate between the two approaches in terms of accuracy. However, as I have discussed several times in this book and in particular shown in Section 11.3 and Figure 11.1, reducing multidimensional problems into single dimensional ones is a poor substitute for multidimensional analysis.

Tsebelis et al. (2001) take a different empirical tack. They use only data from the amendments proposed by the EP to different bills and study the rate of adoption of these amendments. Their method focuses only on the public disagreements among actors. There are disagreements resolved in private before the Commission makes its initial proposal (ignored by the analysis), and there are disagreements that may appear for other strategic reasons (position

---

[19] The Commission cannot ignore Portugal, with five votes, because then it loses the required qualified majority of sixty-two votes.

taking) rather than for the purpose of being legislatively resolved. Tsebelis et al. (2001) defend their approach by arguing that they cannot include "invisible politics" in their analysis and that position taking is not so frequent in E.U. legislation because the E.U. public is not paying attention to legislative politics, as most of the literature indicates. Thus they use the outcomes of the resolution of public disagreements as a proxy measure for the influence of different actors. The same approach has been taken by the EP, which publishes the percentages of its successful amendments, and by most of the literature which reports these measures as an indication of the EP's influence (Corbett, Jacobs, and Shackleton 1995; Westlake 1994; Hix 1999). For example, in 1994 the Commission reported: "Since the Single European Act came into force on July 1 1987, over 50 percent of Parliament's amendments have been accepted by the Commission and carried by the Council. No national Parliament has a comparable success rate in bending the executive to its will" (Commission press release, 15 December 1994, quoted in Earnshaw and Judge 1996: 96).

The data set of Tsebelis et al. (2001) produces the same aggregate results as the EP, namely that EP amendments are more frequently included in the final bill under codecision I than under cooperation. The difference is about ten percentage points. However, this aggregate measure may be not be appropriate for a comparison of the EP's influence under conditional agenda setting or veto. For example, if the Commission disagrees with the EP, the latter is deprived of agenda-setting powers. Similarly, there are no conditional agenda-setting powers if the EP (or, for that matter, the Commission) is confronted with a unanimous Council. Consequently, one has to introduce controls for these possibilities.

Tsebelis et al. (2001) introduced one prerequisite for conditional agenda setting—acceptance by the Commission in their analysis of 230 pieces of legislation involving 5,000 amendments. They begin by controlling for acceptance by the Commission under the cooperation procedure (since it is a condition for conditional agenda setting) but not under codecision (since nobody has claimed that the EP needs the Commission's support under this procedure). They find that the rejection rate by the Council of the EP's amendments that have been accepted by the Commission under cooperation is twenty percentage points lower than for all parliamentary amendments under codecision.

However, one can argue that this is an unfair test, since EP proposals are treated differently in the two procedures (as I said, without any controls, the results are in the opposite direction). This is the relevant equation from Tsebelis et al. (2001) estimating the impact of rejection by the Commission on final rejection by the Council, under both the cooperation and Maastricht codecision procedures:

$$\text{Rejection} = .2708 - .0938\text{SYN} + .3987\text{RCOM} + .3193\text{SYN} * \text{RCOM}$$
$$(6.46) \quad (-1.71) \quad (4.11) \quad (2.66)$$

Where SYN is a dummy with the value 1 for cooperation and 0 for codecision I; RCOM is rejection by the Commission; and SYN * RCOM is the interaction between the two variables (t-statistics in parentheses).

This equation implies the following: first, rejection by the Commission has deleterious consequences for the survival of an EP amendment, and this is true for both cooperation and codecision (the coefficient is substantively large and highly significant). Second, the Commission rejected more EP amendments under cooperation than under the Maastricht version of codecision (the coefficient of the interaction term is also positive and almost as large and statistically significant). Third, controlling for these two factors, the coefficient for amendments made under the cooperation procedure is *negative* (this means that there were *fewer* rejections by the Council of the EP's amendments under cooperation than under codecision). This is a smaller coefficient, and is not as significant as the others (significance at the .05 level using a one-tailed test), so I do not want to make a big issue of it. However, it goes exactly in the direction I have expected.

On the basis of the above statistical results, Tsebelis et al. (2001) calculate the percentage of times that the position of the Commission on an EP amendment is accepted by the Council. They find that on average the Council conforms to the Commission 85 percent under cooperation, and 70 percent under codecision. As a result, the power of the Commission has been significantly reduced under codecision, but certainly not eliminated.

Corbett (2001a: 373–74) has disputed the theoretical arguments on conditional agenda setting versus veto.[20] His major argument has been that codecision I has been de facto altered by Rule 78 (see above), and consequently the Council has not made "take it or leave it" offers to the EP since the 1994 draft directive on open network provision in voice telephony (see above). He interprets the lack of such proposals by the Council as a de facto victory of the EP and does not see any difference between codecision I and II. In his view, the Amsterdam Treaty "did no more than entrench reality into the treaty" (Corbett 2001a: 374). What is mistaken about this analysis is that a successful maneuver by the EP is not equivalent to the text of a treaty, and the lack of take-it-or-leave-it offers by the Council may be due *both* to the fear of the Council and/or the fear of the EP of a disagreement in the conciliation committee. Corbett believes that it was the Council that backed down, but I have found evidence that can be interpreted otherwise.

Table 11.2 presents a breakdown of the 4,904 amendments covered by Tsebelis et al. (2001) into cooperation and codecision I amendments. In addition, it divides these amendments into four groups: introduced for the first time in

---

[20] For the whole debate, see Tsebelis and Garrett (2001), Corbett (2001a), Garrett and Tsebelis (2001), and Corbett (2001b).

TABLE 11.2

Percentages of Different Parliamentary Responses in the Second Round of Cooperation and Codecision I Procedures

	Cooperation			Codecision		
	Number	*Percentage Overall*	*Percentage of Second Round*	*Number*	*Percentage Overall*	*Percentage of Second Round*
New Amendment	272	0.095	0.453	281	0.138	0.533
Modification Amendment	163	0.057	0.272	148	0.073	0.281
Reintroduced "as is" Amendment	165	0.058	0.275	98	0.048	0.186
Not Reintroduced Amendment	2266	0.791		1511	0.741	
Total	2866	1	1	2038	1	1

the second round, reintroduced with modifications, reintroduced verbatim, and not reintroduced. This breakdown indicates that three-quarters of the time amendments are not reintroduced. If, however, they are reintroduced, the EP adopts a more aggressive attitude under cooperation than under codecision I. Indeed, it would reintroduce amendments exactly the same way as in the first round: 50 percent of the time (165 vs. 163) under cooperation and 40 percent of the time (98 vs. 148) under codecision. In addition, the Council introduced modifications that provoked EP response more frequently under codecision (281 of 2038 = .138) than under cooperation (272 of 2866 = .095). Probably a better way to present these numbers is by focusing exclusively on the behavior of different actors in the second round. Under cooperation (see fourth column of Table 11.2), 45 percent of second-round amendments are caused by modifications introduced by the Council, and, of the remaining 55 percent of amendments, half are reintroduced by the EP as they were in the first round, and the other half under a compromise amended form. Under codecision (see the last column of Table 11.2), 53 percent of amendments are caused by modifications introduced by the Council, and the EP reintroduces amendments as they were only 19 percent of the time. In other words, from cooperation to codecision we see an eight percentage point increase of amendments caused by the Council, and an eight-point decrease of the EP adopting an intransigent position. These numbers indicate a more aggressive attitude of the Council, not the EP under codecision.

However, there is one additional interesting point in this debate: the data indicate small differences in the identity of the agenda setter. How can we account for that? It seems to me that the account of the European Union I have presented leaves little doubt that there is a considerable multiplicity of veto players: qualified majorities in the Council, combined with de facto qualified majorities in the EP, and sometimes requirement of agreement by the Commission. Going back to Corollary 1.5.2, the significance of agenda setting declines with the introduction of additional veto players.

Finally, in terms of the powers of the ECJ to interpret law and the Commission as a bureaucratic agent, the predictions above indicate that there will be fluctuations of their powers. Little empirical work has been done on these points. Weiler (1991) suggests that there was a decline in the role of the ECJ in the mid-eighties; however, he is discussing cases where the ECJ referred to treaties while the argument here deals with statutory interpretations. No work has been done with respect to behavioral independence of the Commission, although Franchino (2000) has written several articles demonstrating that the institutional discretion of the Commission declines when decisions in the Council are taken unanimously, because the Council anticipates that the Commission would have more discretion ex post, so it restricts it ex ante. While he presents his findings as an "indirect" negative test of my expectations, it seems to me that he accepts the logic of my arguments, but does not test the implications.[21]

To conclude, let us return to the five questions I asked above:

Question 1: Does the EP have conditional agenda-setting powers under cooperation? On the basis of empirical evidence, it is the case that the EP gained conditional agenda-setting powers with the Single European Act and the cooperation procedure: it introduced thousands of amendments, and overall some 50 percent of them were accepted.

Question 2: Regardless of who has agenda-setting powers, will the outcome be in the qualified majority winset of the Council ($Q(SQ)$), or only in the points that command a qualified majority over everything that the Council can do unanimously ($Q(U(SQ))$)? König's (1997) data contain only cases where $Q(U(SQ))$ is empty. In these cases, the results are located inside $U(SQ)$, as I expect, and not inside $Q(SQ)$.

Question 3: Is there a difference in the influence the EP has between cooperation and codecision I? Is this difference in favor of the EP when it has the Commission on its side and is not confronted with a unanimous Council? The answers to both these questions are affirmative, as the empirical results of Tsebelis et al. (2001) demonstrate.

---

[21] See the arguments I made about institutional and behavioral independence of central banks in Chapter 10.

Question 4: Has the Commission lost agenda-setting powers under codecision I, or have these powers simply been reduced compared to cooperation? The data set of Tsebelis et al. (2001) indicates that when the behavior of the Commission is controlled for, the acceptance rate of EP amendments is higher under cooperation. The unconditional rate of acceptance of EP amendments is higher under codecision than under cooperation because the Commission was more negative and more influential under cooperation than under codecision.

Question 5: Do the Commission as a bureaucracy and the ECJ as the judiciary have constant powers, do their powers increase over time, or do their powers vary as a function of legislative procedures? There is no empirical evidence to corroborate or reject my expectations in bureaucracies and the judiciary in the European Union. Franchino (2000) produces evidence that the institutional power of the Commission is reduced, but he does not address the point of behavioral independence of the Commission. Stone-Sweet (2000) argues for an expansion of the role of the ECJ, while Dehousse (1998) argues for a reduction; however, their arguments are based on constitutional decisions, not on statutory ones.

11.5. Conclusions

The European Union is a complicated and fast-changing polity. In fact, analysts disagree whether it resembles a presidential or parliamentary system at any point of its recent developments. Instead of using the similarities or differences of the E.U. institutions with any particular polity as the basis of my analysis, I described E.U. institutions (Section 11.2) and then modeled them on the basis of veto players theory, and came to a series of conclusions (Section 11.3), which were corroborated by the data (Section 11.4). My expectations regarded not only the legislative system of the European Union, but also the judiciary and the bureaucracies.

At the macro level, my basic conclusions are that the European Union moved from a six, nine, ten, or twelve–veto player system (depending on the number of countries that participated under the Luxembourg Compromise) to a three or two–collective veto player legislative system (from 1987 on). However, these collective veto players were deciding by qualified majorities each: an explicitly-stated-in-the-treaties majority in the Council; a de facto qualified majority in the EP (because of abstentions). As a result, policy stability is very high. The legislative rules may increase it, or decrease it as the analysis in the second half of the third section has shown (Figure 11.3), but we are moving around a very high level of policy stability (large core). All the consequences of policy stability are there: complaints about the important role of "Brussels" (the headquarters of the Commission) in all European countries, as well as the important role of the ECJ (in a comparative perspective).

The Nice Treaty is likely to exacerbate these trends. The qualified majority in the Council is going to increase, and it is supplemented by two more required majorities: a majority of member states, and a qualified majority (62 percent) of the people of the European Union. All these features increase the core of the Council, and therefore of the European Union. In addition, more countries will enter the European Union, which is likely to produce more diversified interests, and as a result an even bigger legislative core and smaller winsets of SQ. The consequences of these changes will be an increase in policy stability, and an increased role for the bureaucracy and the judiciary.

I am not making a normative judgment on whether such changes are beneficial or not. I have already stated that it depends on the position of the judge with respect to the status quo. However, whether we are talking about the behavioral independence of bureaucrats (as my models predict) or the institutional constraints imposed by more detailed legislation that Franchino (2000) describes, it seems that Nice has placed the European Union into a heavy bureaucratization orbit.

Conclusion _____

THIS BOOK HAS INTRODUCED a new framework for the analysis of political institutions. While each of the claims made in particular chapters may have existed already (some of them, as I showed in the Introduction, for centuries or even millennia), the combination provides a different view of institutional analysis. The areas of application of veto players theory are so diversified in terms of traditional institutional analysis (different regimes, parties and party systems, federal and unified countries) and in terms of subject areas (lawmaking, bureaucracies, judiciary, government selection, and duration) that I was able to test an intellectually consistent set of predictions across many different situations and provide several pieces of evidence to corroborate the theory.

Veto players theory focuses on legislative politics, and how lawmaking decisions are made, in order to explain a series of policies and other important characteristics of politics. Its advantage is that it traces the lawmaking process closely, so that its expectations are more likely to be accurate than existing typologies. For example, instead of asking the traditional questions about regime type, party system, types of parties, and so on, it focuses on the interaction between the lawmaking institutions, that is, the veto players. The questions I have addressed are as follows:

1. Who are the veto players? That is, who are the actors whose agreement is necessary for a change in the status quo? How many exist? What are their locations? Is any one of them located in the unanimity core of the others, in which case the absorption rule applies (i.e., a veto player does not "count" because he does not affect outcomes)?

2. How do these veto players decide? Are they single individuals or collective? Do they require simple majority, or qualified majority, or unanimity? Do they decide by a combination of the above (like E.U. institutions)? In each one of these cases, how is the set of possible outcomes affected? Do they have stable or shifting internal coalitions? And how do these features affect the winset of the status quo?

3. How do veto players interact? Do we know a specific sequence of moves, in which case we can restrict the set of outcomes; or do we only know that an agreement among them is necessary, and therefore we have no grounds to select one particular point of the winset of the status quo over another?

4. If we can identify an agenda setter (first mover), what are his institutional and his positional advantages? That is, what are the restrictions imposed on other veto players not to amend the initial proposal? How large is the winset of the status quo of the other veto players (which implies more agenda-setting power)? How centrally is the agenda setter located among the veto players (which also implies more agenda-setting power)?

Answering these questions provides significant insights into the lawmaking process and its outcomes, as well as other structural features of different political systems. I will come to them shortly, but first let me address how standard questions and classifications introduced in the literature relate to these questions.

Regime types differ in terms of their veto players configuration: presidentialism and parliamentarism differ in terms of the number of institutional veto players, as well as who controls the legislative agenda and by how much. Federal and unitary countries also differ along the number of institutional veto players. Multiparty coalitions and single party governments differ in the number of partisan veto players. Strong and weak parties differ in terms of their party cohesion. All systems differ in terms of the distance among veto payers, which affects policy stability.

However, while each one of the standard questions in the literature translates into some feature of veto players, this translation is not direct and straightforward. As I explained in Chapter 6, the same institutions may have different results on the veto player configuration of a country: referendums may increase (usually) or decrease (if both triggering and asking the question are prerogatives of the same player) the number of veto players. Executive decrees may decrease (usually) or increase (as in France) the number of veto players, or may simply alter the distances among them. However, the major reason why institutions cannot be directly translated into statements about veto players is the "absorption rule" that I introduced in Chapter 1. A veto player located in the unanimity core (the Pareto set) of other existing veto players is absorbed, that is, does not alter policy decisionmaking. A second chamber, or a president with veto powers controlled by the same parties as the government, is not going to make a difference if the parties are cohesive, but it might make a difference if they are not. A party located between other parties of a coalition in the left-right dimension will not have an impact on legislation in this dimension, but it might have an impact if, for example, legislation encompasses many different dimensions. In fact, the veto players analysis shows why just counting institutions without looking at their preferences, or assuming policy spaces to be single dimensional when they are multidimensional, or assuming that a country falls in one category (say multiparty system) when the composition of the government changes from a single-party government to a multiparty coalition, might produce misleading or wrong results.

Because of its attention to the legislative process, veto players theory can make accurate predictions about policy outcomes as a function of who controls the agenda, who the veto players are, and the rules under which they decide. In addition, it provides explanations about the relationship between the legislative process and other structural features of a democratic polity, like the role of judges and bureaucrats, or government stability (in parliamentary systems) and regime stability (in presidential ones).

In terms of *specific* predictions, the theory can identify expected outcomes quite accurately when the positions of all veto players, the agenda setter, and the status quo are identified and known by all actors (perfect information). Indeed, as we saw in Chapter 11, the agenda setter can select among the feasible outcomes the one that he prefers the most as long as he makes the relevant actors indifferent between the status quo and his own proposal.

However, most often the identity or the preferences of the agenda setter are not known. Veto players theory responds by identifying the set of all possible outcomes, the winset of the status quo, and expects actors to make inferences from the size of this set. For example, in parliamentary systems it is not clear who controls the agenda inside the government. As a result, the predictions of veto players theory without this agenda-setting information are not as sharp as other theories (e.g., bargaining theories among different actors: Baron and Ferejohn [1989]; Baron [1996]; Tsebelis and Money [1997]; Huber and McCarty [2001]), or situations where most of the decisionmaking power is supposed to reside with one particular actor like the prime minister (Huber [1996]; Strom [2000]) or the corresponding minister (Laver and Shepsle [1996]); as a result, veto players predictions are not as objectionable or controversial as the above. Similarly, in presidential systems, the Congress makes a proposal to the president, but the Congress's proposal usually depends on the compromise struck in a bicameral legislature.

In the absence of such knowledge, veto players theory provides the contours of the possible outcomes on the basis of minimal assumptions: that every veto player will accept only solutions that it prefers over the status quo. It turns out that this assumption of imprecise identity or preferences of the agenda setter and veto players insisting upon having outcomes they prefer over the status quo is quite a good approximation, so that the policy stability expectations of veto players theory turn out to be correct. It also turns out that other actors in the system (governments, bureaucrats, or judges) act upon this expected policy stability.

Thus, while the initial advantage of veto players theory was the precise mapping of the legislative process, it turns out that it has additional derivative advantages. The first advantage is that the assumptions are minimal and not controversial. Indeed, it is very difficult to argue that rational actors will accept policies that they do not prefer over the status quo unless one includes some form of side payments in the analysis. I do not want to argue that such payments are impossible. If they are introduced as a constant feature of the analysis, however, most (if not all) outcomes become possible, and theories become so all-encompassing that they are impossible to test.

Another advantage of the veto players theory is that the underlying models are multidimensional. As a result, I do not apply assumptions that generate median voter outcomes when such median voters may not exist. In fact, I do not generate equilibria when such equilibria might not be there. I just claim that any outcome has to be included in the intersection of the winsets of the different veto players, and study the properties of all these points.

In the theoretical part of this book, I started with the simplifying assumption that veto players are individual decisionmakers, and identified the conditions under which they will count or will be absorbed (Proposition 1.2), and I identify the systems that produce more or less policy stability (Proposition 1.4). All the propositions on policy stability were in the form of necessary but not sufficient conditions. While propositions identifying necessary but not sufficient conditions are very frequent in the social sciences, their methodological implications have not been drawn. In this book I demonstrate that such propositions lead to expectations not only about the mean of the dependent variable (policy stability) but also about its variance (heteroskedasticity). In Chapters 7 and 8 I used the appropriate statistical technique to test both my predictions.

I then expanded the analysis to collective veto players and focused on their decisionmaking rules: majority, qualified majority, or unanimity. I demonstrated that most of the time the qualitative results are not altered if one approximates a collective veto player as if it were an individual one, and that this result holds even when we are considering veto players deciding sequentially (one of them controls the agenda) as opposed to simultaneously.

I applied these simple principles to the important theoretical questions of the comparative politics literature: regime types, federalism, bicameralism, qualified majorities, parties and party systems, and referendums. Here are some of the conclusions of this analysis.

While the existing literature differentiates between presidential and parliamentary regimes, veto players finds a way to unify them and make information about one type of regime inform us about what might happen in the other. While most of the literature focuses on the difference between collaboration and independence of the executive and legislative branches, I point out the importance of agenda setting and cohesion of veto players. Both these variables have an effect on lawmaking, and in both these variables there is wide variation inside each one of the regimes.

However, not all of the literature differentiates between presidential and parliamentary regimes. Arend Lijphart had the sound idea of unifying the study of different regimes by introducing the variable "executive dominance" and locating most parliamentary systems higher than presidential ones on this dimension. While I think that Lijphart's approach has important merits, the equation of executive dominance with government duration is theoretically untenable and empirically weak. I demonstrated that executive dominance depends on government agenda-setting powers, and suggested an exhaustive study on agenda-setting powers in both presidential and parliamentary regimes. Such a study will improve our understanding of politics in both regimes.

Referendums have been a very controversial institution, with some of the literature considering them as the essence of democracy, while other authors criticize the people's lack of information, as well as the fact that they might be a means of empowering particular actors. The veto players theory, instead of focusing on the distinction between direct and indirect democracy, identifies the additional veto player who enters the decisionmaking process in countries with referendums (the "public" or some approximation of the median voter, as I demonstrated in Chapter 5), and focuses on the process of agenda setting in order to understand the properties of different referendum structures. In fact, I have demonstrated that the different approaches of referendums in the literature are based on extrapolations of different agenda-setting structures: the critics of referendums extrapolate from veto player referendums, while the supporters speak of popular initiatives. I have identified other intermediate types of referendums, where legislative power is divided between government and opposition, and where the people are called to decide when such disagreements exist (as in Denmark or Italy).

Federalism has been associated with bicameralism since the creation of the U.S. constitution. However, before that it was associated with qualified majorities. Both institutional settings (qualified majorities and bicameralism) increase the number of veto players, and lead to more policy stability. Their difference is that bicameralism leads to the emergence of one privileged dimension of conflict, while qualified majorities protect all centrally located policies. The theoretical debate concerning the two forms of government can be found in the analyses of Montesquieu and Madison. Today federalism is more frequently associated with bicameralism than with qualified majorities (although polities like the United States and the European Union combine both). Qualified majorities are officially associated with certain important policymaking processes: particularly when different veto players disagree or when an issue is of high significance. However, as I have demonstrated, qualified majorities are much more pervasive and exist de facto when some parties are excluded from decisionmaking or even when absenteeism in parliament turns absolute majorities into qualified majorities.

The empirical chapters of this book demonstrate that policy stability is in fact related to veto players not only when one focuses on legislation (i.e., legislative instruments), but when one studies macroeconomic policies (i.e., legislative outcomes). Chapters 7 and 8 also demonstrated that moving from one to multiple dimensions may be necessary depending on the subject of the study, and that veto players enables research on any number of policy dimensions (if the data are available). This is a significant improvement over most existing theories, which assume a single-dimensional space as a good approximation.

The last part of the book focused on structural differences generated in different democratic countries because of characteristics of their veto players configuration. In terms of government duration as well as government composition, veto players shifts the attention from party systems' characteristics to government characteristics. As we saw, the ideological distance between parties determines who enters government, as well as how long governments last. These features of parliamentary systems can be explained by interpreting the "status quo" as an outcome dependent not only on policies adopted but also on a series of other events prevailing in the political environment (shocks) and the veto players theory.

My analysis indicates that governments are formed by veto players located close to each other, because such veto players will have more points to include in their government program, but will also be able to face exogenous shocks to the economic or political system. When such groups of players exist, they will form a coalition government, while when party dispersion is high, minority governments may be the only solution. These minority governments are using the institutional provisions of government agenda setting more often than other types of government.

The issue of independence of the judiciary and bureaucracies was also studied on the basis of veto players. I distinguished between institutional and behavioral independence, and focused on the second. On the basis of veto players, the underlying difference of the role of the judiciary in a country is not the common law or civil law tradition, but the number (and distances) of veto players. Countries with low policy stability will have low judicial independence, and countries with high policy stability will have more independent judges. I provided empirical evidence to corroborate this prediction, along with evidence that federal systems will have a more independent judiciary, since these judiciaries will be called to adjudicate between different branches of government. I have a similar expectation for presidential systems, but no data to investigate it. I demonstrated that the judiciary should be an additional veto player only in cases where there is judicial review, but I also argued that in most of these cases they get absorbed as an additional veto player because of their mode of appointment.

With respect to bureaucracies, I argued that it is easier to test institutional independence than behavioral independence, because the preferences of the bureaucracy are a necessary component of the analysis. The only case I found where the literature has been unanimous in making such an assumption was the case of central banks, and for these particular bureaucracies I provided existing evidence that my expectation of behavioral independence is corroborated.

Finally, a more global assessment of the veto players predictions could be performed on E.U. institutions, which change significantly and frequently over time. Veto players theory does not rely on "appropriate" or "inappropriate" analogies, but replicates the institutional structure of a polity and studies the policies that it is likely to produce. I demonstrated that legislative power shifts with agenda setting, and provided the reasons for changes over time of the significance of the judiciary and the bureaucracies. I also demonstrated that single dimensional models are not able to assess the powers of the parliament, and hence claimed that a parliament that was making thousands of amendments and had one of every two amendments approved was considered by some of the literature as a weak parliament. Both the theories and the tests in this chapter were significantly more advanced than in the rest of the book. In the case of the theories, this is because the institutions were more complicated and demanded further theoretical developments to address questions like conditional agenda setting. The tests could be more precise because of the existence of sharper theoretical predictions in the literature.

In conclusion, this book contains a series of theoretical arguments and specific expectations. These expectations are frequently different from most of the literature: for example, on how well regime types explain differences among countries, whether party systems or government characteristics are more important explanatory variables for the study of different phenomena, on the role and the significance of referendums, and on the importance and consequences of bicameralism, federalism, and qualified majorities. The policy predictions were corroborated both with respect to legislation (policy instruments) and macroeconomic policies (policy outcomes). The structural predictions were corroborated whether they were on bureaucracies, the judiciary, government composition and duration, or overall assessments about a variable institutional structure like the European Union. On the basis of the arguments produced in this book and the diversity of the supporting evidence, veto players theory can become the basis of an institutional approach to comparative politics.

Bibliography

Ackerman, Bruce. 2000. "The New Separation of Powers." *Harvard Law Review* 113 (3): 633–729.

Alesina, A. 1994. "Political Models of Macroeconomic Policy and Fiscal Reforms." In S. H. and S. B. Webb (eds.), *Voting for Reform*. Washington, D.C.: World Bank; Oxford: Oxford University Press.

Alesina, A., and A. Drazen. 1991. "Why are stabilizations delayed?" *American Economic Review* 81 (December): 1170–88.

Alesina, A., and R. Perotti. 1995. "The Political Economy of Budget Deficits." *International Monetary Fund Staff Papers* 42 (March): 1–31.

Alesina, Alberto, and Lawrence Summers. 1993. "Central Bank Independence and Macroeconomic Performance: Some Comparative Evidence." *Journal of Money, Credit, and Banking* 25 (2): 151–62.

Alivizatos, Nicos. 1995. "Judges as Veto Players." In H. Doering (ed.), *Parliaments and Majority Rule in Western Europe*. New York: St. Martin's Press.

Almond, Gabriel, and Sidney Verba. 1963. *The Civic Culture: Political Attitudes and Democracy in Five Nations*. Princeton: Princeton University Press.

Alt, James E., and Alec Crystal. 1985. *Political Economics*. Berkeley: University of California Press.

Alt, James E., and Robert C. Lowry. 1994. "Divided Government, Fiscal Institutions, and Budget Deficits: Evidence from the States." *American Political Science Review* 88: 811–28.

Ames, Barry. 1995. "Electoral Rules, Constituency Pressures, and Pork Barrell: Bases of Voting in the Brazilian Congress." *Journal of Politics* 57: 324–43.

———. 2001. *The Deadlock of Democracy in Brazil*. Ann Arbor: University of Michigan Press.

Arrow, Kenneth. 1951. *Social Choice and Individual Values*. New York: John Wiley and Sons.

Aspinwall, Mark D., and Gerald Schneider. 2000. "Same Menu, Separate Tables: The Institutionalist Turn in Political Science and the Study of European Integration." *European Journal of Political Research* 38: 1–36.

Axelrod, Robert. 1981. "The Emergence of Cooperation among Egoists." *American Political Science Review* 75: 306–18.

Baron, David P. 1995. "A Sequential Theory Perspective on Legislative Organization." In Kenneth Shepsle and Barry Weingast (eds.), *Positive Theories of Congressional Institutions*. Ann Arbor: University of Michigan Press.

———. 1996. "A Dynamic Theory of Collective Goods Programs." *American Political Science Review* 90: 316–30.

Baron, David P., and John A. Ferejohn. 1989. "Bargaining in Legislatures." *American Political Science Review* 89: 1181–1206.

Baron, David P., and Michael Herron. 1999. "A Dynamic Model of Multidimensional Collective Choice." Unpublished manuscript, Stanford University.

Barro, R. 1996. "Democracy and Growth." *Journal of Economic Growth* 1: 1–27.

Bawn, Kathleen. 1999a. "Constructing 'Us': Ideology, Coalitions and False Consciousness." *American Journal of Political Science* 43 (2): 303–34.

Bawn, Kathleen. 1999b. "Money and Majorities in the Federal Republic of Germany: Evidence for a Veto Players Model of Government Spending." *American Journal of Political Science* 43: (3) 707–36.

Beck, N., and J. Katz. 1995. "What To Do (and Not To Do) with Time-Series-Cross-Section Data." *American Political Science Review* 89 (September): 634–47.

———. 1996. "Nuisance vs. Substance: Specifying and Estimating Time-Series-Cross-Section Models." *Political Analysis* 6 (1): 1–36.

Beck, Thorsten, George Clark, Alberto Groff, Philip Keefer, and Partick Walsh. 1999. "Database on the Institutions of Government Decision Making." Washington, D.C.: World Bank.

Bednar, Jenna, William N. Eskridge, Jr., and John Ferejohn. 2001. "A Political Theory of Federalism." In John Ferejohn, John Riley, and Jack N. Rakove (eds.), *Constitutional Culture and Democratic Rule*. New York: Cambridge University Press.

Bednar, Jenna, John Ferejohn, and Geoffrey Garrett. 1996. "The Politics of European Federalism." *International Review of Law and Economics* 16: 279–94.

Beer, Samuel H. 1993. *To Make a Nation: The Rediscovery of American Federalism*. Cambridge: Harvard University Press.

Berger, Helge, Jakob de Haan, and Sylvester C.W. Eijffinger. 2001. "Central Bank Independence: An Update of Theory and Evidence." *Journal of Economic Surveys* 15 (1): 3–40.

Bernhard, William. 1998. "A Political Explanation of Variations in Central Bank Independence." *American Political Science Review* 92 (2): 311–27.

Bieber, Roland. 1988. "Legislative Procedure for the Establishment of the Single Market." *Common Market Review* 25: 711–12.

Bieber, R., J. Pantalis, and J. Schoo. 1986. "Implications of the Single Act for the European Parliament." *Common Market Law Review* 23: 767–92.

Binder, Sarah. 1999. "The Dynamics of Legislative Gridlock, 1947–96." *American Political Science Review* 93: (3) 519–33.

Birchfield, Vicki, and Markus M. L. Crepaz. 1998. "The Impact of Constitutional Structures and Collective and Competitive Veto Points on Income Inequality in Industrialized Democracies." *European Journal of Political Research* 34: 175–200.

Blanpain, Roger. 1977– . *International Encyclopedia for Labour Law and Industrial Relations*. Amsterdam: Kluwer.

Bogdanor, Vernon. 1994. "Western Europe." In D. Butler and A. Ranney (eds.), *Referendums around the World: The Growing Use of Direct Democracy*. Washington, D.C.: American Enterprise Institute Press.

Boix Charles. 2001. "Democracy, Development, and the Public Sector." *American Journal of Political Science* 45: 1–17.

Bowler, Shaun, and Todd Donovan. 1998. *Demanding Choices*. Ann Arbor: University of Michigan Press.

Braeuninger, Thomas. 2001. "When Weighted Voting Does Not Work: Multi-Chamber Systems For the Representation and Aggregation of Interests in International Organizations." Paper presented at the Twenty-ninth European Consortium of Political Research meeting, Grenoble, France.

Braeuninger, Thomas, and Thomas König. 1999. "The Checks and Balances of Party Federalism: German Federal Government in a Divided Legislature." *European Journal of Political Research* 36: 207–34.

Browne, Eric, Dennis Gleiber, and Carolyn Mashoba. 1984. "Evaluating Conflict of Interest Theory: Western European Cabinet Coalitions, 1945–80." *British Journal of Political Science* 14 (January): 1–32.

Buchanan, James. 1950. "Federalism and Fiscal Equity." *American Economic Review* 40: 583–99.

Butler, D., and A. Ranney. 1978. *Referendums: A Comparative Study of Practice and Theory*. Washington, D.C.: American Enterprise Institute Press.

——— (eds.). 1994. *Referendums around the World: The Growing Use of Direct Democracy*. Washington, D.C.: American Enterprise Institute Press.

Cameron, Charles M. 2000. *Veto Bargaining*. New York: Cambridge University Press.

Cameron, David R. 1992. "The 1992 Initiative: Causes and Consequences." In A. Sbragia (ed.), *Euro-Politics*. Washington, D.C.: Brookings Institution.

Carey, John M., and Matthew Soberg Shugart. 1995. "Incentives to Cultivate a Personal Vote: A Rank Ordering of Electoral Formulas." *Electoral Studies* 14: 417–39.

——— (eds.). 1998. *Executive Decree Authority*. New York: Cambridge University Press.

Castles, Francis G., and Peter Mair. 1984. "Left-Right Political Scales: Some 'Expert' Judgments." *European Journal of Political Research* 12 (March): 73–88.

Chatfield, C. 1996. *The Analysis of Time Series: An Introduction*. New York: Chapman & Hall.

Cheibub, Jose Antonio, and Fernando Limongi. 2001. "Where Is the Difference? Parliamentary and Presidential Democracies Reconsidered." Paper presented at the Eighteenth World Congress of Political Science.

Christiansen, Thomas, Knud Erik Jorgensen, and Antje Wiener. 1999. "The Social Construction of Europe." *Journal of European Public Policy* 6: 528–44.

Clark, William R., and Mark Hallerberg. 2000. "Mobile Capital, Domestic Institutions and Electorally-Induced Monetary and Fiscal Policy." *American Political Science Review* 94: 323–46.

Cohen, Linda, and Roger Noll. 1991. *The Technology Pork Barrel* Washington, D.C.: Brookings Institution.

Condorcet, Marie Jean Antoine Nicolas de Caritat, Marquis de. 1968. *Oeuvres*. Stuttgard-Bad Cannstatt: Friedrich Frommann Verlag.

Cooter, Robert D., and Josef Drexl. 1994. "The Logic of Power in the Emerging European Constitution." *International Review of Law and Economics* 14: 307–26.

Cooter, Robert D., and Tom Ginsburg. 1996. "Comparative Judicial Discretion." *International Review of Law and Economics* 16:295–313.

Corbett, Richard. 2001a. "Academic Modelling of the Codecision Procedure: A Practitioner's Puzzled Reaction." *European Union Politics* 1: 373–81.

———. 2001b. "Academic Modelling of the Codecision Procedure: A Practitioner's Puzzled Reaction." *European Union Politics* 1: 373–81.

Corbett, Richard, Francis Jacobs, and Michael Shackleton. 1995. *The European Parliament*. 3rd ed. London: Longman.

Cosetti, Giancarlo, and Nouriel Roubini. 1993. "The Design of Optimal Fiscal Rules for Europe after 1992." In Francisco Torroes and Francesco Giavazzi (eds.), *Adjust-*

ment and Growth in the European Monetary Union. Cambridge: Cambridge University Press.

Cowhey, Peter F. 1993. "Domestic Institutions and the Credibility of International Commitments: Japan and the United States." *International Organization* 47 (2): 299–326.

Cox, Gary W. 1997. *Making Votes Count.* New York: Cambridge University Press.

Crepaz, Markus M. L. 2002. "Global, Constitutional, and Partisan Determinants of Redistribution in Fifteen OECD Countries." *Comparative Politics* 34 (2): 169–88.

Crombez, Christophe. 1996. Legislative Procedures in the European Community. *British Journal of Political Science* 26: 199–228.

———. 1997. "The Co-Decision Procedure in the Euopean Union." *Legislative Studies Quarterly* 22: 97–119.

Cronin, Thomas. 1989. *Direct Democracy: The Politics of Initiative, Referendum and Recall.* Cambridge: Harvard University Press.

Cukierman, Alex. 1991. *Central Bank Strategy, Credibility and Independence: Theory and Evidence.* Cambridge: MIT Press.

Cukierman, Alex, Steven B. Webb, and Bilin Neyapti. 1992. "Measuring the Independence of Central Banks and Its Effect on Policy Outcomes." *World Bank Economic Review* 6 (3): 353–98.

Dahl, Robert A. 1971. *Polyarchy: Participation and Opposition.* New Haven: Yale University Press.

———. 1982. *Dilemmas of Pluralist Democracy.* New Haven: Yale University Press.

Davidson, Russell, and James G. MacKinnon. 1981. "Several Tests for Model Specification in the Presence of Alternative Hypotheses." *Econometrica* 49 (3): 781–93.

Davoodi, Hamid, and Heng-fu Zou. 1998. "Fiscal Decentralization and Economic Growth: A Cross-Country Study." *Journal of Urban Economics* 43: 244–57.

Dehousse, Renaud. 1998. *The European Court of Justice.* New York: St. Martin's Press.

De Swaan, Abraham. 1973. *Coalition Theories and Cabinet Formation.* Amsterdam: Elsevier.

Dicey, Albert Venn. 1890. "Ought the Referendum to be Introduced in England?" *Contemporary Review* 57: 506.

Diermeier, Daniel, and T. J. Feddersen. 1998. "Cohesion in Legislatures and the Vote of Confidence Procedure." *American Political Science Review* 92: 611–21.

Dinan, Desmond. 1994. *Ever Closer Union?* Boulder, Colo.: L. Rienner.

Di Palma, Guiseppe. 1977. *Surviving without Governing: The Italian Parties in Parliament.* Berkeley: University of California Press.

Dixit, Avinash, and John Londregan. 1998. "Fiscal Federalism and Redistributive Politics." *Journal of Public Economics* 68: 153–80.

Dodd, Lawrence C. 1976. *Coalitions in Parliamentary Government.* Princeton: Princeton University Press.

Doering, Herbert. http://www.uni-potsdam.de/u/ls_vergleich/index.htm

———. 1995a. *Parliaments and Majority Rule in Western Europe.* New York: St. Martin's Press.

———. 1995b. "Time as a Scarce Resource: Government Control of the Agenda." In H. Doering (ed.), *Parliaments and Majority Rule in Western Europe.* New York: St. Martin's Press.

————. 1995c. "Is Government Control of the Agenda Likely to Keep Legislative Inflation at Bay?" In H. Doering (ed.), *Parliaments and Majority Rule in Western Europe*. New York: St. Martin's Press.

————. Forthcoming. "Time-Saving Government Prerogatives—A Case for Contentiousness?" In H. Doering (ed.), *Parliamentary Organization and Legislative Outcomes in Western Europe*.

Dogan, Mattei. 1989. "Irremovable Leaders and Ministerial Instability in European Democracies." In M. Dogan (ed.), *Pathways to Power: Selecting Rulers in Pluralist Democracies*. Boulder, Colo.: Westview Press.

Downs, Anthony. 1957. *An Economic Theory of Democracy*. New York: Harper and Row.

Duverger, Maurice. 1954 (1969). *Political Parties: Their Organization and Activity in the Modern State*. London: Methuen.

Earnshaw, David, and David Judge. 1996. "From Co-operation to Co-decision: The European Parliament's Path to Legislative Power." In J.J. Richardson (ed.), *European Union: Power and Policy-Making*. London: Routledge.

Eaton, Kent. 2000. "Parliamentarism versus Presidentialism in the Policy Arena." *Comparative Politics* 32 (3): 355–73.

Edin, P.-A., and H. Ohlsson. 1991. "Political Determinants of Budget Deficits: Coalition Effects versus Minority Effects." *European Economic Review* 35 (December): 1597–1603.

Eichengreen, B. 1992. *Golden Fetters: The Gold Standard and the Great Depression, 1919–1939*. Oxford: Oxford University Press.

Elgie, R. 1998. "The classification of Democratic Regime Types: Conceptual Ambiguity and Contestable Assumptions." *European Journal of Political Research* 33 (2): 219–38.

Epstein, David, and Sharyn O'Halloran. 1999. *Delegating Powers: A Transaction Cost Politics Approach to Policy Making Under Separate Powers*. Cambridge: Cambridge University Press.

Eskridge, W. 1991. "Overriding Supreme Court Statutory Interpretation Decisions." *Yale Law Journal* 101: 331.

Feld, Lars P., and Marcel R. Savioz. 1997. "Direct Democracy Matters for Economic Performance: An Empirical Investigation." *Kyklos* 50 (4): 507–38.

Ferejohn, John. 1974. *Pork Barrel Politics: Rivers and Harbors Legislation, 1947–68*. Stanford: Stanford University Press.

Ferejohn, John A., Richard D. McKelvey, and Edward W. Packell. 1984. "Limiting Distributions for Continuous State Markov Voting Models." *Social Choice and Welfare* 1: 45–67.

Ferejohn, John, and Charles Shipan. 1990. "Congressional Influence on Bureaucracy." *Journal of Law, Economics and Organization* 6: 1–20.

Ferejohn, John, and Barry Weingast. 1992a. "A Positive Theory of Statutory Interpretation." *International Review of Law and Economics* 12: 263–79.

Ferejohn, John, and Barry Weingast. 1992b. "Limitation of Statues: Strategic Statutory Interpretation." *Georgetown Law Journal* 80: 565–82.

Finer, Samuel E. 1980. *The Changing British Party System, 1945–79*. Washington, D.C.: American Enterprise Institute Press.

Fiorina, Morris P. 1992. *Divided Government*. New York: Macmillan.

Fitzmaurice, John. 1988. "An Analysis of the European Community's Co-operation Procedure." *Journal of Common Market Studies* 4: 389–400.

Franchino, Fabio. 2000. "Delegating Powers in the European Union." Unpublished manuscript.

Franzese, Robert J., Jr. 2002. *Macroeconomic Policies of Developed Democracies*. Cambridge: Cambridge University Press.

Frey, Bruno S., and Goette, Lorenz. 1998. "Does the Popular Vote Destroy Civil Rights?" *American Journal of Political Science*. 42 (4): 1343–48.

Gallagher, Michael, Michael Laver, and Peter Mair. 1995. *Representative Government in Modern Europe*. New York: McGraw-Hill.

Gamble, Barbara. 1997. "Putting Civil Rights to a Popular Vote." *American Journal of Political Science* 41 (1): 245–69.

Garrett, Geoffrey. 1992. "International Cooperation and Institutional Choice: The European Community's Internal Market." *International Organization* 46: 533–60.

———. 1995a. "The Politics of Legal Integration in the European Union." *International Organization* 49: 171–81.

———. 1995b. "From the Luxembourg Compromise to Codecision: Decision Making in the European Union." *Electoral Studies* 14: 289–308.

Garrett, Geoffrey, R. Daniel Kelemen, and Heiner Schulz. 1998. "The European Court of Justice, National Governments and Legal Integration in the European Union." *International Organization* 52: 149–76.

Garrett, Geoffrey, and George Tsebelis. 1996. "An Institutional Critique of Intergovernmentalism." *International Organization* 50: 269–300.

———. 1997. "More on the Codecision Endgame." *Journal of Legislative Studies* 3 (4): 139–43.

———. 2001. "Understanding Better the EU Legislative Process." *European Union Politics* 2 (3): 353–61.

Garrett, Geoffrey, and Barry Weingast. 1993. "Ideas, Interests, and Institutions: Constructing the European Community's Internal Market." In Judith Goldstein and Robert Keohane (eds.), *Ideas and Foreign Policy*. Ithaca: Cornell University Press.

Gaulle, Charles de. 1960. "Press Conference." In *Major Addresses, Statements, and Press Conferences, May 19, 1958–January 31, 1964*. New York: French Embassy, Press, and Information Division.

———. 1971. *Memoirs of Hope: Renewal and Endeavor*. New York: Simon and Schuster.

Gely, R., and P. T. Spiller. 1990. "A Rational Choice Theory of Supreme Court Statutory Decisions with Applications to *State Farm* and *Grove City* Cases." *Journal of Law, Economics and Organization* 6: 263–300.

Gerber, Elisabeth R. 1996. "Legislative Response to the Threat of Popular Initiatives." *American Journal of Political Science* 40: 99–128.

———. 1999. *The Populist Paradox: Interest Group Influence and the Promise of Direct Legislation*. Princeton: Princeton University Press.

Gerber, Elisabeth R., and Simon Hug. 1999. "Legislative Response to Direct Legislation." Unpublished manuscript, University of California, San Diego.

Gilligan, Thomas W., and Keith Krehbiel. 1987. "Organization and Informative Committees by a Rational Legislation." *American Journal of Political Science* 34: 531–64.

Golden, Miriam, Michael Wallerstein, and Peter Lange. 1999. "Postwar Trade Union Organization and Industrial Relations in Twelve Countries." In H. Kitschelt, P. Lange, G. Marks, and J. Stephens (eds.), *Continuity and Change in Contemporary Capitalism*, 194–230. Cambridge: Cambridge University Press.

Greenberg, Joseph. 1979. "Consistent Majority Rule over Compact Sets of Alternatives." *Econometrica* 47: 627–36.

Grilli, Vittorio, Donato Masciandaro, and Guido Tabellini. 1991. "Political and Monetary Institutions and Public Finance Policies in the Industrialized Democracies." *Economic Policy* 10: 342–92.

Haan, J. de, and J.-E. Sturm. 1997. "Political and Economic Determinants of OECD Budget Deficits and Government Expenditures: A Reinvestigation." *European Journal of Political Economy* 13 (December): 739–50.

Haas, Ernst B. 1961. "International Integration: The European and the Universal Process." *International Organization* 15: 366–92.

Hallerberg, Mark. 2001a. *The Maastricht Treaty and Domestic Politics: The Effects of the European Union on the Making of Budgets*. Unpublished manuscript, University of Pittsburgh.

———. Forthcoming. "Veto Players and the Choice of Monetary Institutions." *International Organization*.

Hallerberg, Mark, and Scott Basinger. 1998. "Internationalization and Changes in Tax Policy in OECD Countries: The Importance of Domestic Veto Players." *Comparative Political Studies* 31 (3): 321–52.

Hallerberg, Mark, and Jürgen von Hagen. 1999. "Electoral Institutions, Cabinet Negotiations, and Budget Deficits within the European Union." In James Poterba and Jürgen von Hagen (eds.), *Fiscal Institutions and Fiscal Performance*, 209–32. Chicago: University of Chicago Press.

Hallerberg, Mark, Rolf Strauch, and Juergen von Hagen. 2001. "The Use and Effectiveness of Budgetary Rules and Norms in EU Member States." Report prepared for the Dutch Ministry of Finance. Institute of European Integration Studies.

Hamilton, Alexander, James Madison, and John Jay. 1961 (1787–88). *The Federalist Papers*. Edited by Jacob E. Cooke. Middletown, Conn. Wesleyan University Press.

Hammond, Thomas H. 1996. "Formal Theory and the Institutions of Governance." *Governance* 9:2 (April): 107–85.

Hammond, Thomas H., and Jack H. Knott. 1996. "Who Controls the Bureaucracy? Presidential Power, Congressional Dominance, Legal Constraints, and Bureaucratic Autonomy in a Model of Multi-Institutional Policymaking." *Journal of Law, Economics, & Organization* 12 (1): 119–66.

———. 1999. "Political Institutions, Public Management, and Policy Choice." *Journal of Public Administration Research and Theory* 9: 33–85.

Hammond, Thomas H., and Gary J. Miller. 1987. "The Core of the Constitution." *American Political Science Review* 81: 1155–74.

Hayek, Friedrich von. 1939. "The Economic Conditions of Interstate Federalism." Reprinted in *Individualism and the Economic Order* (1948). Chicago: University of Chicago Press.

Heller, William, B. 1999. "Making Policy Stick: Why the Government Gets What It Wants in Multiparty Parliaments." Paper presented at the meeting of the Midwest Political Science Association, Chicago.

Henisz, Witold J., 2000a. "The Institutional Environment for Economic Growth." *Economics & Politics* 12 (1): 1–31.

————. 2000b. "The Institutional Environment for Multinational Investment." *Journal of Law, Economics & Organization* 16 (2): 334–64.

Hicks, Ursula K. 1978. *Federalism: Failure and Success, A Comparative Study.* New York: Oxford University Press.

Hix, Simon. 1994. "The Study of the European Community: The Challenge to Comparative Politics." *West European Politics* 17: 1–30.

————. 1999. *The Political System of the EU.* New York: St. Martin's Press.

————. Forthcoming. "Constitutional Agenda-Setting Through Discretion in Rule Interpretation: Why the European Parliament Won at Amsterdam." *British Journal of Political Science.*

Horowitz, Donald L. 1996. "Comparing Democratic Systems." In L. Diamond and M. F. Platter (eds.), *The Global Resurgence of Democracy.* 2nd ed. Baltimore: Johns Hopkins University Press.

Huang, S. 2001. "MECH." *American Mechanical Review* 1 (Jan.): 1–30.

Huber, John D. 1996. "The Vote of Confidence in Parliamentary Democracies." *American Political Science Review* 90: 269–82.

Huber, John D., and Arthur Lupia. 2000. "Cabinet Instability and Delegation in Parliamentary Democracies." *American Journal of Political Science* 45 (1): 18–33.

Huber, John D., and Nolan McCarty. 2001. "Cabinet Decision Rules and Political Uncertainty in Parliamentary Bargaining." *American Political Science Review* 95 (2): 345–60.

Huber, John D., and G. Bingham Powell. 1994. "Congruence Between Citizens and Policy-Makers in 2 Visions of Liberal Democracy." *World Politics* 46 (3): 291–326.

Huber, John D., and Charles Shipan. 2002. *Laws and Bureaucratic Autonomy in Modern Democracies: Wise and Salutary Neglect?* Cambridge: Cambridge University Press.

Hug, Simon. 2001. "Policy Consequences of Direct Legislation in the States: Theory, Empirical Models and Evidence." Unpublished manuscript, University of Texas at Austin.

Hug, Simon, and George Tsebelis. 2002. "Veto Players and Referendums around the World." *Journal of Theoretical Politics* 14 (4).

Humphreys, Macartan. 2000. "The Political Economy of Obstruction: A Model of Votes and Vetoes in Many Dimensions." Unpublished manuscript, Harvard University.

————. 2001. "Core Existence in Multigroup Spatial Games." Unpublished manuscript, Harvard University.

Inman, Robert P., and Daniel L. Rubinfeld. 1997. "Rethinking Federalism." In *Symposia: Fiscal Federalism. The Journal of Economic Perspectives* 11 (4): 43–64.

International Labour Office. NATLEX. The Labour and Social Security Legislation Database. (Permission to be obtained from International Labour Office. CH-1211 Geneva 22 Switzerland. ILO homepage www.ilo.org.)

Inter-Parliamentary Union. 1986. *Parliaments of the World.* 2nd ed. Aldershot, Eng.: Gower House.

Jacobs, Francis. 1997. "Legislative Co-decision: A Real Step Forward?" Paper presented at the Fifth Biennial European Communities Studies Association Conference, Seattle.

Jones, David. 2001a. "Party Polarization and Legislative Gridlock." *Political Research Quarterly* 53: 125–41.

———. 2001b. *Political Parties and Policy Gridlock in American Government.* Lewiston, N.Y.: The Edwin Mellen Press.

Kalandrakis, Anastassios. 2000. "General Equilibrium Political Competition." Ph.D. dissertation, UCLA.

Katzenstein, Peter J. 1985. *Small States in World Markets: Industrial Policy in Europe.* Ithaca: Cornell University Press.

Keefer, Philip, and David Stasavage. 2000. "Bureaucratic Delegation and Political Institutions: When Are Independent Central Banks Irrelevant?" Unpublished manuscript, World Bank.

———. Forthcoming. "Checks and Balances, Private Information, and the Credibility of Monetary Commitments." *International Organization.*

Kelly, Sean Q. 1993. "Divided We Govern? A Reassessment." *Polity* 25: 473–84.

Kiewiet, D. R., and M. D. McCubbins. 1991. *The Logic of Delegation.* Chicago: University of Chicago Press.

Kilroy, Bernadette. 1999. *Integration through the Law: ECJ and Governments in the EU.* Ph.D. dissertation, UCLA.

King, Gary, James Alt, Nancy Burns, and Michael Laver. 1990. "A Unified Model of Cabinet Dissolution in Parliamentary Democracies." *American Journal of Political Science* 32: 846–71.

Koehler, D. H. 1990. "The Size of the Yolk: Computations for Odd and Even-Numbered Committees." *Social Choice and Welfare* 7: 231–45.

König, Thomas. 1997. *Europa auf dem Weg zum Mehrheitssystem. Gründe und Konsequenzen nationaler und parlamentarischer Integration.* Opladen: Westdeutscher Verlag.

———. 2001. "Bicameralism and Party Politics in Germany. An Empirical Social Choice Analysis." *Political Studies* 49: 411–37.

König, Thomas, and Vera Tröger. 2001. "Haushaltspolitik und Vetospieler." Paper presented at the Jahrestagung der Deutschen Vereinigung für Politikwissenschaft, Berlin.

König, Thomas, and Mirja Pöter. 2002. "Examining the EU Legislative Process: The Relative Importance of Agenda and Veto Power." *European Union Politics.*

Krause, G. 2000. "Partisan and Ideological Sources of Fiscal Deficits in the United States." *American Journal of Political Science* 44 (July): 541–59.

Krehbiel, Keith. 1988. "Spatial Models of Legislative Choice." *Legislative Studies Quarterly* 3: 259–319.

———. 1991. *Information and Legislative Organization.* Ann Arbor: University of Michigan Press.

———. 1998. *Pivotal Politics: A Thoery of U.S. Lawmaking.* Chicago: University of Chicago Press.

Kreppel, Amie. 1997. "The Impact of Parties in Government on Legislative Output in Italy." *European Journal of Political Research* 31: 327–50.

Kreppel, Amie, and George Tsebelis. 1999. "Coalition Formation in the European Parliament." *Comparative Political Studies* 32 (8): 933–66.

Kydland, Finn E., and Edward C. Prescott. 1977. "Rules Rather than Discretion: The Inconsistency of Optimal Plans." *Journal of Political Economy* 85: 473–91.

Lambertini, L., and C. Azariadis. 1998. "The Fiscal Politics of Big Governments: Do Coalitions Matter?" Unpublished manuscript, UCLA.

Lange, Peter. 1992. "The Politics of the Social Dimension." In A. Sbragia (ed.), *Euro-Politics*. Washington, D.C.: Brookings Institution.

Lange, Peter, and Hudson Meadwell. 1985. "Typologies of Democratic Systems: From Political Inputs to Political Economy." In Howard Wiarda (ed.), *New Directions in Comparative Politics*. Boulder, Colo.: Westview Press.

Lascher, E., M. Hagen, and S. Rochliln. 1996. "Gun Behind the Door: Ballot Initiatives, State Politics and Public Opinion." *Journal of Politics* 58: 760–75.

Laver, Michael, and W. Ben Hunt. 1992. *Policy and Party Competition*. New York: Routledge, Chapman and Hall.

Laver, Michael, and Norman Schofield. 1990. *Multiparty Government: The Politics of Coalition in Europe*. Oxford: Oxford University Press.

Laver, Michael, and Kenneth A. Shepsle. 1996. *Making and Breaking Governments: Cabinets and Legislatures in Parliamentary Democracies*. New York: Cambridge University Press.

———. 1999. "Understanding Government Survival: Empirical Exploration or Analytical Models?" *British Journal of Political Science* 29: 395–401.

Lijphart, Arend. 1984. "Measures of Cabinet Durability: A Conceptual and Empirical Evaluation." *Comparative Political Studies* 17: 265–79.

———. 1989. "Democratic Political Systems: Types, Cases, Causes, and Consequences." *Journal of Theoretical Politics* 1: 33–48.

———. 1992. *Parliamentary versus Presidential Government*. Oxford: Oxford University Press.

———. 1994. *Electoral Systems and Party Systems: A Study of Twenty-Seven Democracies, 1945–1990*. Oxford: Oxford University Press.

———. 1999. *Patterns of Democracy: Government Forms and Performance in Thirty-Six Countries*. New Haven: Yale University Press.

Lindberg, Leon N. 1963. *The Political Dynamics of European Integration*. Stanford: Stanford University Press.

Linder, Wolf. 1994. *Swiss Democracy*. New York: St. Martin's Press.

Linz, Juan J. 1994. "Presidential or Parliamentary Democracy: Does it Make a Difference?" In J. Linz and A. Valenzuela (eds.), *The Failure of Presidential Democracy*. Baltimore: Johns Hopkins University Press.

———. 1996. "The Perils of Presidentialism." In L. Diamond and M. F. Platter (eds.), *The Global Resurgence of Democracy*. 2nd ed. Baltimore: Johns Hopkins University Press.

Lipset, Seymour M. 1996. "The Centrality of Political Culture." In L. Diamond and M. F. Platter (eds.), *The Global Resurgence of Democracy*. 2nd ed. Baltimore: Johns Hopkins University Press.

Lodge, Juliet. 1983. "Integration Theory." In Juliet Lodge (ed.), *The European Community*. London: Frances Pinter.

———. 1987. "The Single European Act and the New Legislative Cooperation Procedure: A Critical Analysis." *Journal of European Integration* 11: 5–28.

Lohmann, Susanne. 1998. "Federalism and Central Bank Independence: The Politics of German Monetary Policy, 1957–1992." *World Politics* 51: 401–46.

Londregan, John. 2000. *Legislative Institutions and Ideology in Chile*. New York: Cambridge University Press.

Lowell, A. Lawrence. 1896. *Governments and Parties in Continental Europe*. Boston: Houghton Mifflin.

Lowenstein, Daniel H. 1982. "Campaign Spending and Ballot Propositions: Recent Experience, Public Choice Theory, and the First Amendment." *UCLA Law Review* 29: 505–641.

Lupia, Arthur. 1992. "Busy Voters, Agenda Control, and the Power of Information." *American Political Science Review* 86: 390–404.

———. 1993. "Credibility and the Responsiveness of Direct Legislation." In William A. Barnett, Norman J. Schofield and Melvin J. Hinich (eds.), *Political Economy: Institutions, Competition, and Representation*. Cambridge: Cambridge University Press.

Lupia, Arthur, and Mathew D. McCubbins. 2000. "Representation or Abdication? How Citizens Use Institutions to Help Delegation Succeed." *European Journal of Political Research* 37: 291–307.

Lupia, Arthur, and Kaare Strom. 1995. "Coalition Termination and the Strategic Timing of Parliamentary Elections." *American Political Science Review* 89: 648–65.

Macpherson, C. B. 1973. *Democratic Theory: Essays in Retrieval*. Oxford: Clarendon Press.

Manin, Bernard. 2001. "Rousseau." In P. Perrineau and D. Reynié (eds.), *Dictionnaire du Vote*, 814–16. Paris: Presses Universitaires de France.

Maor, Moshe. 1992. "Intra-Party Conflict and Coalitional Behavior in Denmark and Norway: The Case of 'Highly Institutionalized' Parties." *Scandinavian Political Studies* 15: 99–116.

Marjolin, Robert. 1980. *Europe in Search of its Identity*. New York: Council on Foreign Relations.

Marks, Gary, Liesbet Hooghe, and Kermit Blank. 1996. "European Integration from the 1980s: State-Centric v. Multi-level Governance." *Journal of Common Market Studies* 34: 341–78.

Marshall, T. H. 1965. *Class, Citizenship, and Social Development*. New York: Anchor.

Martin, Lanny W., and Randolph T. Stevenson. 2001. "Government Formation in Parliamentary Democracies." *American Journal of Political Science* 45: 33–50.

Matsusaka, John G. 1992. Economics of Direct Legislation. *Quarterly Journal of Economics* 107 (May): 541–71.

———. 1995. "Fiscal Effects of the Voter Initiative: Evidence from the Last 30 Years." *Journal of Political Economy* 103 (3): 587–623.

———. 2000. "Fiscal Effects of the Voter Initiative in the First Half of the Twentieth Century." *Journal of Law and Economics* 43: 619–44.

Mattli, Walter, and Anne-Marie Slaughter. 1998. "Revisiting the European Court of Justice." *International Organization* 52: 177–210.

Mayhew, David R. 1991. *Divided We Govern*. New Haven: Yale University Press.

———. 1993. "Reply: Let's Stick With the Longer List." *Polity* 25: 485–88.

McCarty, Nolan, Keith T. Poole, and Howard Rosenthal. 2001. "The Hunt for Party Discipline in Congress." *American Political Science Review* 95 (3): 673–88.

McCubbins, Mathew D. 1985. "Legislative Design of Regulatory Structure." *American Journal of Political Science* 29: 721–48.

McCubbins, Mathew D. 1991. "Government on Lay-Away: Federal Spending and Deficits under Divided Party Control." In Gary W. Cox and Samuel Kernell (eds.), *The Politics of Divided Government*. Boulder, Colo.: Westview Press.

McCubbins, Mathew D., Roger G. Noll, and Barry R. Weingast. 1987. "Administrative Procedures as Instruments of Political Control." *Journal of Law Economics and Organization* 3: 243–77.

———. 1989. "Structure and Process, Politics and Policy: Administrative Arrangements and the Political Control of Agencies." *Virginia Law Review* 75: 430–82.

McCubbins, Mathew D., and Thomas Schwartz. 1984. "Congressional Oversight Overlooked: Police Patrols versus Fire Alarms." *American Journal of Political Science* 28 (1): 165–79.

McKelvey, Richard D. 1976. "Intransitivities in Multidimensional Voting Models and Some Implications for Agenda Control." *Journal of Economic Theory* 12: 472–82.

Meltzer, A. H., and S. F. Richard. 1981. "A Rational Theory of the Size of Government." *Journal of Political Economy* 89: 914–27.

Mikva, Abner, and Jeffrey Bleich. 1991. "When Congress Overrules the Court." *California Law Review* 79 (3): 729–50.

Miller, Nicholas R. 1980. "A New 'Solution Set' for Tournaments and Majority Voting." *American Journal of Political Science* 24: 68–96.

Miller, Nicholas R., Bernard Grofman, and Scott L. Feld. 1989. "The Geometry of Majority Rule." *Journal of Theoretical Politics* 4: 379–406.

Moe, Terry M. 1990. "Political Institutions: The Neglected Side of the Story." *Journal of Law, Economics and Organization* 6: 213–53.

Moe, Terry M., and Michael Caldwell. 1994. "The Institutional Foundations of Democratic Government." *Journal of Institutional and Theoretical Economics* 150: 171–95.

Montesquieu, Charles-Louis de Secondat, Baron de. 1977. *The Spirit of Laws*. Edited by David Wallace Carrithers. Berkeley: University of California Press.

Moore, Barrington, Jr. 1966. *Social Origins of Dictatorship and Democracy*. Boston: Beacon Press.

Moravcsik, Andrew. 1998. *The Choice for Europe*. Ithaca: Cornell University Press.

———. 1999. "Is Something Rotten in the State of Denmark? Constructivism and European Integration." *Journal of European Public Policy* 6: 669–81.

Moravcsik, Andrew, and Kalypso Nicolaïdis. 1999. "Explaining the Treaty of Amsterdam: Interests, Influence, Institutions." *Journal of Common Market Studies* 37 (1): 59–85.

Moser, Peter. 1996. "The European Parliament as a Conditional Agenda Setter: What are the Conditions?" *American Political Science Review* 90: 834–38.

———. 1999. "Checks and Balances, and the Supply of Central Bank Independence." *European Economic Review* 43: 1569–93.

Mueller, Dennis C. 1996. *Constitutional Democracy*. Oxford: Oxford University Press.

Mueller, Wolfgang C. 2000. "Political Parties in Parliamentary Democracies: Making Delegation and Accountability Work." *European Journal of Political Research* 37: 309–33.

Norton, Philip (ed.). 1990. *Legislatures*. Oxford: Oxford University Press.

Nugent, Neill. 1994. *The Government and Politics of the European Union*. 3rd ed. Durham, N.C.: Duke University Press.

Nurmi, Hannu. 1998. "Voting Paradoxes and Referendums." *Social Choice and Welfare* 15: 333–50.

Oates, Wallace E. 1972. *Fiscal Federalism*. New York: Harcourt Brace Jovanovich.

Parrish, Scott. 1998. "Presidential Decree Power in Russia: 1991–95." In J. Carey and M. Shugart (eds.), *Executive Decree Authority*. New York: Cambridge University Press.

Perotti, R., and Y. Kontopoulos. 1998. "Fragmented Fiscal Policy." Unpublished manuscript, Columbia University.

Persson, Torsten, and Guido Tabellini. 1999. "The Size and Scope of Government: Comparative Politics with Rational Politicians." *European Economic Review* 43: 699–735.

———. 2000. *Political Economics: Explaining Economic Policy* Cambridge: MIT Press.

Persson, Torsten, Gerard Roland, and Guido Tabellini. 2000. "Comparative Politics and Public Finance." *Journal of Political Economy* 108: 1121–61.

Pindyck, Robert S., and Daniel L. Rubinfeld. 1998. *Econometric Models and Economic Forecasts*. New York: McGraw-Hill.

Plot, Charles R. 1967. "A Notion of Equilibrium and Its Possibility under Majority Rule." *American Economic Review* 57: 787–806.

Pollack, Mark A. 1997. "Delegation, Agency and Agenda Setting in the EC." *International Organization* 51: 99–134.

———. 2001. "International Relations Theory and European Integration." *Journal of Common Market Studies* 39 (2): 197–220.

Pommerehne, Werner W. 1978. "Institutional Approaches to Public Expenditure: Empirical Evidence from Swiss Municipalities." *Journal of Public Economics* 9: 255–80.

Poterba, J. 1994. "State Responses to Fiscal Crises: The Effects of Budgetary Institutions and Politics." *Journal of Political Economy* 102 (August): 799–822.

Powell, G. Bingham. 1982. *Contemporary Democracies: Participation, Stability and Violence*. Cambridge: Harvard University Press.

———. 2000. *Elections as Instruments of Democracy: Majoritarian and Proportional Visions*. New Haven: Yale University Press.

Prud'homme, Remy. 1995. "On the Dangers of Decentralization." *World Bank Research Observer* 10 (2): 201–20.

Przeworski, Adam. 1991. *Democracy and the Market*. New York: Cambridge University Press.

———. 1999. "Minimalist Conception of Democracy: A Defense." In Ian Shapiro and Casiano Hacker-Cordon (eds.), *Democracy's Value*. New York: Cambridge University Press.

Przeworski, Adam, and Fernando Limongi. 1997. "Modernization: Theories and Facts." *World Politics* 49: 155–83.

Przeworski, Adam, Michael E. Alvarez, Jose Antonio Cheibub, and Fernando Limongi. 2000. *Democracy and Development*. New York: Cambridge University Press.

Qian, Yingyi, and Gérard Roland. 1998. "Federalism and the Soft Budget Constraint." *American Economic Review* 5: 1143–62.

Qvortrum, Mads. 1999. "A. V. Dicey: The Referendum as the People's Veto." *History of Political Thought* 20: 531–46.

Rae, Douglas. 1967. *The Political Consequences of Electoral Laws* New Haven: Yale University Press.

Rasch, Bjorn Eric. 2000. "Parliamentary Floor Procedures and Agenda Setting in Europe." *Legislative Studies Quarterly* 25: 3–23.

Remmer, Karen. 1989. *Military Rule in Latin America*. Boston: Unwin Hyman.

Riker, William H. 1962. *The Theory of Political Coalitions*. New Haven: Yale University Press.

———. 1964. *Federalism: Origin, Operation, Significance*. Boston: Little, Brown.

———. 1975. "Federalism." In Fred Greenstein and Nicholas Polsby (eds.), *Handbook of Political Science*, Vol. 5. Reading, Mass.: Addison-Wesley.

———. 1982a. "The Two-Party System and Duverger's Law: An Essay on the History of Political Science." *American Political Science Review* 76: 753–66.

———. 1982b. *Liberalism Against Populism*. San Fransisco: W. H. Freeman.

Robertson, John D. 1983. "The Political Economy and the Durability of European Coalition Governments: New Variations on a Game Theoretic Perspective." *Journal of Politics* 45: 932–57.

Rogowski, Ronald. 1987. "Trade and the Variety of Democratic Institutions." *International Organization* 41: 203–23.

Rose-Ackerman, Susan. 1981. "Does Federalism Matter? Political Choice in a Federal Republic." *Journal of Political Economy* 89 (11): 152–65.

———. 1990. "Comment on Ferejohn and Shipan's 'Congressional Influence on Bureaucracy.'" *Journal of Law Economics and Organization* 6: 21–27.

Ross, George. 1995. *Jacques Delors and European Integration*. New York: Oxford University Press.

Roubini, N., and Jeffrey Sachs. 1989a. "Political and Economic Determinants of Budget Deficits in the Industrial Democracies." *European Economic Review* 33 (May): 903–34.

———. 1989b. "Government Spending and Budget Deficits in the Industrialized Countries." *Economic Policy* 8: 700–732.

Rousseau, Jean-Jacques. 1947 (1762). *The Social Contract*. Trans. Charles Frankel. New York: Hafner.

Rueschemeyer, Dietrich, Evelyn Huber Stephens, and John Stephens. 1992. *Capitalist Development and Democracy*. Chicago: University of Chicago Press.

Sanders, David, and Valentine Herman. 1977. "The Stability and Survival of Governments in Western Democracies." *Acta Politica* 12: 346–77.

Sandholtz, Wayne. 1992. *Hi-Tech Europe*. Berkeley: University of California Press.

Sandholtz, Wayne, and John Zysman. 1989. "Recasting the European Bargain." *World Politics* 42: 95–128.

Sani, Giacomo, and Giovanni Sartori. 1983. "Polarization, Competition, and Fragmentation in Western Democracies." In Hans Daalder and Peter Mair (eds.), *Western European Party Systems: Continuity and Change*. Beverly Hills: Sage.

Sartori, Giovanni. 1976. *Parties and Party Systems*. New York: Cambridge University Press.

———. 1996. *Comparative Constitutional Engineering: An Inquiry into Structures, Incentives, and Outcomes*. New York: NYU Press.

Sbragia, Alberta M. (ed.). 1992. *Euro-Politics*. Washington, D.C.: Brookings Institution.

Scharpf, Fritz W. 1970. *Die politischen Kosten des Rechtsstaats: Eine vergleichende Studie der deutschen und amerikanischen Verwaltungskontrollen.* Tübingen: J. C. B. Mohr.

———. 1988. "The Joint-Decision Trap: Lessons From German Federalism and European Integration." *Public Administration* 66: 239–78.

Schofield, Norman. 1977. "Transitivity of Preferences on a Smooth Manifold of Alternatives." *Journal of Economic Theory* 14: 149–71.

———. 1978. "Instability of Simple Dynamic Games." *Review of Economic Studies* 45: 575–94.

———. 1987. "Stability of Coalition Governments in Western Europe." *European Journal of Political Economy* 3: 555–91.

Scholtz, Evi, and Georgios Trantas. 1995. "Legislation on Benefits and on Regulatory Matters: Social Security and Labor Matters." In H. Doering (ed.), *Parliaments and Majority Rule in Western Europe.* New York: St. Martin's Press.

Schumpeter, Joseph R. 1950. *Capitalism, Socialism, and Democracy.* New York: Harper and Row.

Schwartz, Thomas. 1990. "Cyclic Tournaments and Cooperative Majority Voting: A Solution." *Social Choice and Welfare* 7: 19–29.

Scully, Roger M. 1997. "The European Parliament and the Codecision Procedure: A Reassessment." *Journal of Legislative Studies* 3 (3): 58–73.

Shapiro, Ian. 2001. "The State of Democratic Theory." In Ira Katznelson and Helen Milner (eds.), *Political Science: The State of the Discipline.* Washington, D.C.: American Political Science Association.

Shaw, Malcolm. 1979. "Conclusions." In J. D. Lees and M. Shaw (eds.), *Committees in Legislatures.* Durham, N.C.: Duke University Press.

Shepsle, Kenneth A. 1979. "Institutional Arrangements and Equilibrium In Multidimensional Voting Models." *American Journal of Political Science* 23: 27–57.

———. 1986. "Institutional Equilibria and Equilibrium Institutions." In Herbert Weisberg (ed.), *Political Science: The Science of Politics.* New York: Agathon.

Shepsle, Kenneth A., and Barry R. Weingast. 1981. "Structure Induced Equilibrium and Legislative Choice." *Public Choice* 37: 503–19.

———. 1984. "Uncovered Sets and Sophisticated Outcomes with Implications for Agenda Institutions." *American Journal of Political Science* 29: 49–74.

———. 1987. "The Institutional Foundations of Committee Power." *American Political Science Review* 81: 85–104.

Shugart, Matthew S., and John M. Carey. 1992. *Presidents and Assemblies: Constitutional Design and Electoral Dynamics* Cambridge: Cambridge University Press.

Siegfried, Andre. 1956. "Stable Instability in France." *Foreign Affairs* 34: 394–404.

Smith, Gordon. 1975. "The Referendum and Political Change." *Government and Opposition* 10: 294–305.

Smith, Steven S. 1988. "An Essay On Sequence, Position, Goals, and Committee Power." *Legislative Studies Quarterly* 13: 151–76.

Snyder, James M., and Tim Groseclose. 2001. "Estimating Party Influence on Roll Call Voting: Regression Coefficients versus Classification Success." *American Political Science Review* 95 (3): 689–98.

Spolaore, E. 1993. "Macroeconomic Policy, Institutions and Efficiency." Ph.D. dissertation, Harvard University.

Stepan, Alfred, and Cindy Skach. 1993. "Constitutional Frameworks and Democratic Consolidation: Parliamentarism versus Presidentialism." *World Politics* 46: 1–22.

Steunenberg, Bernard. 1992. "Referendum, Initiative, and Veto Power." *Kyklos* 45: 501–29.

———. 1994. "Decision-Making under Different Institutional Arrangements: Legislation by the European Community." *Journal of Institutional and Theoretical Economics* 16: 329–44.

Steunenberg, Bernard, Christian Koboldt, and Dieter Schmidtchen. 1996. "Policy Making, Comitology and the Balance of Power in the European Union." *International Review of Law and Economics* 16: 329–44.

Stone-Sweet, Alec. 1992. *The Birth of Judicial Politics in France: The Constitutional Council in Comparative Perspective.* Oxford: Oxford University Press.

———. 2000. *Governing with Judges: Constitutional Politics in Europe.* New York: Oxford University Press.

Stone-Sweet, Alec, and Sandholtz, Wayne. 1997. "European Integration and Supranational Governance." *Journal of European Public Policy* 4: 297–317.

Strom, Kaare. 1988. "Contending Models of Cabinet Stability." *American Political Science Review* 79: 738–54.

———. 1990. *Minority Government and Majority Rule.* New York: Cambridge University Press.

———. 2000. "Delegation and Accountability in Parliamentary Democracies." *European Journal of Political Research* 37: 261–89.

Suksi, Markku. 1993. *Bringing in the People: A Comparison of Constitutional Forms and Practices of the Referendum.* Dordrecht: Martinus Nijhoff.

Sundquist, James L. 1988. "Needed: A Political Theory for the New Era of Coalition Government in the United States." *Political Science Quarterly* 103: 614–24.

Tanzi, Vito. 1995. "Fiscal Federalism and Decentralization: A Review of Some Efficiency and Macroeconomic Aspects." In *Annual World Bank Conference on Development Economics.* Washington, D.C.: World Bank.

Thies, Michael F. 2001. "Keeping Tabs on One's Partners: The Logic of Delegation in Coalition Governments." *American Journal of Political Science* 45 (3): 580–98.

Tiebout, Charles. 1956. "A Pure Theory of Local Expenditure." *Journal of Political Economy* 64 (October): 416–24.

Treisman, Daniel. 2000a. "The Causes of Corruption: A Cross-National Study." *Journal of Public Economics* 76 (3): 399–458.

———. 2000b. "Decentralization and the Quality of Government." Unpublished manuscript, UCLA.

———. 2000c. "Decentralization and Inflation: Commitment, Collective Action, or Continuity?" *American Political Science Review* 94 (4): 837–58.

Tsebelis, George. http://www.polisci.ucla.edu/tsebelis.

Tsebelis, George. 1994. "The Power of the European Parliament as a Conditional Agenda-Setter." *American Political Science Review* 88: 128–42.

———. 1995a. "Decision Making in Political Systems: Veto players in Presidentialism, Parliamentarism, Multicameralism, and Multipartyism." *British Journal of Political Science* 25: 289–326.

————. 1995b. "Veto players and Law Production in Parliamentary Democracies." In H. Doering (ed.), *Parliaments and Majority Rule in Western Europe*. New York: St. Martin's Press.

————. 1995c. "Conditional Agenda-Setting and Decisionmaking *Inside* the European Parliament." *Journal of Legislative Studies* 1: 65–93.

————. 1997. "Maastricht and the Democratic Deficit." *Aussenwirtschaft* 52: 29–56.

————. 1999. "Veto Players and Law Production in Parliamentary Democracies: An Empirical Analysis." *American Political Science Review* 93 (3): 591–608.

————. 2000. "Veto Players and Institutional Analysis." *Governance* 13 (4): 441–74.

Tsebelis, George, and Eric Chang. 2001. "Veto Players and the Structure of Budgets in Advanced Industrialized Countries." Unpublished manuscript, UCLA.

Tsebelis, George, and Geoffrey Garrett. 2000. "Legislative Politics in the European Union." *European Union Politics* 1: 9–36.

————. 2001. "The Institutional Determinants of Supranationalism in the EU." *International Organization* 55 (2): 357–90.

Tsebelis, George, Christian B. Jensen, Anastassios Kalandrakis, and Amie Kreppel. 2001. "Legislative Procedures in the European Union: An Empirical Analysis." *British Journal of Political Science* 31: 573–99.

Tsebelis, George, and Anastassios Kalandrakis. 1999. "The European Parliament and Environmental Legislation: The Case of Chemicals." *European Journal of Political Research* 36 (1): 119–54.

Tsebelis, George, and Amie Kreppel. 1998. "The History of Conditional Agenda Setting in European Institutions." *European Journal of Political Research* 33: 41–71.

Tsebelis, George, and Jeannette Money. 1997. *Bicameralism*. New York: Cambridge University Press.

Tsebelis, George, and Xenophon A. Yataganas. Forthcoming. "Veto Players and Decisionmaking in the EU after Nice: Legislative Gridlock and Bureaucratic/Judicial Discretion." *Journal of Common Market Studies*.

Uleri, Pier Vincenzo. 1996. "Introduction." In Michael Gallagher and Pier Vincenzo Uleri (eds.), *The Referendum Experience in Europe*. London: Macmillan.

Ursprung, Tobias. 1994. "The Use and Effect of Political Propaganda in Democracies." *Public Choice* 78: 259–82.

Van Hees, Martin, and Bernard Steunenberg. 2000. "The Choices Judges Make: Court Rulings, Personal Values, and Legal Constraints." *Journal of Theoretical Politics* 12: 299–317.

Volcansek, M. L. 2001. "Constitutional Courts as Veto Players: Divorce and Decrees in Italy." *European Journal of Political Research* 39 (3): 347–72.

Von Hagen, J., and I. J. Harden. 1995. "Budget Processes and Commitment to Fiscal Discipline." *European Economic Review* 39 (April): 771–79.

Vreeland, James R. 2001. "Institutional Determinant of IMF Agreements." Unpublished manuscript, Yale University.

Wallace, Helen, William Wallace, and Carol Webb (eds.). 1983. *Policy Making in the European Community*. 2nd ed. New York: John Wiley and Sons.

Wallace, William. 1982. "Europe as a Confederation: The Community and the Nation State." *Journal of Common Market Studies* 21: 57–68.

Wallace, William. 1983. "Less Than a Federation, More Than a Regime: The Community as a Political System." In Helen Wallace, William Wallace, and Carol Webb (eds.), *Policy Making in the European Community*. 2nd ed. New York: John Wiley and Sons.

Waltman, Jerold L., and Kenneth M. Holland. 1988. *The Political Role of Law Courts in Modern Democracies*. New York: Macmillan.

Warwick, Paul. 1994. *Government Survival in Western European Parliamentary Democracies*. New York: Cambridge University Press.

————. 1999. "Ministerial Autonomy or Ministerial Accommodation? Contested Bases of Government Survival in Parliamentary Democracies." *British Journal of Political Science* 29: 369–94.

Weaver, R. Kent, and Bert A. Rockman. 1993. *Do Institutions Matter?* Washington, D.C.: Brookings Institution.

Weiler, Joseph, J. 1991. "The Transformation of Europe." *Yale Law Journal* 100: 2403–83.

Weingast, Barry R. 1992. "Fighting Fire with Fire: Amending Activity and Institutional Change in the Postreform Congress." In Roger H. Davidson (ed.), *In the Postreform Congress*. New York: St. Martin's Press.

————. 1995. "The Economic Role of Political Institutions: Market-Preserving Federalism and Economic Development." *Journal of Law, Economics, and Organization* 11: 1–31.

————. 1997. "Political Foundations of Democracy and the Rule of Law." *American Political Science Review* 91: 245–63.

Weingast, Barry, Kenneth Shepsle, and Christopher Johnsen. 1981. "The Political Economy of Benefits and Costs: A Neoclassical Approach to Distributive Politics." *Journal of Political Economy* 89 (4): 642–64.

Westlake, Martin. 1994. *A Modern Guide to the European Parliament*. London: Pinter Publishers.

White, H. 1980. "A Heteroskedasticity-Consistent Covariance Matrix Estimator and a Direct Test for Heteroskedasticity." *Econometrica* 48: 81–38.

Winter, Lieven de. Forthcoming. "Living up to One's Promises: Government Declarations and Law Production." In H. Doering (ed.), *Parliamentary Organization and Legislative Outcomes in Western Europe*.

Woldendorp, J., H. Keman, et al. 1998. "Party Government in 20 Democracies: An Update." *European Journal of Political Research* 33 (January): 125–64.

Wornall, Robyn B. 2001. "Harmonic Dissidents? An Analysis of Party Cohesion in the German Bundestag." Ph.D. dissertation, UCLA.

Wright, Vincent. 1978. "France." In D. Butler and A. Ranney (eds.), *Referendums: A Comparative Study of Practice and Theory*. Washington, D.C.: American Enterprise Institute Press.

Yataganas, Xenophon A. 2001. "The Treaty of Nice: The Sharing of Power and the Institutional Balance in the European Union-A Continental Perspective." *European Law Journal* 7 (3): 239–88.

Index

absorption rule, 12, 26–30; criticism of, 86–87, 89; in different regimes, 78, 80; judiciary/judges and, 227; policy stability and, 158; political parties and, 165

Ackerman, B., 7, 138, 237

administrative law, 235–37

agenda setting/setters, 2, *104*; competition and, 10, 132, 134–35; conditional, 256, 260–62, 264, 272, 277, 280; executive decrees and, 81, 100, 113–14, 159, 226; executive dominance and, 109–14, 219–20; labor legislation and, 177–78, 180–85; ministerial discretion and, 106–9; in parliamentary regimes, 3, 33n, 67, 82–84, 93–115, 180–85, 219, 285; policy stability and, 2–3, 35, 97, 108; positional advantages in, 35, 91, 93–99, 106, 109, 130; in presidential regimes, 3, 67, 82–84, 112–14, 285; referendums and, 116, 126–34, 158–59; rules of, 91, 99–105, 106, 109; sequence of moves and, 33–37, 55–60, 222–25, 235. *See also specific countries and institutions*

Alesina, A., 189, 241

Alivizatos, N., 229, 230, 232, 234

Almond, G., 4, 106

Alt, J. E., 189, 195

alternation, 165, 171–72, 176–80, 194, 196–201, 234

amendments, 99, 104, 219, 256, 276–79

Ames, B., 75, 113

Amsterdam Treaty, 252, 257–58, 265, 278

anti-system parties, 152, 211, 218

Argentina, 77, 138, 151

Arrow, K., 43, 68

Australia, 147, 225, 232

Austria: agenda setting in, 101–3; bicameralism in, 144; decisionmaking in, 147; government duration in, 212; judiciary/judges in, 230; labor legislation in, 167; referendums in, 117n; regime type of, 112n

authoritarian regimes, 67–70, 76–77, 90, 131

Axelrod, R., 58

Banks set, 58

Barber Protocol, 251

Baron, D., 59

Barro, R., 204

Basinger, S., 203, 206

Bawn, K., 192–93, 206

Bednar, J., 139–40, 142–43

Belgium: agenda setting in, 101–3; civil law in, 225; decisionmaking rules in, 51, 151; government duration in, 212; labor legislation in, 167, 178, 179; political constraints in, 205

Bernhard, W., 241, 242

bicameral core, 50, 145, 147, 150

bicameralism: diversity and, 143–45; federalism and, 13, 136, 140–41, 287; number of veto players and, 158, 287; qualified majority and, 136, 153–57, 272; weak political parties and, 145–49; winset of, 141–42

Bieber, R., 261

Binder, S., 149

Birchfield, V., 87–88

Bogdanor, V., 118

Boix, C., 75

Botswana, 111

Bowler, S., 120–21, 122

Braeuninger, T., 35n, 145n6, 157

Brandt, W., 94–95

Brazil, 74, 112, 113, 138

Browne, E., 168

Buchanan, J., 136

budgets: deficits in, 8n.5, 14, 187–92, 205; structure of, 192–201, 205. *See also* public finance issues

bureaucracies and bureaucrats: administrative law and, 235–37; central bank independence and, 240–46, 247; empirical evidence on, 239–46; of European Union, 265–72, 273, 280, 281; federalism and, 158; independence of, 3, 15, 208, 236–37, 239, 242, 288; oversight of, 224–25; regime types and, 237–39; research on, 235–39

Bush, G.H.W., 81

Printed in Great Britain
by Amazon

78744374R00194